THE OFFICIAL 1981 BLACKBOOK PRICE GUIDE OF UNITED STATES COINS
NINETEENTH EDITION
BY MARC HUDGEONS

Y0-EIJ-359

© 1980 The House of Collectibles, Inc.
All rights reserved. No part of this book may be reproduced or utilized in any form or by any means, electronic or mechanical, including photocopying, recording, or by any information storage and retrieval system, without permission in writing from the publisher.

Published by: The House of Collectibles, Inc.
773 Kirkman Road, No. 120,
Orlando, FL 32811

Printed in the United States of America
Library of Congress Card Number 68-57353
ISBN: 0-87637-164-0

TABLE OF CONTENTS

Introduction 3	**VALUES:**
The American Numismatic Association 3	Colonial Coins, Patterns and Tokens 80
The Effects of the Gold and Silver Rush on the Coin Market 6	First United States Mint Issues 128
Coin Investing 10	Half Cents 130
The Future of the Susan B. Anthony Dollar 13	Large Cents 133
The Future For United States Coins and Numismatics 15	Small Cents 143
	Two Cent Pieces 151
Colonial Coins, Patterns and Tokens 16	Three Cent Pieces 153
The United States Mint 18	Nickels 155
Early Mint Operations 20	Half Dimes 164
Coins of the Civil War and Late 19th Century 21	Dimes 169
Coins of the 20th Century 22	Twenty Cent Pieces 181
The Rare Metals—Copper 24	Quarters 182
The Rare Metals—Silver 24	Half Dollars 194
The Rare Metals—Gold 24	Dollars 209
Silver Coin Melt Valve Chart 25	Gold Dollars 222
Gold Coin Melt Value Chart 25	Gold $2.50 Pieces 225
How United States Coins Are Minted 26	Gold $3.00 Pieces 231
What Is Coin Collecting 29	Gold $4.00 Pieces 233
Condition of Coins 29	Gold $5.00 Pieces 233
Scarcity 29	Gold $10.00 Pieces 242
Geographic Location 30	Gold $20.00 Pieces 248
Where To Buy and Sell Coins 30	Silver Commemorative Coinage 257
Cleaning Coins 31	Gold Commemorative Coinage 262
How to Use This Book 31	Confederate Coinage 265
Official ANA Grading System 32	U.S. Proof Cents 266
	Detecting Altered Coins 269
	Index 278

OFFICIAL BOARD OF CONTRIBUTORS TO THE NINETEENTH EDITION

Col. Grover C. Criswell	Mr. Lawrence Goldberg	Mr. Julian Leidman
Mr. Kurt R. Krueger	Mr. Roger Bryan	Mr. Curtis Iversen
Mr. Q David Bowers	Mr. Dennis Forgue	Mr. Robert L. Hughes
Mr. Robert Cornely	Mr. Kamal M. Ahwash	Mr. Glenn Smedley
Mr. Clifford Mishler	Mr. Aubrey E. Bebee	Mr. Rick Sundman

The publisher also wishes to express thanks to the American Numismatic Association and Krause Publications for photographs and illustrations. Certain photographs are courtesy of Bowers and Ruddy Galleries, Inc. and Diversified Numismatics, Inc.

PUBLISHER'S NOTE

This book is presented as a guide to the values of U.S. coins, as an aid for the beginner, advanced collector and dealer. We are not dealers. We do not buy or sell coins. Prices listed are intended as a guide only and are not warranted for accuracy.

INTRODUCTION

We have tried to make this book more than just another coin guide. Now, more than ever before, there is a real need for up-to-date, reliable information on coins for anyone interested in collecting or investing. We have carefully analyzed all circumstances of the recent gold and silver rush and tried to interpret them as usefully as possible. While we are not in the business of making predictions we've set forth our best opinions about what the future may hold in store, and tried to summarize the events of the very hectic past six months or so. But we also realize that coins remain, first and foremost, a collectors' hobby and have designed this book not only for the collector/investor but the beginner, the mildly experienced numismatist, and the coin buff who is just as interested in the art and history of coins as in their cash prices. It has often been said that coins mirror the past and that a study of them can be as informative as a library of history books. Their role in the future — in the world economics and politics — may be greater than at any period in history.

THE AMERICAN NUMISMATIC ASSOCIATION

Most of today's coin collectors probably know that there is an American Numismatic Association, and that it is the largest organization of "coin" collectors in the world. But many may not realize that as of October 1980 the Association will be 89 years old with an operating budget of over a million dollars.

The American Numismatic Association is an educational and nonprofit organization. It invites and welcomes to membership all worthy persons eleven years of age and over who have a sincere interest in numismatics, whether they collect coins, paper money, tokens or medals; whether advanced collectors or those only generally interested in the subject without being collectors at all. Members, located in every state of the Union and in many other countries, total some 30,000.

A factor in the operation of the Association and a deterrent to its development during its first three-quarters of a century was the geographical dispersal of its functional offices. As the situation was finally coming to an end, the executive secretary was in Phoenix, Ariz.; treasurer in Washington, D.C.; editor in Chicago; and the librarian was in Lincoln, Nebr. None of these employees were on full-time pay and mostly they operated out of their homes or private offices. Obviously, this situation limited and slowed communication and made for inefficient operation in general.

The ANA operations have been centered in a headquarters building in Colorado Springs since 1967. A board of governors, which establishes policy is determining all bylaws and regulations, is elected on a regular basis from the membership at large and serves without pay. To implement established policy there is a full time salaried professional staff in Colorado Springs that includes an executive vice president, editor, librarian, authenticators, and their assistants and clerical staff.

To advance the knowledge of numismatics and to bring about better cooperation and closer relations between numismatists are the principal

A.N.A. HEADQUARTERS IN COLORADO SPRINGS, COLORADO

objectives of the Association. Collectors will find that the annual dues of membership low compared to the tremendous value to be found in the prestige and services that membership offers.

The ANA does not buy or sell coins. Its revenue comes from dues paid by members, supplemented by gifts, bequests and contributions. It receives no operating funds from any governmental body. Any net income from various activities is used on behalf of its members and for the advancement of the hobby.

**DR. GEORGE F. HEATH,
FOUNDER OF A.N.A.**

**GEORGE HATIE
CURRENT A.N.A. PRESIDENT**

When the ANA was organized in October 1891, Dr. George F. Heath, the motivational force behind it, was honored with membership no. 1. Member no. 1,000 was admitted in March 1908; no. 10,000 in March 1944; no. 50,000 in August 1963; and no.100,000 in August 1979. Of course, the passing of time has taken its toll, and today's membership is slightly less than a third of the total number enrolled during its 89-year membership lifetime.

The Association's monthly magazine, *The Numismatist,* is actually older than ANA itself, having been started privately by Dr. Heath in 1888 (Sept.-Oct.) and continued to be published privately through 1910. It did, however, cooperate with and champion the cause of the Association — before and after its organization. In 1910 the vice president of ANA, W. W. C. Wilson of Montreal, purchased the magazine from publisher Farran

Zerve and gifted it to the Association that has continued its publication without interruption.

The Numismatist continues to be the official publication and mouthpiece of the Association. Published monthly, it contains well illustrated articles on various phases of collecting, identifying and caring for coins, tokens, medals and paper money. Included are news items regarding Association activities, new issues of coins, medals and paper money, and developments within the hobby.

The advertising pages of the magazine are open to ANA members only, who agree to abide by a strict "Code of Ethics". Members, except Associates, receive the magazine as one of the advantages of membership.

Following the magazine, one of the earliest services offered was use of a numismatic library that has grown to be the world's largest such facility loaning books to its members. Its 7,500 reference books, in addition to periodicals and other items, are loaned by mail to members and are available to non-members for use in the Colorado Springs headquarters.

Related to the library and actually a part of it is a visual education service that maintains and loans numismatic slide sets to member clubs for their meeting programs. These sets cover many different phases of numismatics and are available without cost except for the shipping charges.

An important date in the history of ANA is May 9, 1912, when it was granted a Federal Charter by the U. S. Congress. Signed by President William H. Taft, the Act gave the Charter a fifty-year life. A Congressional amendment dated April 10, 1962, allowed for an increase in the number of ANA board members and perpetuated the Charter indefinitely. One of the very few such charters ever granted, it has given the Association prestige and has been a stabilizing influence on its management.

While the ANA does not sell "in print" books, it does offer some pamphlet-type reprints of articles previously published in the *The Numismatist*, a few books of previous editions that have been donated to it, back copies of *The Numismatist*, etc. A copy of a price list of such material may be obtained without cost from the ANA library.

In addition to the official magazine, the editorial department publishes the bimonthly *Club Bulletin*, primarily to disseminate information about the activities of member clubs. The illustrated booklet is available to any ANA member who requests that his name be put on the mailing list.

More recent and rapidly growing is the Certification Service, available to the public but with lower fees to members. The ANACS staff examines and makes nondestructive tests on numismatic items and furnishes the person submitting an item with a statement of expert opinion of the item's genuineness and grade. A permanent record is kept by ANACS of all items it examines.

Collectors between the ages of 10 and 18 (11 to 17 years inclusive) are encouraged by a special lower-dues class of membership, by special articles in *The Numismatist*, by special exhibit classes and programs at conventions and in other ways.

Classes of membership are as follows: **Regular** — adults 18 years of age and older who want to be eligible for all benefits, including receipt of *The Numismatist;* **Club** — nonprofit numismatic organizations, entitled to all benefits; **Junior** — 11 through 17 years of age who are entitled to all benefits, but cannot hold office; **Associate** — limited to the spouse or child of a Regular or Life Member, who may not hold office or receive *The Numismatist;* and **Life Members** — corresponding to Regular members but who pay a one-time fee for lifetime memership. Memberships are not transferrable from one person to another, and membership numbers are never reassigned.

The amounts of dues and a few other details of membership follow:

DUES
Regular (U. S. only)

☐ 1 Yr.-$15.00   ☐ 3 Yr.-$40.00   ☐ 5 Yr.-$60.00

Regular (all other countries)	$ 18.00*
Club (wherever located)	15.00*
Junior (11 through 17 years old)	9.00
Associate (child or spouse of R or LM)	2.00
Life (adult individual)	350.00
Installment ($60 with application**, plus $25 per month for 12 months)	
Life (club)	1000.00

*Add $5 application fee, first year only
**Includes $10 bookkeeping fee, deducted from final payment if made within 90 days of application. Life Membership is not effective until full $350 fee is paid.

Nonmember annual subscription (U. S. only)	15.00
Subscription (all other countries)	18.00

Persons having specific questions, wanting to see a copy of *The Numismatist* or obtain an application for membership are invited to write to: ANA Executive Vice President, P. O. Box 2366, Colorado Springs, CO 80901. Such an inquiry or request does not obligate the writer in any way.

THE EFFECTS OF THE GOLD AND SILVER RUSH ON THE COIN MARKET

Early in 1979 the price of gold bullion was around $240 an ounce and silver was being traded at $8. A year later gold had reached $800 and silver was up to $49.00. Never in the world's history had precious metal jumped so high in a single year — not even during times of financial panic, which 1979 was not. The effect on coins made of these metals was overwhelming. They skyrocketed in price, in jumps so rapid and dizzying that coin dealers gave up running prices in their ads. "Call for latest quotes," they advised. And if you called, the price was usually guaranteed for only 48 hours. Since the market hit its peak in January, 1980, things have cooled down a bit, but aftershocks are still being felt.

What caused this unprecedented stampede to buy gold and silver? Investment analysts are still shaking their heads. Few of them foresaw the extent or impact. A major factor was inflation, not just in the U. S. (which reached 17% in 1979) but nearly every industrialized nation. When money declines rapidly in value or purchasing power, so-called paper investments of money tend to decline along with it. A study made from 1965 to 1975 showed that everyone who had a savings account during that period lost 6%. Yes, they lost only $94 worth of buying power in 1975, even with the interest included. Those who bought government bonds, the presumably failsafe investments, took an even worse beating. They lost 17%. Corporate bonds? You lost 19% in purchasing power by buying them. A portfolio of bluechip Dow Jones Industrials resulted in a loss of 25¢ on every dollar, not counting brokers' fees.

The problem with all these investments was that they just didn't grow fast enough to keep pace with inflation. Many small investors and individuals with modest savings accounts aren't even aware that their capital is being eroded. They look at interest gains and presume they've come out ahead. The professional investors and big-money people have long been aware that most investments of this type are a losing game. In 1979 they began looking elsewhere, in earnest. And they got a big boost from the international monetary situation.

As most large world nations import a great deal of fuel oil from the Mideast, billions of dollars worth of their currency are siphoned out of the country into Arab hands. This creates a "balance of payments" deficit (i.e., more money flowing out of a country than coming in) and the currency of that country weakens. A sort of domino-theory reaction sets in. Foreigners holding large amounts of that country's currency get panicky. They want to get rid of it — trade it for something that isn't declining in value. Until recently the usual procedure, when the U. S. dollar was down, was for foreign investors to swap their dollars for German marks or Swiss francs or Japanese yen. But, since inflation and "balance of payments" problems then began to effect just about every currency, they sought other investments. Some bought art and antiques. Others tried real estate. And some did well with these things. But they lacked the advantage of gold and silver. Art and antiques and real estate usually take a long while to show substantial gains. There's some risk attached to them because suitable buyers might prove hard to find. They can't be cashed in, on the spot, immediately. And the commissions involved in selling them can run high. Gold and silver appeared to be the perfect investments. Once the rush to buy it began, a "bandwagon" fervor developed. Investors everywhere sold whatever they had and used the proceeds to buy precious metal.

Profit-taking in February and March, 1980, forced the price of gold down about $200 an ounce from its peak. But this wasn't regarded as any weakness in the market or a sign that investors were turning away from precious metals. It was looked upon only as a temporary situation. After all, once their profits had been taken, they were left with money again and faced the old dilemma of what to do with it. What better than buy more gold and silver?

Gold's upturn in the market, while impressive to be sure, did not startle the general public so much as silver's. Everyone has a respect for gold as something rare and precious and valuable. But silver? Isn't that the stuff grandma's knives and forks are made from? Didn't we have ample supplies of silver coins in our pockets just a while ago? How can silver be something to get all excited about? Well, silver *is* more plentiful than gold and will never be worth as much as gold. But as a precious metal, silver has myriad industrial and commercial uses: jewelry, eyeglass frames and wristwatch cases being just a few. When gold prices become exorbitant, the use of silver always increases as a substitute. If gold wasn't so expensive, many watch cases (and other things) would be made of gold today and the demand for silver wouldn't be nearly as strong. Like gold, silver is still being mined, but quantities of new silver brought into the world market are not enough to satisfy the need. Smelters — those who melt down silver and recycle it — depend upon supplies obtained from dealers in scrap silver, who buy tableware, jewelry and the like from the public. As these are gradually exhausted, coins become the logical substitute. It is no longer illegal to melt coins for their metal content, so smelters are well within the law to take coinage and process it in the same fashion as old knives and spoons.

Just what has all this done to the coin market?

Plenty, obviously. But the effects have not been easy to analyze.

Many people not versed in coin investment believe that all coins made of gold or silver advance in value at the same pace, in step with the metal's price advance. This is simply not so. Every coin, it is true, made of precious metal has increased substantially in value since early 1979. Many, however, would have done so anyway, even without a "metal rush" of quite such large proportions, simply because of the increasing numbers of coin investors and collectors.

Here are the increases, based on average retail prices, of some gold and silver coins *before* the big surge of metal investing:

	1974 price	1979 price
$10 Gold 1843-O MS-60	150.00	1,700.00
$20 Gold 1857-S MS-60	500.00	1,800.00
$2.50 Gold 1838 MS-60	325.00	2,000.00

	1963 price	1979 price
$1 Silver 1879-CC MS-60	90.00	900.00
$1 Silver 1866 proof	95.00	1,350.00

Nobody is buying these coins for their metal content. Even at the height of the market in January, 1980, that 1838 $2.50 gold piece would have brought only about $125 for its gold. And an 1866 proof $1 has less than $30 worth of silver in it — meaning there's over $1,300.00 in numismatic value attached to this coin. Obviously, there are two groups of investors buying coins: one concentrating on rarities that have shown past growth performance, regardless of metal, the other buying coins whose metal value advances faster than their numismatic value (or "melters," as they've come to be called).

Common-date silver dollars in average condition are a good example of the latter. There is no numismatic investment in these coins, for the simple reason that dealers and coin people in general are not interested in them. But a common-date silver dollar in average condition — worn, scratched, nicked or otherwise defaced — contains just as much silver as the 1879-CC MS-60. These are bullion coins and their fate is the smelter's furnace. For those who owned such coins in 1979 they proved extremely profitable. They were even pretty fair short-term investments. In January, 1979, common-date silver dollars (not "Ikes" but the old ones that did not merely look like silver but *were* silver) could be bought from any coin shop at $10 each, sometimes less if the dealer was overloaded and anxious to move them. In January, 1980, dealers in scrap silver were paying as much as $20 for these coins — coins *they themselves* could have bought by the ton for half the price just 12 months earlier.

If you wonder why the buying price of bullion coins reached only around $20 an ounce while silver was being quoted at $37, the answer lies in the profits and commissions along the way. The smelters, more than anyone else, control this market. They won't pay the full market price because this leaves them no profit margin. Also, smelters will sometimes cut down or totally cease their buying when the price goes high, preferring to process already-bought bullion and bide their time. Since all bullion silver ends up in the hands of smelters, the price *they* pay determines the price dealers in scrap silver will *pay* you.

Now for the side-effects, which may have far-reaching consequences.

Right now, as you read this, thousands of silver dollars and other silver coins are being shoveled into smelters' furnaces. The process goes on constantly, every day. Nobody could even estimate the number of silver dollars melted down within the past six months — it must be well into the millions. Now, as we have said, most of these are common dates and/or not in the best condition. But not everyone who sells these coins, and not everyone who buys them, has the ability to recognize good dates. Nor do they pay great attention to condition. Some better-grade silver dollars are getting melted, too — you can be sure of that. Even so far as the commonest are concerned, such vast quantities cannot be destroyed for a long period of time without these coins gradually becoming less common. The supply is not endless. Except for 1921, the biggest minting for any Morgan dollar was less than 40 million. Most were minted in quantities under 20 million. This is not a huge total by any means, especially considering that there are believed to be 28 million coin collectors in the country and at least 200 million worldwide. Collectors of foreign coins are well aware of issues that became scarce as a result of being melted down to build cannons in times of war. It could well be that our silver dollars will get into that category, too, if the present situation continues.

With gold, things are rather different. Gold coins aren't being melted down to anything approaching the volume of silver, simply because most gold coins are worth more numismatically than for the metal content. It is not impossible, however, depending on the market, that the time will come when large-scale melting of $20 gold pieces begins.

The big question is: what should the coin investor do now? There are no easy answers but one undeniable fact comes through. The better gold and silver coins (and base-metal ones, too) showed very satisfactory growth before the 1979/80 metal rush. They continued showing it during the metal rush. And there was no indication, when the buying and selling fever started to cool down, that they would not continue going along as if nothing extraordinary had happened. Why? Because rare coins — not just super-rarities but all good collectible coins in VF or better condition — have a life of their own apart from the metals game. They have their own audience of buyers and connoisseurs and investors. Great attention is focused on them in times of precious metal upsurges, but even without newspaper headlines and public comment they do pretty well for themselves.

COIN INVESTING

Coin investing from a purely speculative point of view — buying coins solely for the purpose of making money on them — is no longer confined to professional dealers. In fact it is likely that the volume of coins bought for profit by the public exceeds purchases by dealers. Investment groups have sprung up, in which investors band together and contribute sums toward the purchase of expensive rarities that they could not individually afford. They then own "shares" of the coin, shares which of course pay no dividends until the coin is sold. There are coin investment clubs and dealers who make a specialty of "investment parcels," sometimes with a guarantee to buy back the coins at full cost or a slight advance after a stated period of time.

This kind of coin investment thrives regardless of gold and silver bullion prices. It concentrates upon coins of established numismatic popularity, in VF or better condition.

Coin investing is a complex subject which we have space here to deal with only briefly. Some comment on the matter seems called for, now that coin investing has extended well beyond the realm of numismatists and attracted the interest of many financial experts.

It is undeniable that coin investing offers the potential for very satisfactory capital growth, based on past market performances. Frank Pick of Barron's Magazine went so far as to call rare coins "the number one hedge against inflation." The following increases in average retail values of certain coins (not all of them terribly rare by any means) from 1948 to 1979 can be matched by few commodities or other types of investments:

	1948 value	1979 value
1853 Half Dime, Type III	1.50	400.00
1880 $3 Gold	50.00	2,500.00
1804 Half Cent	16.50	1,000.00
1901 Quarter	4.00	260.00
1864 2¢ Piece	1.00	200.00

As is clearly evident, these coins are not all extremely old, nor are they all made of precious metal. It should not be assumed that *every* U. S. coin has advanced at this rate, which is certainly not the case. Most, however, have demonstrated healthy price jumps.

There are many questions the potential investor should ask before plunging ahead.

Is coin investing "safe"?

No investment is 100% safe. In numismatics the safer investments are coins that are not valued chiefly for their metallic content. This shouldn't be taken to mean gold and silver coins are bad investments. They can be quite the reverse, provided coins are chosen in which the numismatic value is greater than the metal value. For example: common-date silver dollars are not good speculative investments. Their value is almost entirely in their metal. To gain a worthwhile profit on common date silver dollars (or any common date silver coins), silver would need to double its current price. It may do this. But this could take a very long time, during which inflation would probably be rising, and the resulting net gain would be negligible. On the other hand, key-date or key-mark silvers are an attractive investment as they tend to appreciate at a fairly steady rate regardless of the bullion market's ups and downs. Why? Because of these two important factors:

1. Many investors are buying them.
2. In addition to investors, these coins always have a demand with collectors.

Why have certain coins, whose values inched slowly upward for years, suddenly doubled and tripled in price?

Because of increased investor activity. Coin collectors alone — people buying coins strictly as a hobby with no thought of profit — could never make such sharp impacts on the market. Collectors have an influence and their influence is growing but investors account for most of the wildly spiraling prices. The more investors, the higher prices will go. And as better returns are shown on coin investments, as they have been recently, the more investors you will have entering the market. Everyone who buys a rare coin is aiding persons who already own a specimen of that coin.

Don't prices come down just as far when investors sell as they were before they bought?

No. It isn't necessary that a coin be scarcer on the market to be more valuable. So long as buying activity is increased, the same coins can keep coming up for sale and still gain in price. Buying activity is the key. Investors are not influenced by rarity. They're influenced only by whether a coin is showing value gains.

How long must coins be held to show a satisfactory profit?

This depends on what is meant by satisfactory. The question is difficult to answer at any rate because there is no established or reliable growth rate. In a boon year, such as 1979, rare coins in general can double in price in just twelve months. Some even did better. But there have been years, even in the recent past, when the overall rate of increase was less than 20%. It is impossible to forecast what the future holds. This, however, should be taken into account. Just as with any investment, the paper profit on coins is not necessarily the actual profit. For coins to be converted into cash they must be sold and the dealer or agent to whom you sell will not pay the full retail price. When you buy you pay the full retail price but in selling you receive the retail price less the dealer's margin of profit, which is figured into the next sale. Unlike you, the dealer is not interested in holding his coins for years until they appreciate greatly in value. He wants to sell them immediately, as soon as they reach his hands, and would rather have a 20% profit on a coin today than wait a year and sell it for much more. The margin of profit depends on the type of coin and its value. For a popular U. S. key coin worth $1,000 in uncirculated condition, which the dealer knows he will have no trouble selling quickly, you are likely to be paid as much as 80% of the retail value, especially if you sell at a time of strong demand. If the coin is not so popular, or is less than VF in condition, the dealer will probably pay from 60% to 70% of his retail selling price.

You can calculate your potential success as an investor based upon this situation *plus* the rate of inflation. Obviously, future trends taken by the inflation rate are very difficult to predict. Assuming it to be 10% annually over the next five years, this would present the following prospects:

```
Coin bought for $1,000 in 1980 ........................ $1,000
Coin increases to $5,000 by 1985
Coin is sold for $5,000 less 20% ......................  4,000
Inflation has reduced buying power of the dollar
  by 50%, so your $4,000 becomes ................... $2,000
                                    net profit      1,000
```

This is a very simplistic example which should not be taken too seriously. It merely shows how to operate the arithmetic.

Assuming one has decided to invest in coins, should he trust his own abilities or rely on the services of a numismatic broker?

While brokers are of invaluable aid to persons uninformed about coins and the coin market there is no question but that a well-educated investor can do as well, or better, on his own. Often, "investment parcels" made up by so-called brokers (a title that can be used indiscriminately, without license) consist of coins that a broker, in his regular trading as a coin dealer, was unable to sell profitably. The likelihood of their being sound investments is slim. If you need expert advice, a reputable dealer is usually the best source, one to whom you can speak personally. If you purchase good key coins from his stock in uncirculated condition they are likely to prove as good an investment as any broker could supply.

What price range should the investor buy in? If I have $1,000 to spend, should I buy a single $1,000 coin or five for $200? Or ten for $100?

There is no established "best way" in this situation. Generally, a $1,000 coin with a proven record of growth would be a more attractive investment than several coins of lower value. Selection of the coins to buy is more important than their price range. You must confine yourself to VF or Uncirculated only. It is true that many early coins are not available in such high grades of condition but these are not considered prime investment pieces. Be careful that the coins are not overgraded and that you aren't buying above the market. Shop around and compare prices but don't take too long doing this: the price may go up.

Obviously the best time to invest in any coin is before a stampede for it develops. Investors with the foresight to purchase 1864 2¢ pieces in 1948 at $1 each got in virtually on the ground floor, before much notice was taken of this coin by other investors or collectors. There are no opportunities comparable to this today, no coin purchasable for $1 that could be expected to rise 200 times in value in 30 years, because no coins are that far undervalued any longer. The coin hobby is much bigger than it was in 1948. The 1864 2¢ piece was really worth more than $1 in 1948. It wasn't bringing more because few people were buying it. As things stand now, copper coins would seem the investments of the future. With so much attention focused on gold and silver, much of the cash that would be spent on coppers is being directed away from them. Early coppers are almost sure to become an investment favorite, as well as key-date Lincolns. The nickel is another coin that could very likely profit when and if the current precious metal mania subsides.

Do we advise coin investment? We neither advise or discourage it. The purpose of this book is to point out the realities of buying and selling coins and provide potential buyers (investors and collectors) with the information they need to make their own decisions.

THE FUTURE OF THE SUSAN B. ANTHONY DOLLAR

The Susan B. Anthony dollar came into existence as a daring experiment. Unlike its recent predecessor, the Eisenhower dollar, it was not designed for limited circulation to banks and gambling casinos and collectors. It was intended as a coin for general use, to be minted in large quantities, just as was the old "Morgan dollar" and other silver dollars of the 19th-century. Treasury Department officials have hopes that the Anthony dollar will be accepted by the public and that this will enable the government to discontinue printing paper dollars.

Why would the government prefer us to use $1 coins instead of $1 notes? Because Uncle Sam will save money if we use coins. A dollar coin may not be cheaper to manufacture than a piece of paper money, but notes wear out quickly and replacement costs are high. Coins can be circulated for a much longer time. If a bill lasts five years, it's shown remarkable longevity; coins often circulate for 50 years or longer.

The government realizes, of course, that the $1 bill may die hard, if at all. Substituting coins for bills would place a certain burden on the public. Coins are a lot bulkier than notes, but to those who claim that bulkiness will prove the Anthony dollar's downfall, the Treasury Department is quick to point out that old silver dollars were twice as big and nobody seems to have complained about the task of carrying them around. The Anthony dollar is only about the size of a quarter — so close, in fact, that many have been dropped into coin-operated machines calling for quarters.

It would be natural enough to assume that the Anthony dollar is smaller than earlier silver dollars because silver is worth much more today. In fact, the Anthony dollar is not silver at all but made of a metal composition known as cupro-nickel, the same used in other U.S. coins that once were minted from pure silver.

Many politicians and lawmakers are in the Anthony dollar's corner, rooting for it to replace paper notes. Others feel that the basic concept, while sound, should not be pushed forward too quickly. They fear that the Treasury Department might discontinue printing dollars too soon, before the coin has been sufficiently tested, and that great confusion (not to mention embarrassment) is likely to ensue. Just getting enough $1 coins into circulation — which is now well on the way to being accomplished — is not the answer, they say. Suppose an ample quantity is circulated, the Treasury ceases manufacturing notes, and the coins are either hoarded by speculators or thrown into cookie jars by people who do not want the bother of carrying them around? Then the nation would possibly be faced with a dollar shortage, just as it was faced with a penny shortage several years ago when aluminum pennies were discontinued as potential replacements for copper.

Some legislators are sufficiently disturbed by this prospect to start a "save the paper dollar" movement. A bill has been introduced into the House banking subcommittee that seeks to restrain the Treasury Department from shelving the $1 note before all the facts are in. It reads, in part: "If America wants to use the new $1 coin, it will be a success. But that success must come because people choose to use the coin. Freedom is one of the great values of this land. George Washington was important in leading the fight for that freedom, and establishing the new United States. It is ironic that his portrait on the $1 note could become a casualty of government action to restrict that freedom."

Hogwash, retort the coin's supporters. This kind of thing has happened many times in the past. Was any loss of freedom involved when the government abandoned odd-denomination coinage? Or when gold coins ceased to be struck in the Roosevelt administration? Didn't these measures, if not necessarily well-received at the time, prove in the long run to be wise and sound? Isn't it equally true, they continue, that many foreign governments have done exactly the same thing replacing their lowest-denomination notes with coins, with no visible ill effects?

It is entirely possible, say the dollar's detractors, that a Domino Theory may occur. First the $1 note disappears, then the $5, then the $10 and so on, until the public has nothing to do business with but checks, credit cards and a lot of bulky coins. This, they argue, would be a giant step backward — back to pre-Civil War days, when there was no federal paper currency. It worked then, only because the nation had a small population and most day-to-day commercial transactions were for amounts under $1.

As of now, there is not even any positive proof that the Treasury **will** save money if $1 coins replace $1 notes. The Treasury strongly believes it would, but a number of Congressmen think otherwise. Thomas B. Evans Jr. (R-Del.) stated, "while the $1 coin may last longer than the $1 bill, it also costs a great deal more to warehouse and ship than the $1 bill." Actually, the Treasury appears to be looking into the distant rather than immediate future for most of its revenue-savings on dollar manufacture. With inflation at its current rate, driving up the price of just about everything, dollars are sure to be in greater demand 5-10 years from now than they are today. It is almost sure that dollar production — either coins or bills, or both — would be increased during the 1980's at a faster rate than production of "small change".

The $1 note's demise, if it comes, might mean stepped-up production of the long-controversial $2 bill. After ceasing production of $2 notes for almost two and a half years, the Bureau of Engraving and Printing resumed their production last August. While there was no official word that the new $2 bill output was related to the Anthony dollar situation, speculation leaned strongly in that direction. One Federal Reserve official went so far as to link the two in an announcement. Philip E. Coldwell, Federal Reserve governor, told a Bank Administration Institute Conference in New Orleans that by "early 1980" there should be a sufficient quantity of $1 coins and $2 notes in circulation to halt printing of $1 notes.

When the small $1 coin was first seriously discussed, in 1976 (it was not yet known as the Anthony dollar because no decision had been made on design), belief was held by some that collectors would gobble down the first wave of such coins placed in circulation and that it would be a very long while before they circulated freely. Collectors, being rather intelligent folk, realized that a coin minted in quantities large enough for vast general circulation would hardly be an item to salt away for possible future gain — especially as it was not made of precious or semi-precious metal. Numismatists have shown interest in the coin, but only, apparently, to the extent of adding single uncirculated specimens to their collection, not hoarding every example that reaches their hands. Some minor varieties have shown up, which naturally attract collectors, but this would not seem to hinder the coin's availability for general use.

What will be the future of the Anthony dollar? At this point, it's anyone's guess. The politicians are agreeing on only one thing. If it fails, neither party takes the blame, as it was conceived in a Republican administration and released in a Democratic. But, then, who gets the credit?

THE FUTURE FOR UNITED STATES COINS AND NUMISMATICS

Coin collecting developed from a casual pastime into America's biggest hobby. It's taken on an entirely new character within the past few years, because of massive media publicity, investor activity, and the big metal rush of 1979/80. Coin dealing is now a major industry. Its executives command salaries equal to those of giant corporations. Telex machines now flash the latest price quotes to coin shops where, 20 years ago, the only electronic instrument was a telephone. There are full-time investment brokers who handle nothing but coins, and investment consultants who don't even handle coins but earn a handsome living by giving advice on buying and selling them. The world of coins has grown so huge and complex that everyone except the wealthy would seem to be crowded out. But that just isn't so. For every millionaire who buys a Continental dollar, for every investment group that ponders whether or not to sell its gold portfolio, there are hundreds of quite ordinary people digging into their pockets to look for "wheat" cents or working to complete their sets of Jefferson nickels. Coins are a hobby that offers something for everybody.

No matter how many coins are melted down for bullion an equal number — probably even greater — will go into the albums and cabinets of collectors. There is still, despite ever-growing investing, no shortage of persons who merely enjoy owning coins and get a thrill from building up a set or series or making a "find." Swappers still swap. And coin conventions are still places of wide-eyed wonderment for newcomers to the hobby. There is no lessening of interest in the "collecting" aspects of coins: their designs, their history and other details. If the market goes up or down, the dyed-in-the-wool numismatist merely shrugs. He bought enjoyment when he bought his coins and he's gotten his money's worth.

But of course, one should try to be an informed buyer. Otherwise there's risk of acquiring faked or incorrectly graded coins, or building a mishmash accumulation rather than a collection. Any collection gathered with care and intelligence can be taken pride in. The value is secondary. If money was all that counted, the rich would win every award at coin shows. But many awards are taken by persons who never spent more than $20 or $30 on a coin.

Right now, the hobby is in a volatile period. Non-investor numismatists are complaining because investor activity has boosted many coins beyond their price range. For every coin that gets too expensive for the average budget, though, others — previously ignored — begin to gain attention and collectibility. The rate at which Mercury and early Roosevelt dimes are being melted down has brought once-common dates into the "mildly scarce" category. The speculation that some material other than copper will be used for minting pennies has focused interest on these coins. Pennies could well prove as big an item, at some time in the future, as silver coins did in 1979/80. No one can predict. And that's half the fun. Coin collecting is an adventure and it can lead just about anywhere.

COLONIAL COINS, PATTERNS AND TOKENS

The history of our coinage begins not with the first federal issues but the coin used earlier by colonists. This period in American coin use, from exploration of Florida and the first Virginia settlements up to 1792, spans 200 years and is considered one of the most fascinating specialties for collectors. It is rich in types, designs and methods of production. While a great deal of colonial coinage is rare, some falls into the moderate price range. Here are historical objects of undisputed significance, purchasable in some cases for less than the cost of key-date modern coins. The celebrated "Rosa Americana," circulated before George Washington was born, can be had in good condition for less than $100. Even some of the 17th century "elephant tokens" sell for under $100, though this series also includes rarities of high price. The belief that colonial coinage is only for the wealthy just isn't so.

The story of this nation's beginnings is probably better told by its early money than by any other antiquities. Pilgrim settlers are often pictured as hunters and trappers living off the land. This is partly true but even in the 1600's there were cities with shops and a real need existed for coinage. When nothing better was available the old barter system was resorted to, as used in ancient times, with goods traded for other goods of similar value. In Massachusetts iron nails were accepted as legal tender, as well as Indian wampum (shells strung together on cords, each having a set value). As early as the 1640's, 20 years after the Mayflower, serious thought was given by the Bay Colony to striking its own money. In 1652 the Massachusetts General Court authorized experimental efforts in this direction, the first attempts being no more than rough metal discs stamped with small symbols. Compared to Europe's elaborate coinage they were meager but proved that this country had the ability to produce a medium of exchange. These were followed by improved domestic efforts as well as importation of coins from abroad, struck expressly for colonial use. These include the "Lord Baltimore" coins of Maryland and the Colonial Plantation Token. By the 17th century's close a variety of coins and pseudo-coins circulated. Some were private or merchant tokens, of British or Dutch manufacture. There were largely speculative issues brought to this country in large quantities by persons hoping to acquire vast land parcels. There was little confidence in the integrity of such coinage but it was nevertheless accepted, on the basis of weight.

Coins of both England and Spain, brought over by immigrants and traders, circulated pretty freely. Other foreign coins were also met with. Rather than being changed at face value they were, in the early years, valued on metal content, every merchant having a scale to weigh coins brought to him. Spain's dollar or "piece of eight" became the most familiar coin in the colonies, replaced thereafter by the coins of Great Britain. By the time of the Revolution, probably as many as 90% of the coins in American circulation were of British mintage.

Because colonial coins and tokens were not issued by a central government and were produced under challenging conditions, standardization cannot be expected. Sizes, denominations and quality of workmanship all vary sometimes to an extreme degree. Included are crude pieces hardly recognizable as coins, and works of considerable artistic merit. Some were not milled but hammered, struck by hammering the dies into metal blanks just as the Romans and Greeks made their coins 2,000 years ago. They also vary in scarcity. The collector should not be duped into paying inflated prices for coins merely on grounds of their being pre-Revolutionary. This in itself is no assurance of rarity. Each issue has its own established value, as shown in the listings section of this book. Allowance must be made for the condition of hammered pieces (whose shape will be somewhat irregular) and for specimens of great rarity, as these are almost impossible to find in the kind of condition one would expect of later coins. On the whole, condition standards are less rigid for colonial than federal issues. On the other hand, the buyer should not accept badly damaged examples in the belief that nothing better can be found.

THE UNITED STATES MINT

For 16 years following the Declaration of Independence this country still relied upon British and other foreign coinage. This was not only unsatisfactory but objectionable to many citizens, as Britain's coins bore the likeness of the not-too-popular George III. In 1791 Congress approved the establishment of a federal Mint. Presses for milling were purchased, designers and die-cutters hired. But the question remained whether to fashion U. S. coinage after Britain's or devise an entirely new series with different denominations. After much debate the latter plan was adopted, with the dollar (named for Thalers of the Dutch, who were not our enemies) as the chief currency unit and our coinage based upon divisions or multiples of it. The metal standard was fixed at 15 parts silver to one part of gold. When finalized on April 2, 1792, the Mint Act provided for coins in values of $10, $5, $2.50, $1, 50¢, 25¢, 10¢, 5¢, 1¢ and ½¢. The 1¢ and ½¢ were of copper, other denominations up to $1 silver, those over $1 gold. The $5 piece was regarded as the equivalent to Britain's pound sterling, the 25¢ to the British shilling, while the ½¢ was the counterpart to Britain's farthing or "fourthling" (¼th part of a British penny). It may seem odd that necessity was felt for a coin valued under one cent but at this remote period even the penny had considerable buying power and fractional pricing of goods was common — apples at 1¢ each or 5½¢ per half dozen for example. If such a coin was not available the situation would have invited an onslaught of merchant tokens.

Philadelphia was selected as home for the first Mint building, whose cornerstone was laid July 31, 1792. George Washington, then serving as President, contributed silverware from which the first federal coins were struck — a few half dimes or half dismes as they were called (5¢ pieces). Proceeding cautiously, the Mint's first purchase of metal was six pounds of copper. This was used for cents and half cents, delivered to the Treasurer of the United States in 1793. The following year a deposit of $80,715.73½ worth of French silver coins was made to the Mint by the State of Maryland, to be melted down and used for coinage. They yielded a quantity of 1794-dated dollars and half dollars. Gold was not obtained until 1795 when a Boston merchant turned over $2,276.72 in ingots, which were quickly transformed (apparently along with gold from other sources) into 744 Half Eagles ($5 pieces). Later that year 400 Eagles ($10) were produced. By the close of the year 1800 the Mint had milled $2,534,000 worth of coins and succeeded in distributing them pretty widely throughout the then-inhabited regions of the country, as far west as Michigan and Missouri. The operation was of course far more modest than it subsequently became. In 1974 the Mint attained the following output:

```
    8,800,000,000 1¢ pieces
       88,100,000 5¢
    1,000,000,000 10¢
      587,000,000 25¢
      193,000,000 50¢
    ─────────────
    $475,000,000 face value
```

The Philadelphia Mint in 1792. Painting by E. Lamasure

The New Philadelphia Mint

EARLY MINT OPERATIONS

The Mint's early history is a subject of considerable interest. U. S. coins were quite different in their evolution than those of major European nations. In most areas of Europe coins had been struck since Roman times and each new government or regime acquired the mints and materials of its predecessor, consisting of all necessary equipment and storehouses of bullion. There was already an established coinage and all that was necessary was to change its designs and denominations. As this was not the situation in the U. S., where coinage began literally from "scratch," problems faced in the Mint's developing years were sizable. Those assigned to the various tasks were inexperienced and blunders occurred often. Though the Mint possessed milling machines its equipment was not fully up to European standards. Dies were sometimes poorly cut and resulted in misstrikes or unusual variations. Not all dies used for a coin were identical in design, either, yielding varieties such as found on the 1793 Flowing Hair cent. It is normally presumed by beginners that these "types" represent intentional changes in design but such was not the case (aside, of course, from major alterations such as the switch from Flowing Hair to Liberty Cap on the cent). Die-cutters apparently had basic designs or sketches from which to work and added small touches, or left them off, as they saw fit. It is doubtful that much notice was taken of such variations originally but they've spawned a fertile collecting ground for numismatists. Even as late at 1839 die variations occurred on the cent, producing the "Booby Head" and "Silly Head" portraits.

There were other difficulties, too, of a more serious nature. The bullion content of our precious metal coins was undervalued by foreign standards and traders reaped handsome profits shipping our coins abroad. As this activity increased the coinage supply dwindled and the Mint found itself unable to produce coins fast enough. In an effort to stifle speculation, President Jefferson placed a moratorium on the striking of silver dollars in 1804 and Eagles in 1806. A new monetary standard was adopted in 1834, setting the value of silver at 1/16th that of gold, compared to the old ratio of 1/15th. This proved successful for a time, though the later 19th century witnessed heated political squabbles over the market price of gold (most prominent in the 1896 McKinley/Bryan campaign). Today, of course, gold and silver are traded freely, something which it was then felt would bring worldwide economic ruin. What happened to the 16-to-1 ration? Well, if we take the market values during the "metal rush" of January, 1980, when gold was $800 per ounce and silver $49.00, this works out to roughly 16½ to 1.

So far as their designs were concerned, this was another challenge faced by our early coiners. There was the choice of showing national leaders, classical types, or rely on the kind of abstract symbolism used on certain foreign coins. As Washington was not only President but the chief national hero there was strong sentiment to place his likeness on coinage. This was decided against, on grounds that the English portrayed their king on coinage and we as a people had no wish to regard our President as a king. Many other possibilities were advanced. Finally the decision was made to use a portrait of Liberty on obverses, symbolic of the liberty achieved from colonial domination. The principal reverse type, though not used on every coin, was the American eagle. It was not until the 20th century that an American citizen appeared on our coinage, this distinction belonging to Lincoln when his likeness was introduced to the penny in 1909. (An objection may be made on grounds that Lincoln's predecessor on the penny, the Indian, was also an American citizen; but this portrait was merely an emblem, not intended as the likeness of a specific person.)

It is generally agreed that the early representations of Liberty are something less than artistic marvels. The mythological goddess is shown either with craggy features, stringy hair, or unbecomingly chubby. Things improved somewhat after 1836 when Christian Gobrecht, a Dutchman, was engaged as assistant engraver. By the 1870's America's coins were as handsome as those of any European nation, the Morgan dollar far surpassing most foreign "crowns."

Early U. S. Gold Coinage. Gold played a relatively minor role, as outlined above, in U. S. coinage until the late 1840's, when major gold discoveries in California reshaped the nation's economy. Vast quantities of bullion reaching the market brought about renewed melting of silver dollars so the government stepped up production of gold coinage to take its place. Most significant was introduction of the Double Eagle, a gold piece with a $20 value. This remained an important banking coin for 80 years, though its use in day to day commerce was limited. Finally in 1933, as part of President Roosevelt's "New Deal" to counteract effects of the Depression, production of gold coinage was suspended and a recall made of all such coins in circulation. To this day the U. S. has not resumed minting gold coins.

Gold Coins in the Future? The question was raised, during the recent "gold rush" in January, 1980, whether our government could or should alleviate gold speculation and strengthen the dollar by resuming gold coinage. This seems a very remote possibility. The Treasury Department owns ample gold for coinage use, more than 250 million ounces. But the problems faced by such a move are insurmountable. Gold coins, if struck, would be too high a face value to freely circulate. Even a $10 denomination coin would weigh only about 1/60th of an ounce and be little bigger than a pinhead. Also, the rapidly fluctuating value of gold would make it impossible for face values to be maintained. The coins would end up merely being traded as bullion. There is no greater likelihood of a resumption of silver coinage either.

COINS OF THE CIVIL WAR AND LATE 19TH CENTURY

The Civil War brought about a currency emergency in the north and in most states of the Union. Coin supply became extremely short, resulting in trade tokens and the use of encased postage stamps — set into metal discs covered with a thin sheet of transparent mica — for currency. These failed to solve the problem and in some instances made matters worse, as merchants could go out of business or disappear without redeeming tokens. Paper notes were resorted to but as these lacked government backing there was little confidence in them. So the Federal Government stepped in and began to print its own notes, with face values equivalent to those of coinage. They came to be known as "greenbacks" because of the green paper stock on which they were printed. As the notes were not redeemable for gold or silver, this enhanced the value of precious metal and premiums were given for it in trading. A merchant selling an aritcle for $1.25 might accept $1 in silver. As copper was available in much more abundant quantities than gold or silver, the Treasury Department introduced a new coin, the 2¢ piece, designed to alleviate the drain on coinage. This was the first American coin to carry the motto "In God We Trust." Subsequently a three-cent piece was coined, in 1865. Finally the first true "nickel" or five-cent piece composed of base metal (as opposed to the half dime of earlier vintage) was issued in 1866, superseding the 2¢ and 3¢ denominations. Information on coinage of the Confederacy will be found at the appropriate place in the listings section of this book.

Reconstruction following the war made heavy demands upon coinage and paper money, originally regarded as an emergency measure only, was continued. From 1874 through 1877 no silver dollars were struck but the series was resumed in 1878. The new coin, authorized by the Bland Allison Act, featured a portrait of Liberty by George T. Morgan and came to be known as the Morgan Dollar — the most famous design of the entire silver $1 series. It was also important in another respect, as its purpose was to renew public confidence in silver and create new markets for the metal.

At the 19th century closed, the following designs were in use for coinage:

1¢ - Indian Head	$1 - Liberty ("Morgan")
5¢ - Liberty Head	$2.50 (gold) - Liberty Head
10¢ - Liberty Head ("Barber")	$5 (gold) - Liberty Head
25¢ - Liberty Head ("Barber")	$10 (gold) - Liberty Head
50¢ - Liberty Head ("Barber")	$20 (gold) - Liberty Head

As can be seen there was little variety, no more in fact than on coinage of the Mint's first years of operation. This situation was to change markedly in the next century.

COINS OF THE 20TH CENTURY

The 20th has proved by far the most exciting century for America's coins. Though the number of denominations was not so great as in the 19th, with the absence of so-called fractional cents, designs finally achieved some variety, rather than the endless repetition of Liberty Heads used in the 1800's. In 1909 the Indian cent was replaced by one picturing President Lincoln. This was followed in 1913 by the introduction of a truly classic coin, the Indian/Buffalo 5¢ piece, and in 1916 by a redesigned dime portraying Liberty. The quarter was likewise redesigned in 1916 and retained Liberty as its obverse type but this was time in a full-length standing pose. A variation of this theme graced the new half dollar (also in 1916), with Liberty in full-length but walking instead of standing. Never in the nation's history had so many fresh designs been installed on coinage within so short a period of time. Shortly after World War I, in 1921, the new $1 silver piece made its debut, the famous Peace dollar, named in recognition of the fact that America was no longer at war. Like its predecessor the Morgan dollar it featured a portrait of Liberty but drawn in a more modernistic, also Art Deco style. More information on these coins will be found in the appropriate places in the listings section.

The Liberty was the last U. S. silver dollar. It was discontinued in 1935, at the height of the economic depression, and when finally $1 coins were resumed in the 1970's they were no longer struck from silver, the metal by then having so greatly in value that a silver dollar would have been an unfashionable small coin. The Eisenhower or "Ike" dollar in uncirculated and proof condition contains 40% silver and 60% copper. Another dollar coin, intended not as a collectors' piece but for general circulation, was introduced in 1979. It pictured Susan B. Anthony and was of reduced size but not struck from precious metal. To date this coin has enjoyed limited success and its future is uncertain. (See the article on the future of Susan B. Anthony dollar located elsewhere in this edition.)

The economic depression also brought about a cessation of gold coinage. It was the belief of President Roosevelt that, if gold coinage and bullion were removed from circulation and placed in the government's hands, this would permit far greater quantities of paper notes to be printed (redeemable for bullion) and thus pump life into the economy. The price of gold was then set at $35 per ounce. A special provision was made for the retention of gold coins by collectors, which of course was abused by many persons who claimed to be collectors for the purpose of hoarding gold Eagles and Double Eagles.

Perhaps the most significant development of the 20th century was the measure taken in 1965, as the result of Congress' Coinage Act, to revise the metallic composition of coins previously minted of silver. The new dime and quarter contained no silver whatever, while the half dollar was reduced to 40% silver. Later in 1971 the 40% silver content of the half dollar was also dropped completely. This was brought about by the rising cost of silver, which threatened to surpass the face values of coins made from it, and the gradual disappearance of silver coins from circulation, as persons hoarded them in hopes of financial gain. While this alleviated the shortage it left the U. S. with coins as thoroughly debased as those of the most notorious Roman emperors. The new coinage has been referred to by critics as "token money" because of its negligible intrinsic value. During the mid-1970's there was strong speculation that the copper penny might be replaced with one made of aluminum or some other material. This possibility has now resurfaced.

THE RARE METALS — COPPER

To the general public, copper coins (and those of other base metal such as zinc) lack the glamor of gold and silver. The precious-metal rush of recent months has created an impression that coins of these metals are far better investments. The facts simply do not prove this out. The 1823 Large Cent in VF condition jumped from $80 in 1964 to $600 in 1979, while the 1871 2¢ MS-60 went from $40 to $350 in that same period — an increase comparable to the better silver coins and only slightly behind gold. Now that gold has risen beyond the reach of many collectors, quite a few who might have collected gold are turning to copper. In terms of design and historical significance, U. S. copper coinage rates high. Two of the most celebrated U. S. coins, the Large Cent and the Indian Head Penny, are copper. As for common-date modern cents as a metal investment, hoarding has already begun by hopeful individuals.

THE RARE METALS — SILVER

Most collectors are familiar with the events surrounding silver coinage in the past 15-20 years. In the early 1960's our dime, quarter and 50¢ piece were still being made of silver. Silver's market price was rising then (not so rapidly as later, but rising) and a point was being reached where, if it continued rising, the dime would contain more than 10¢ worth of silver and other coins likewise more than their face values. This could not be allowed to happen so in 1965 the government changed the metal content of these coins, constructing their centers of a mixture of copper and nickel and coating them with a silver plating. At first it was doubted that the old silver specimens would ever increase sufficiently in value to gain any profit in selling ordinary common dates. Within a few years they had all but disappeared from circulation and dealers began offering to pay advances of 10% or 20% over the face value. Today, silver-content coins dated before 1964 are worth about 11 to 12 times their face values, just for the metal content. As more and more are melted down they're sure to gain greater collector and investor status. Silver has traded for as much as $49.00 an ounce in the open market, and currently it is being traded in the area of $15.00 to $18.00. There is good reason to believe it will eventually go as high as $100.00.

THE RARE METALS — GOLD

The situation with gold has been rather different than the other metals. Gold coins are not being melted down in wholesale quantities but still their values soar. Less than 20 years ago a customer in any coin shop could have his pick of common-date $20 gold pieces for just double the face value. The average increase since than has been more than 2,000%, with prices — already high in January, 1979 — tripling in just the past year. Obviously, non-numismatic investor activity has been largely responsible. But no matter the cause, gold coins now have attained an aura of desirability, both to collector and investor, well beyond any they had previously possessed. In January, 1980, gold was traded for as much as $800 per ounce. At the time of going to press it was down to around the $625.00 to $650.00 range, but predictions are that gold will eventually reach $1,000.

SILVER COIN VALUE CHART
Prices Reflect Melt Value of Individual Coins

Silver Price Per Ounce	Amount of Pure Silver	15.00	20.00	25.00	30.00	35.00	40.00	45.00	50.00	55.00	60.00	65.00	70.00	Change in Value per Dollar
1942-45 5¢ U.S.	.05626 oz.	.85	1.13	1.41	1.69	1.97	2.25	2.54	2.82	3.10	3.38	3.66	3.94	.056
1965-70 5¢ U.S. 50¢	.14792 oz.	2.22	2.96	3.70	4.44	5.18	5.92	6.66	7.40	8.14	8.88	9.62	10.36	.148
U.S. $1	.31625 oz.	4.75	6.33	7.91	9.49	11.07	12.65	14.24	15.82	17.40	18.98	20.56	22.14	.316
1964 & Earlier U.S. 10¢	.07234 oz.	1.09	1.45	1.81	2.17	2.54	2.90	3.26	3.62	3.98	4.34	4.71	5.07	.072
1964 & Earlier U.S. 25¢	.18084 oz.	2.72	3.62	4.53	5.43	6.33	7.24	8.14	9.05	9.95	10.85	11.76	12.66	.18
1964 & Earlier U.S. 50¢	.36169 oz.	5.43	7.24	9.05	10.85	12.66	14.47	16.28	18.09	19.90	21.71	23.51	25.32	.362
1935 & Earlier U.S. $1	.77344 oz.	11.61	15.47	19.34	23.21	27.07	30.94	34.81	38.68	42.54	46.41	50.28	54.14	.772

Dealers who purchase silver coins to be melted normally pay 15% to 25% under melt value in order to cover their cost of handling.

GOLD COIN VALUE CHART
Prices Reflect Melt Value of Individual Coins

Gold Price Per Ounce	Amount of Pure Gold	200.00	300.00	400.00	500.00	550.00	600.00	650.00	700.00	800.00	900.00	1000.00	Change in Value per Dollar
U.S. $1.00	.04837 oz.	9.68	14.52	19.35	24.19	26.61	29.03	31.44	33.86	38.70	43.54	48.37	.048
U.S. $2.50	.12094 oz.	24.19	36.29	48.38	60.47	66.52	72.57	78.62	84.66	96.76	108.85	120.94	.121
U.S. $5.00	.14512 oz.	29.03	43.54	58.05	72.56	79.82	87.08	94.33	101.59	116.10	130.61	145.12	.145
U.S. $5.00	.24187 oz.	48.38	72.57	96.75	120.94	133.03	145.13	157.22	169.31	193.50	217.69	241.87	.242
U.S. $10.00	.48375 oz.	96.75	145.13	193.50	241.88	266.07	290.25	314.44	338.63	387.00	435.38	483.75	.484
U.S. $20.00	.96750 oz.	193.50	290.25	387.00	483.75	532.13	580.50	628.88	677.25	774.00	870.75	967.50	.967

Dealers normally purchase U.S. Gold Coins for a premium over melt. As an example, with Gold at $635.00/ounce you could expect a dealer to pay $700.00 for a common dated twenty dollar gold coin in extremely fine or better condition.

HOW UNITED STATES COINS ARE MINTED
THE COIN ALLOY CONTENT

In the coinage process, the first step is to prepare the alloy to be used. Except for nickels and one cent pieces, the alloys formerly (1964 and earlier) used in the coining of United States coins, were as follows:

a. **Silver coins**—90% silver and 10% copper
b. **Five-cent pieces**—75% copper and 25% nickel
c. **One-cent pieces**—95% copper and 5% zinc
(The cents of 1943 consisted of steel coated with zinc; and the nickels of 1942 to 1945 consisted of 35% silver, 56% copper, and 9% manganese.)

WHAT ARE THE NEW CLAD COINS MADE OF?

a. **(1971 TO DATE)** cupro-nickel dollars, and half dollars.
(1965 TO DATE) quarters and dimes. The outer surfaces are 75% copper and 25% nickel and the inner core is 100% copper.
b. **(1965-1970)** half dollars. The outer surface is 80% silver and 20% copper. The inner core is 21% silver and 79% copper. The overall silver content of the coin is 40%.

When clad coinage was introduced in 1965, the designs then in use were retained: the Roosevelt dime, Washington quarter and Kennedy half. (The U. S. was not at that time minting dollar coins.) The only alteration since then was for the special 1976 Bicentennial designs.

Because of the ever-increasing demand for coinage, the mint introduced new time-saving steps in its coin minting. Raw metal is cast into giant ingots 18 feet long, 16 inches wide and 6 inches thick, weighing 6,600 pounds. Previously they had weighed 400 pounds and were 16 times smaller in measurement. The ingot is rolled red hot and scaled to remove imperfections. It's then ready for the coins to be stamped; no longer are blanks made and annealed (heated). The excess metal that's left behind is used to make new ingots, in a continuing, never-ending process. The new coins are electronically scanned, counted and automatically bagged. These facilities are in use at the new, ultra-modern Mint in Philadelphia. It has a production capacity of eight billion coins per year and is open to the public, featuring interesting displays and guided tours.

HOW PROOF COINS ARE MINTED

1. Perfect planchets are picked out.
2. They are washed with a solution of cream of tartar.
3. Washed again and alcohol dipped.
4. The dies for making proof coins receive a special polishing for mirror-like finish.
5. The planchets are then milled.
6. The coins are minted by special hydraulic presses at a much slower rate than regular coins. The fine lines are much more visible on a proof coin.

MINTING: FROM METAL TO COINS

© 1965 by The New York Times Company. Reprinted by permission.

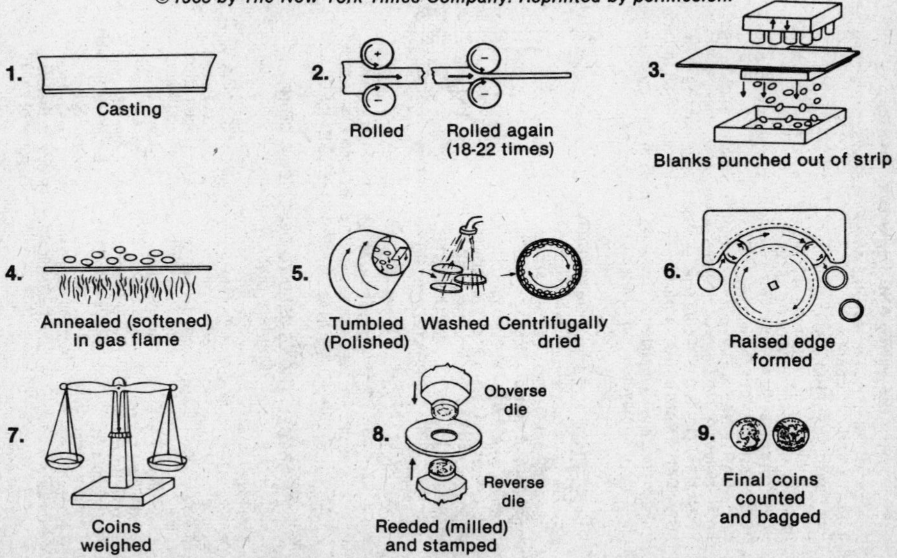

1. Casting

2. Rolled — Rolled again (18-22 times)

3. Blanks punched out of strip

4. Annealed (softened) in gas flame

5. Tumbled (Polished) — Washed — Centrifugally dried

6. Raised edge formed

7. Coins weighed

8. Obverse die — Reverse die — Reeded (milled) and stamped

9. Final coins counted and bagged

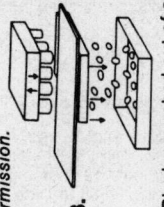
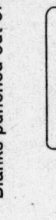

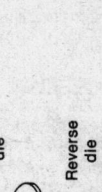
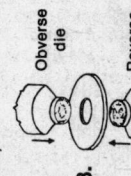
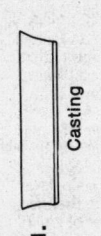

27

THE MINTS AND THEIR MINT MARKS

By separate Acts of Congress, the government has established mints in different parts of the country.

1. **"P"** PHILADELPHIA, *Pennsylvania* — 1973 to date — No Mint Mark. The coins minted at Philadelphia have never carried a mint mark except for nickels 1942 to 1945.
2. **"C"** CHARLOTTE, *North Carolina* — gold coins only 1838 to 1861.
3. **"CC"** CARSON CITY, *Nevada* — 1870 to 1893.
4. **"D"** DAHLONEGA, *Georgia* — on gold coins only 1838 to 1861.
5. **"D"** DENVER, *Colorado* — 1906 to Date.
6. **"O"** NEW ORLEANS, *Louisiana* — 1838 to 1861 and 1879 to 1909.
7. **"S"** SAN FRANCISCO, *California* — 1854 to 1955. 1968 to Date.

The mint mark is a small letter, denoting which mint made the coin. Mint marks appear on obverse and reverse of coins.

DESCRIPTIVE IDENTIFICATION OF A COIN

BORDERS
BEADED ·······
ORNAMENTED ·—·—·
SERRATED ━━ OR ▬▬ AND ∽∽∽

EDGES
MILLED • LETTERED • ORNAMENTED • VINE & BARS

• PLAIN • DIAGONALLY REEDED • ENGRAILED

ABBREVIATIONS USED TO DESCRIBE A COIN...
(Courtesy *Coins* Magazine)

FA = Fair	*Rev* = Reverse	*MM* = Mint Mark
G = Good	*Sm* = Small	*SL* = Small Letters
VG = Very Good	*Lg* = Large	*LL* = Large Letters
F = Fine	*Stg* = Standing	*SD* = Small Date
VF = Very Fine	*Std* = Seated	*LD* = Large Date
XF = Extra Fine	*Var* = Variety	*Eagle* = $10 gold
AU = About Uncirculated	*Avg* = Average	½ *Eagle* = $5 gold
Unc = Uncirculated	*W.C.* = With Cent	¼ *Eagle* = $2.50 gold
BU = Brilliant Uncirculated	*N.C.* = No Cent	*Double Eagle* = $20 gold
Prf = Proof	*42/41* = Overdate	*V.D.B.* = Initials of
Obv = Obverse	*Dupl* = Duplicate	Victor D. Brenner, designer of Lincoln cent.

WHAT IS COIN COLLECTING

Coin collecting or "numismatics" is a 2,000-year-old-hobby that began when the Romans started to collect Greek coins. For many years the physical beauty of coins was their chief attraction to collectors. Today there is greater interest in their origins, scarcity, and in building set or series. A typical series collection would include one specimen of each Lincoln penny issued from 1909 to date. The advanced specialist collects not only by date but mint mark. "Type" collecting, another popular approach, disregards dates and concentrates on designs. A type collection of 5¢ pieces would include the shield, liberty, buffalo and Jefferson. Topical collecting, yet another possibility, is more adaptable to foreign than to U. S. coins.

CONDITION OF COINS

This is an important matter that the beginner should not take lightly. Anyone who has started out collecting be saving pocket change or swapping with friends has generally formed a mistaken notion about condition. He believes that so long as a coin has a readable date and is not seriously marred the condition is acceptable. Actually there are various grades of condition, from Average to Uncirculated. The grade into which a coin falls greatly influences its value. An Uncirculated coin can be worth ten times as much as an Average. Don't be fooled by the word "average." This doesn't mean the usual grade of condition for that coin, but denotes a specimen that is well worn and far below "collector" condition. However there are many coins, especially very old ones, that are just about impossible to find in the best condition. In these situations an Average or Good specimen will be looked upon less disdainfully. The rarer a coin is, the more desirable it will be even if the condition is substandard. But don't pay Very Fine prices for Good or Very Good coins! The correct grading of coins — that is, classifying them by condition — is by no means simple and even the experts sometimes disagree. In the earlier days of numismatics, dealers were often accused of overgrading. Today the complains are not as numerous, but it's a fact of life that anything a seller owns, whether the seller is a dealer or private party, is likely to have more beauty in his eyes than those of a prospective purchaser. Please refer to our Official ANA grading section of this book explanations on coin grading.

SCARCITY

Scarcity comes in many shades of meaning. One of the chief satisfactions in collecting is owning coins that are scarce, or hard to get, or at least harder to get than those in everyday pocket change. But scarcity is hard to define. The 1913S Lincoln cent is far scarcer than any cent in your pocket but can be supplied by any coin dealer. There is no scarcity of it on the market. Price is not a true indication of scarcity because factors in addition to scarcity influence price, such as condition and demand. Strong demand can result in a high price for a coin which isn't especially scarce. A good example are "key" coins needed to complete sets or runs. Generally the coin with the lowest mintage in a series is the scarcest and sells for the highest price but this is not invariably so.

GEOGRAPHIC LOCATION

This plays some role in the availability of modern or recent coins. Coins take a long while to disperse evenly across the country. On the West Coast you will find a greater proportion of "S" mintmarks (coins struck at San Francisco) than in the east, while Philadelphia-minted coins are not as frequently found west of the Rockies. However, the effect of geographic location on coin prices is becoming negligible, now that so many dealers operate nationwide by mail and phone.

WHERE TO BUY AND SELL COINS

There are many potential sources for buying and selling coins: coin shops, auction sales, approval selections, coin shows and conventions, mail order and other collectors. If a coin shop is located in your area, this is the best place to begin buying. By examining the many coins offered in a shop you will become familiar with grading standards. Later you may wish to try buying at auction. When buying from dealers be sure to do business only with reputable parties. Be wary of rare coins offered at bargain prices as they could be counterfeits or improperly graded. Some bargain coins are specimens that have been amateurishly cleaned and are not considered desirable by collectors. The best "bargains" are popular coins in good condition, offered at fair prices.

Selling Coins to a Dealer. All coin dealers buy from the public. They must replenish their stock and the public is a much more economical source of supply than buying from other dealers. Damaged, very worn, or common coins are worthless to a dealer. So, too, usually, are sets in which the "key" coins are missing. If you have a large collection or several valuable coins to sell it might be wise to check the pages of coin publications for addresses of dealers handling major properties, rather than selling to a local shop.

Other outlets for selling your gold and silver coins, bars and sterling flatware are firms that only buy periodically, depending on market conditions. Every effort should be made only to sell to reputable and established persons; try to avoid selling to the "traveling dealer" who uses hotel rooms as a location for buying.

Visit a coin show or convention. There you will find many dealers at one time, and you will experience the thrill of an active trading market in coins. You will find schedules of conventions and meetings of regional coin clubs listed in such publications as:

Coin World ($18.00/yr.)
Post Office Box 150
Sidney, OH 45367

The Numismatist ($15.00/yr.)
Published by the A.N.A.
P.O. Box 2366
Colorado Springs, CO 80901

Coins Magazine ($9.00/yr.) or
Numismatic News ($13.50/yr.)
700 E. State Street
Iola, WI 54945

The Coin Wholesaler ($10.00/yr.)
2970 Peachtree Road, N.W.
Atlanta, GA 30305

To find your local dealer, check the phone book under *"Coin Dealers"*.

CLEANING COINS

Under no circumstances should any effort be made to clean coins. Their value is likely to be reduced by such attempt.

HOW TO USE THIS BOOK

This book contains a complete record of all coins minted by the federal government from 1793 to date as well as many of the more important Colonial issues. It is broken down into denomination and series, with the coins of each series listed chronologically. Listings give the coin's date; its mint mark, if any, and additional information that may be needed for identification; quantity minted; average buying price; and retail values in various grades of condition. Please note that the grades of condition for which prices are given vary throughout the book. For example there are listings for proof specimens of recent coins but not for early ones, where proofs would be impossible to get. For colonial coinage the best grade of condition that can reasonably be expected is "fine," due to the vast age of these coins and the fact that many were produced by old-fashioned hand hammering.

A.B.P. or *AVERAGE BUYING PRICE.* The average buying price is just that, the price most dealers will pay for that particular coin in good condition. Keep in mind that buying prices vary just as much as selling prices. When the selling price of a coin is up, the buying price should be as well.

OFFICIAL ANA GRADING SYSTEM

The descriptions of coin grades given in this book are intended for use in determining the relative condition of coins in various states of preservation. The terms and standards are based on the commonly accepted practices of experienced dealers and collectors. Use of these standards is recommended by the American Numismatic Association to avoid misunderstandings during transactions, cataloging and advertising.

The method of grading described in this book should be referred to as the Official ANA Grading System. When grading by these standards, care must be taken to adhere to the standard wording, abbreviations and numbers used in this text.

When a coin first begins to show signs of handling, abrasion, or light wear, only the highest parts of the design are affected. Evidence that such a coin is not Uncirculated can be seen by carefully examining the high spots for signs of a slight change in color, surface texture, or sharpness of fine details.

In early stages of wear the highest points of design become slightly rounded or flattened, and the very fine details begin to merge together in small spots.

After a coin has been in circulation for a short time, the entire design and surface will show light wear. Many of the high parts will lose their sharpness, and most of the original mint luster will begin to wear except in recessed areas.

Further circulation will reduce the sharpness and relief of the entire design. High points then begin to merge with the next lower parts of the design.

After the protective rim is worn away the entire surface becomes flat, and most of the details blend together or become partially merged with the surface.

It should be understood that because of the nature of the minting process, some coins will be found which do not conform exactly with the standard definitions of wear as given in this text. Specific points of wear may vary slightly. Information given in the notes at the end of some sections does not cover all exceptions, but is a guide to the most frequently encountered varieties.

Also, the amount of mint luster (for the highest several grades) is intended more as a visual guide rather than a fixed quantity. The percentage of visible mint luster described in the text is the *minimum* allowable amount, and a higher percentage can usually be expected. Luster is not always brilliant and may be evident although sometimes dull or discolored.

A *Choice* coin in any condition is one with an attractive, above average surface relatively free from nicks or bag marks. A *Typical* coin may have more noticeable minor surface blemishes.

In all cases, a coin in lower condition must be assumed to include all the wear features of the next higher grade in addition to its own distinguishing points of wear.

Remarks concerning the visibility of certain features refer to the *maximum* allowable amount of wear for those features.

NOTE: The official ANA Grading System used in this book is with the permission of the American Numismatic Association.

RECORD KEEPING

For your convenience, we suggest you use the following record-keeping system to note condition of your coin in the checklist box.

ABOUT GOOD ◘   FINE ◘   UNCIRCULATED ◘
GOOD ◘   VERY FINE ◘   PROOF ■
VERY GOOD ◘ EXTREMELY FINE ◘

GRADING ABBREVIATIONS

Corresponding numbers may be used with any of these descriptions.

PROOF-70	Perfect Proof	Perf. Proof	Proof-70
PROOF-65	Choice Proof	Ch. Proof	Proof-65
PROOF-60	Proof	Proof	Proof-60
MS-70	Perfect Uncirculated	Perf. Unc.	Unc.-70
MS-65	Choice Uncirculated	Ch. Unc.	Unc.-65
MS-60	Uncirculated	Unc.	Unc.-60
AU-55	Choice About Uncirculated	Ch. Abt. Unc.	Ch. AU
AU-50	About Uncirculated	Abt. Unc.	AU
EF-45	Choice Extremely Fine	Ch. Ex. Fine	Ch. EF
EF-40	Extremely Fine	Ex. Fine	EF
VF-30	Choice Very Fine	Ch. V. Fine	Ch. VF
VF-20	Very Fine	V. Fine	VF
F-12	Fine	Fine	F
VG-8	Very Good	V. Good	VG
G-4	Good	Good	G
AG-3	About Good	Abt. Good	AG

PROOF COINS

The mirrorlike surface of a brilliant proof coin is much more susceptible to damage than are the surfaces of an Uncirculated coin. For this reason, proof coins which have been cleaned often show a series of fine hairlines or minute striations. Also, careless handling has resulted in certain proofs acquiring marks, nicks and scratches.

Some proofs, particularly nineteenth century issues, have "lintmarks." When a proof die was wiped with an oily rag, sometimes threads, bits of hair, lint, and so on would remain. When a coin was struck from such a die, an incuse or recessed impression of the debris would appear on the piece. Lintmarks visible to the unaided eye should be specifically mentioned in a description.

Proofs are divided into the following classifications:

Proof-70 (Perfect Proof). A Proof-70 or Perfect Proof is a coin with no hairlines, handling marks, or other defects; in other words, a flawless coin. Such a coin may be brilliant or may have natural toning.

Proof-65 (Choice Proof). Proof-65 or Choice Proof refers to a proof which may show some fine hairlines, usually from friction-type cleaning or friction-type drying or rubbing after dipping. To the unaided eye, a Proof-65 or a Choice Proof will appear to be virtually perfect. However, 5x magnification will reveal some minute lines. Such hairlines are best seen under strong incandescent light.

Proof-60 (Proof). Proof-60 refers to a proof with some scattered handling marks and hairlines which will be visible to the unaided eye.

Impaired Proofs; Other Comments. If a proof has been excessively cleaned, has many marks, scratches, dents or other defects, it is described as an impaired proof. If the coin has seen extensive wear then it will be graded one of the lesser grades — Proof-55, Proof-45 or whatever. It is not logical to describe a slightly worn proof as "AU" (Almost Uncirculated) for it never was "Uncirculated" to begin with — in the sense that Uncirculated describes a top grade normal production strike. So, the term "impaired proof" is appropriate. It is best to describe fully such a coin, examples being: "Proof with extensive hairlines and scuffing," or "Proof with numerous nicks and scratches in the field," or "Proof-55, with light wear on the higher surfaces."

UNCIRCULATED COINS

The term "Uncirculated," interchangeable with "Mint State," refers to a coin which has never seen circulation. Such a piece has no wear of any kind. A coin as bright as the time it was minted or with very light natural toning can be described as "Brilliant Uncirculated." A coin which has natural toning can be described as "Toned Uncirculated." Except in the instance of copper coins, the presence or absence of light toning does not affect an Uncirculated coin's grade. Indeed, among silver coins, attractive natural toning often results in the coin bringing a premium.

The quality of luster or "mint bloom" on an Uncirculated coin is an essential element in correctly grading the piece, and has a bearing on its value. Luster may in time become dull, frosty, spotted or discolored. Unattractive luster will normally lower the grade.

With the exception of certain Special Mint Sets made in recent years for collectors, Uncirculated or normal production strike coins were produced on high speed presses, stored in bags together with other coins, run through counting machines, and in other ways handled without regard to numismatic posterity. As a result, it is the rule and not the exception for an Uncirculated coin to have bag marks and evidence of coin-to-coin contact, although the piece might not have seen actual commercial circulation. The amount of such marks will depend upon the coin's size. Differences in criteria in this regard are given in the individual sections under grading descriptions for different denominations and types.

Uncirculated coins can be divided into three major categories:

MS-70 (Perfect Uncirculated). MS-70 or Perfect Uncirculated is the finest quality available. Such a coin under 4x magnification will show no bag marks, lines, or other evidence of handling or contact with other coins.

A brilliant coin may be described as "MS-70, Brilliant" or "Perfect Brilliant Uncirculated." A lightly toned nickel or silver coin may be described as "MS-70, toned" or "Perfect Toned Uncirculated." Or, in the case of particularly attractive or unusual toning, additional adjectives may be in order such as "Perfect Uncirculated with attractive iridescent toning around the borders."

Copper and bronze coins: To qualify as MS-70 or Perfect Uncirculated, a copper or bronze coin must have its full luster and natural surface color, and may not be toned brown, olive, or any other color. (Coins with toned surfaces which are otherwise perfect should be described as MS-65 as the following text indicates.)

MS-65 (Choice Uncirculated). This refers to an above average Uncirculated coin which may be brilliant or tones (and described accordingly) and which has fewer bag marks than usual; scattered occasional bag marks on the surface or perhaps one or two very light rim marks.

MS-60 (Uncirculated). MS-60 or Uncirculated (typical Uncirculated without any other adjectives) refers to a coin which has a moderate number of bag marks on its surface. Also present may be a few minor edge nicks and marks, although not of a serious nature. Unusually deep bag marks, nicks and the like must be described separately. A coin may be either brilliant or toned.

Striking and Minting Peculiarities on Uncirculated Coins

Certain early United States gold and silver coins have mint-caused planchet or adjustment marks, a series of parallel striations. If these are visible to the naked eye they should be described adjectively in addition to the numerical or regular descriptive grade. For example: "MS-60 with adjustment marks," or "MS-65 with adjustment marks," or "Perfect Uncirculated with very light adjustment marks," or something similar.

If an Uncirculated coin exhibits weakness due to striking or die wear, or unusual (for the variety) die wear, this must be adjectivally mentioned in addition to the grade. Examples are: "MS-60, lightly struck," or "Choice Uncirculated, lightly struck," and "MS-70, lightly struck."

CIRCULATED COINS

Once again a coin enters circulation it begins to shows signs of wear. As time goes on the coin becomes more and more worn until; after a period of many decades, only a few features may be left.

Dr. William H. Sheldon devised a numerical scale to indicate degrees of wear. According to this scale, a coin in condition 1 or "Basal State" is barely recognizable. At the opposite end, a coin touched by even the slightest trace of wear (below MS-60) cannot be called Uncirculated.

While numbers from 1 through 59 are continuous, it has been found practical to designate specific intermediate numbers to define grades. Hence, this text uses the following descriptions and their numerical equivalents:

AU-55 (Choice About Uncirculated). Only a small trace of wear is visible on the highest points of the coin. As is the case with the other grades here, specific information is listed in the following text under the various types, for wear often occurs in different spots on different designs.

AU-50 (About Uncirculated). With traces of wear on nearly all of the highest areas. At least half of the original mint luster is present.

EF-45 (Choice Extremely Fine). With light overall wear on the coin's highest points. All design details are very sharp. Mint luster is usually seen only in protected areas of the coin's surface such as between the star points and in the letter spaces.

EF-40 (Extremely Fine). With only slight wear but more extensive than the preceding, still with excellent overall sharpness. Traces of mint luster may still show.

VF-30 (Choice Very Fine). With light even wear on the surface; design details on the highest points lightly worn, but with all lettering and major features sharp.

VF-20 (Very Fine). As preceding but with moderate wear on highest parts.

F-12 (Fine). Moderate to considerable even wear. Entire design is bold. All lettering, including the word LIBERTY (on coins with this feature on the shield or headband), visible, but with some weaknesses.

VG-8 (Very Good). Well worn. Most fine details such as hair strands, leaf details, and so on are worn nearly smooth. The word LIBERTY, if on a shield or headband, is only partially visible.

G-4 (Good). Heavily worn. Major designs visible, but with faintness in areas. Head of Liberty, wreath, and other major features visible in outline form without center detail.

AG-3 (About Good). Very heavily worn with portions of the lettering, date and legends being worn smooth. The date barely readable.

Note: The exact descriptions of circulated grades vary widely from issue to issue. It is essential to refer to the specific text when grading any coin.

SPLIT AND INTERMEDIATE GRADES

It is often the case that because of the peculiarities of striking or a coin's design, one side of the coin will grade differently from the other. When this is the case, a diagonal mark is used to separate the two. For example, a coin with an AU-50 obverse and a Choice Extremely Fine-45 reverse can be described as: AU/EF or, alternately, 50/45.

The ANA standard numerical scale is divided into the following steps: 3, 4, 8, 12, 20, 30, 40, 45, 50, 60, 65 and 70. Most advanced collectors and dealers find that the gradations from AG-3 through Choice AU-55 are sufficient to describe nearly every coin showing wear. The use of intermediate grade levels such as EF-42, EF-43 and so on is not encouraged. Grading is not that precise, and using such finely split intermediate grades is imparting a degree of accuracy which probably will not be able to be verified by other numismatists. As such, it is discouraged.

A split or intermediate grade, such as that between VF-30 and EF-40, should be called Choice VF-35 rather than VF-EF or About EF.

An exception to intermediate grades can be found among Mint State coins, coins grading from MS-60 through MS-70. Among Mint State coins there are fewer variables. Wear is not a factor; the considerations are the amount of bag marks and surface blemishes. While it is good numismatic practice to adhere to the numerical classifications of 60, 65 and 70, it is permissible to use intermediate grades.

In all instances, the adjectival description must be of the next lower grade. For example, a standard grade for a coin is MS-60 or Uncirculated Typical. The next major category is MS-65 or Uncirculated Choice. A coin which is felt to grade, for example, MS-64, must be described as "MS-64, Uncirculated Typical." It may not be described as Choice Uncirculated, for the minimum definition of Choice Uncirculated is MS-65. Likewise, a MS-69 coin must be described as: MS-69, Uncirculated Choice. It is not permissible to use Uncirculated Perfect for any coin which is any degree less than MS-70.

The ANA grading system considers it to be good numismatic practice to adhere to the standard 60, 65 and 70 numerical designations. Experienced numismatists can generally agree on whether a given coin is MS-60 or MS-65. However, not even the most advanced numismatists can necessarily agree on whether a coin is MS-62 or MS-63; the distinction is simply too minute to permit accuracy. In all instances, it is recommended that intermediate grades be avoided, and if there is any doubt, the lowest standard grade should be used. The use of plus or minus signs is also not accepted practice.

SMALL CENTS — INDIAN HEAD 1859-1909

REVERSE
(without shield, 1859)

OBVERSE

REVERSE
(with shield, 1860-1909)

MINT STATE *(Absolutely no trace of wear.)*

MS-70 (Perfect Uncirculated)
A flawless coin exactly as it was minted, with no trace of wear or injury. Must have full mint luster and brilliance of light toning. Any unusual die or planchet traits must be described.

MS-65 (Choice Uncirculated)
No trace of wear; nearly as perfect as MS-70 except for some small blemish. Has full mint luster but may be unevenly toned or lightly fingermarked. A few barely noticeable nicks or marks may be present.

MS-60 (Uncirculated)
A strictly Uncirculated coin with no trace of wear, but with blemishes more obvious than for MS-65. May lack full mint luster, and surface may be dull or spotted. Check points for signs of abrasion: hair above ear; curl to right of ribbon; bow knot.

ABOUT UNCIRCULATED *(Small trace of wear visible on highest points.)*

AU-55 (Choice About Uncirculated)
OBVERSE: Only a trace of wear shows on the hair above the ear.
REVERSE: A trace of wear shows on the bow knot. Three-quarters of the mint lust is still present.

AU-50 (About Uncirculated)
OBVERSE: Traces of wear show on the hair above ear and curl to right of ribbon.
REVERSE: Traces of wear show on the leaves and bow knot. Half of the mint luster is still present.

EXTREMELY FINE *(Very light wear on only the highest points.)*

EF-45 (Choice Extremely Fine)
OBVERSE: Wear shows on hair above ear, curl to right of ribbon and on the ribbon end. All of the diamond design and letters in LIBERTY are very plain.
REVERSE: High points of the leaves and bow are lightly worn. Traces of mint luster still show.

EF-40 (Extremely Fine)
OBVERSE: Feathers well defined and LIBERTY is bold. Wear shows on hair above ear, curl to right of ribbon and on the ribbon end. Most of the diamond design shows plainly.
REVERSE: High points of the leaves and bow are worn.

VERY FINE *(Light to moderate even wear. All major features are sharp.)*

VF-30 (Choice Very Fine)
OBVERSE: Small flat spots of wear on tips of feathers, ribbon and hair ends. Hair still shows half of details. LIBERTY slightly worn but all letters are sharp.
REVERSE: Leaves and bow worn but fully detailed.

VF-20 (Very Fine)
OBVERSE: Headdress shows considerable flatness. Nearly half of the details still show in hair and on ribbon. Head slightly worn but bold. LIBERTY is worn but all letters are complete.
REVERSE: Leaves and bow are almost fully detailed.

FINE *(Moderate to heavy even wear. Entire design clear and bold.)*

F-12 (Fine)
OBVERSE: One-quarter of details show in the hair. Ribbon is worn smooth. LIBERTY shows clearly with no letters missing.
REVERSE: Some details visible in the wreath and bow. Tops of leaves are worn smooth.

VERY GOOD *(Well worn. Design clear but flat and lacking details.)*

VG-8 (Very Good)
OBVERSE: Outline of feather ends shows but some are smooth. Legend and date are visible. At least three letters in LIBERTY show clearly, but any combination of two full letters and parts of two others are sufficient.

REVERSE: Slight detail in wreath shows, but the top is worn smooth. Very little outline showing in the bow.

GOOD *(Heavily worn. Design and legend visible but faint in spots.)*

G-4 (Good)
OBVERSE: Entire design well worn with very little detail remaining. Legend and date are weak but visible.
REVERSE: Wreath is worn flat but completely outlined. Bow merges with wreath.

ABOUT GOOD *(Outlined design. Parts of date and legend worn smooth.)*

AG-3 (About Good)
OBVERSE: Head is outlined with nearly all details worn away. Legend and date readable but very weak and merging into rim.
REVERSE: Entire design partially worn away. Bow is merged with the wreath.

SMALL CENTS — LINCOLN 1909 TO DATE

REVERSE
(wheatline, 1909-1958)

OBVERSE

REVERSE
(memorial, 1959-date)

MINT STATE *(Absolutely no trace of wear.)*

MS-70 (Perfect Uncirculated)
A flawless coin exactly as it was minted, with no trace of wear or injury. Must have full mint luster and brilliance of light toning. Any unusual die or planchet traits must be described.

MS-65 (Choice Uncirculated)
No trace of wear; nearly as perfect as MS-70 except for some small blemish. Has full mint luster but may be unevenly toned or lightly fingermarked. A few barely noticeable nicks or marks may be present.

MS-60 (Uncirculated)
A strictly Uncirculated coin with no trace of wear, but with blemishes more obvious than for MS-65. May lack full mint luster, and surface may be dull or spotted. Check points for signs of abrasion: high points of cheek and jaw; tips of wheat stalks.

ABOUT UNCIRCULATED *(Small trace of wear visible on highest points.)*

AU-55 (Choice About Uncirculated)
OBVERSE: Only a trace of wear shows on the highest point of the jaw.
REVERSE: A trace of wear on the top of wheat stalks. Almost all of the mint luster is still present.

AU-50 (About Uncirculated)
OBVERSE: Traces of wear show on the cheek and jaw.
REVERSE: Traces of wear show on the wheat stalks. Three-quarters of the mint luster is still present.

EXTREMELY FINE *(Very light wear on only the highest points.)*
EF-45 (Choice Extremely Fine)
OBVERSE: Slight wear shows on hair above ear, on the cheek, and at the jaw.
REVERSE: High points of wheat stalks are lightly worn, but each line is clearly defined. Half of the mint luster still shows.

EF-40 (Extremely Fine)
OBVERSE: Wear shows on hair above ear, on the cheek, and on the jaw.
REVERSE: High points of wheat stalks are worn, but each line is clearly defined. Traces of mint luster still show.

VERY FINE *(Light to moderate even wear. All major features are sharp.)*
VF-30 (Choice Very Fine)
OBVERSE: There are small flat spots of wear on cheek and jaw. Hair still shows details. Ear and bow tie slightly worn but show clearly.
REVERSE: Lines in wheat stalks are lightly worn but fully detailed.

VF-20 (Very Fine)
OBVERSE: Head shows considerable flatness. Nearly all the details still show in hair and on the face. Ear and bow tie worn but bold.
REVERSE: Lines in wheat stalks are worn but plain and without weak spots.

FINE *(Moderate to heavy even wear. Entire design clear and bold.)*
F-12 (Fine)
OBVERSE: Some details show in the hair. Cheek and jaw are worn nearly smooth. LIBERTY shows clearly with no letters missing. The ear and bow tie are visible.
REVERSE: Most details are visible in the stalks. Top wheat lines are worn but separated.

VERY GOOD *(Well worn. Design clear but flat and lacking details.)*
VG-8 (Very Good)
OBVERSE: Outline of hair shows but most details are smooth. Cheek and jaw are smooth. More than half of bow tie is visible. Legend and date are clear.
REVERSE: Wheat shows some details and about half of the lines at the top.

GOOD *(Heavily worn. Design and legend visible but faint in spots.)*
G-4 (Good)
OBVERSE: Entire design well worn with very little detail remaining. Legend and date are weak but visible.
REVERSE: Wheat is worn nearly flat but is completely outlined. Some grains are visible.

ABOUT GOOD *(Outlined design. Parts of date and legend worn smooth.)*
AG-3 (About Good)
OBVERSE: Head is outlined with nearly all details worn away. Legend and date readable but very weak and merging into rim.
REVERSE: Entire design partially worn away. Parts of wheat and motto merged with the wreath.

Note: The Memorial cents from 1959 to date can be graded by using the obverse descriptions.

The following characteristic traits will assist in grading but must not be confused with actual wear on the coins:
  Matte proof cents of 1909 through 1916 are often spotted or stained.
  Branch mint cents of the 1920's are usually not as sharply struck as later dates.

Many of the early dates of Lincoln cents are weakly struck either on the obverse or the reverse, especially the following dates: 1911-D, 1914-D, 1917-D, 1918-D, 1921, 1922-D, 1923, 1924, 1927-D, 1927-S and 1929-D.

1922 "plain" is weakly struck at the head, has a small l and joined RT in LIBERTY. Sometimes the wheat heads are weak on the reverse.

1924-D usually has a weak mint mark.

1931-S is sometimes unevenly struck.

1936 proof cents: early strikes are less brilliant than those made later that year.

1955 doubled die: hair details are less sharp than most cents of the period.

NICKEL FIVE CENTS — LIBERTY HEAD 1883-1912

OBVERSE   "NO CENTS" REVERSE   REVERSE

MINT STATE *(Absolutely no trace of wear.)*

MS-70 (Perfect Uncirculated)
A flawless coin exactly as it was minted, with no trace of wear or injury. Must have full mint luster but this may range from brilliant to frosty. Any unusual die or striking traits must be described.

MS-65 (Choice Uncirculated)
No trace of wear; nearly as perfect as MS-70 except for some small weakness or blemish. Has full mint luster but may be unevenly toned, frosty, or lightly fingermarked. A few barely noticeable nicks or marks may be present.

MS-60 (Uncirculated)
A strictly Uncirculated coin with no trace of wear, but with blemishes more obvious than for MS-65. May lack full mint luster, and surface may be dull or spotted. Check points for signs of abrasion: high points of hair left of ear and at forehead. Corn ears at bottom of wreath.

ABOUT UNCIRCULATED *(Small trace of wear visible on highest points.)*

AU-55 (Choice About Uncirculated)
OBVERSE: Only a trace of wear shows on the highest points of hair left of ear.
REVERSE: A trace of wear shows on corn ears. Half of the mint luster is still present.

AU-50 (About Uncirculated)
OBVERSE: Traces of wear show on hair left of ear and at forehead.
REVERSE: Traces of wear show on the wreath and on corn ears. Part of the mint luster is still present.

EXTREMELY FINE *(Very light wear on only the highest points.)*

EF-45 (Choice Extremely Fine)
OBVERSE: Slight wear shows on high points of hair from forehead to the ear.
REVERSE: High points of wreath are lightly worn. Lines in corn are clearly defined. Traces of mint luster may still show.

EF-40 (Extremely Fine)
OBVERSE: Wear shows on hair from forehead to ear, on the cheek, and on curls.
REVERSE: High points of wreath are worn, but each line is clearly defined. Corn shows some wear.

VERY FINE *(Light to moderate even wear. All major features are sharp.)*

VF-30 (Choice Very Fine)
OBVERSE: Three-quarters of hair details show. The coronet has full bold lettering.
REVERSE: Leaves are worn but most of the ribs are visible. Some of the lines in the corn are clear unless weakly struck.

VF-20 (Very Fine)
OBVERSE: Over half the details still show in hair and curls. Head worn but bold. Every letter on coronet is plainly visible.
REVERSE: Leaves are worn but some of the ribs are visible. Most details in the wreath are clear unless weakly struck.

FINE *(Moderate to heavy even wear. Entire design clear and bold.)*

F-12 (Fine)
OBVERSE: Some details show in curls and hair at top of head. All letters of LIBERTY are visible.
REVERSE: Some details visible in wreath. Letters in the motto are worn but clear.

VERY GOOD *(Well worn. Design clear but flat and lacking details.)*

VG-8 (Very Good)
OBVERSE: Bottom edge of coronet, and most hair details, are worn smooth. At least three letters in LIBERTY are clear. Rim is complete.
REVERSE: Wreath shows only bold outline. Some letters in the motto are very weak. Rim is complete.

GOOD *(Heavily worn. Design and legend visible but faint in spots.)*

G-4 (Good)
OBVERSE: Entire design well worn with very little detail remaining. Stars and date are weak but visible.
REVERSE: Wreath is worn flat and not completely outlined. Legend and motto are worn nearly smooth.

ABOUT GOOD *(Outlined design. Parts of date and legend worn smooth.)*

AG-3 (About Good)
OBVERSE: Head is outlined with nearly all details worn away. Date readable but very weak and merging into rim.
REVERSE: Entire design partially worn away.

Note: The 1912-D, 1912-S and 1883 "no cents" variety are often weakly struck.

NICKEL FIVE CENTS — BUFFALO 1913-1938

MINT STATE *(Absolutely no trace of wear.)*

MS-70 (Perfect Uncirculated)
A flawless coin exactly as it was minted, with no trace of wear or injury. Must have full mint luster. Any unusual die or striking traits must be described.

MS-65 (Choice Uncirculated)
No trace of wear; nearly as perfect as MS-70 except for some small weakness or blemish. Has full mint luster but may be unevenly toned or lightly fingermarked. A few barely noticeable nicks or marks may be present.

NICKEL FIVE CENTS — BUFFALO 1913-1938

OBVERSE    REVERSE

MS-60 (Uncirculated)
A strictly uncirculated coin with no trace of wear, but with blemishes more obvious than for MS-65. May lack full mint luster and surface may be dull or spotted. Check points for signs of abrasion: high points of Indian's cheek. Upper front leg, hip, tip of tail. Shallow or weak spots in the relief are usually caused by improper striking and not wear.

ABOUT UNCIRCULATED *(Small trace of wear visible on highest points.)*

AU-55 (Choice About Uncirculated)
OBVERSE: Only a trace of wear shows on high point of cheek.
REVERSE: A trace of wear shows on the hip. Half of the mint luster is still present.

AU-50 (About Uncirculated)
OBVERSE: Traces of wear show on hair above and to left of forehead, and at the cheek bone.
REVERSE: Traces of wear show on tail, hip and hair above and around the horn. Traces of mint luster still show.

EXTREMELY FINE *(Very light wear on only the highest points.)*

EF-45 (Choice Extremely Fine)
OBVERSE: Slight wear shows on the hair above the braid. There is a trace of wear on the temple and hair near cheek bone.
REVERSE: High points of hip and thigh are lightly worn. The horn and tip of tail are sharp and nearly complete.

EF-40 (Extremely Fine)
OBVERSE: Hair and face are lightly worn but well defined and bold. Slight wear shows on lines of hair braid.
REVERSE: Horn and end of tail are worn but all details are visible.

VERY FINE *(Light to moderate even wear. All major features are sharp.)*

VF-30 (Choice Very Fine)
OBVERSE: Hair shows nearly full details. Feathers and braid are worn but sharp.
REVERSE: Head, front leg and hip are worn. Tail shows plainly. Horn is worn but full.

VF-20 (Very Fine)
OBVERSE: Hair and cheek show considerable flatness, but all details are clear. Feathers still show partial detail.
REVERSE: Hair on head is worn. Tail and point of horn are visible.

FINE *(Moderate to considerable even wear. Entire design clear and bold.)*

F-12 (Fine)
OBVERSE: Three-quarters of details show in hair and braid. LIBERTY is plain but merging with rim.
REVERSE: Major details visible along the back. Horn and tail are smooth but three-quarters visible.

VERY GOOD *(Well worn. Design clear but flat and lacking details.)*
VG-8 (Very Good)
OBVERSE: Outline of hair is visible at temple and near cheek bone. LIBERTY merges with rim. Date is clear.
REVERSE: Some detail shows in head. Lettering is all clear. Horn is worn nearly flat but is partially visible.

GOOD *(Heavily worn. Design and legend visible but faint in spots.)*
G-4 (Good)
OBVERSE: Entire design well worn with very little detail remaining in central part. LIBERTY is weak and merged with rim.
REVERSE: Buffalo is nearly flat but is well outlined. Horn does not show. Legend is weak but readable. Rim worn to tops of letters.

ABOUT GOOD *(Outlined design. Parts of date and legend worn smooth.)*
AG-3 (About Good)
OBVERSE: Design is outlined with nearly all details worn away. Date and motto partially readable but very weak and merging into rim.
REVERSE: Entire design partially worn away. Rim is merged with the letters.

Note: Buffalo nickels were often weakly struck, and lack details even on Uncirculated specimens. The following dates are usually unevenly struck with weak spots in the details:
1913-S I and II, 1917-D, 1917-S, 1918-D, 1918-S, 1919-S, 1920-D, 1920-S, 1921-S, 1923-S, 1924-D, 1924-S, 1925-D, 1925-S, 1926-D, 1926-S, 1927-D, 1927-S, 1928-D, 1928-S, 1929-D, 1931-S, 1934-D and 1935-D.
1913 through 1916 matte proof coins are sometimes spotted or stained.

NICKEL FIVE CENTS — JEFFERSON 1938 TO DATE

OBVERSE   "WARTIME" REVERSE 1942-1945   REVERSE

MINT STATE *(Absolutely no trace of wear.)*
MS-70 (Perfect Uncirculated)
A flawless coin exactly as it was minted, with no trace of wear or injury. Must have full mint luster and brilliance. Any unusual striking or planchet traits must be described.

MS-65 (Choice Uncirculated)
No trace of wear; nearly as perfect as MS-70 except for some small weakness or blemish. Has full mint luster but may be unevenly toned or lightly fingermarked. A few barely noticeable nicks or marks may be present.

MS-60 (Uncirculated)
A strictly Uncirculated coin with no trace of wear, but with weaknesses and blemishes more obvious than for MS-65. May lack full mint luster, and surface may be dull or spotted. Check points for signs of abrasion: cheek bone and high points of hair. Triangular roof above pillars. Shallow or weak spots in the relief, particularly in the steps below pillars, are usually caused by improper striking and not wear.

ABOUT UNCIRCULATED *(Small trace of wear visible on highest points.)*

AU-55 (Choice About Uncirculated)
OBVERSE: Only a trace of wear shows on cheek bone.
REVERSE: A trace of wear shows on the beam above pillars. Three-quarters of the mint luster is still present.

AU-50 (About Uncirculated)
OBVERSE: Traces of wear show on cheek bone and high points of hair.
REVERSE: Traces of wear show on the beam and triangular roof above pillars. Half of the mint luster is still present.

EXTREMELY FINE *(Very light wear on only the highest points.)*

EF-45 (Choice Extremely Fine)
OBVERSE: Slight wear shows on cheek bone, and central portion of hair. There is a trace of wear at bottom of the bust.
REVERSE: High points of the triangular roof and beam are lightly worn. Traces of mint luster still show.

EF-40 (Extremely Fine)
OBVERSE: Hair is lightly worn but well defined and bold. Slight wear shows on cheek bone and bottom of the bust. High points of hair are worn but show all details.
REVERSE: Triangular roof and beam are worn but all details are visible.

VERY FINE *(Light to moderate even wear. All major features are sharp.)*

VF-30 (Choice Very Fine)
OBVERSE: Hair worn but shows nearly full details. Cheek line and bottom of bust are worn but sharp.
REVERSE: Triangular roof and beam worn nearly flat. Most of the pillar lines show plainly.

VF-20 (Very Fine)
OBVERSE: Cheek line shows considerable flatness. Over half the hair lines are clear. Parts of the details still show in collar.
REVERSE: Pillars are worn but clearly defined. Triangular roof is partially visible.

FINE *(Moderate to heavy even wear. Entire design clear and bold.)*

F-12 (Fine)
OBVERSE: Some details show in hair around face. Cheek line and collar plain but very weak.
REVERSE: Some details visible behind pillars. Triangular roof is very smooth and indistinct.

VERY GOOD *(Well worn. Design clear but flat and lacking details.)*
VG-8 (Very Good)
OBVERSE: Cheek line is visible but parts are worn smooth. Collar is weak but visible. Only a few hair lines show separations.
REVERSE: Slight details shows throughout building. The arch is worn away. Pillars are weak but visible.

GOOD *(Heavily worn. Design and legend visible but faint in spots.)*
G-4 (Good)
OBVERSE: Entire design well worn with very little detail remaining. Motto is weak and merged with rim.
REVERSE: Building is nearly flat but is well outlined. Pillars are worn flat. Rim worn to tops of letters.

ABOUT GOOD *(Outlined design. Parts of date and legend worn smooth.)*
AG-3 (About Good)
OBVERSE: Design is outlined with nearly all details worn away. Date and legend readable but very weak and merging into rim.
REVERSE: Entire design partially worn away. Rim is merged with the letters.

Note: Jefferson nickels are frequently seen weakly struck, and with the horizontal step lines joined even on Uncirculated specimens. Many of the 1950 and 1955 nickels are unevenly struck with weak spots in the details.

DIMES — BARBER 1892-1916

OBVERSE   REVERSE

MINT STATE *(Absolutely no trace of wear.)*
MS-70 (Perfect Uncirculated)
A flawless coin exactly as it was minted, with no trace of wear or injury. Must have full mint luster and brilliance or light toning. Any unusual die or striking traits must be described.

MS-65 (Choice Uncirculated)
No trace of wear; nearly as perfect as MS-70 except for some small blemish. Has full mint luster but may be unevenly toned or lightly fingermarked. A few barely noticeable nicks or marks may be present.

MS-60 (Uncirculated)
A strictly Uncirculated coin with no trace of wear, but with blemishes more obvious than for MS-65. May lack full mint luster, and surface may be dull, spotted, or heavily toned. Check points for signs of abrasion: high points of cheek, and hair below LIBERTY. Ribbon bow and tips of leaves.

ABOUT UNCIRCULATED *(Small trace of wear visible on highest points.)*
AU-55 (Choice About Uncirculated)
OBVERSE: Only a trace of wear shows on highest points of hair below LIBERTY.

REVERSE: A trace of wear shows on ribbon bow, wheat grains and leaf near O. Three-quarters of the mint luster is still present.

AU-50 (About Uncirculated)
OBVERSE: Traces of wear show on cheek, top of forehead and hair below LIBERTY.
REVERSE: Traces of wear show on ribbon bow, wheat grains and tips of leaves. Half of the mint luster is still present.

EXTREMELY FINE *(Very light wear on only the highest points.)*

EF-45 (Choice Extremely Fine)
OBVERSE: Slight wear shows on high points of upper leaves, cheek and hair above forehead. LIBERTY is sharp and band edges are bold.
REVERSE: High points of the wreath and bow lightly worn. Lines in leaves are clearly defined. Part of the mint luster is still present.

EF-40 (Extremely Fine)
OBVERSE: Light wear shows on leaves, cheek, cap and hair above forehead. LIBERTY is sharp and band edges are clear.
REVERSE: High points of wreath and bow are worn, but all details are clearly defined. Traces of mint luster may still show.

VERY FINE *(Light to moderate even wear. All major features are sharp.)*

VF-30 (Choice Very Fine)
OBVERSE: Wear spots show on leaves, cap, hair and cheek. Bottom row of leaves is weak but has some visible details. LIBERTY and band are complete.
REVERSE: Wear shows on the two bottom leaves but most details are visible. Nearly all the details in the ribbon bow and corn kernels are clear.

VF-20 (Very Fine)
OBVERSE: Over half the details still show in leaves. Hair worn but bold. Every letter in LIBERTY is visible.
REVERSE: The ribbon is worn, but some details are visible. Half the details in leaves are clear. Bottom leaves and upper stalks show wear spots.

FINE *(Moderate to heavy even wear. Entire design clear and bold.)*

F-12 (Fine)
OBVERSE: Some details show in hair, cap and facial features. All letters in LIBERTY are weak but visible. Upper row of leaves is outlined, but bottom row is worn smooth.
REVERSE: Some details in the lower leaf clusters are plainly visible. Bow is outlined but flat. Letters in legend are worn but clear.

VERY GOOD *(Well worn. Design clear but flat and lacking details.)*

VG-8 (Very Good)
OBVERSE: Entire head weak, and most of the details in the face are worn smooth. Three letters in LIBERTY are clear. Rim is complete.
REVERSE: Wreath shows only a small amount of detail. Corn and grain are flat. Some of the bow is very weak.

GOOD *(Heavily worn. Design and legend visible but faint in spots.)*

G-4 (Good)
OBVERSE: Entire design well worn with very little detail remaining. Legend is weak but visible. LIBERTY is worn away.
REVERSE: Wreath is worn flat but is completely outlined. Corn and grains are worn nearly smooth.

ABOUT GOOD *(Outlined design. Parts of date and legend worn smooth.)*
AG-3 (About Good)
OBVERSE: Head is outlined with nearly all details worn away. Date readable but partially worn away. Legend merging into rim.
REVERSE: Entire wreath partially worn away and merging into rim.

DIMES — MERCURY 1916-1945

OBVERSE    REVERSE

MINT STATE *(Absolutely no trace of wear.)*
MS-70 (Perfect Uncirculated)
A flawless coin exactly as it was minted, with no trace of wear or injury. Must have full mint luster and brilliance or light toning. Any unusual die or striking traits must be described.

MS-65 (Choice Uncirculated)
No trace of wear; nearly as perfect as MS-70 except for some small blemish. Has full mint luster but may be unevenly toned or lightly fingermarked. A few barely noticeable nicks or marks may be present.

MS-60 (Uncirculated)
A strictly Uncirculated coin with no trace of wear, but with blemishes more obvious than for MS-65. May lack full mint luster, and surface may be dull, spotted or heavily toned. Check points for signs of abrasion: high points of hair and in front of ear. Diagonal bands on fasces.

ABOUT UNCIRCULATED *(Small trace of wear visible on highest points.)*
AU-55 (Choice About Uncirculated)
OBVERSE: Only a trace of wear shows on highest points of hair above forehead and in front of ear.
REVERSE: A trace of wear shows on the horizontal and diagonal fasces bands. Three-quarters of the mint luster is still present.

AU-50 (About Uncirculated)
OBVERSE: Traces of wear show on hair along face, above forehead and in front of ear.
REVERSE: Traces of wear show on the fasces bands but edges are sharply defined. Half of the mint luster is still present.

EXTREMELY FINE *(Very light wear on only the highest points.)*
EF-45 (Choice Extremely Fine)
OBVERSE: Slight wear shows on high points of feathers and at hair line. Hair along face is sharp and detailed.
REVERSE: High points of the diagonal fasces bands are lightly worn. Horizontal lines are clearly defined but not fully separated. Part of the mint luster is still present.

EF-40 (Extremely Fine)
OBVERSE: Wear shows on high points of feathers, hair and at neck line.
REVERSE: High points of fasces bands are worn, but all details are clearly defined and partially separated. Traces of mint luster may still show.

VERY FINE *(Light to moderate even wear. All major features are sharp.)*

VF-30 (Choice Very Fine)
OBVERSE: Wear spots on hair along face, cheek and neck line. Feathers are weak but have nearly full details.
REVERSE: Wear shows on the two diagonal bands but most details are visible. All vertical lines are sharp. All details in the branch are clear.

VF-20 (Very Fine)
OBVERSE: Three-quarters of the details still show in feathers. Hair worn but bold. Some details in hair braid are visible.
REVERSE: Wear shows on the two diagonal bands but most details are visible. All vertical lines are sharp. All details in the branch are clear.

FINE *(Moderate to considerable even wear. Entire design clear and bold.)*

F-12 (Fine)
OBVERSE: Some details show in hair. All feathers are weak but partially visible. Hair braid is nearly worn away.
REVERSE: Vertical lines are all visible but lack sharpness. Diagonal bands show on fasces but one is worn smooth at midpoint.

VERY GOOD *(Well worn. Design clear but flat and lacking details.)*

VG-8 (Very Good)
OBVERSE: Entire head is weak, and most details in the wing are worn smooth. All letters and date are clear. Rim is complete.
REVERSE: About half the vertical lines in the fasces are visible. Rim is complete.

GOOD *(Heavily worn. Design and legend visible but faint in spots.)*

G-4 (Good)
OBVERSE: Entire design well worn with very little detail remaining. Legend and date are weak but visible. Rim is visible.
REVERSE: Fasces is worn nearly flat but is completely outlined. Sticks and bands are worn smooth.

ABOUT GOOD *(Outlined design. Parts of date and legend worn smooth.)*

AG-3 (About Good)
OBVERSE: Head is outlined with nearly all details worn away. Date readable but worn. Legend merging into rim.
REVERSE: Entire design partially worn away. Rim worn half way into the legend.

Note: Coins of this design are sometimes weakly struck in spots, particularly in the lines and horizontal bands of the fasces.
  The following dates are usually found poorly struck and lacking full details regardless of condition: 1916-D, 1918-S, 1921, 1921-D, 1925-D, 1925-S, 1926-S, 1927-D and 1927-S.
  1920 and 1920-D usually show the zero joined to the rim.
  1921 usually has a weakly struck date, especially the last two digits.
  1923 often has the bottom of the three weakly struck and joined to the rim.
  1945 is rarely seen with full cross bands on the fasces.

DIMES — ROOSEVELT 1946 TO DATE

OBVERSE    REVERSE

MINT STATE *(Absolutely no trace of wear.)*

MS-70 (Perfect Uncirculated)
A flawless coin exactly as it was minted, with no trace of wear or injury. Must have full mint luster and brilliance or light toning. Any unusual striking traits must be described.

MS-65 (Choice Uncirculated)
No trace of wear; nearly as perfect as MS-70 except for some small blemish. Has full mint luster but may be unevenly toned or lightly fingermarked. A few barely noticeable nicks or marks may be present.

MS-60 (Uncirculated)
A strictly Uncirculated coin with no trace of wear, but with blemishes more obvious than for MS-65. Has full mint luster, but surface may be dull, spotted, or toned. Check points for signs of abrasion: high points of cheek and hair above ear. Tops of leaves and details in flame.

ABOUT UNCIRCULATED *(Small trace of wear visible on highest points.)*

AU-55 (Choice About Uncirculated)
OBVERSE: Only a trace of wear shows on highest points of hair above ear.
REVERSE: A trace of wear shows on highest spots of the flame. Three-quarters of the mint luster is still present.

AU-50 (About Uncirculated)
OBVERSE: Traces of wear show on hair above ear.
REVERSE: Traces of wear show on flame but details are sharply defined. Half of the mint luster is still present.

EXTREMELY FINE *(Very light wear on only the highest points.)*

EF-45 (Choice Extremely Fine)
OBVERSE: Slight wear shows on high points of hair above ear. Ear is sharp and detailed.
REVERSE: High points of flame are lightly worn. Torch lines are clearly defined and fully separated. Part of the mint luster is still present.

EF-40 (Extremely Fine)
OBVERSE: Wear shows on high points of hair and at cheek line. Ear shows slight wear on the upper tip.
REVERSE: High points of flame, torch and leaves are worn, but all details are clearly defined and partially separated. Traces of mint luster may still show.

VERY FINE *(Light to moderate even wear. All major features are sharp.)*

VF-30 (Choice Very Fine)
OBVERSE: Wear spots show on hair, ear, cheek and chin. Hair lines are weak but have nearly full visible details.
REVERSE: Wear shows on flame but some details are visible. All vertical lines are plain. Most details in the torch and leaves are clear.

VF-20 (Very Fine)
OBVERSE: Three-quarters of the details still show in hair. Face worn but bold. Some details in the ear are visible.
REVERSE: Wear shows on the flame but a few lines are visible. All torch lines are worn but bold. Most details in leaves are clear.

FINE *(Moderate to heavy even wear. Entire design clear and bold.)*

F-12 (Fine)
OBVERSE: Half the details show in hair. All of the face is weak but boldly visible. Half of inner edge of ear is worn away.
REVERSE: Vertical lines are all visible, but horizontal bands are worn smooth. Leaves show some detail. Flame is nearly smooth.

VERY GOOD *(Well worn. Design clear but flat and lacking details.)*

VG-8 (Very Good)
OBVERSE: Entire head is weak, and most of the details in hair and ear are worn smooth. All letters and date are clear. Rim is complete.
REVERSE: About half the outer vertical lines in torch are visible. Flame is only outlined. Leaves show very little detail. Rim is complete.

GOOD *(Heavily worn. Design and legend visible but faint in spots.)*

G-4 (Good)
OBVERSE: Entire design well worn with very little detail remaining. Ear is completely outlined. Legend and date are weak but visible. Rim is visible.
REVERSE: Torch is worn nearly flat but is completely outlined. Leaves are worn smooth. Legend is all visible.

ABOUT GOOD *(Outlined design. Parts of date and legend worn smooth.)*

AG-3 (About Good)
OBVERSE: Head is outlined with nearly all details worn away. Date readable but worn. Legend merging into rim.
REVERSE: Entire design partially worn away. Rim merges into the legend.

QUARTERS — BARBER 1892-1916

OBVERSE   REVERSE

MINT STATE *(Absolutely no trace of wear.)*

MS-70 (Perfect Uncirculated)
A flawless coin exactly as it was minted, with no trace of wear or injury. Must have full mint luster and brilliance or light toning. Any unusual die or striking traits must be described.

MS-65 (Choice Uncirculated)
No trace of wear; nearly as perfect as MS-70 except for some small blemish. Has full mint luster but may be unevenly toned or lightly fingermarked. A few barely noticeable nicks or marks may be present.

MS-60 (Uncirculated)
A strictly Uncirculated coin with no trace of wear, but with blemishes more obvious than for MS-65. May lack full mint luster, and surface may be dull, spotted, or heavily toned. Check points for signs of abrasion: high points of cheek and hair below LIBERTY. Eagle's head and tips of tail and wings.

ABOUT UNCIRCULATED *(Small trace of wear visible on highest points.)*

AU-55 (Choice About Uncirculated)
OBVERSE: Only a trace of wear shows on highest points of hair below BER in LIBERTY.
REVERSE: A trace of wear shows on head, tip of tail and tips of wings. Three-quarters of the mint luster is still present.

AU-50 (About Uncirculated)
OBVERSE: Traces of wear show on cheek, tips of leaves and hair below LIBERTY.
REVERSE: Traces of wear show on head, neck, tail and tips of wings. Half of the mint luster is still present.

EXTREMELY FINE *(Very light wear on only the highest points.)*

EF-45 (Choice Extremely Fine)
OBVERSE: Slight wear shows on high points of upper leaves, cheek and hair above forehead. LIBERTY is sharp and band edges are bold.
REVERSE: High points of head, neck, wings and talons lightly worn. Lines in center tail feathers are clearly defined. Part of the mint luster is still present.

EF-40 (Extremely Fine)
OBVERSE: Light wear shows on leaves, cheek, cap and hair above forehead. LIBERTY is sharp and band edges are clear.
REVERSE: High points of head, neck, wings and tail are lightly worn, but all details are clearly defined. Leaves show trace of wear at edges. Traces of mint luster may still show.

VERY FINE *(Light to moderate even wear. All major features are sharp.)*

VF-30 (Choice Very Fine)
OBVERSE: Wear spots show on leaves, cap, hair and cheek. Bottom row of leaves is weak but has some visible details. LIBERTY and band are complete. Folds in cap are distinct.
REVERSE: Wear shows on shield but all details are visible. Most of the details in neck and tail are clear. Motto is complete.

VF-20 (Very Fine)
OBVERSE: Over half the details still show in leaves. Hair and ribbon worn but bold. Every letter in LIBERTY is visible.
REVERSE: The shield is worn, but most details are visible. Half the details in feathers are clear. Wings and legs show wear spots. Motto is clear.

FINE *(Moderate to heavy even wear. Entire design clear and bold.)*
F-12 (Fine)
OBVERSE: Some details show in hair, cap and facial features. All letters in LIBERTY are weak but visible. Upper row of leaves is outlined, but bottom row is worn nearly smooth. Rim is full and bold.
REVERSE: Half of the feathers are plainly visible. Wear spots show in center of neck, motto and arrows. Horizontal shield lines are merged; vertical lines are separated. Letters in legend are worn but clear.

VERY GOOD *(Well worn. Design clear but flat and lacking details.)*
VG-8 (Very Good)
OBVERSE: Entire head weak, and most details in face are worn smooth. Three letters in LIBERTY are clear. Rim is complete.
REVERSE: Eagle shows only a small amount of detail. Arrows and leaves are flat. Most of the shield is very weak. Part of the eye is visible.

GOOD *(Heavily worn. Design and legend visible but faint in spots.)*
G-4 (Good)
OBVERSE: Entire design well worn with very little detail remaining. Legend is weak but visible. LIBERTY is worn away.
REVERSE: Eagle worn flat but is completely outlined. Ribbon worn nearly smooth. Legend weak but visible. Rim worn to tops of letters.

ABOUT GOOD *(Outlined design. Parts of date and legend worn smooth.)*
AG-3 (About Good)
OBVERSE: Head is outlined with nearly all details worn away. Date readable but partially worn away. Legend merging into rim.
REVERSE: Entire design partially worn away and legend merges with rim.

QUARTERS — LIBERTY STANDING, VARIETY I 1916-1917
LIBERTY STANDING, VARIETY II 1917-1924

OBVERSE  | TYPE I REVERSE | TYPE II REVERSE

MINT STATE *(Absolutely no trace of wear.)*
MS-70 (Perfect Uncirculated)
A flawless coin exactly as it was minted, with no trace of wear or injury. Must have full mint luster and brilliance or light toning. Head details* are an important part of this grade and must be specifically designated. Any other unusual die or striking traits must be described.

MS-65 (Choice Uncirculated)
No trace of wear; nearly as perfect as MS-70 except for some small blemish. Has full mint luster but may be unevenly toned or lightly fingermarked, may be weakly struck in one small spot. A few barely noticeable nicks or marks may be present. Head details* may be incomplete.

MS-60 (Uncirculated)
A strictly Uncirculated coin with no trace of wear, but with blemishes more obvious than for MS-65. May lack full mint luster, and surface may be dull, spotted or heavily toned. One or two small spots may be weakly struck. Head details* may be incomplete. Check points for signs of abrasion: mail covering breast, knee, high points of gown and shield; high points of eagle's breast and wings. Coins of this design frequently show weakly struck spots and usually lack full head details.

ABOUT UNCIRCULATED *(Small trace of wear visible on highest points.)*

AU-55 (Choice About Uncirculated)
OBVERSE: Only a trace of wear shows on highest points of mail covering breast, inner shield and right knee.
REVERSE: A trace of wear shows on breast and edges of wings. Three-quarters of the mint luster is still present.

AU-50 (About Uncirculated)
OBVERSE: Traces of wear show on breast, knee and high points of inner shield.
REVERSE: Traces of wear show on edges of wings and at center of breast. All of the tail feathers are visible. Half of the mint luster is still present.

EXTREMELY FINE *(Very light wear on only the highest points.)*

EF-45 (Choice Extremely Fine)
OBVERSE: Light wear spots show on upper right leg and knee. Nearly all of the gown lines are clearly visible. Shield details are bold. Breast is lightly worn and may show small flat spot.
REVERSE: Small flat spots show on high points of breast and on front wing edges. Tail feathers have nearly full details. Part of the mint luster is still present.

EF-40 (Extremely Fine)
OBVERSE: Wear shows on breast, and right leg above and below knee. Most of the gown lines are visible. Shield details are bold. Breast is well rounded but has small flat spot.
REVERSE: High points of eagle are lightly worn. Central part of edge on right wing is well worn. Traces of mint luster may still show.

VERY FINE *(Light to moderate even wear. All major features are sharp.)*

VF-30 (Choice Very Fine)
OBVERSE: Wear spots show on breast, shield and leg. Right leg is rounded but worn from above knee to ankle. Gown line crossing thigh is partially visible. Half of mail covering breast can be seen. Circle around inner shield is complete.
REVERSE: Breast and leg are worn but clearly separated, with some feathers visible between them. Feather ends and folds are visible in right wing.

VF-20 (Very Fine)
OBVERSE: Right leg is worn flat in central parts. Wear spots show on head, breast, shield and foot. Beads on outer shield are visible, but those next to body are weak. Inner circle of shield is complete.
REVERSE: Entire eagle is lightly worn but most major details are visible. Breast and edge of right wing are worn flat. Top tail feathers are complete.

FINE *(Moderate to considerable even wear. Entire design clear and bold.)*
F-12 (Fine)
OBVERSE: Gown details worn but show clearly across body. Left leg is lightly worn. Right leg nearly flat and toe is worn. Breast worn but some mail is visible. Date may show some weakness at top. Rim is full. Outer edge of shield is complete.
REVERSE: Breast is worn almost smooth. Half of the wing feathers are visible although well worn in spots. The rim is full.

VERY GOOD *(Well worn. Design clear but flat and lacking details.)*
VG-8 (Very Good)
OBVERSE: Entire design is weak, and most details in gown are worn smooth. All letters and date are clear but tops of numerals may be flat. Rim is complete. Drapery across breast is partially outlined.
REVERSE: About one-third of the feathers are visible, and large feathers at ends of wings are well separated. Eye is visible. Rim is full and all letters are clear.

GOOD *(Heavily worn. Design and legend visible but faint in spots.)*
G-4 (Good)
OBVERSE: Entire design well worn with very little detail remaining. Legend and date are weak but visible. Top of date may be worn flat. Rim is complete.
REVERSE: Eagle worn nearly flat but is completely outlined. Lettering and stars worn but clearly visible. Rim worn to tops of legend.

ABOUT GOOD *(Outlined design. Parts of date and legend worn smooth.)*
AG-3 (About Good)
OBVERSE: Figure is outlined with nearly all details worn away. Legend visible but half worn away and may merge with rim. Date weak and readable.
REVERSE: Entire design partially worn away. Some letters merging into rim.

Note: Coins of this design are sometimes weakly struck in spots, particularly at Liberty's head, breast, knee and shield and on the eagle's breast and wings.

*Specimens with "full head" must show the following details: Three well defined leaves in hair; complete hairline along brow and across face; small indentation at ear. Coins of any grade other than MS-70 can be assumed to lack full head details unless the amount of visible features are specifically designated.

QUARTERS — WASHINGTON 1932 TO DATE

OBVERSE   REVERSE

MINT STATE *(Absolutely no trace of wear.)*

MS-70 (Perfect Uncirculated)
A flawless coin exactly as it was minted, with no trace of wear or injury. Must have full mint luster and brilliance or light toning. Any unusual striking traits must be described.

MS-65 (Choice Uncirculated)
No trace of wear; nearly as perfect as MS-70 except for some small blemish. Has full mint luster but may be unevenly toned or lightly fingermarked. A few barely noticeable nicks or marks may be present.

MS-60 (Uncirculated)
A strictly Uncirculated coin with no trace of wear, but with blemishes more obvious than for MS-65. May lack full mint luster, and surface may be dull, spotted or heavily toned. Check points for signs of abrasion: high points of cheek and hair in front and back of ear. Tops of legs and details in breast feathers.

ABOUT UNCIRCULATED *(Small trace of wear visible on highest points.)*

AU-55 (Choice About Uncirculated)
OBVERSE: Only a trace of wear shows on highest points of hair in front and in back of ear.
REVERSE: A trace of wear shows on highest spots of breast feathers. Nearly all of the mint luster is still present.

AU-50 (About Uncirculated)
OBVERSE: Traces of wear show on hair in front and in back of ear.
REVERSE: Traces of wear show on legs and breast feathers. Three-quarters of the mint luster is still present.

EXTREMELY FINE *(Light wear on most of the highest points.)*

EF-45 (Choice Extremely Fine)
OBVERSE: Slight wear shows on high points of hair around ear and along hairline up to crown. Hairlines are sharp and detailed.
REVERSE: High points of legs are lightly worn. Breast feathers are worn but clearly defined and fully separated. Half of the mint luster is still present.

EF-40 (Extremely Fine)
OBVERSE: Wear shows on high points of hair around and at hairline up to crown.
REVERSE: High points of breast, legs and claws are lightly worn, but all details are clearly defined and partially separated. Part of the mint luster is still present.

VERY FINE *(Light to moderate even wear. All major features are sharp.)*

VF-30 (Choice Very Fine)
OBVERSE: Wear spots show on hair at forehead and ear, cheek and jaw. Hair lines are weak but have nearly full visible details.
REVERSE: Wear shows on breast but a few feathers are visible. Legs are worn smooth. Most details in the wings are clear.

FINE *(Moderate to considerable even wear. Entire design clear and bold.)*

F-12 (Fine)
OBVERSE: Details show only at back of hair. Motto is weak but clearly visible. Part of cheek edge is worn away.
REVERSE: Feathers in breast and legs are worn smooth. Leaves show some detail. Parts of wings are nearly smooth.

VERY GOOD *(Well worn. Design clear but flat and lacking details.)*

VG-8 (Very Good)
OBVERSE: Entire head is weak, and most details in hair are worn smooth. All letters and date are clear. Rim is complete.
REVERSE: About half of the wing feathers are visible. Breast and legs only outlined. Leaves show very little detail. Rim is complete.

GOOD *(Heavily worn. Design and legend visible but faint in spots.)*

G-4 (Good)
OBVERSE: Hair is well worn with very little detail remaining. Half of motto is readable. LIBERTY and date are weak but visible. Rim merges with letters.
REVERSE: Eagle is worn nearly flat but is completely outlined. Leaves, breast and legs are worn smooth. Legend is all visible but merges with rim.

ABOUT GOOD *(Outlined design. Parts of date and legend worn smooth.)*

AG-3 (About Good)
OBVERSE: Head is outlined with nearly all details worn away. Date readable but worn. Traces of motto are visible. Legend merging into rim.
REVERSE: Entire design partially worn away. Rim merges into legend.

Note: The obverse motto is always weak on coins of 1932 and early issues of 1934.
The reverse rim and lettering has a tendency to be very weak, particularly on coins dated 1934-D, 1935-D and S, 1936-D and S, 1937-D and S (especially), 1938-D and S, and 1939-D and 1940-D.

HALF DOLLARS — BARBER 1892-1915

OBVERSE    REVERSE

MINT STATE *(Absolutely no trace of wear.)*

MS-70 (Perfect Uncirculated)
A flawless coin exactly as it was minted, with no trace of wear or injury. Must have full mint luster and brilliance or light toning. Any unusual die or striking traits must be described.

MS-65 (Choice Uncirculated)
No trace of wear; nearly as perfect as MS-70 except for some small blemish. Has full mint luster but may be unevenly toned or lightly fingermarked. A few barely noticeable nicks or marks may be present.

MS-60 (Uncirculated)
A strictly Uncirculated coin with no trace of wear, but with blemishes more obvious than for MS-65. May lack full mint luster, and surface may be dull, spotted or heavily toned. Check points for signs of abrasion: high points of cheek and hair below LIBERTY. Eagle's head and tips of tail and wings.

ABOUT UNCIRCULATED *(Small trace of wear visible on highest points.)*

AU-55 (Choice About Uncirculated)
OBVERSE: Only a trace of wear shows on highest points of hair below BER in LIBERTY.
REVERSE: A trace of wear shows on head, tip of tail and tips of wings. Three-quarters of the mint luster is still present.

AU-50 (About Uncirculated)
OBVERSE: Traces of wear show on cheek, tips of leaves and hair below LIBERTY.
REVERSE: Traces of wear show on head, neck, tail and tips of wings. Half of the mint luster is still present.

EXTREMELY FINE *(Very light wear on only the highest points.)*

EF-45 (Choice Extremely Fine)
OBVERSE: Slight wear shows on high points of upper leaves, cheek and hair above forehead. LIBERTY is sharp and band edges are bold.
High points of head, neck, wings and talons lightly worn. Lines in reverse center tail feathers are clearly defined. Part of the mint luster is still present.

EF-40 (Extremely Fine)
OBVERSE: Light wear shows on leaves, cheek, cap and hair above forehead. LIBERTY is sharp and band edges are bold.
REVERSE: High points of head, neck and tail are lightly worn, but all details are clearly defined. Leaves show trace of wear at edges. Traces of mint luster may still show.

VERY FINE *(Light to moderate even wear. All major features are sharp.)*

VF-30 (Choice Very Fine)
OBVERSE: Wear spots show on leaves, cap, hair and cheek. Bottom row of leaves is weak but has some visible details. LIBERTY and band are complete. Folds in cap are distinct.
REVERSE: Wear shows on shield but all details are visible. Most of the details in neck and tail are clear. Motto is complete.

VF-20 (Very Fine)
OBVERSE: Over half the details still show in leaves. Hair and ribbon worn but bold. Every letter in LIBERTY is visible. Bottom folds in cap are full.
REVERSE: Shield is worn, but all details are visible. Half the details in feathers are clear. Wings, tail and legs show small wear spots. Motto is clear.

FINE *(Moderate to considerable even wear. Entire design clear and bold.)*

F-12 (Fine)
OBVERSE: Some details show in hair, cap and facial features. All letters in LIBERTY are weak but visible. Upper row of leaves is outlined, but bottom row is worn nearly smooth. Rim is full and bold.
REVERSE: Half the feathers are plainly visible. Wear spots show in center of neck, motto and arrows. Horizontal shield lines are merged; vertical lines are separated. Letters in legend are worn but clear.

VERY GOOD *(Well worn. Design clear but flat and lacking details.)*

VG-8 (Very Good)
OBVERSE: Entire head weak, and most details in face are heavily worn. Three letters in LIBERTY are clear. Rim is complete.
REVERSE: Eagle shows only a small amount of detail. Arrows and leaves are flat. Most of shield is very weak. Parts of eye and motto visible.

GOOD *(Heavily worn. Design and legend visible but faint in spots.)*

G-4 (Good)
OBVERSE: Entire design well worn with very little detail remaining. Legend and date weak but visible. LIBERTY is worn away.
REVERSE: Eagle worn flat but is completely outlined. Ribbon worn nearly smooth. Legend weak but visible. Rim worn to tops of letters.

ABOUT GOOD *(Outlined design. Parts of date and legend worn smooth.)*

AG-3 (About Good)
OBVERSE: Head is outlined with nearly all details worn away. Date readable but partially worn away. Legend merging into rim.
REVERSE: Entire design partially worn away and legend merges with rim.

HALF DOLLARS — LIBERTY WALKING 1916-1947

OBVERSE   REVERSE

MINT STATE *(Absolutely no trace of wear.)*

MS-70 (Perfect Uncirculated)
A flawless coin exactly as it was minted, with no trace of wear or injury. Must have full mint luster and brilliance or light toning. Any unusual die or striking traits must be described.

MS-65 (Choice Uncirculated)
No trace of wear; nearly as perfect as MS-70 except for some small blemish. Has full mint luster but may be unevenly toned or lightly fingermarked. May be weakly struck in one of two small spots. A few minute nicks or marks may be present.

MS-60 (Uncirculated)
A strictly Uncirculated coin with no trace of wear, but with blemishes more obvious than for MS-65. May lack full mint luster, and surface may be dull, spotted or heavily toned. A few small spots may be weakly struck. Check points for signs of abrasion: hair above temple, right arm, left breast; high points of eagle's head, breast, legs and wings. Coins of this design frequently show weakly struck spots, and usually lack full head and hand details.

ABOUT UNCIRCULATED *(Small trace of wear visible on highest points.)*

AU-55 (Choice About Uncirculated)
OBVERSE: Only a trace of wear shows on highest points of head, breast and right arm.
REVERSE: A trace of wear shows on left leg between breast and left wing. Three-quarters of the mint luster is still present.

AU-50 (About Uncirculated)
OBVERSE: Traces of wear show on head, breast, arms and left leg.

REVERSE: Traces of wear show on high points of wings and at center of head. All leg feathers are visible. Half of the mint luster is still present.

EXTREMELY FINE *(Very light wear on only the highest points.)*

EF-45 (Choice Extremely Fine)
OBVERSE: Light wear spots show on head, breast, arms, left leg and foot. Nearly all gown lines are clearly visible. Sandal details are bold and complete. Knee is lightly worn but full and rounded.
REVERSE: Small flat spots show on high points of breast and legs. Wing feathers have nearly full details. Part of the mint luster is still present.

EF-40 (Extremely Fine)
OBVERSE: Wear shows on head, breast, arms and left leg. Nearly all gown lines are visible. Sandal details are complete. Breast and knee are nearly flat.
REVERSE: High points of eagle are lightly worn. Half the breast and leg feathers are visible. Central part of feathers below neck is well worn. Traces of mint luster may still show.

VERY FINE *(Light to moderate even wear. All major features are sharp.)*

VF-30 (Choice Very Fine)
OBVERSE: Wear spots on head, breast, arms and legs. Left leg is rounded but worn from above knee to ankle. Gown line crossing body is partially visible. Knee is flat. Outline of breast can be seen.
REVERSE: Breast and legs are moderately worn but clearly separated, with some feathers visible in right wing. Pupil in eye is visible.

VF-20 (Very Fine)
OBVERSE: Left leg is worn nearly flat. Wear spots show on head, breast, arms and foot. Lines on skirt are visible, but may be weak on coins before 1921. Breast is outlined.
REVERSE: Entire eagle is lightly worn but most major details are visible. Breast, central part of legs and top edge of right wing are worn flat.

FINE *(Moderate to considerable even wear. Entire design clear and bold.)*

F-12 (Fine)
OBVERSE: Gown stripes worn but show clearly, except for coins before 1921 where only half are visible. Right leg is lightly worn. Left leg nearly flat and sandal is worn but visible. Center of body worn but some of the gown is visible. Outer edge of rim is complete.
REVERSE: Breast is worn smooth. Half the wing feathers are visible although well worn in spots. Top two layers of feathers are visible in left wing. Rim is full.

VERY GOOD *(Well worn. Design clear but flat and lacking details.)*

VG-8 (Very Good)
OBVERSE: Entire design is weak; most details in gown are worn smooth except for coins after 1921, where half the stripes must show. All letters and date are clear but top of motto may be weak. Rim is complete. Drapery across body is partially visible.
REVERSE: About one-third of the feathers are visible, and large feathers at ends of wings are well separated. Eye is visible. Rim is full and all letters are clear.

GOOD *(Heavily worn. Design and legend visible but faint in spots.)*

G-4 (Good)
OBVERSE: Entire design well worn with very little detail remaining. Legend and date weak but visible. Top of date may be worn flat. Rim is flat but nearly complete.
REVERSE: Eagle worn nearly flat but is completely outlined. Lettering and motto worn but clearly visible.

ABOUT GOOD *(Outlined design. Parts of date and legend worn smooth.)*
AG-3 (About Good)
OBVERSE: Figure is outlined with nearly all details worn away. Legend visible but half worn away. Date weak but readable. Rim merges with lettering.
REVERSE: Entire design partially worn away. Letters merge with rim.

Note: Coins of this design are sometimes weakly struck in spots, particularly at Liberty's head, hand holding branch and drapery lines of dress, and on the eagle's leg feathers.

HALF DOLLARS — FRANKLIN 1948-1963

OBVERSE    REVERSE

MINT STATE *(Absolutely no trace of wear.)*
MS-70 (Perfect Uncirculated)
A flawless coin exactly as it was minted, with no trace of wear or injury. Must have full mint luster and brilliance or light toning. Any unusual striking traits must be described.
MS-65 (Choice Uncirculated)
No trace of wear; nearly as perfect as MS-70 except for some small blemish. Has full mint luster but may be unevenly toned or lightly fingermarked. A few barely noticeable nicks or marks may be present.
MS-60 (Uncirculated)
A strictly Uncirculated coin with no trace of wear, but with blemishes more obvious than for MS-65. May lack full mint luster, and surface may be dull, spotted or heavily toned. Check points for signs of abrasion: high points of cheek, shoulder and hair left of ear. Straps around beam, lines and lettering on bell.

ABOUT UNCIRCULATED *(Small trace of wear visible on highest points.)*
AU-55 (Choice About Uncirculated)
OBVERSE: Only a trace of wear shows on highest spots of cheek and hair left of ear.
REVERSE: A trace of wear shows on highest points of lettering on bell. Nearly all of the mint luster is still present.
AU-50 (About Uncirculated)
OBVERSE: Traces of wear show on cheek and hair on shoulder and left of ear.
REVERSE: Traces of wear show on bell at lettering and along ridges at bottom. Three-quarters of the mint luster is still present.

EXTREMELY FINE *(Very light wear on only the highest points.)*
EF-45 (Choice Extremely Fine)
OBVERSE: Slight wear shows on cheek and high points of hair behind ear and along shoulder. Hair lines at back of head are sharp and detailed.

REVERSE: High points of straps on beam are lightly worn. Lines at bottom of bell are worn but clearly defined and separated. Lettering on bell is very weak at center. Half of the mint luster is still present.

EF-40 (Extremely Fine)
OBVERSE: Wear shows on high points of cheek and hair behind ear and at shoulder.
REVERSE: High points of beam straps, and lines along bottom of bell are lightly worn, but details are clearly defined and partially separated. Lettering on bell is worn away at center. Part of the mint luster is still present.

VERY FINE *(Light to moderate even wear. All major features are sharp.)*

VF-30 (Choice Very Fine)
OBVERSE: Wear spots show on hair at shoulder and behind ear, on cheek and jaw. Hair lines are weak but have nearly full visible details.
REVERSE: Wear shows on bell lettering but some of the details are visible. Straps on beam are plain. Half of line details at bottom of bell are worn smooth.

VF-20 (Very Fine)
OBVERSE: Three-quarters of the lines still show in hair. Cheek lightly worn but bold. Some hair details around the ear are visible.
REVERSE: Wear shows on beam but most details are visible. Bell is worn but bold. Lines across bottom of bell are flat near crack.

FINE *(Moderate to considerable even wear. Entire design clear and bold.)*

F-12 (Very Fine)
OBVERSE: Hair details show only at back and side of head. Designer's initials weak but clearly visible. Part of cheek is worn flat.
REVERSE: Most of lines at bottom of bell are nearly smooth. Parts of straps on beam are nearly smooth. Rim is full.

VERY GOOD *(Well worn. Design clear but flat and lacking details.)*

VG-8 (Very Good)
OBVERSE: Entire head is weak, and most details in hair from temple to ear are worn smooth. All letters and date are bold. Ear and designer's initial are visible. Rim is complete.

HALF DOLLARS — KENNEDY 1964 TO DATE

OBVERSE    REVERSE

MINT STATE *(Absolutely no trace of wear.)*

MS-70 (Perfect Uncirculated)
A flawless coin exactly as it was minted, with no trace of wear or injury. Must have full mint luster and brilliance or light toning. Any unusual striking traits must be described.

MS-65 (Choice Uncirculated)
No trace of wear; nearly as perfect as MS-70 except for some small blemish. Has full mint luster but may be unevenly toned or lightly fingermarked. A few barely noticeable nicks or marks may be present.

MS-60 (Uncirculated)
A strictly Uncirculated coin with no trace of wear, but with blemishes more obvious than for MS-65. Has full mint luster, but surface may be dull, spotted or heavily toned. Check points for signs of abrasion: high points of cheek and jawbone, center of neck, hair below part. Bundle of arrows, center tail feather, right wing tip.

ABOUT UNCIRCULATED *(Small trace of wear visible on highest points.)*

AU-55 (Choice About Uncirculated)
OBVERSE: Only a trace of wear shows on highest points of cheek, jawbone and hair below part.
REVERSE: A trace of wear shows on central tail feather. Nearly all of the mint luster is still present.

EXTREMELY FINE *(Very light wear on only the highest points.)*

EF-40 (Extremely Fine)
OBVERSE: Slight wear shows on cheek, along jawbone and on high points of hair below part. Hair lines are sharp and detailed.
REVERSE: High points of arrows and right wing tip are lightly worn. Central tail feathers are worn but clearly defined and fully separated. Three-quarters of the mint luster is still present.

VERY FINE *(Light to moderate even wear. All major features are sharp.)*

VF-30 (Choice Very Fine)
OBVERSE: Wear spots show on hair below part, and along cheek and jaw. Hair lines are weak but have nearly full visible details.
REVERSE: Wear shows on arrow points but some details are visible. All central tail feathers are plain. Wing tips are lightly worn.

DOLLARS — MORGAN 1878-1921

OBVERSE   REVERSE

MINT STATE *(Absolutely no trace of wear.)*

MS-70 (Perfect Uncirculated)
A flawless coin exactly as it was minted, with no trace of wear or injury. Must have full mint luster and brilliance or light toning. Any unusual striking traits must be described.

MS-65 (Choice Uncirculated)
No trace of wear; nearly as perfect as MS-70 except for a few minute bag marks or

surface mars. Has full mint luster but may be unevenly toned. Any unusual striking traits must be described.

MS-60 (Uncirculated)
A strictly Uncirculated coin with no trace of wear, but with bag marks and other abrasions more obvious than for MS-65. May have a few small rim mars and weakly struck spots. Has full mint luster but may lack brilliance, and surface may be spotted or heavily toned. For these coins, bag abrasions and scuff marks are considered different from circulation wear. Full mint luster and lack of any wear are necessary to distinguish MS-60 from AU-55. Check points for signs of wear: hair above eye and ear, edges of cotton leaves and blossoms, high upper fold of cap. High points of eagle's breast and tops of legs. Weakly struck spots are common and should not be confused with actual wear.

ABOUT UNCIRCULATED *(Small trace of wear visible on highest points.)*

AU-55 (Choice About Uncirculated)
OBVERSE: Slight trace of wear shows on hair above ear and eye, edges of cotton leaves, and high upper fold of cap. Luster fading from cheek.
REVERSE: Slight trace of wear shows on breast, tops of legs and talons. Most of the mint luster is still present, although marred by light bag marks and surface abrasions.

AU-50 (About Uncirculated)
OBVERSE: Traces of wear show on hair above eye and ear, edges of cotton leaves, and high upper fold of cap. Partial detail visible on tops of cotton blossoms. Luster gone from cheek.
REVERSE: There are traces of wear on breast, tops of legs, wing tips and talons. Three-quarters of the mint luster is still present. Surface abrasions and bag marks are more noticeable than for AU-55.

EXTREMELY FINE *(Very light wear on only the highest points.)*

EF-45 (Choice Extremely Fine)
OBVERSE: Slight wear on hair above date, forehead and ear. Lines in hair well detailed and sharp. Slight flat spots on edges of cotton leaves. Minute signs of wear on cheek.
REVERSE: High points of breast are lightly worn. Tops of legs and right wing tip show wear. Talons are slightly flat. Half of the mint luster is still present.

EF-40 (Extremely Fine)
OBVERSE: Wear shows on hair above date, forehead and ear. Lines in hair well detailed. Flat spots visible on edges of cotton leaves. Cheek lightly worn.
REVERSE: Almost all feathers gone from breast. Tops of legs, wing tips and feathers on head show wear. Talons are flat. Partial mint luster is visible.

VERY FINE *(Light to moderate even wear. All major features are sharp.)*

VF-30 (Choice Very Fine)
OBVERSE: Wear shows on high points of hair from forehead to ear. Some strands visible in hair above ear. There are smooth areas on cotton leaves and at top of cotton blossoms.
REVERSE: Wear shows on leaves of wreath and tips of wings. Only a few feathers visible on breast and head.

VF-20 (Very Fine)
OBVERSE: Smooth spots visible on hair from forehead to ear. Cotton leaves heavily worn but separated. Wheat grains show wear.
REVERSE: Some leaves on wreath are well worn. Breast is smooth, and only a few feathers show on head. Tips of wings are weak but lines are complete.

FINE *(Moderate to heavy even wear. Entire design clear and bold.)*
F-12 (Fine)
OBVERSE: Hairline along face is clearly defined. Lower two cotton leaves smooth but distinct from cap. Some wheat grains merging. Cotton blossoms flat but the two lines in each show clearly.
REVERSE: One-quarter of eagle's right wing and edge of left wing are smooth. Head, neck and breast are flat and merging. Tail feathers slightly worn. Top leaves in wreath show heavy wear.

VERY GOOD *(Well worn. Design clear but flat and lacking details.)*
VG-8 (Very Good)
OBVERSE: Most details in hair are worn smooth. All letters and date are clear. Cotton blossoms flat and leaves merging in spots. Hair of eagle's right wing and one-third of left wing are smooth. All leaves in wreath are worn. Rim is complete.

GOOD *(Heavily worn. Design and legend visible but faint in spots.)*
G-4 (Good)
OBVERSE: Hair is well worn with very little detail remaining. Date, letters and design clearly outlined. Rim is full.
REVERSE: Eagle is worn nearly flat but is completely outlined. Design elements smooth but visible. Legend is all visible; rim is full.

ABOUT GOOD *(Outlined design. Parts of date and legend worn smooth.)*
AG-3 (About Good)
OBVERSE: Head is outlined with nearly all details worn away. Date readable but worn. Legend merging into rim.
REVERSE: Entire design partially worn away. Rim merges into legend.

Note: Some of these dollars have a prooflike surface; this should be mentioned in any description of such pieces.

Portions of the design are often weakly struck, especially on the hair above the ear and on the eagle's breast.

DOLLARS — PEACE 1921-1935

OBVERSE  REVERSE

MINT STATE *(Absolutely no trace of wear.)*
MS-70 (Perfect Uncirculated)
A flawless coin exactly as it was minted, with no trace of wear or injury. Must have full mint luster or light toning. Any unusual striking traits must be described.
MS-65 (Choice Uncirculated)
No trace of wear; nearly as perfect as MS-70 except for a few minute bag marks or surface mars. Has full mint luster but may be unevenly toned.

MS-60 (Uncirculated)
A strictly Uncirculated coin with no trace of wear, but with bag marks and other abrasions more obvious than for MS-65. May have a few small rim mars, and may be weakly struck. Has full mint luster but may lack brilliance, and surface may be spotted or heavily toned. For these coins, bag abrasions and scuff marks are considered different from circulation wear. Full mint luster and lack of any wear are necessary to distinguish MS-60 from AU-55. Check points for signs of wear: high points of cheek and hair. High points of feathers on right wing and leg. Weakly struck spots are common and should not be confused with actual wear.

ABOUT UNCIRCULATED *(Small trace of wear visible on highest points.)*

AU-55 (Choice About Uncirculated)
OBVERSE: Trace of wear shows on hair over ear and above forehead. Slight wear visible on cheek.
REVERSE: High points of feathers on right wing show a trace of wear. Most of the mint luster is still present, although marred by light bag marks and surface abrasions.

AU-50 (About Uncirculated)
OBVERSE: Traces of wear visible on neck, and hair over ear and above forehead. Cheek shows slight wear.
REVERSE: Traces of wear show on head and high points of feathers on right wing. Three-quarters of the mint luster is still present. Surface abrasions and bag marks are more noticeable than for AU-55.

EXTREMELY FINE *(Very light wear on only the highest points.)*

EF-45 (Choice Extemely Fine)
OBVERSE: Hair around face shows slight wear, but most hair strands are visible. Lower edge of neck lightly worn.
REVERSE: Top of neck and head behind eye show slight wear. Central wing and leg feathers lightly worn. Half of the mint luster is still present.

EF-40 (Extremely Fine)
OBVERSE: Slight flattening visible on high points of hair; most hair strands clearly separated. Entire face and lower edge of neck lightly worn.
REVERSE: Wear shows on head behind eye and top of neck. Some flat spots visible on central wing and leg feathers. Partial mint luster is visible.

DOLLARS — EISENHOWER 1971 TO DATE

OBVERSE   REVERSE

MINT STATE *(Absolutely no trace of wear.)*

MS-70 (Perfect Uncirculated)
A flawless coin exactly as it was minted, with no trace of wear or injury. Must have full mint luster and brilliance or light toning. Any unusual striking traits must be described.

MS-65 (Choice Uncirculated)
No trace of wear; nearly as perfect as MS-70 except for some small blemish. Has full mint luster but may be unevenly toned or lightly fingermarked. A few minute nicks or marks may be present.

MS-60 (Uncirculated)
A strictly Uncirculated coin with no trace of wear, but with blemishes more obvious than for MS-65. Has full mint luster, but surface may be dull, spotted or heavily toned. Check points for signs of abrasion: high points of cheek and jawbone, center of neck, edge of bust. Head, high points of ridges and feathers in wings and legs.

ABOUT UNCIRCULATED *(Small trace of wear visible on highest points.)*

AU-55 (Choice About Uncirculated)
OBVERSE: Only a trace of wear shows on highest points of jawbone and at center of neck.
REVERSE: A trace of wear shows on high points of feathers in wings and legs. Nearly all of the mint luster is still present.

EXTREMELY FINE *(Very light wear on only the highest points.)*

EF-45 (Choice Extremely Fine)
OBVERSE: Slight wear shows on cheek, along jawbone and on high points at edge of bust. Hair lines are sharp and detailed.
REVERSE: High points of head, legs and wing ridges are lightly worn. Central feathers are all clearly defined. Three-quarters of the mint luster is still present.

VERY FINE *(Light to moderate even wear. All major features are sharp.)*

VF-30 (Choice Very Fine)
OBVERSE: Wear spots show on hair below part, and along cheek and jaw. Hair lines are weak but have nearly full visible details. Slight wear shows at center of neck and along edge of bust.
REVERSE: Wear shows on head, and feathers in wings and legs but all details are visible. All central tail feathers are plain. Wing and leg ridges are lightly worn.

GOLD DOLLARS — TYPE I 1849-1854

OBVERSE    REVERSE

MINT STATE *(Absolutely no trace of wear.)*

MS-70 (Perfect Uncirculated)
A flawless coin exactly as it was minted, with no trace of wear or injury. Must have full mint luster and brilliance. Any unusual die or planchet traits must be described.

MS-65 (Choice Uncirculated)
No trace of wear; nearly as perfect as MS-70 except for some small blemish. Has full mint luster and brilliance but may show slight discoloration. A few barely noticeable nicks or marks may be present.

MS-60 (Uncirculated)
A strictly Uncirculated coin with no trace of wear, but with blemishes more obvious than for MS-65. May lack full mint luster and brilliance. Check points for signs of abrasion: hair near coronet; tips of leaves.

ABOUT UNCIRCULATED *(Small trace of wear visible on highest points.)*

AU-55 (Choice About Uncirculated)
OBVERSE: There is a trace of wear at upper hairline below coronet.
REVERE: Trace of wear visible on tips of leaves. Three-quarters of the mint luster is still present.

AU-50 (About Uncirculated)
OBVERSE: There is a trace of wear on hairlines near coronet, and below the ear.
REVERSE: Trace of wear visible on tips of leaves. Half of the mint luster is still present.

EXTREMELY FINE *(Very light wear on only the highest points.)*

EF-45 (Choice Extremely Fine)
OBVERSE: Slight wear shows on highest wave of hair, hairline and below ear. All major details are sharp. Beads at top of coronet are well defined.
REVERSE: Leaves show visible wear at tips, but central details are clearly defined. Part of the mint luster is still present.

EF-40 (Extremely Fine)
OBVERSE: Slight wear shows on highest wave of hair, hairline and below ear. All major details are sharp. Beads at top of coronet are well defined.
REVERSE: Leaves show visible wear at tips but central details are clearly defined. Traces of mint luster will show.

VERY FINE *(Light to moderate even wear. All major features are sharp.)*

VF-30 (Choice Very Fine)
OBVERSE: Beads on top of coronet are well defined. LIBERTY is complete. Hair

around face and neck slightly worn but strands fully separated. Star centers show some details.
REVERSE: These is light even wear on legend and date. Some details show in center of leaves.

VF-20 (Very Fine)
OBVERSE: Beads at top of coronet are partially separated. LIBERTY is complete. Hair around face and neck noticeably worn but well outlined. Some star centers show details.
REVERSE: There is light even wear on legend and date. Only traces of leaf ribs are visible. Bow knot is flat on high point.

FINE *(Moderate to heavy even wear. Entire design clear and bold.)*
F-12 (Fine)
OBVERSE: LIBERTY is complete but weak. Ear lobe is visible. Hairlines and beads on coronet, are worn smooth. Stars are clearly outlined, but centers are flat.
REVERSE: Legend within wreath is worn and weak in spots. Leaves and wreath are well outlined. Rim is full and edge beveled.

VERY GOOD *(Well worn. Design clear but flat and lacking details.)*
VG-8 (Very Good)
OBVERSE: Only the outline of hair is visible. Four letters in LIBERTY are clear.
REVERSE: Only the outline of leaves is visible. Legend and numeral are worn and very weak.

GOOD *(Heavily worn. Design and legend visible but faint in spots.)*
G-4 (Good)
OBVERSE: Head is outlined with nearly all details worn away. Stars are weak. Full rim shows.
REVERSE: Date and legend well worn but readable. Leaves are outlined. Full rim shows.

Note: The gold dollars stuck at Charlotte and Dahlonega are crude compared to those of the Philadelphia Mint. Frequently they have rough edges, and the die work appears to be generally inferior. In grading coins from these branch mints, consideration must be made for these factors.

QUARTER EAGLES — CORONET HEAD 1840-1907

OBVERSE   REVERSE

MINT STATE *(Absolutely no trace of wear.)*
MS-70 (Perfect Uncirculated)
A flawless coin exactly as it was minted, with no trace of wear or injury. Must have full mint luster and brilliance. Any unusual die or planchet traits must be described.

MS-65 (Choice Uncirculated)
No trace of wear; nearly as perfect as MS-70 except for some small blemish. Has full mint luster and brilliance but may show slight discoloration. A few barely noticeable nicks or marks may be present.

MS-60 (Uncirculated)
A strictly Uncirculated coin with no trace of wear, but with blemishes more obvious than for MS-65. May lack full mint luster and brilliance. Check points for signs of abrasion: tip of coronet, hair; wings, claws.

ABOUT UNCIRCULATED *(Small trace of wear visible on highest points.)*

AU-55 (Choice About Uncirculated)
OBVERSE: There is a trace of wear on tip of coronet and above eye.
REVERSE: Trace of wear visible on wing tips. Three-quarters of the mint luster is still present.

AU-50 (About Uncirculated)
OBVERSE: There is a trace of wear on coronet and on hair above ear, eye and forehead.
REVERSE: Trace of wear visible on wing tips, below eye and on claw. Half of the mint luster is still present.

EXTREMELY FINE *(Very light wear on only the highest points.)*

EF-45 (Choice Extremely Fine)
OBVERSE: There is light wear on coronet, and on hair above ear, eye, forelocks and top of head.
REVERSE: Light wear shows on edges and tips of wings, on neck, below eye and on claws. Part of the mint luster is still present.

EF-40 (Extremely Fine)
OBVERSE: Light wear shows on coronet, hair above ear and eye, on forelocks, and on cheek. All major details sharp.
REVERSE: Light wear shows on edges and tips of wings, on neck, below eye, on feathers and claws. Shield well defined. Traces of mint luster will show.

VERY FINE *(Light to moderate even wear. All major features are sharp.)*

VF-30 (Choice Very Fine)
OBVERSE: Light wear visible on coronet; hair is worn but shows considerable detail. Most stars show details. LIBERTY bold and clear.
REVERSE: Light wear shows on edges and tips of wings. Some detail shows on head and neck feathers. Vertical shield lines complete but some not separated; horizontal lines worn in center.

VF-20 (Very Fine)
OBVERSE: Hair outlined with very little detail. Only a few stars show any details. LIBERTY clear but not bold.
REVERSE: Half of wing feathers visible. Half of lines in shield are clear.

FINE *(Moderate to heavy even wear. Entire design clear and bold.)*

F-12 (Fine)
OBVERSE: Hair and cheek smooth. Stars outlined with no visible details. LIBERTY worn but visible.
REVERSE: Wings show very little detail. Head and one claw outlined only, with no details visible. Neck almost smooth. Most of shield lines merge.

Note: Coins of this type seldom appear in grades lower than Fine. Pieces made at Charlotte, Dahlonega and New Orleans are frequently found weakly struck. Those from San Francisco often lack feather details.

QUARTER EAGLES — INDIAN HEAD 1908-1929

OBVERSE   REVERSE

MINT STATE *(Absolutely no trace of wear.)*

MS-70 (Perfect Uncirculated)
A flawless coin exactly as it was minted, with no trace of wear or injury. Must have full mint luster and brilliance. Any unusual die or planchet traits must be described.

MS-65 (Choice Uncirculated)
No trace of wear; nearly as perfect as MS-70 except for some small blemish. Has full mint luster and brilliance but may show slight discoloration. A few barely noticeable nicks or marks may be present.

MS-60 (Uncirculated)
A strictly Uncirculated coin with no trace of wear, but with blemishes more obvious than for MS-65. May lack full mint luster and brilliance. Check points for signs of abrasion: cheekbone, headdress, headband feathers; shoulder of eagle's left wing.

ABOUT UNCIRCULATED *(Small trace of wear visible on highest points.)*

AU-55 (Choice About Uncirculated)
OBVERSE: There is a trace of wear on cheekbone.
REVERSE: Trace of wear visible on shoulder of eagle's left wing. Three-quarters of the mint luster is still present.

AU-50 (About Uncirculated)
OBVERSE: There is a trace of wear on cheekbone and headdress.
REVERSE: Trace of wear visible on shoulder of wing, head and breast. Half of the mint luster is still present.

EXTREMELY FINE *(Very light wear on only the highest points.)*

EF-45 (Choice Extremely Fine)
OBVERSE: There is light wear on cheekbone, headdress and headband.
REVERSE: Light wear shows on upper portion of wing, head, neck and breast.

EF-40 (Extremely Fine)
OBVERSE: Light wear shows on cheekbone, jaw and headband. Slight wear visible on feathers of headdress. Stars sharp.
REVERSE: Light wear shows on wing, head, neck and breast. Leg has full feather detail. Traces of mint luster will show.

VERY FINE *(Light to moderate even wear. All major features are sharp.)*

VF-30 (Choice Very Fine)
OBVERSE: Cheekbone shows flat spot. Small feathers clear; large feathers show some detail. Most of headband detail visible.
REVERSE: Wear shows on wing and neck. Some breast feathers show details. Most of leg feathers visible.

VF-20 (Very Fine)
OBVERSE: Cheekbone worn about halfway. Small feathers clear but large feathers show a little detail. Hair cord knot is distinct. Headband shows some detail.
REVERSE: Little detail shows on breast and leg feathers. Top of wing and neck worn. Second layer of wing feathers shows.

FINE *(Moderate to heavy even wear. Entire design clear and bold.)*
F-12 (Fine)
OBVERSE: Cheekbone worn; all feathers worn with very little detail visible. Stars outlined, with no details visible. Hair cord knot is worn but visible.
REVERSE: Wing worn, with only partial feathers at bottom visible. All lettering worn but visible.

Note: Coins of this type are seldom collected in grades lower than Fine. Mint marks are often weakly struck.

HALF EAGLES — CORONET HEAD 1839-1908

OBVERSE   REVERSE

MINT STATE *(Absolutely no trace of wear.)*
MS-70 (Perfect Uncirculated)
A flawless coin exactly as it was minted, with no trace of wear or injury. Must have full mint luster and brilliance. Any unusual die or planchet traits must be described.

MS-65 (Choice Uncirculated)
No trace of wear; nearly as perfect as MS-70 except for some small blemish. Has full mint luster and brilliance but may show slight discoloration. A few barely noticeable bag marks and surface abrasions may be present.

MS-60 (Uncirculated)
A strictly Uncirculated coin with no trace of wear, but with blemishes more obvious than for MS-65. Has full mint luster but may lack brilliance. Surface may be lightly marred by minor bag marks and abrasions. Check points for signs of wear: hair, coronet; wings.

ABOUT UNCIRCULATED *(Small trace of wear visible on highest points.)*
AU-55 (Choice About Uncirculated)
OBVERSE: There is a trace of wear on tip of coronet and hair above eye.
REVERSE: Trace of wear visible on wing tips. Three-quarters of the mint luster is still present.

AU-50 (About Uncirculated)
OBVERSE: There is a trace of wear on coronet, above ear and eye.
REVERSE: Trace of wear visible on wing tips, below eye and on claw. Half of the mint luster is still present.

EXTREMELY FINE *(Light wear on only the highest points.)*

EF-45 (Choice Extremely Fine)
OBVERSE: There is light wear on coronet, and on hair above ear, eye, forelocks and top of head.
REVERSE: Light wear shows on edges and tips of wings, on neck, below eye and on claws. Part of the mint luster is still present.

EF-40 (Extremely Fine)
OBVERSE: Light wear shows on coronet, on hair above ear and eye, on the forelock, on top of head and on cheek. All major details are sharp.
REVERSE: Light wear visible on edges and tips of wings, on neck, below eye, on feathers and claws. Shield is well defined. Traces of mint luster will show.

VERY FINE *(Light to moderate even wear. All major features are sharp.)*

VF-30 (Choice Very Fine)
OBVERSE: Light wear shows on coronet, hair and stars but most details are visible. LIBERTY bold.
REVERSE: Light wear visible on edges and tips of wings. Head and neck feathers show some detail. Vertical lines in shield complete but some not separated; horizontal lines worn in center.

VF-20 (Very Fine)
OBVERSE: Hair worn but major details visible. Top line of coronet broken. Some stars show partial detail. LIBERTY clear but not bold.
REVERSE: Half of wing feathers are visible. Half of lines in shield are clear.

FINE *(Moderate to heavy even wear. Entire design clear and bold.)*

F-12 (Fine)
OBVERSE: Hair and cheekbone smooth. Top line of coronet worn. LIBERTY worn but visible.
REVERSE: Wings show very little detail. Head and one claw outlined only, with no details visible. Neck almost smooth. Most of shield lines merge. (For the 1866 through 1908 group, the motto is worn but readable.)

Note: Coins of this type are seldom collected in grades lower than Fine.

HALF EAGLES — INDIAN HEAD 1908-1929

OBVERSE    REVERSE

MINT STATE *(Absolutely no trace of wear.)*

MS-70 (Perfect Uncirculated)
A flawless coin exactly as it was minted, with no trace of wear or injury. Must have full mint luster and brilliance. Any unusual die or planchet traits must be described.

MS-65 (Choice Uncirculated)
No trace of wear; nearly as perfect as MS-70 except for some small blemish. Has full mint luster and brilliance but may show slight discoloration. A few barely noticeable bag marks and surface abrasions may be present.

MS-60 (Uncirculated)
A strictly Uncirculated coin with no trace of wear, but with blemishes more obvious than for MS-65. Has full mint luster but may lack brilliance. Surface may be lightly marred by minor bag marks and abrasions. Check points for signs of wear: cheekbone, headdress, headband feathers; shoulder of eagle's left wing.

ABOUT UNCIRCULATED *(Small trace of wear visible on highest points.)*

AU-55 (Choice About Uncirculated)
OBVERSE: There is a trace of wear on cheekbone.
REVERSE: Trace of wear visible on shoulder of eagle's left wing. Three-quarters of the mint luster is still present.

AU-50 (About Uncirculated)
OBVERSE: There is a trace of wear on cheekbone and headdress.
REVERSE: Trace of wear visible on shoulder of wing, head and breast. Half of the mint luster is still present.

EXTREMELY FINE *(Light wear on only the highest points.)*

EF-45 (Choice Extremely Fine)
OBVERSE: There is light wear on cheekbone, headdress and headband.
REVERSE: Light wear shows on upper portion of wing, head, neck and breast. Part of mint luster is still present.

EF-40 (Extremely Fine)
OBVERSE: Light wear shows on cheekbone, jaw and headband. Slight wear visible on feathers of headdress. Stars are sharp.
REVERSE: Light wear shows on wing, head, neck and breast. Leg has full feather detail. Traces of mint luster will show.

VERY FINE *(Light to moderate even wear. All major features are sharp.)*

VF-30 (Choice Very Fine)
OBVERSE: Cheekbone shows flat spot. Small feathers clear; large feathers show some details. Most of headband detail visible.
REVERSE: Wear shows on wing and neck. Some breast feathers show details. Most of leg feathers visible.

VF-20 (Very Fine)
OBVERSE: Cheekbone worn about half-way. Headdress feathers show some details. Hair cord knot is distinct. Headband shows only a little detail.
REVERSE: Little detail shows on breast and leg feathers. Top of wing and neck worn. Second layer of wing feathers shows.

FINE *(Moderate to heavy even wear. Entire design clear and bold.)*

F-12 (Fine)
OBVERSE: Cheekbone worn; all feathers worn with very little detail visible. Stars outlined, with no details visible. Hair cord knot is worn but visible.
REVERSE: Wing worn, with only partial feathers at bottom visible. All lettering worn but visible.

Note: Coins of this type are seldom collected in grades lower than Fine. Mint marks are often very weakly struck.

EAGLES — CORONET HEAD 1838-1907

OBVERSE REVERSE

MINT STATE *(Absolutely no trace of wear.)*

MS-70 (Perfect Uncirculated)
A flawless coin exactly as it was minted, with no trace of wear or injury. Must have full mint luster and brilliance. Any unusual die or planchet traits must be described.

MS-65 (Choice Uncirculated)
No trace of wear; nearly as perfect as MS-70 except for some small blemish. Has full mint luster and brilliance but may show slight discoloration. A few barely noticeable bag marks and surface abrasions may be present.

MS-60 (Uncirculated)
A strictly Uncirculated coin with no trace of wear, but with blemishes more obvious than for MS-65. Has full mint luster but may lack brilliance. Surface may be lightly marred by minor bag marks and abrasions. Check points for signs of wear: hair, coronet; wings.

ABOUT UNCIRCULATED *(Small trace of wear visible on highest points.)*

AU-55 (Choice About Uncirculated)
OBVERSE: There is a trace of wear on hair above eye and on coronet.
REVERSE: Trace of wear visible on wing tips. Three-quarters of the mint luster is still present.

AU-50 (About Uncirculated)
OBVERSE: There is a trace of wear on hair at ear and above eye, and on coronet.
REVERSE: Trace of wear visible on wing tips, below eye and on claw. Half of the mint luster is still present.

EXTREMELY FINE *(Light wear on only the highest points.)*

EF-45 (Choice Extremely Fine)
OBVERSE: There is light wear on coronet, and on hair above ear, eye, forelocks and top of head.
REVERSE: Light wear shows on edges and tips of wings, on neck, below eye and on claws. Part of the mint luster is still present.

EF-40 (Extremely Fine)
OBVERSE: Light wear shows on coronet, hair, cheek and stars. All major details sharp.
REVERSE: Light wear visible on wings, head, neck and claws. Shield is well defined. Traces of mint luster will show.

VERY FINE *(Light to moderate even wear. All major features are sharp.)*

VF-30 (Choice Very Fine)
OBVERSE: There is light wear on coronet, hair and stars, but most details are visible. There is a break on top line of coronet over two letters in LIBERTY. Cheek worn. LIBERTY bold.

REVERSE: Light wear visible on wings and head but some details show. Vertical lines in shield complete but some are not separated; horizontal lines worn in center.

VF-20 (Very Fine)
OBVERSE: Hair worn but major details visible. Break on top line of coronet extends over at least three letters in LIBERTY. Cheek well worn. Stars worn but show most details. LIBERTY clear but shows wear.
REVERSE: About half of wing feathers are visible. Very little detail shows in head.

FINE *(Moderate to heavy even wear. Entire design clear and bold.)*

F-12 (Fine)
OBVERSE: Hair and cheekbone smooth. Top line of coronet worn. Some details show in stars. LIBERTY worn but visible.
REVERSE: Wings show very little detail. Head and one claw outlined only, with no details visible. Neck is almost smooth. Most of shield lines merge. (In the 1866 through 1907 group, the motto is worn but readable.)

Note: Coins of this type are seldom collected in grades lower than Fine.

EAGLES — INDIAN HEAD 1907-1933

OBVERSE    REVERSE

MINT STATE *(Absolutely no trace of wear.)*

MS-70 (Perfect Uncirculated)
A flawless coin exactly as it was minted, with no trace of wear or injury. Must have full mint luster and brilliance. Any unusual die or planchet traits must be described.

MS-65 (Choice Uncirculated)
No trace of wear; nearly as perfect as MS-70 except for some small blemish. Has full mint luster and brilliance but may show some slight discoloration. A few minute bag marks and surface abrasions may be present.

MS-60 (Uncirculated)
A strictly Uncirculated coin with no trace of wear, but with blemishes more obvious than for MS-65. Has full mint luster but may lack brilliance. Surface may be lightly marred by minor bag marks and abrasions. Check points for signs of wear: above eye, cheek, wing.

ABOUT UNCIRCULATED *(Small trace of wear visible on highest points.)*

AU-55 (Choice About Uncirculated)
OBVERSE: There is a trace of wear above eye.
REVERSE: Trace of wear visible on wing. Three-quarters of the mint luster is still present.

AU-50 (About Uncirculated)
OBVERSE: There is a trace of wear on hair above eye and on forehead.
REVERSE: Trace of wear visible on wing. Half of the mint luster is still present.

EXTREMELY FINE *(Light wear on only the highest points.)*

EF-45 (Choice Extremely Fine)
OBVERSE: There is light wear on hair above eye and on forehead, and on cheekbone.
REVERSE: Light wear shows on wing and head. Part of the mint luster is still present.

EF-40 (Extremely Fine)
OBVERSE: Light wear shows on hair, cheekbone and feathers.
REVERSE: Light wear visible on wing and head. Traces of mint luster will show.

VERY FINE *(Light to moderate even wear. All major features are sharp.)*

VF-30 (Choice Very Fine)
OBVERSE: There is light wear along forehead, but most detail shows. Moderate wear visible on cheekbone. Light wear shows where feathers meet headband.
REVERSE: Left wing shows more than half the details. Some details in head are visible.

VF-20 (Very Fine)
OBVERSE: About half the hair detail is visible. Moderate wear shows on cheekbone. Some feathers do not touch headband.
REVERSE: There is moderate wear on left wing which shows only about one-quarter detail. Head almost smooth. All lettering bold.

FINE *(Moderate to heavy even wear. Entire design clear and bold.)*

F-12 (Very Fine)
OBVERSE: Hair smooth with no details; cheekbone almost smooth. No feathers touch headband but most feather details visible.
REVERSE: Left wing top and head are worn smooth. Lettering worn but visible.

Note: Coins of this type are seldom collected in grades lower than Fine.

DOUBLE EAGLES — LIBERTY HEAD 1850-1907

OBVERSE 　　　　　　REVERSE

MINT STATE *(Absolutely no trace of wear.)*

MS-70 (Perfect Uncirculated)
A flawless coin exactly as it was minted, with no trace of wear or injury. Must have full mint luster and brilliance. Any unusual die or planchet traits must be described.

MS-65 (Choice Uncirculated)
No trace of wear; nearly as perfect as MS-70 except for some small blemish. Has full mint luster and brilliance but may show slight discoloration. A few minute bag marks and surface abrasions are usually present.

MS-60 (Uncirculated)
A strictly Uncirculated coin with no trace of wear, but with blemishes more obvious than for MS-65. Has full mint luster but may lack brilliance. Surface is usually lightly marred by minor bag marks and abrasions. Check points for signs of wear: hair, coronet; eagle's neck and wing, top of shield.

ABOUT UNCIRCULATED *(Small trace of wear visible on highest points.)*

AU-55 (Choice About Uncirculated)
OBVERSE: There is a trace of wear on hair.
REVERSE: Trace of wear visible on wing tips and neck. Three-quarters of the mint luster is still present.

AU-50 (About Uncirculated)
OBVERSE: There is a trace of wear on hair at top and over eye, and on coronet.
REVERSE: Trace of wear visible on wing tips, neck and at top of shield. Half of the mint luster is still present.

EXTREMELY FINE *(Light wear on only the highest points.)*

EF-45 (Choice Extremely Fine)
OBVERSE: There is light wear on hair and coronet prongs.
REVERSE: Light wear shows on edges and tips of wings, on head and neck, and on horizontal shield lines. Part of the mint luster is still present.

EF-40 (Extremely Fine)
OBVERSE: Light wear shows on hair, coronet prongs and cheek.
REVERSE: Light wear visible on wings, head, neck, horizontal shield lines and tail. Traces of mint luster will show.

VERY FINE *(Light to moderate even wear. All major features are sharp.)*

VF-30 (Choice Very Fine)
OBVERSE: About one-quarter of hair detail below coronet visible; half the detail shows above coronet. Cheek and some coronet prongs worn. Stars show wear but all details visible.
REVERSE: Most of wing details visible. Top part of shield shows moderate wear. About half the detail in tail visible.

VF-20 (Very Fine)
OBVERSE: Less than half the hair detail above coronet visible. About half the coronet prongs are considerably worn. Stars are flat but show most details. LIBERTY shows wear but is very clear.
REVERSE: Some wing details visible. Shield shows very little detail at top. Tail is worn with very little detail.

FINE *(Moderate to heavy even wear. Entire design clear and bold.)*

F-12 (Fine)
OBVERSE: All hairlines are well worn with very little detail visible. About one-quarter of details within coronet visible. Stars show little detail. LIBERTY readable.
REVERSE: Wings show very little detail. Head and neck smooth. Eye visible. Tail and top of shield smooth.

Note: Coins of this type are seldom collected in grades lower than Fine. The hair curl under the ear is sometimes weakly struck.

In the group between 1866 and 1876, the reverse motto is sometimes weakly struck.

Pieces made at the Carson City mint are usually found weakly struck and heavily bag marked.

DOUBLE EAGLES — SAINT-GAUDENS 1907-1932

OBVERSE

REVERSE

MINT STATE *(Absolutely no trace of wear.)*

MS-70 (Perfect Uncirculated)
A flawless coin exactly as it was minted, with no trace of wear or injury. Must have full mint luster and brilliance. Any unusual die or planchet traits must be described.

MS-65 (Choice Uncirculated)
No trace of wear; nearly as perfect as MS-70 except for some small blemish. Has full mint luster and brilliance but may show slight discoloration. A few minute bag marks and surface abrasions are usually present.

MS-60 (Uncirculated)
A strictly Uncirculated coin with no trace of wear, but with blemishes more obvious than for MS-65. Has full mint luster but may lack brilliance. Surface is usually lightly marred by minor bag marks and abrasions. Check points for signs of wear: forehead, breast, knee, nose; eagle's wings and breast.

ABOUT UNCIRCULATED *(Small trace of wear visible on highest points.)*

AU-55 (Choice About Uncirculated)
OBVERSE: There is a trace of wear on left breast and left knee.
REVERSE: Trace of wear visible on high point of wing. Three-quarters of the mint luster is still present.

AU-50 (About Uncirculated)
OBVERSE: There is a trace of wear on nose, breast and knee.
REVERSE: Trace of wear visible on wings. Half of the mint luster is still present.

EXTREMELY FINE *(Light wear on only the highest points.)*

EF-45 (Choice Extremely Fine)
OBVERSE: There is light wear on forehead, nose, breast and knee.
REVERSE: Light wear shows on wings and breast, but all feathers are bold. Part of the mint luster is still present.

EF-40 (Extremely Fine)
OBVERSE: Light wear shows on forehead, nose, breast, knee and just below left knee. Drapery lines on chest visible.
REVERSE: Light wear visible on wings and breast but all feathers bold. Traces of mint luster will show.

VERY FINE *(Light to moderate even wear. All major features are sharp.)*

VF-30 (Choice Very Fine)
OBVERSE: There is light wear on all features, extending above and below left knee and along part of right leg. Some of garment lines on chest are visible.
REVERSE: Light wear visible on left wing and breast; feathers show but some are weak.

VF-20 (Very Fine)
OBVERSE: Forehead moderately worn. Contours of breast worn. Only a few garment lines on chest are visible. Entire right leg shows moderate wear.
REVERSE: Half of feathers are visible in wings and breast.

FINE *(Moderate to heavy even wear. Entire design clear and bold.)*
F-12 (Fine)
OBVERSE: Forehead and garment smooth; breasts flat. Both legs worn with right bottom missing.
REVERSE: Less than half the wing details are visible. Only a little breast detail is visible.

Note: Coins of this type are seldom found in grades lower than Fine.

COLONIAL COINS, PATTERNS AND TOKENS

The most extensively circulated — and faithfully trusted — coin of early colonial America was the Spanish silver dollar or "piece of eight." Introduced to this country by the Spanish explorers and later imported in abundance by traders, it had a value of eight *reals*, each real of "bit" being worth 12½ cents. Thus the quarter or 25 cent piece came to be known as "two bits".

"Two-bits"

"Four-bits"

THE SPANISH MILLED DOLLAR
The "Piece of Eight"

The following pages comprise descriptions and price valuations for most types of monies used in the American colonies, excluding foreign coins intended to serve currency needs abroad. Most can only be classed as tokens as they either had no face value or were struck without government sanction. These include merchant pieces and other speculative issues. However the colonists, being ever-resourceful, attempted from time to time to strike semi-official or official coinage, and these will be found listed as well. Colonial coinage on the whole is not handsome. It was generally produced under conditions inferior to that of governmentally issued money, often designed struck by persons who had little or no prior experience in such work. It is nevertheless of great interest from both a numismatic and historical point of view and much of it extremely rare. As a general rule the collector should be wary of counterfeits and reproductions, as the majority of these pieces have at one time or other been facsimilized, either as legitimate souvenirs or fraudulently.

SOMMER ISLANDS (BERMUDA)

This so-called "Hog money" is thought to be the first coinage of the American colonies. A hog is pictured on one side and a sailing vessel on the other. The workmanship is English. Hogs were not native to the islands but introduced around 1515 by the Spaniard Juan Bermudez, from whom Bermuda takes its name. The apparently increased and multiplied vastly within the next hundred years, serving as an important article of food for the inhabitants. The suggestion that the coins were intended to represent the market value of a hog, just as early Greek coins were sometimes stamped with a likeness of an animal whose price they equaled, is no longer given serious consideration. It was used merely as an emblem. These coins are of lightly silvered brass, inscribed "SOMMER ISLANDS." The edges are, as to be expected, irregular, having been produced by the hammering technique rather than milling.

SHILLING

TYPE OF COIN	ABP	AG-3 About Good	G-4 Good	F-12 Fine
☐ Shilling	1000.00	1250.00	1750.00	7250.00

SIXPENCE

TYPE OF COIN	ABP	AG-3 About Good	G-4 Good	F-12 Fine
☐ Sixpence	650.00	800.00	1650.00	6750.00
☐ Threepence		VERY RARE		
☐ Twopence	650.00	800.00	1800.00	7750.00

MASSACHUSETTS-NEW ENGLAND COINAGE

This is the earliest coinage struck on the North American continent. Its history is briefly detailed in the section on Colonial Coins, Patterns and Tokens. This crude coinage may not be appealing aesthetically but its historical significance is as great, or greater, than any coins subsequently issued in this country. It was produced in limited quantities for local circulation in the Boston area and is extremely rare. When the decision was reached to attempt a native currency, the Massachusetts General Court appointed John Hull "mintmaster." The "mint" was an iron works operated by Joseph Jenks at Saugus, just north of Boston. These coins were made of silver by the ancient process of hammering — beating the designs into them by holding the die against the metal blank and striking it with a mallet. There was in fact no design at all. The coins were issued in three denominations — threepence, sixpence and twelvepence (shilling) — and each carried the letters "NE" on one side and the value in roman numerals on the other, most of the surface being blank. Variations in size, shape and placement of the markings are usual. They date to 1652 but no date appears upon them.

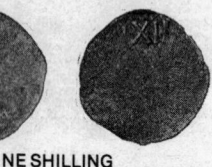

NE SHILLING

NE SIXPENCE

NE THREEPENCE

TYPE OF COIN		ABP	G-4 Good	F-12 Fine
☐ NE Shilling		5000.00	8250.00	14000.00
☐ NE Sixpence	Less than 7 known	15000.00	22000.00	30000.00
☐ NE Threepence	Less than 3 known			EXTREMELY RARE

WILLOW TREE COINS

After about four months of circulation of the Massachusetts-New England coinage (above), it was decided they were unsatisfactory. The legend and numeral of value were so simplistic that anyone possessing smith's tools could reproduce them. There was the further problem — not a new one, as it was faced by English mints in the middle ages — that the large expanses of unstamped metal invited "clipping," a practice in which unscrupulous persons trimmed down the edges and collected quantities of silver while still passing the coins at face value. It was impossible to improve the method of manufacture, there being no milling machines available. But the designs could be improved by the use of more fully engraved dies. This was accomplished with the so-called Willow Tree Coinage, introduced in 1653. On the obverse appears a very abstract rendition of a willow tree, surrounded by the placename, with the date and value designation on the reverse (III stood for threepence, VI for sixpence and XII for shilling). Although struck at odd moments from 1653 to 1660 (there was no regular or continuous production), all specimens are dated 1652. Two theories are advanced to explain the sameness of date. The first is that the reverse die was engraved in 1652 and, because of the limited use to which it was placed, it was considered not worthwhile to revise it. The second, far more historically intriguing, holds that the colonists feared reprisals from Britain for striking coinage and wished to pretend that no such activity was taking place after 1652.

SHILLING

SIXPENCE

THREEPENCE

TYPE OF COIN	ABP	G-4 Good	F-12 Fine
☐ Willow Tree Shilling	3500.00	7500.00	14000.00
☐ Willow Tree Sixpence	12000.00	16500.00	22500.00
☐ Willow Tree Threepence			EXTREMELY RARE

OAK TREE COINS

Successors to the Willow Tree Coins, these were likewise of Massachusetts origin and, like them, showed a tree on the obverse with the date and numeral of value on the reverse. They were introduced in 1660, the year of the English Restoration (the return of the Stuarts to the throne), an item of no small significance numismatically. While the previous regime, the Protectorate of Oliver Cromwell, was composed of politicians who supported the pilgrim cause, there was genuine fear that the new king — Charles II — might deal harshly with the colonists for being so bold as to strike coins. They attemped to camouflage this activity by retaining the old date, 1652, during the eight years that Oak Tree Coins were struck; and in fact it remained unaltered for the 16 years of their successors, Pine Tree Coins. In terms of design these Oak Tree Coins were an improvement on their predecessors, being much sharper and bolder. Whether this can be attributed to more deeply engraved dies, more careful hammering, or (an usually overlooked possibility) better annealing or heating of the blanks is uncertain. The Mintmaster was still the same: John Hull. But this much is sure, the Oak Tree Coins were turned out in far larger quantities than previous Massachusetts coins.

SHILLING  **SIXPENCE**  **THREEPENCE**

TYPE OF COIN	ABP	G-4 Good	F-12 Fine	EF-40 Ex. Fine
☐ Shilling	225.00	350.00	600.00	1400.00
☐ Sixpence	225.00	350.00	650.00	1375.00
☐ Threepence	225.00	350.00	650.00	1600.00
☐ Twopence	225.00	350.00	600.00	1600.00

PINE TREE COINS

The final version of the Bay Colony *"tree"* coin, it featured a much clearer if not more botanically accurate portrait of a tree. Though struck in the same three denominations as the earlier types, there is a "Large Planchet" and "Small Planchet" version of the shilling, the large being slightly rarer. Both are of the same weight; the metal was simply hammered thinner on the "Large Planchet." It had been demonstrated, by the use of large planchets for the Willow and Oak Tree shillings, that the coin did not stand up well to handling and could be rendered sturdier by reducing its size and thereby increasing the thickness. It was also possible to strike the design more deeply with a thicker planchet. All coins from this series are dated 1652. They were actually struck from 1667 to 1682, during the reign of Britain's Charles II. After 1682 the issuing of coinage was discontinued by the Bay Colony. Many varieties exist in this series.

SHILLING, Large Planchet  **SHILLING, Small Planchet**

SIXPENCE  **THREEPENCE**

TYPE OF COIN	ABP	G-4 Good	F-12 Fine	EF-40 Ex. Fine
☐ Shilling, Large Planchet	200.00	275.00	600.00	1200.00
☐ Shilling, Small Planchet	180.00	250.00	500.00	950.00
☐ Sixpence	200.00	275.00	600.00	1200.00
☐ Threepence	180.00	250.00	400.00	925.00

MARYLAND

Maryland was the second colony, next to Massachusetts, to have coinage of its own. The origins of these coins bear little relation to those of the Bay Colony. While the Massachusetts pieces had been natively designed and struck, Maryland's coins were entirely a foreign product. They date from 1658. At this time Maryland was very sparsely inhabited, its only residents being small colonies of English immigrants, and could not have suffered too seriously from a shortage of coinage. Though not strictly classified as private issues they might well merit that designation. Maryland's first coins were the brainchild of Cecil Calvert, Lord Baltimore (for whom the colony's chief city was named). Calvert did not, as popularly supposed, "own Maryland." He did however possess large areas of its land and had the title of Lord Proprietor of Maryland. As an English lord with typical lordly pride, Calvert looked with disdain upon the prospect of Englishmen — his subjects, technically — trading with beads or iron or other objects of barter. So he ordered a batch of English-quality coins to be struck in Britain for use in the colony. They comprised a shilling, sixpence, fourpence or groat, and a penny. The first three were of silver, following the British tradition, the penny in copper. As a result of their production in an established, well-equipped mint, these coins are considerably more professional in appearance than those of Massachusetts. Lord Calvert placed his own portrait upon them. There was no need to fear censure from the king for this brazen act as the English Civil War had already swept the king (Charles I) from his throne and Britain was not to again be ruled by a king until 1660. The reverses of the silver pieces carry Calvert's heraldic bearings with the value in roman numerals. The penny's obverse shows a regal crown surmounted by staffs and banners. There is no numeral of value on the penny but instead the word "denarium," the name of an ancient Roman coin from which the British penny evolved. (To this day the symbol for "penny" in Britain is the letter "d," meaning denarium. The cent sign, ¢, is never used.) Lord Calvert's portrait is a shoulder-length bust without crown, wreath of laurel or other symbol of rulership. The penny is the scarcest of the denominations, as this is believed to have been a pattern only, no actually placed in use.

DENARIUM   SIXPENCE

SHILLING

TYPE OF COIN	ABP	G-4 Good	F-12 Fine
☐ Shilling	750.00	1500.00	4000.00
☐ Sixpence	500.00	1000.00	3000.00
☐ Fourpence	750.00	1500.00	5000.00
☐ Denarium (Penny)		EXTREMELY RARE	

MARK NEWBY OR ST. PATRICK HALFPENCE

The coinage shortage in the early colonies, and the voraciousness with which anything resembling coinage was seized upon as a medium of exchange, is clearly demonstrated by the Newby or St. Patrick Halfpence. The coins are really misnamed, as they existed not only in halfpence but farthing denomination (in the British currency system a farthing or "fourthling" was equal to one quarter of a penny). Mark Newby was neither an explorer or royal governor but apparently a private Irish citizen who came from Dublin and settled in New Jersey in the year 1681. He brought with him a quantity of tokens — they could only very charitably be called coins — which are thought to have been struck at Dublin about eight years earlier. These were coppers. On the obverse they depict a crowned king kneeling and playing a harp, almost certainly intended as the Biblical king David who is often represented in art as a harpist. St. Patrick, the legendary and patron saint of Ireland, appears on the reverses. On the halfpence he holds a crozier and cross (often mistaken for a clover) while giving benediction to a worshipper; on the farthing he is shown in a similar pose, driving the snakes out of Ireland, one of the many accomplishments with which this saint is credited. The obverse legend is "FLOREAT REX," which can be translated as "PROSPERITY TO THE KING." These are not at all bad-looking pieces and they feature an intriguing detail: the large crown on the obverse was inlaid in brass, to contrast in color with the copper and give the appearance of being golden. It is, however, sometimes lacking. The origin of this St. Patrick Money is not clearly known. The possibility that it was struck for circulation in America seems very remote, as (a) there is no record of supportive legislation on either side of the Atlantic, and (b) the coins were apparently not brought to this country until long after striking, which hardly would have been the case had they been designed for use here. In any event the General Assembly of the New Jersey Province authorized their use as legal tender in May, 1682, and for some while thereafter they served as the common currency of New Jersey. The most logical conclusion to be drawn is that Newby was a commercial trader who sought to profit from the shortage of coinage in America, and that he settled in New Jersey because this area was virtually without money of any kind. If so, he would not have been the only colonist to do this. Silver and gold patterns of the farthing were struck, of which the silver is very rare and the gold unique. There may have been similar patterns of the ½ penny but they have not been discovered. In their normal metal, copper, neither is a coin of extreme scarcity.

ST. PATRICK HALFPENCE ST. PATRICK FARTHING

TYPE OF COIN	ABP	G-4 Good	F-12 Fine
☐ St. Patrick Halfpence	95.00	150.00	325.00
☐ St. Patrick Farthing (Brass Insert on Obverse)	50.00	80.00	225.00
☐ St. Patrick Farthing (Without Brass Insert)	50.00	80.00	225.00
☐ St. Patrick Farthing (Silver Pattern)	1000.00	1200.00	2000.00
☐ St. Patrick Farthing (Gold Pattern)			UNIQUE

COLONIAL PLANTATION TOKEN

The so-called Plantation Token was the first coinage authorized for use in the American colonies by the British government. Its history is of great interest. Throughout the middle 17th century it was well known in England that the American provinces or "plantations" as they were called abroad (largely by persons unaware of the extent of population) suffered from a shortage of coinage. In 1688 an Englishman named John Holt petitioned the king (James II) for a patent or franchise for the striking of coinage for distribution in the colonies. In Britain at this time the system of "patents of exclusivity" was commonplace. Printers would pay a fee to have the exclusive right on putting out Bibles; merchants paid for a franchise to sell a particular product without fear of competition. The fee, which was considerable, had to be paid each year while the franchise was in force. Holt was convinced that the supply of coinage to America would be a very profitable endeavor. The government approved his request for a franchise and shortly thereafter he began to strike his coins, better called tokens. Large in size, they were made of tin and had the face value of 1/24th of a Spanish real or "piece of eight," say about fourpence. On their obverse they pictured an equestrian likeness of James II, regal-looking in this design but soon to be driven out of the country into exile. It is important to note that they were not intended for use in any special region but could be exchanged anywhere in the provinces; thus they carry no placename. The original dies were preserved and restrikes made from them in the late 1820's, whose appearance is quite similar to the original and could well be a cause of confusion to beginners. A very rare variety exists, in which the numeral "4" in the value legend on the reverse is positioned vertically instead of horizontally.

PLANTATION TOKEN

TYPE OF COIN	ABP	G-4 Good	F-12 Fine	EF-40 Ex. Fine	MS-60 Unc.
☐ James II Plantation Token ..	100.00	175.00	275.00	500.00	1200.00
☐ James II Plantation Token, vertical "4"			RARE		

Restrikes exist which are worth slightly less.

ELEPHANT TOKENS

These extremely popular, intriguing pieces have been the subject of much study and debate. Their origins are only sketchily known. There are three specific types: London token, Carolina token and New England token. All have the same obverse, a portrait of an elephant without legend or inscription of any kind. These pieces are coppers and were modeled as halfpennies, though they carry no indication of value. The extent to which they circulated in the American colonies is not established. Based on what little information is available their history may be pieced together as follows.

First in the series was the London token, which on some specimens carries the wording "God Preserve London" on the reverse, on others merely "London," accompanying a heraldic shield. The belief is that they were struck in 1664 when the population of that city was being decimated by an outbreak of bubonic plague, which apparently is the danger from which preservation was sought. So far this theory makes some historical sense though it fails to explain the selection of an elephant as the obverse symbol. Could it be that this was a reference to "stamping out" the plague, and that the elephant, as the largest of creatures, would be best equipped to do so? That elephants were well known at London in the 1660's is well established. There were no zoos for the display of wild beasts but elephants and tigers (both from India) were kept in enclosed dungeons in the Tower of London for the amusement of visitors. Natural history drawing was still in an archaic state at that time, which explains why the elephant on Elephant Tokens looks rather strange. For a long while thereafter there appears to have been no effort to revive the Elephant Token, perhaps because the plague subsided. Then in 1694 it reappeared, in an edition bearing two different reverses: "God Preserve Carolina and the Lord's Proprietors" and "God Preserve New England." Just how these pieces came to be, what their intent was, and how they were circulated, it totally unknown. It may be presumed that "God Preserve" was used merely in the sense of "God Bless," after the fashion of the slogan "God Save the King," not as implication that either Carolina or New England suffered from any specific difficulty. There is little doubt, based on physical evidence, that they were struck in England, as these tokens are handsomely milled (not hammered) and it is doubtful that such work could have been accomplished in the colonies. It has been said that the London variety was intended for circulation in Tangier but even if that were so, there is no evidence of it being an official issue. The Carolina and New England pieces could have been entirely speculative. Their distribution may have been local (in England) with no intention of exporting or using them for actual currency in the colonies. This seems the logical answer, especially in view of the extremely small quantities struck. Of the London token there were considerably larger numbers struck but to classify this as a piece designed for colonial use seems very presumptive. Some specimens undoubtedly reached the colonies at an early date but, if they did, it was only accidentally, in the baggage or pockets of immigrants or traders, just as almost everything else made abroad found its way across the Atlantic.

There are a number of types and varieties. The London token exists in both thin and thick planchet; with interlacing in the central portion of the shield; with sword in the second quarter of the shield (transposed from the first, where it is commonly found); and with the inscription "London" rather than "God Preserve London." Of these the transposed sword is the rarest. The chief variety on the Carolina issue is the alteration from "Proprieters" to the more correct spelling, "Proprietors," accomplished not by the introduction of a fresh die but re-engraving the original. If closely inspected the letter "e," or what remains of it, can be observed.

1664 NEW ENGLAND   **1664 PROPRIETORS**

1664 PROPRIETORS

1664 GOD PRESERVE LONDON

1664 GOD PRESERVE LONDON

1664 LONDON

TYPE OF COIN	ABP	G-4 Good	F-12 Fine
☐ 1664 God Preserve London (thin)	65.00	80.00	225.00
☐ 1664 God Preserve London (thick)	50.00	65.00	175.00
☐ 1664 God Preserve London (diag.)	80.00	125.00	300.00
☐ 1664 God Preserve London (swords)		EXTREMELY RARE	
☐ 1664 Lon Don	400.00	675.00	1800.00
☐ 1694 New England		EXTREMELY RARE	
☐ 1694 Proprietors (overstrike)	800.00	1200.00	5500.00
☐ 1694 Proprietors		EXTREMELY RARE	

NEW YORKE TOKEN

The New York colony (referring to the state, not the city) had no coinage of its own in the 17th century. Though settled somewhat later than Massachusetts, the population of New York came close to equaling it by the century's close and the volume of business transacted was at least comparable. It is curious that tiny Maryland and equally tiny New Jersey had coins during the 17th century while New York did not. The closest it came to having one was the New Yorke Token, but this can hardly be classed with the Massachusetts, Maryland or even the New Jersey coinage as there is no evidence it received official sanction. It was very likely nothing more than a merchant token. This is a smallish piece, roughly equal to our nickel, of which some were struck in brass and others in pewter. On the obverse it carries a rather scrawny eagle with an allegorical design (Cupid is one of the figures) on the reverse. The obverse legend reads "NEW YORKE IN AMERICA." Of its origins practically nothing is known. The belief that this coin was struck in Holland is founded more upon assumption, because of

90

New York's extensive Dutch population, than evidence. Its date has been the subject of controversy. The spelling of New York as "New Yorke" suggests a dating in the 17th century, but as this spelling lingered on into the 18th century it is quite possible that the coin or token is not so old as commonly presumed. It is very likely that even in the second quarter of the 18th century a European designing such a piece would have used the "New Yorke" spelling, even if it was no longer current in America. The likelihood that the New Yorke Token was struck in Manhattan from dies prepared in Holland is a romantic but not convincing theory.

TYPE OF COIN	ABP	G-4 Good	F-12 Fine
☐ New Yorke Token, undated: Brass	1000.00	1800.00	4250.00
☐ New Yorke Token, undated: Tin (Pewter)	3450.00	4800.00	9000.00

GLOUCESTER TOKEN

Very few specimens exist of this early amateur token and information about it is likewise scanty. It is apparently the first private token struck on American soil. The composition is brass, leading to the assumption that it might have been a pattern for a silver shilling that was never produced. Whether the brass pieces were intended to circulate is highly doubtful. The Gloucester Token is thought to have been the work of Richard Dawson of Gloucester, Virginia. On one side appears a five-pointed star, with a building of modest design on the other. Known specimens are so thoroughly worn that the inscription surrounding this building is unreadable. The best guess is that it was intended to represent the Gloucester County Courthouse or some other public structure. It does not appear to be a place of worship. The Gloucester Token dates to 1714.

TYPE OF COIN	ABP	G-4 Good	F-12 Fine
☐ Gloucester shilling (brass)	EXTREMELY RARE		

ROSA AMERICANA

These extremely handsome coins, thoroughly European in appearance and workmanship, are often referred to as Wood Tokens — not from being made of wood (their composition is copper, zinc and silver) but from William Wood, the Englishman who originated them. Nearly 40 years before their appearance, John Holt, another Englishman, had gained a patent from the then-king, James II, to strike coinage for circulation in the American colonies. Upon expiration of the Holt patent or franchise there had been little enthusiasm for its renewal, as Holt's coins — the so-called Plantation Tokens — had not proved very successful. As time passed and the population of such cities as Boston, New York and Philadelphia increased, the prospects for coinage seemed to brighten. William Wood, of whom there is not very much known, obtained a franchise from George I to supply coinage to America, as well as to Ireland. This resulted in the Rosa Americana tokens. These were struck in small denominations only, from a halfpence to twopence. The earliest, which apparently were struck in 1722, carried no date. Later a date was added and these pieces saw fairly large production in the years 1722, 1723 and 1724. After an interval of nearly ten years in which none were produced a Rosa Americana pattern proof was struck off in 1733. As best as can be ascertained, the Wood patent had fallen into other hands, as Wood died in 1730. His successors probably toyed with the idea of reinstituting the Rosa Americana coins but never got beyond the stage of this single proof. To judge by the relative commonness of the coin (except for certain varieties, which are rare), they must have been turned out at least in the hundreds and possibly the thousands. The obverses are all alike, picturing George I in profile facing the viewer's right (it was switched to the left on the 1733 trial proof). This is not the king against whom America went to war in the Revolution but the first English monarch of that name, a German who could speak but a few words of English. Surrounding the portrait is, generally, a legend giving the names of the countries over which the king ruled: Great Britain, France and Hibernia (Ireland). The claim that he ruled France was a purely speculative one, a reference to the victories of Marlborough over Louis XIV's armies which had ended France's ambition to capture England but in no way gave England rulership over that nation. The reverse shows the Rose, sometimes alone, sometimes surmounted by a crown. There is one variation (on the 1724 penny) where the rose is not pictured symbolicly but as an actual flower growing up from the ground. These pieces gain their name from the reverse inscription, not present on all, reading "ROSA AMERICANA UTILE DULCI," or, roughly, "American Rose, utility and pleasure." The rose had been a symbol of the Tudor kings and queens well before colonization of America. In the extent and variety the Rosa Americana coins are unmatched by any others intended for circulation in America. The opinion held of them today was not shared by colonists, however, who protested that the coins were short weighted and refused to accept them.

1722 PENNY   **1723 TWOPENCE**

TYPE OF COIN	ABP	G-4 Good	F-12 Fine	EF-40 Ex. Fine
☐ Twopence, No Date	75.00	125.00	200.00	425.00
☐ Twopence, No Date, Motto Sans Label		EXTREMELY RARE		
☐ 1722 Halfpenny, D. G. REX	65.00	100.00	175.00	375.00
☐ 1722 Halfpenny, DEL GRATIA REX	50.00	80.00	125.00	300.00
☐ 1722 Halfpenny, VTILE DVLCI		EXTREMELY RARE		
☐ 1722 Twopence, Period after REX	40.00	85.00	175.00	375.00
☐ 1722 Twopence, No Period after REX	50.00	95.00	180.00	385.00
☐ 1722 Penny, UTILE DULCI	45.00	80.00	125.00	300.00
☐ 1722 Penny, VTILE DVLCI	40.00	60.00	115.00	275.00
☐ 1722 Penny, Georgivs		EXTREMELY RARE		
☐ 1723 Twopence	50.00	75.00	175.00	375.00
☐ 1723 Penny	45.00	65.00	125.00	275.00
☐ 1723 Halfpenny	45.00	65.00	125.00	275.00
☐ 1723 Halfpenny, Rose without Crown		EXTREMELY RARE		
☐ 1724 Penny (Pattern)		EXTREMELY RARE		
☐ 1724 Penny, No Date, ROSA:SINE:SPINA		EXTREMELY RARE		
☐ 1724 Twopence (Pattern)		EXTREMELY RARE		
☐ 1723 Twopence (Pattern Proof)		EXTREMELY RARE		

WOODS COINAGE OR HIBERNIA

These coins, more properly called tokens, were issued under the patent granted to William Wood to strike coinage for America and Ireland (see Rosa Americana). "Hibernia" was the Latin name for Ireland. They are included here because these pieces proved unpopular in Ireland — just as did the Rosa Americanas in America — and Wood sought to recover his investment by circulating them in America. History does not record their fate on this side of the Atlantic but it is doubtful that they received a warm reception. They were struck in some enormous numbers, thanks to excessive over-confidence, that most types can be had inexpensively. George I appears on the obverse. There are two reverse types, both picturing a seated female with a harp representing Hibernia, the Irish equivalent of Britannia.

1723 OVER 22 HALFPENNY

1723 HALFPENNY

TYPE OF COIN	ABP	G-4 Good	F-12 Fine	EF-40 Ex. Fine
☐ 1722 Farthing, D.G.REX	95.00	165.00	250.00	425.00
☐ 1722 Halfpenny, Harp Facing Left	22.00	40.00	75.00	140.00
☐ 1722 Halfpenny, Harp Facing Right	22.00	40.00	75.00	175.00
☐ 1722 Halfpenny, D.G.REX		EXTREMELY RARE		
☐ 1723 Halfpenny	20.00	40.00	80.00	120.00
☐ 1723 Over 22 Halfpenny	35.00	60.00	100.00	200.00
☐ 1723 Halfpenny, Silver (Pattern)		EXTREMELY RARE		
☐ 1723 Farthing, Silver (Pattern)	600.00	875.00	1000.00	1500.00
☐ 1723 Farthing, DEL. GRATIA REX	25.00	45.00	75.00	135.00
☐ 1723 Farthing, D.G. REX	80.00	160.00	275.00	500.00
☐ 1724 Halfpenny	35.00	75.00	100.00	150.00
☐ 1724 Farthing	40.00	80.00	100.00	200.00

HIGLEY COINAGE

The Higley or Granby tokens were entirely private issues. Had they been imported for circulation from abroad they might be of modest interest at best but these are, in fact, **the first privately produced tokens struck on American soil that actually reached circulation.** All are extremely rare. Dr. Samuel Higley, a Connecticut resident and graduate of Yale University, deplored the coinage shortage in his state and took matters into his own hands. Unsupported by legislation and unsponsored by government funds, Higley engraved his own dies and for coin metal used copper from a mine he owned located near Granby, Connecticut (hence the alternate title of these pieces). Considering their amateur origin the designs and workmanship are of higher quality than might be expected. On the obverse appears a deer surrounded by inscription. There are two reverse types, one featuring a trio of small hammers, the other a broad-bladed cleaver. As originally issued in 1737 they carried the value of threepence, stated on the obverse legend. Though well received at first, protest was later raised by persons skeptical of their copper content. This inspired the ever-resourceful Higley to add the inscription "I AM GOOD COPPER." When this failed to silence critics, who persisted in their belief that the face value was too high and that Higley was gaining a profit from circulating them, the statement of value was replaced by the not-too-subtle suggestion to "VALUE ME AS YOU PLEASE." Even so, the Roman numeral III remained. This placed them in the category of bartering pieces which could be exchanged on basis of weight. We are told that the local supply was numerous but this is hardly reflected by their present rarity. It can only be assumed that many individuals hoarded the Higley tokens and melted them. The inscription on the second reverse type (the cleaver) states "I CUT MY WAY THROUGH." The "I" is sometimes stated to be a "J," but in fact was intended merely to represent an ornamental "I" with loop at the base.

The collector is cautioned that reproductions of the Higley Tokens exist, made by electrotyping and casting, and are of sufficient quality to confuse an inexperienced buyer.

1737 THREEPENCE

1737 COPPER

1737 COPPER

1737 COPPER

TYPE OF COIN	ABP	G-4 Good	VG-8 Very Good
☐ 1737 THE VALVE OF THREEPENCE (3 hammers CONNECTICVT)	3750.00	6500.00	10000.00
☐ 1737 THE VALVE OF THREEPENCE (3 hammers, I AM GOOD COPPER)	5000.00	8500.00	12000.00
☐ 1737 VALUE ME AS YOU PLEASE (3 hammers, I AM GOOD COPPER)	4500.00	6000.00	10000.00
☐ 1737 VALVE ME AS YOU PLEASE (3 hammers, I AM GOOD COPPER)	EXTREMELY RARE		
☐ 1737 VALVE ME AS YOU PLEASE (broad axe, I CUT MY WAY THROUGH)	5000.00	7000.00	11000.00
☐ 1739 VALUE ME AS YOU PLEASE (broad axe, I CUT MY WAY THROUGH)	6500.00	10000.00	20000.00

VOCE POPULI COINAGE

These impressive pieces are exclusively private issues and not of American origin. They were struck in Dublin, Ireland, in 1760 by a firm whose chief occupation was the making of buttons for military uniforms. Its proprietor was named Roche. The 17th and 18th centuries both witnessed an inordinate quantity of private tokens and pseudo-money struck in Ireland, much of which reached America. It could all logically be included within the realm of Americana but the Voce Populi Tokens have become special favorites of collectors, probably on strength of design more than anything else. The obverse features a classical style portrait profile crowned with laurel wreath. It has traditionally been assumed to be George III but no actual evidence exists to support this belief. The inscription makes no reference to the king but merely carries the words "VOCE POPULI," or "Voice of the People." Various interpretations (too lengthy to be discussed here) could be placed upon the use of this common slogan. The reverse pictures a female with harp, a standard Irish symbol, and the word "HIBERNIA." This was the Latin name for Ireland. The date is shown in the exergue beneath the figure. It should always be 1760; however, on one occasion a defective die was used for the halfpenny, causing it to read 1700. That the token was actually struck in 1700 can easily be refuted on stylistic as well as other evidence. There is also a variety in which the inscription reads "VOOE POPULI."

1700 HALFPENNY   1760 HALFPENNY

TYPE OF COIN	ABP	G-4 Good	F-12 Fine
☐ 1700 Halfpenny (diecutters error)	550.00	800.00	1500.00
☐ 1760 Halfpenny	20.00	35.00	75.00
☐ 1760 Halfpenny, P beneath bust	45.00	75.00	120.00
☐ 1760 Halfpenny, P beside face	45.00	75.00	120.00
☐ 1760 Halfpenny VOOE POPULI	27.50	40.00	90.00
☐ 1760 Farthing	125.00	200.00	500.00
☐ 1760 Farthing, small lettering	EXTREMELY RARE		

PITT TOKENS

William Pitt, for whom Pittsburgh is named, is associated with these tokens only to the extent that his portrait appears on them. He apparently was connected in no way with their issuance. Two denominations were struck, or rather pieces in the **sizes** of two denominations (as they bear no value markings): farthing and halfpenny. They carry the date 1766. Just what their purpose was is not clear. The suggestion has been put forward that they were issued in the nature of medals as an honor to Pitt, who, for his stand against the British stamp tax, was held in high regard by agitators for self-government. The long-held popular belief that Pitt Tokens were designed by Paul Revere would probably be best relegated to the ranks of numismatic folklore until some firm evidence is discovered. Similarly long-held belief that the engraver was Smithers of Philadelphia is more acceptable. The obverse has Pitt's likeness in profile with the legend "NO STAMPS:THE RESTORE OF COMMERCE:1766." The reverse shows a handsomely rendered sailing ship with the inscription "THANKS TO THE FRIENDS OF LIBERTY AND TRADE." Next to the ship is the word "AMERICA," which apparently suggests that the vessel is traveling from some foreign port with cargo for this country. "The Restore of Commerce" (it would probably have been spelled Restoration had there been more space) was a reference to the fact that British-imposed taxes were periling American commerce by rendering goods so costly that the public could not buy nearly so much as it wished to. The halfpenny is known to have been used briefly as coinage. No such use has been established for the farthing, which is much rarer.

1766 HALFPENNY   1766 FARTHING

TYPE OF COIN	ABP	G-4 Good	F-12 Fine
☐ 1766 Halfpenny	150.00	250.00	450.00
☐ 1766 Farthing	2500.00	4000.00	6000.00

FRENCH COLONIES IN AMERICA

A number of coins were struck in France for use in that nation's colonies during the 18th century. These were non-geographical pieces that could be exchanged in any French province and carried inscriptions in French and Latin rather than in local languages. It is important to remember in collecting these coins that they were **not** expressly struck for use in America, though they did see use in areas such as Louisiana (named for Louis XIV). The earliest of these issue dates to 1670. It was authorized by the king on February 19, 1670, and consisted of a 5 sols and 15 sols denomination.

Some 200,000 of the former and 40,000 of the latter were minted (these are incidentally the earliest "American" coins, if they can be so classified, for which mintage totals are known). Plans were put forward to strike a 2 sols piece as well but never materialized; a single pattern specimen exists. The 5 and 15 sols were silver and struck at the central French mint at Paris, at that time the most modern and well-equipped facility of its kind in the world. As the Parisian mint was too busy to strike the 2 sols denomination, intended as a copper piece, its production was assigned to the regional mint at Nantes. Just why it was never manufactured is unknown. Very likely some political difficulty intervened; or a last-minute decision may have been made to test acceptance of the silvers before going further. To say that the 5 and 15 sols were well received would be an understatement. They proved extremely popular — but not for their intended use. Instead of changing these coins as currency, they were hoarded and melted down to obtain the silver. An effort to halt this activity, by raising their face values while maintaining the same metal content, was attempted in 1672 but did little good. By 1680 they had all but disappeared from circulation and no further were struck. Thus, in spite of the large quantities turned out (large for that time), these are still scarce coins, the 15 sols ranking as a prime rarity.

Louis XIV now recognized that a silver coinage could not be successful in the colonies. For more than 30 years no coins of any sort were produced for colonial use, until in 1709 the well-known series of billon pieces was introduced. At first only a 30 deniers denomination was struck. It was subsequently followed by values of 15 deniers, a ½ sou marque, and a full sou marque, the latter two not appearing until 1738. The smaller denominations were manufactured only at provincial mints but the others were struck at Paris as well as elsewhere. There are no reliable records of quantities but to judge from their easy availability it may be concluded that fair numbers were produced. Design-wise they were not up to French standards of the time but can be considered attractive in their way. While they were in circulation a copper coinage was also instituted for the colonies, which suffered a much different fate. Louis XV authorized a copper 6 deniers and 12 deniers in December, 1716, production to be commenced the following year at the provincial mint at Perpignan. It was suspended after the striking of only a handful of pieces, owing to the lack of the metal's purity. A further attempt was made in 1720 to get these coins into circulation but again failed, the only memorial of that effort being a single unique pattern of the 6 deniers. No 12 deniers coins dated 1720 have been found.

France simply lacked a suitable supply of copper, a metal which, in other countries, was not scarce. In 1721, still determined to produce a copper coin for the colonies, the government imported blanks from Sweden. The new piece had a value of nine deniers, midway between the two previous coins and designed as a replacement for both. It was struck at the provincial mints of LaRochelle and Rouen in 1721 and 1722. Though manufactured for only two years it was coined in heavy numbers. A total of 534,000 were allotted to New France (Louisiana), or more than ten for every citizen. As the colonists preferred to trade with silver they viewed this coin with extreme skepticism. Of the more than half million imported for disbursement, only slightly more than 8,000 were actually circulated. The remainder were housed in vaults and, when it became evident that no progress could be made in popularizing the coin, eventually shipped back to France.

There is also another coin issued for use in the French Colonies, that may reasonably be collected as "American colonial," the 1767 sou. There was no intention to distribute this piece in Louisiana; it was intended mainly for the West Indies. Some did, nevertheless, reach America merely in the course of trade and travel. The two varieties to be encountered are the plain specimens and those bearing the letters "R.F." in the central portion of the reverse design, the latter being the special West Indies batch.

1722 SOU

1767 SOU

1767 SOU

TYPE OF COIN	ABP	G-4 Good	F-12 Fine
☐ 1670 5 sols	75.00	130.00	475.00
☐ 1670 15 sols	3000.00	4500.00	12000.00
☐ 1709-1713 30 deniers, mint mark AA	40.00	65.00	150.00
☐ 1709-1713 30 deniers, mint mark D	40.00	65.00	150.00
☐ 1710-1713 15 deniers	55.00	85.00	225.00
☐ 1738-1748 ½ sou marque	30.00	45.00	90.00
☐ 1738-1760 sou marque	18.00	25.00	45.00
☐ 1717 6 deniers	650.00	1000.00	1875.00
☐ 1720 6 deniers	EXTREMELY RARE		
☐ 1717 12 deniers	850.00	1350.00	2200.00
☐ 1721 SOU, mint mark B for ROUEN	35.00	60.00	125.00
☐ 1721 SOU, mint mark H for ROCHELLE	20.00	30.00	75.00
☐ 1722 SOU, mint mark H	20.00	30.00	75.00
☐ 1722 Over 1721	30.00	60.00	125.00
☐ 1767 SOU	20.00	40.00	95.00
☐ 1767 SOU, counterstamped RF	20.00	30.00	60.00

VIRGINIA

Plagued by a coinage shortage, Virginia's colonists petitioned George III for supplies of trading pieces. He responded by authorizing the striking of a copper halfpenny, with his likeness on the obverse and the Virginia seal on its reverse. Proposals were also made for a penny and shilling, or coins which, to judge by the size of the few specimens struck, were intended for these denominations. They never reached circulation and are very rare. The halfpenny was struck in large quantities.

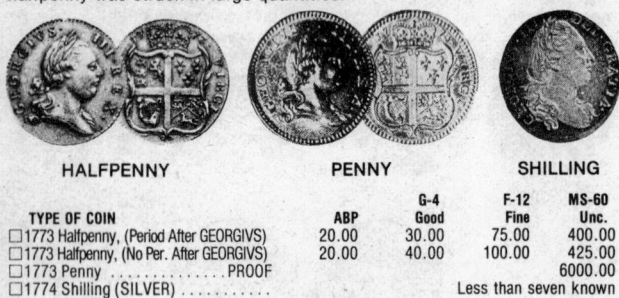

| HALFPENNY | PENNY | SHILLING |

TYPE OF COIN	ABP	G-4 Good	F-12 Fine	MS-60 Unc.
☐ 1773 Halfpenny, (Period After GEORGIVS)	20.00	30.00	75.00	400.00
☐ 1773 Halfpenny, (No Per. After GEORGIVS)	20.00	40.00	100.00	425.00
☐ 1773 Penny ....PROOF				6000.00
☐ 1774 Shilling (SILVER)			Less than seven known	

STATE OF NEW HAMPSHIRE

New Hampshire has the distinction of being the first state to attempt a local coinage following the Declaration of Independence. In 1776 it authorized William Moulton to produce an experimental batch of copper pieces. The small numbers that have been traced indicate this coin never attained general circulation, though it probably circulated in a small way. The chief type has a tree on the obverse and a harp on the reverse. Other types are known but their status has not been positively established.

| 1776 COPPER | 1776 COPPER WM |

TYPE OF COIN		VG-8 Very Good
☐ 1776 New Hampshire Copper		6500.00
☐ 1776 New Hampshire Copper, WM in center	EXTREMELY RARE	

STATE OF VERMONT

Vermont's post-revolutionary coinage, probably the best known for its designs of any regional pieces, was struck by Reuben Harmon of Rupert, Vermont, and some by Thomas Machin of Newburgh, New York. This extensive series most often employed portraits of George III but is best known for its "plough money," an obverse design picturing a farm plough in a field against a background of tree-laden mountains. This is sometimes referred to as the most original, creative and authentically American design to be found on our colonial or federal-era coins. William Coley, a New York goldsmith, was the die-cutter for this design.

1786 VERMONTENSIUM

BABY HEAD

1786 BUST

1787 BRITANNIA

TYPE OF COIN	ABP	G-4 Good	F-12 Fine
☐ 1785 Immune Colombia	1600.00	2500.00	5000.00
☐ 1785 VERMONTS	60.00	100.00	400.00
☐ 1785 VERMONTS	110.00	200.00	500.00
☐ 1786 VERMONTENSIUM	40.00	85.00	325.00
☐ 1786 Baby Head	80.00	175.00	600.00
☐ 1786 Bust faces left	65.00	100.00	325.00
☐ 1787 Bust faces right	40.00	75.00	200.00

☐ 1787 BRITANNIA reverse; it is thought that the reverse of the Brittania piece was struck from a worn discarded die for a counterfeit British halfpenny 35.00 70.00 175.00
☐ 1788 Cent 35.00 70.00 200.00
☐ 1788 ET LIB INDE 75.00 150.00 400.00
☐ 1788 VERMON AUCTORI; reversed C .... VERY RARE
☐ 1788 GEORGIVS III REX 90.00 145.00 435.00

STATE OF CONNECTICUT

Connecticut struck more coins in the period from the Revolution to the establishment of a federal currency than any other state. Or, it might be better put, more varieties, as they represent numerous variations of three basic issues. The mint at which they were struck was established by authority of the state in 1785. It was located at New Haven. The chief die-cutters were Abel Buel and James Atlee.

1.
1785 CENT

2.
1785 CENT

3.
1785 CENT

4.
1786 CENT

5.
1786 CENT

6.
1786 CENT

7.
1786 CENT

8.
1787 CENT

9.
1787 CENT

10.
1787 CENT

11.
1787 CENT

12.
1787 CENT

13.
1787 CENT

14.
1788 CENT

15.
1788 CENT

16.
1788 CENT

TYPE OF COIN	ABP	G-4 Good	F-12 Fine
☐ 1. 1785 Cent, Bust right	20.00	35.00	100.00
☐ 2. 1785 Cent, Bust right: African head	25.00	40.00	135.00
☐ 3. 1785 Cent, Bust left	75.00	125.00	300.00
☐ 3a. 1786 Cent, ET LIB INDE	30.00	65.00	125.00
☐ 4. 1786 Cent, Large Bust Faces Right	30.00	65.00	175.00
☐ 5. 1786 Cent, Mailed Bust Left	20.00	40.00	80.00
☐ 6. 1786 Cent, Mailed Bust Left (Hercules Head)	40.00	80.00	180.00
☐ 7. 1786 Cent, Draped Bust	45.00	75.00	175.00
☐ 8. 1787 Cent, Mailed Bust, Small Head Faces Right, ET LIB ENDE	40.00	75.00	180.00
☐ 9. 1787 Cent, Mailed Bust Faces Left, INDE ET LIB	40.00	75.00	200.00
☐ 10. 1787 Cent, Muttonhead: INDE ET LIB	35.00	65.00	175.00
☐ 11. 1787 Cent, Mailed Bust Faces Left	20.00	30.00	65.00
☐ 11a. 1787 Cent, Horned Bust	20.00	35.00	75.00
☐ 12. 1787 Cent, CONNECT	35.00	75.00	175.00
☐ 13. 1787 Cent, Draped Bust Faces Left	15.00	20.00	40.00
☐ 13a. 1787 Cent, Bust Left: AUCIORI	15.00	35.00	75.00
☐ 13b. 1787 Cent: AUCTOPI	15.00	30.00	75.00
☐ 13c. 1787 Cent: AUCTOBI	20.00	40.00	80.00
☐ 13d. 1787 Cent: CONNFC	35.00	60.00	125.00
☐ 13e. 1787 Cent: FNDE	15.00	30.00	75.00
☐ 13f. 1787 Cent: ETLIR	15.00	30.00	75.00
☐ 13g. 1787 Cent: ETIIB	15.00	30.00	70.00
☐ 14. 1788 Cent, Mailed Bust Faces Right	20.00	40.00	85.00
☐ 14a. 1788 Cent: Small Head	90.00	165.00	475.00
☐ 15. 1788 Cent, Mailed Bust Faces Left	25.00	35.00	80.00
☐ 15a. 1788 Cent, Mailed Bust Left: CONNLC	20.00	40.00	100.00
☐ 16. 1788 Cent, Draped Bust Faces Left	20.00	35.00	80.00
☐ 16a. Same: CONNLC	40.00	70.00	150.00
☐ 16b. 1788 Same: INDL ET LIB	25.00	50.00	120.00

STATE OF NEW JERSEY

No coinage was struck for New Jersey in the colonial period. As the state's population increased a serious coin shortage was experienced and on June 1, 1786, its legislature authorized the striking of three million copper pieces, each to weigh "six pennyweight and six grains apiece." The contract for these token was awarded to Thomas Goadsby, Walter Mould and Albion Cox. The full quantity was to be delivered by June 1788, with partial deliveries to be made in quarterly installments of 300,000 each. Soon after work had begun, Goadby and Cox requested and were granted permission to divide up the quantities and strike them separately, each operating his own facility. Mould set up at Morristown, New Jersey, Cox at Rahway. Goadsby's location is not established but is thought to also have been Rahway. The obverses of all these tokens show a horse's head and a plough, symbolic of the state's economy being founded largely on agriculture. The legend "NOVA CAESAREA" is simply New Jersey in Latin. On the reverse is a U.S. shield and "E PLURIBUS UNUM." A number of varieties are to be encountered.

TYPE OF COIN	ABP	G-4 Good	F-12 Fine
☐ 1. 1786 Date Under Plow Handle		VERY RARE	
☐ 2. 1786 Normal Legends (NOT ILLUS.)	20.00	37.50	75.00
☐ 3. 1786 No Coulter	75.00	120.00	325.00
☐ 4. 1786 Bridle Variety (NOT ILLUS.)	17.50	35.00	75.00
☐ 5. 1786 Narrow Shield (NOT ILLUS.)	35.00	50.00	100.00
☐ 6. 1786 Wide Shield (NOT ILLUS.)	45.00	65.00	130.00
☐ 7. 1787 Normal Legends (NOT ILLUS.)	10.00	20.00	45.00
☐ 8. 1787 PLURIBS	25.00	40.00	125.00
☐ 9. 1787 "Serpent Head" (NOT ILLUS.)	60.00	85.00	190.00
☐10. 1788 Normal Legends (NOT ILLUS.)	12.00	25.00	65.00
☐11. 1788 Horses Head Faces Right, Running Fox	45.00	75.00	120.00
☐12. 1788 Horses Head Left	60.00	180.00	350.00

STATE OF NEW YORK

The history of New York's local coinage prior to the Revolution reveals only the supposed Dutch merchant token discussed above and various coins and tokens struck for use elsewhere that, in the ordinary course of trade, found their way to the state. For more than a hundred years it was without locally authorized coinage. This void was filled by Dutch, British, French and, to a lesser extent, Spanish monies, which came to New York through its great port and disseminated throughout the region. Apparently no pressing need was felt for a local coinage because none was official instituted, even after independence. However, quantities of privately struck money did circulate. Some were the work of Thomas Machin of Newburgh, New York (where Washington had a headquarters during the war), who operated what he surreptitiously called a "hardware manufactory." It was in fact a copper mill, whose chief products were tokens. Other New York coins were produced at Rupert, Vermont, by a team of millers (Reuben Harmon and William Coley) who also made coins for Vermont and Connecticut. There is much yet to be learned about New York's federal-era coinage but quite a good deal has already been determined. The theory, once popularly maintained, that coins bearing the inscription "NOVA EBORAC" are of foreign origin, is now known to be false. Nova Eborac is not some sort of mysterious foreign term. It is simply New York in Latin. (If you wonder how there could be a Latin name for New York, when there are none for railroad and television and other things discovered after the Latin language died, the explanation is quite simple. The Romans did not know of New York but they certainly knew of **old** York in Britain, which they called Eborac. To change this into New York you need only add the Latin word for new — nova — and you have Nova Eborac.)

All the New York coins (or tokens) are coppers. They carry various designs, of which the portrait of George Clinton is most famous. There was also an Indian figure (not too impressively portrayed), a New York coat-of-arms, and profile bust pretty confidently believed to be George Washington. Though the designs are not very well drawn the coins themselves are very professionally struck.

1. 1786

2. 1787

3.
1787

4.
1787

5.
1787

6.
1787

TYPE OF COIN	ABP	F-12 Fine	VF-20 V.Fine
☐1. 1786 NON VI VIRTUtE VICI; Thought to be the head of George Washington	2500.00	5500.00	10000.00
☐2. 1787 EXCELSIOR; Eagle on Obv. faces left (NOT ILLUS.)	900.00	1400.00	3500.00
☐3. 1787 EXCELSIOR; Eagle on Obv. faces right	1000.00	1450.00	3750.00
☐3a. 1787 EXCELSIOR; Large Eagle on reverse (NOT ILLUS.)		VERY RARE	
☐3b. 1787 EXCELSIOR; George Clinton reverse (NOT ILLUS.)	4500.00	7500.00	16000.00
☐3c. 1787 EXCELSIOR; Indian Standing reverse (NOT ILLUS.)	2500.00	4000.00	7500.00
☐3d. 1787 EXCELSIOR; Indian Standing Eagle on globe (NOT ILLUS.)	2750.00	4500.00	8500.00
☐4. 1787 LIBERTATEM; Indian Standing, George III (NOT ILLUS.)		EXTREMELY RARE	
☐5. 1787 NOVA EBORAC; Rev. seated figure faces left	100.00	180.00	275.00
☐5a. 1787 NOVA EBORAC; Rev. seated figure faces right	125.00	200.00	375.00
☐5b. 1787 NOVA EBORAC; Small head (NOT ILLUS.)	400.00	850.00	1600.00
☐5c. 1787 NOVA EBORAC; Large head (NOT ILLUS.)	200.00	450.00	950.00

BRASHER DOUBLOONS

Perhaps the most celebrated, at any rate the most glamorized, U.S. colonial coin is the Brasher Doubloon. Though traditionally referred to as colonial it should correctly be termed a federal-era piece, as it was struck after our independence had been gained. This is a private issue. Ephraim Brasher was a goldsmith from New York who became acquainted with George Washington when the latter resided there following the war. To classify this handsome goldpiece as a speculative coin would be mistaken. Brasher, artist and patriot, appears to have manufactured it not for purposes of general circulation but as a memorial to the nation's independence and, possibly, a model from which federal coiners could gain inspiration. It dates to 1787, before the introduction of federal coinage but not before much speculation and debate on the matter. The Brasher Doubloon, as the name suggests, was modeled after the Spanish coin of that name. It contained 408 grains of gold. As a goldsmith Brasher would have encountered no difficulty securing the needed bullion for a small quantity of such pieces, but it is doubtful that he had either the resources or intention to strike this coin in large numbers. The obverse pictures the sun rising over a mountain, with the American eagle emblem on the back. The reverse bears the impressed letters E.B., the initials of Brasher's name. Obviously they were not clandestine issues or their origin would not have been so plainly identified. At the time of its issue the Brasher Doubloon had a value of about $16. There was also a Half Doubloon worth $8. All are extremely rare, the variety in which the initials appear on the eagle's breast being preserved in a single specimen only.

EB Punch on Wing

TYPE OF COIN
☐ 1787 (GOLD) DOUBLOON, EB punch on breast ....
☐ 1787 (GOLD) DOUBLOON, EB punch on wing ....
☐ 1787 (GOLD) HALF DOUBLOON ....
*Garret Sale November, 1979........$750,000.00

ALL TYPES EXTREMELY RARE

STATE OF MASSACHUSETTS

Massachusetts, the first colony to strike its own coins in pre-revolution days, also had its own coinage in the period between independence and the establishment of the U.S. Mint. On October 17, 1786, the General Court of that state authorized the setting up of a mint, "for the coinage of gold, silver and copper." A stipulation was made that the design for coinage should employ the "figure of an Indian with bow and arrow and a star on one side with the word Commonwealth, on the reverse a spread eagle with the words Massachusetts 1787." The ambitiousness of this project was never fully realized. While coppers were struck in some quantities, a coinage of silver and gold never appeared. In 1789 the mint was abandoned, having proven costly to operate.

1787 CENT

1787 HALF CENT

TYPE OF COIN	ABP	G-4 Good	F-12 Fine
☐ 1787 Cent, Arrows in Left Talon	20.00	30.00	65.00
☐ 1787 Cent, Arrows in Right Talon	VERY RARE		
☐ 1787 Cent, Horned Eagle (Die Break)	20.00	30.00	60.00
☐ 1787 Half Cent	22.50	45.00	75.00
☐ 1788 Cent	20.00	35.00	65.00
☐ 1788 Half Cent	25.00	55.00	75.00

MASSACHUSETTS PINE TREE COPPER

The origin of this unique coin is undetermined. Only one specimen is known, undoubtedly a pattern piece, and but for the greatest of good luck it would have been undiscovered. It turned up, buried beneath a Boston street, during an excavation in the 1800's, having probably been entombed nearly a century. Only the sharp eyes of a laborer prevented it from being discarded along with rubbish. Despite this imprisonment its condition is surprisingly good. It shows a pine tree on the obverse, obviously inspired by the Pine Tree Coinage of a century earlier, and a figure of Liberty posed as Britannia on the reverse, complete with globe and dog. The date 1776 appears beneath the reverse figure. Whether this was the year of striking or was used merely symbolicly to denote our independence from Britain is unknown. The obverse inscription is "MASSACHUSETTS STATE" while the reverse reads "LIBERTY AND VIRTUE." This unique item is owned today by the Massachusetts Historical Society. Reproductions exist

1776 PINE TREE (UNIQUE)

MASSACHUSETTS HALFPENNY

This intriguing coin, classical in appearance, is dated 1776 and is often referred to as the Janus Copper or Janus Halfpenny. This is a reference (though not quite historically accurate) to the obverse design, which shows a three-sided head with faces looking forward, left and right. The mythological god Janus had only two faces, looking right and left (the month of January is named for him; one face looks to the old year, one to the new). On the reverse is a seated representation of Liberty. The Massachusetts Halfpenny is a unique pattern piece.

MASSACHUSETTS HALFPENNY

KENTUCKY TOKEN

This novel piece was not of American origin but struck in England around the year 1792. It is thought to have been occasioned by admission of Kentucky into the Union. On the obverse is a hand holding a petition reading "OUR CAUSE IS JUST" surrounded by the wording "UNANIMITY IS THE STRENGTH OF SOCIETY." The reverse is composed of a star in which are circular ornaments, each bearing the initial letter of a state. As K for Kentucky appears at the top of this piece is identified with that state. Some specimens have plain edges while others are stamped "Payable at Bedworth," "Payable in Lancaster," etc.

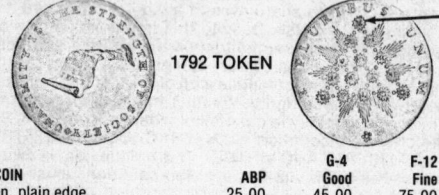

1792 TOKEN — "K"

TYPE OF COIN	ABP	G-4 Good	F-12 Fine	MS-60 Unc.
☐ 1792 Token, plain edge	25.00	45.00	75.00	400.00
☐ 1792 Token, engrailed edge	60.00	175.00	350.00	900.00
☐ 1792 Token, lettered edge, Payable at I. Fielding, etc.		EXTREMELY RARE		
☐ 1792 Token, lettered edge, Payable at Bedworth, etc.		EXTREMELY RARE		
☐ 1792 Token, lettered edge, Payable at Lancaster, London, or Bristol	50.00	75.00	165.00	485.00

MARYLAND - CHALMERS

The Chalmers tokens were the second group of coins to be struck for circulation in Maryland, preceded by the Lord Baltimore money of a century earlier. Unlike these early pieces, which were of foreign manufacture, the Chalmers coins evolved locally. They were minted at Annapolis in 1783. Apparently they came into being because of the coinage shortage which then existed in Maryland and the hesitency of that state's legislature to take official action. John Chalmers, their maker, was a goldsmith. He struck them in silver in denominations of threepence, sixpence and one shilling (twelve pence). Their odd geometrical designs give them almost a cabbalistic appearance. All are quite scarce but the majority are obtainable.

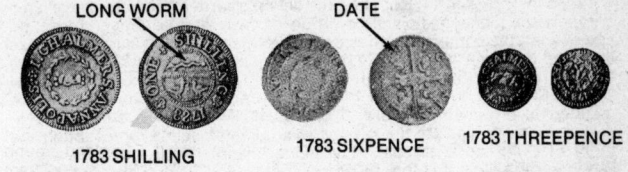

LONG WORM   **DATE**

1783 SHILLING   **1783 SIXPENCE**   **1783 THREEPENCE**

TYPE OF COIN	ABP	G-4 Good	F-12 Fine
☐ 1783 Shilling, short worm	225.00	350.00	1250.00
☐ 1783 Shilling, long worm	275.00	450.00	1400.00
☐ 1783 Shilling, rings on reverse	EXTREMELY RARE		
☐ 1783 Sixpence, small date	450.00	900.00	2000.00
☐ 1783 Sixpence, large date	450.00	750.00	1850.00
☐ 1783 Threepence	400.00	600.00	1700.00

BALTIMORE, MARYLAND/STANDISH BARRY

Standish Barry was a private citizen of Baltimore who worked at various craft trades including watchmaking and silversmithing. In 1790 he struck, in very limited quantities, a silver threepenny token bearing a portrait on one side and the words "THREE PENCE" on the other. Due to the low face value and the fact of its being made of silver the physical size is quite small, about comparable to our dime. Barry's motive is not known with certainty. That he wished to alleviate the shortage of small-denomination coinage in his neighborhood is a possibility, but he produced so few specimens that this goal, if such was his intent, could not have been achieved. A more likely suggestion is that the Barry token was intended chiefly as an advertising piece. This is supported by the appearance of his name, spelled out in full on the reverse, which commonly was done only with tradesmens' tokens. The obverse portrait is thought to have been intended as George

Washington, which fails to resemble him only because of artistic inability. Not only the year but the month is stated and the day as well: July 4, 90. The whole appearance is crude and amateurish, but collectors treasure it.

TYPE OF COIN	ABP	G-4 Good	F-12 Fine
☐ 1790 Silver Threepence	4000.00	7500.00	10000.00

RHODE ISLAND TOKEN

The Rhode Island Ship Token has been variously classified as a coin, token and medal, and its status is hardly clearer today than when research first began. Struck in 1778 or 1779 (the obverse carries one date, the reverse another), the piece is known in a variety of base metals: copper, brass, tin and pewter, the composition having little influence on its value. That it was intended as a coin for ordinary circulation and exchange appears remote as it carries no mark of value and would have had to trade on the basis of weight. Being made of different metals, the weight varies and would have resulted in no small measure of confusion. The obverse shows a well-drawn ocean vessel. On the reverse is a complex scene representing the flight of Continental troops from Rhode Island. The inscriptions are in Dutch but the old belief that this production was of Dutch or Dutch-American origin is now given little support. Based upon the reverse theme it could well have been struck in England or by royalists in America. It should be kept in mind that the Revolutionary war had not yet ended in 1778-9 and coins or medals had a certain propaganda value. Reproductions are known to exist.

1778-1779 "VLUTENDE" REMOVED   **1778-1779 WREATH**

TYPE OF COIN	ABP	VF-20 V. Fine	EF-40 Ex. Fine
☐ 1778-1779 "VLUGTENDE" Below Ship		RARE	
☐ 1778-1779 "VLUGTENDE" Removed	275.00	475.00	900.00
☐ 1778-1779 "WREATH" Below Ship	300.00	500.00	1000.00

1776 CONTINENTAL CURRENCY

The Continental Dollar and its affiliates were struck as pattern pieces only, based upon the latest research, and never reached general circulation. They are believed to represent the first attempt at coinage by the Continental Congress, at any rate the first to achieve physical form. Upon declaring its independence from Britain the United States was cut off from supplies of British currency and anticipated an extreme shortage within the coming months. Actually this shortage did not materialize to the degree feared. Continental Currency is crown-size and struck in silver, pewter and brass. Though the sizes are identical and the coins bear no indication of value it is presumed the silver pieces were intended as dollars and the base metal varieties as divisions thereof. The exact history of their origin is not recorded, the documentation of it having apparently been swept away in the turbulent times of war. We know that the engraver bore the initials E.G. because he signed his work. An exhaustive search of goldsmiths, silversmiths and other metalworkers active at that time, having the initials E.G., has led to the conclusion that the 1776 Continental Currency was the work of Elisha Gallaudet of Philadelphia. If this is the case they would undoubtedly have been struck in that city as well. Which, considering that it was headquarters of the Continental Congress, seems to fit together historically. The legends include "WE ARE ONE" and "MIND YOUR BUSINESS," the latter not, probably, having been directed toward the British but used merely as a piece of sage advice in the spirit of Ben Franklin. Copies exist, struck at the 1876 Centennial exposition.

1776
CURENCY
Brass, Pewter, Silver

1776
CURRENCY
Pewter

1776 CURRENCY
E. G. FECIT
Pewter, Silver

TYPE OF COIN	ABP	F-12 Fine	EF-40 Ex. Fine
☐ 1776 CURENCY, Brass		UNIQUE	
☐ 1776 CURENCY, Pewter	1500.00	2500.00	5000.00
☐ 1776 CURENCY, Silver		UNIQUE	
☐ 1776 CURRENCY, Pewter	2000.00	3500.00	6500.00
☐ 1776 CURRENCY, E.G. FECIT, Pewter	1800.00	2750.00	6000.00
☐ 1776 CURRENCY, E.F. FECIT, Silver		UNIQUE	
☐ 1776 CURRENCY, Pewter		UNIQUE	

NOVA CONSTELLATIO SILVER

These Nova Constellatio silvers are pattern pieces for a federal coinage, the first such pattern pieces of silver struck by the newly born government. They date from 1783, shortly after the war for Independence had been concluded. Supposedly the brainchild of Gouverneur Morris, a signer of the Declaration of Independence and Assistant Financier of the Confederation, their designer was Benjamin Dudley. At this point the system of cents and dollars, later agreed upon, had not yet evolved; but there was no wish to continue use of the British pound standard. Morris evolved a currency system in which the chief denomination was a mark, consisting of 1,000 units. Divisions of this coin — also included among the Nova Constellatio patterns — were the quint, equal to 500 units or half a mark, and the bit, with a value of 100 units or a tenth of a mark. Further divisions could then supposedly be made of base metal, in 50 or 10 units or whatever seemed practical. If we think of Morris' mark as the equivalent of the dollar (which in reality it was), then the 500 unit piece was the counterpart of 50¢ and the 100 unit piece of 10¢. Morris won little support for his currency proposals and the patterns were never approved for general circulation. Just one specimen is known to exist of each example, however there are two types (and consequently two known specimens) of the 500 unit piece, one having an inscription on the obverse and the other bearing no inscription.

1783 MARK

1783 QUINT

SECOND VARIETY **1783 QUINT**

1783 CENT

TYPE OF COIN
- 1783 MARK — 1000 Mills, Silver
- 1783 QUINT — 500 Mills, Silver
- 1783 QUINT — Second Variety, Silver
- 1783 Cent — 100 Mills, Silver

ALL TYPES EXTREMELY RARE

NOVA CONSTELLATIO COPPERS

Though their name and design is similar to the Nova Constellatio silvers, it is important to note that these coins had quite different origins and purposes. The concept for both was that of Gouveneur Morris, who, in addition to being a legislator was also a prominent businessman in the late colonial/early federal age. While the silvers were pattern pieces for a proposed federal coinage, these coppers were struck as a personal speculative venture. It is quite likely that their place of origin was not America but Birmingham, England, and that their dies were engraved by an Englishman named Wyon. Upon importation to this country Morris placed them into circulation as best he could. To judge from the fairly large quantities that exist of most types their production must have reached the tens of thousands if not higher.

1783 CENT   **1785 CENT**

115

TYPE OF COIN	ABP	G-4 Good	F-12 Fine
☐ 1783 Cent, CONSTELLATIO, Pointed Rays, Large U.S.	18.00	25.00	85.00
☐ 1783 Cent, CONSTELLATIO, Pointed Rays, Small U.S.	18.00	25.00	75.00
☐ 1783 Cent, CONSTELLATIO, Blunt Rays	15.00	20.00	85.00
☐ 1785 Cent, CONSTELLATIO, Blunt Rays	20.00	35.00	100.00
☐ 1785 Cent, CONSTELLATIO, Point Rays	15.00	25.00	60.00
☐ 1786 Cent, CONSTALLATIO, Point Rays	VERY RARE		

IMMUNE COLUMBIA

It is believed that this token, whose obverse designs are in some instances similar to those of the Nova Constellatio Coppers, were struck from dies engraved by Thomas Wyon of Birmingham, England. Their history is otherwise shrouded in mystery. That they represent pattern pieces which did not actually circulate seems unquestionable as they exist in extremely limited quantities. There are several varieties, chiefly in copper but the piece does exist in silver. A single gold specimen, dated 1785, is included in the government's collection at Washington. It was obtained by trade with the collector Stickney, who accepted a duplicate 1804 silver dollar for it. A later version of the Immune Columbia token, dated 1787, was struck from dies by James Atlee. Justice with scales is the reverse theme with a number of different obverses, including a portrait of the then-not-too-popular George III.

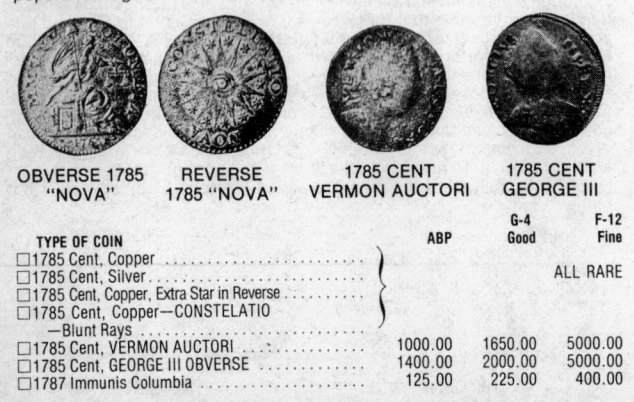

OBVERSE 1785 "NOVA" — REVERSE 1785 "NOVA" — 1785 CENT VERMON AUCTORI — 1785 CENT GEORGE III

TYPE OF COIN	ABP	G-4 Good	F-12 Fine
☐ 1785 Cent, Copper			
☐ 1785 Cent, Silver			ALL RARE
☐ 1785 Cent, Copper, Extra Star in Reverse			
☐ 1785 Cent, Copper—CONSTELATIO —Blunt Rays			
☐ 1785 Cent, VERMON AUCTORI	1000.00	1650.00	5000.00
☐ 1785 Cent, GEORGE III OBVERSE	1400.00	2000.00	5000.00
☐ 1787 Immunis Columbia	125.00	225.00	400.00

CONFEDERATIO

The Confederatio Cent, also known as Confederatio Coppers, is a hybrid coin found with various obverse and reverse designs. Regardless of the designs these are all pattern pieces that never reached circulation and all are extremely rare. Identity of the die cutters is not known but it is believed that at least some were the work of Thomas Wyon of Birmingham, England, and undoubtedly they were struck abroad. One of the obverse motifs features George Washington.

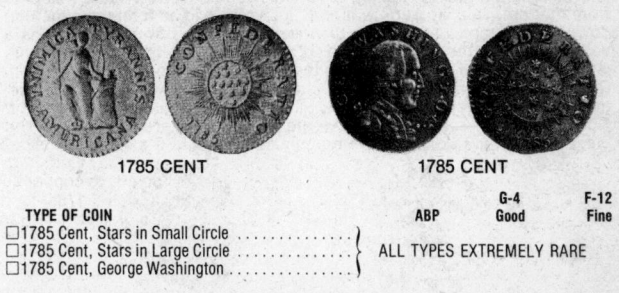

1785 CENT   1785 CENT

TYPE OF COIN	ABP	G-4 Good	F-12 Fine
☐ 1785 Cent, Stars in Small Circle			
☐ 1785 Cent, Stars in Large Circle	ALL TYPES EXTREMELY RARE		
☐ 1785 Cent, George Washington			

SPECIMEN PATTERNS

A number of copper pattern pieces were struck in or about 1786 for possible use as token currency. Their history is not well established and all are extremely rare. The shield design and "E PLURIBUS UNUM" inscription on the reverses of some were subsequently used on New Jersey tokens, but the following patterns cannot be classified as belonging to any given locality.

TYPE OF COIN	ABP	G-4 Good	F-12 Fine
☐ 1786 IMMUNIS COLUMBIA, shield reverse	EXTREMELY RARE		
☐ 1786 IMMUNIS COLUMBIA, eagle reverse	EXTREMELY RARE		
☐ 1786 Eagle on obverse	EXTREMELY RARE		
☐ 1786 Washington/eagle	EXTREMELY RARE		
☐ Undated, Washington obverse	EXTREMELY RARE		

NORTH AMERICAN TOKEN

This is a private piece, one of a number issued following the Revolution that circulated in this country. Its origin is Irish, having been struck in Dublin. Undoubtedly it represented the effort of an Irish merchant or metalsmith to take advantage of America's coin shortage. The date shown is 1781 but belief is strong that it was actually produced at some later time, possibly in the late 1790's or early 1800's. The U.S. was experiencing a coin shortage during the Presidency of Thomas Jefferson, so it could well date from that era. This situation was well known abroad as foreigners melting down our coinage were chiefly responsible. On the obverse it pictures a sailing ship with the word "COMMERCE" and a seated likeness of Hibernia (symbol of Ireland) with her harp on the reverse, inscribed "NORTH AMERICAN TOKEN." It may well be that the side of this token traditionally regarded as the obverse was intended as the reverse. Quantities in which the North American Token were distributed in the U.S. are not known. The piece is far from rare. Its size is roughly equivalent to a quarter.

TYPE OF COIN	ABP	G-4 Good	F-12 Fine
☐ 1781 Token	15.00	20.00	40.00

MACHIN COPPERS

Thomas Machin operated a copper mill at Newburgh, New York. From 1786 to 1789 he was active in the production of tokens, some designed for use in the State of New York (listed under New York) and others that were nothing but counterfeits of the British copper halfpenny. He attempted to profit by placing these counterfeits, of lighter than standard weight, into immense circulation. To avoid suspicion he used a variety of dates, going back as far as 1747, but the majority are dated in the early 1770's. The design is always the same: a portrait of the king on the obverse with Britannia on the reverse. As these pieces are not collected by date, their values are constant irrespective of date. They can easily be distinguished from genuine British halfpennies by their cruder die engraving. However, the Machin fakes were not the only ones made of this coin.

TYPE OF COIN	ABP	G-4 Good	F-12 Fine
☐ Halfpenny, various dates	40.00	75.00	150.00

GEORGIUS TRIUMPHO TOKEN

This controversial coin, dating from 1783, is made of copper. On the obverse is a male portrait in profile with the inscription "GEORGIUS TRIUMPHO," which cannot be translated in any other fashion but "George Has Triumphed." Considering that the was for indpendence had recently ended with an American victory, the triumphal George should be Washington. But the portrait much more closely resembles George III, the British monarch who sought to preserve American colonization. Just how this George could be regarded to have triumphed at that moment is puzzling. Perhaps the explanation is that Washington was intended but the engraver, being unskilled and having no likeness at hand from which to copy, merely fashioned the portrait after that on English money. A similar situation prevailed at the time among illustrators who designed copperplate portraits for books, the likeness often being guessed at. As photography did not exist and few citizens actually saw celebrities in the flesh, it was not really known if such works were accurate, and it may further be presumed that the great significance we attach to such matters was not a factor then. The reverse pictures Liberty holding an olive branch, and thirteen bars representing the confederation. Its inscription is "VOCE POPULI," an error for Voce Populi or "Voice of the People."

TYPE OF COIN	ABP	G-4 Good	F-12 Fine	VF-20 V. Fine
☐ 1783 GEORGIUS TRIUMPHO	30.00	60.00	125.00	300.00

AUCTORI PLEBIS TOKEN

Not much is known of this copper piece, other than the fact that it closely resembles the early coinage of Connecticut. It is thought to have been struck in England and may never have been intended for American circulation. It has, however, traditionally been included in American colonial and federal-era collections. It bears a date of 1787 and carries a male portrait profile on the obverse with a seated figure of Liberty on the reverse. The workmanship is not especially skilled.

TYPE OF COIN	ABP	G-4 Good	F-12 Fine	VF-20 V. Fine
☐ 1787 AUCTORI PLEBIS Token	25.00	50.00	135.00	275.00

MOTT TOKEN

An early trade token, this piece had no official sanction nor any legal value as money. Its issuers were William and John Mott, who operated a business at Water Street in the downtown area of Manhattan. Mott Street, now the central boulevard of New York's Chinatown, was named for this family. The Mott Token is of copper, picturing on one side the American eagle emblem and (quite unusual) a shelf clock on the other. The clock served an advertising purpose as the Motts dealt in goldware, silverware and fancy goods, including importations. This token dates from 1789. Of too high a quality for local production, it seems evident they were manufactured in England.

TYPE OF COIN	ABP	G-4 Good	F-12 Fine	EF-40 Ex. Fine
☐ 1789 Mott Token, thick planchet	30.00	65.00	150.00	400.00
☐ 1789 Mott Token, thin planchet	40.00	85.00	200.00	650.00
☐ 1789 Mott Token, engrailed edge	65.00	110.00	375.00	1000.00

BAR CENT

The Bar Cent is a very simply designed coin whose name derives from the fact that its reverse design is composed of a grid containing thirteen bars (one for each state of the confederation). On the obverse are the letters USA in large size, intertwined. Beyond this there is no further ornament or inscription and the origin of this piece has proven a dilemma. It is almost surely a foreign product, made possibly by Wyon (of Nova Constellatio copper fame) of Birmingham, England. Its first public appearance was made at New York in late 1785. It may be presumed that the date of minting was either that year or possibly 1784. Reproductions were produced during the Civil War, against which collectors are cautioned.

TYPE OF COIN	ABP	G-4 Good	F-12 Fine	EF-40 Ex. Fine
☐ Undated, Bar Cent	125.00	225.00	775.00	1250.00

TALBOT, ALLUM AND LEE CENTS

These are trade tokens, circulated by a firm of importers known as Talbot, Allum and Lee, who were headquartered at 241 Pearl Street, New York, in what is now the financial district but then was given over largely to import/export because of its access to the Battery docks. There is no question but that they were struck in England. The corporation's name appears on one side, sometimes with and sometimes without its place of location. The earliest date is 1794 and at this point they carried a value legend of one cent. In 1794 this was removed, possibly out of fear of government protest, and an inscription added to the edge: "WE PROMISE TO PAY THE BEARER ONE CENT." There are, however, specimens of the 1795 edition with unlettered edge, which are considerably scarcer. This practice of issuing tokens redeemable at a certain place of business became widespread in the 19th century, especially during the small-change shortage of the Civil War.

TYPE OF COIN	ABP	G-4 Good	F-12 Fine	EF-40 Ex. Fine
☐ 1794 Cent w/"NEW YORK"	15.00	30.00	80.00	150.00
☐ 1794 Cent without "NEW YORK"	75.00	150.00	300.00	750.00
☐ 1795 Cent	15.00	25.00	50.00	150.00

GEORGE WASHINGTON PIECES

Following the Revolution, George Washington became a national hero and idol to such degree that he was virtually worshipped. Books were written on his life, engravers published pictures of him, and his likeness was set into snuff boxes, jewelry cases and other fancy goods. It is only natural that Washington would also be the subject of numerous tokens and pseudo-coins. These were issued beginning in 1783 and (for practical purposes) ceasing about 1795, after official federal coinage began circulating. No exact date can be placed on their discontinuance, however, as token and medals honoring Washington appeared from time to time thereafter. Those listed below are not strictly classed as commemoratives but might just as well be. They were primarily coppers and contained a cent's worth of that metal. They could therefore be used as money but the extent to which this was done is not known and can be presumed to have been limited, as none was struck in large quantities. The best title for them might be "celebration pieces." Building a complete collection is outside the realm of possibility, because of the extreme scarcity of some issues. A fair assembly of them can, however, be made. Their origins are not well established. Some are believed to have been designed and struck in England. This would seem logical on the basis of workmanship. Those made abroad were surely not designed for circulation there, but for export and distribution within the United States. One of the Washington tokens — in ½ penny value — declares itself a Welsh product; it carries the inscription "NORTH WALES" on the reverse. Another was a London tradesman's token. As for their dates, the presumption is that some, at least, were struck subsequent to the year indicated, perhaps in the first decade of the 19th century or even later. Most have distinctive reverses and are known chiefly by these reverse types. So far as the portraiture is concerned, there is a rich and interesting variety, differing not only in artistic quality but concept. On some, Washington is shown as a Roman-style emperor, wearing a laurel wreath. The majority portray him in military dress. Though a few coins of amateurish design are included in this group there are likewise several of the most skilled and impressive workmanship, which, if executed as sculptures, would be regarded as important works of art. The likelihood that Washington sat for any of the die-cutters is remote, but apparently they either had prior experience drawing or sculpting him or worked from some of the better oil pictures, such as those of Stuart. They could not have achieved such faithful portraiture merely from descriptions of his physical appearance.

1.
1783 CENT

2.
1783 CENT

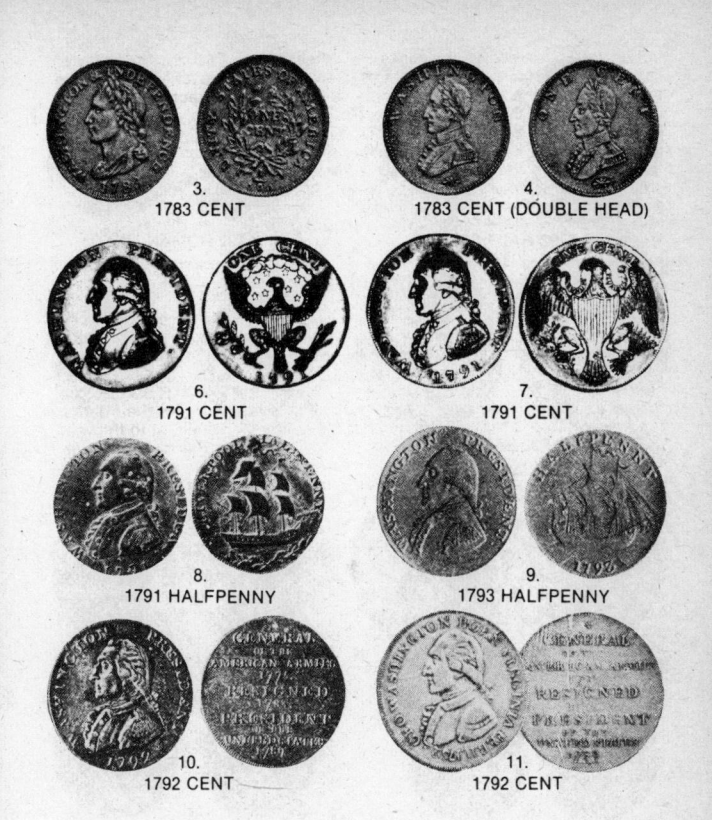

3.
1783 CENT

4.
1783 CENT (DOUBLE HEAD)

6.
1791 CENT

7.
1791 CENT

8.
1791 HALFPENNY

9.
1793 HALFPENNY

10.
1792 CENT

11.
1792 CENT

12.
1792 HALF DOLLAR

13.
1792 ROMAN HEAD

14.
1792 EAGLE

15.
1795 HALFPENNY

16.
1795 PENNY

17.
1795 PENNY

18.
TOKEN

20.
1795 HALFPENNY

19.
TOKEN

124

TYPE OF COIN	ABP	G-4 Good	F-12 Fine
☐ 1. 1783 Cent, Large Military Bust	15.00	30.00	75.00
☐ 1a. 1783 Cent, Small Military Bust	25.00	45.00	100.00
☐ 1b. 1783 Cent, Small Military Bust, engrailed edge	35.00	65.00	150.00
☐ 2. 1783 Cent, Draped Bust	20.00	40.00	100.00
☐ 2a. 1783 Cent, Draped Bust, button on cloak	40.00	75.00	150.00
☐ 2b. 1783 Cent, Draped Bust, silver restrike		PROOF: $450.00	
☐ 3. 1783 Cent, Draped Bust: Unity States	25.00	40.00	110.00
☐ 4. 1783 Cent (Undraped) Double Head	35.00	60.00	85.00
☐ 5. 1784 (Ugly Head) (NOT ILLUS.)		RARE	
☐ 6. 1791 Cent, Small Eagle	75.00	140.00	250.00
☐ 7. 1791 Cent, Large Eagle	65.00	125.00	225.00
☐ 8. 1791 Liverpool Halfpenny	400.00	750.00	1000.00
☐ 9. 1792 Cent, WASHINGTON PRESIDENT	1200.00	6000.00	8500.00
☐10. 1792 Cent, BORN VIRGINIA	1200.00	2500.00	4000.00
☐11. 1792 Silver		EXTREMELY RARE	
☐11a. 1792 Copper	1600.00	3800.00	5000.00
☐11b. 1792 Large Eagle		UNIQUE	
☐12. 1792 Roman Head	PROOF RARE		12000.00
☐13. 1792 Eagle, Copper	}		
☐13a. 1792 Eagle, Silver	} EXTREMELY RARE		
☐13b. 1792 Eagle, Gold	}		
☐14. 1793 Ship Halfpenny	45.00	85.00	175.00
☐15. 1795 Halfpenny, Reeded Edge, "GRATE", small buttons	65.00	160.00	225.00
☐15a. 1795 Halfpenny, Reeded Edge, "GRATE" large buttons	40.00	65.00	85.00
☐15b. 1795 Halfpenny, Lettered Edge, "GRATE" large buttons	125.00	250.00	375.00
☐16. 1795 Penny, Undated, LIBERTY AND SECURITY	75.00	135.00	260.00
☐17. 1795 Halfpenny, Dated LIBERTY AND SECURITY, London	50.00	100.00	225.00
☐17a. 1795 Halfpenny, LIBERTY AND SECURITY, Birmingham	65.00	125.00	275.00
☐17b. 1795 Halfpenny, Dated, LIBERTY AND SECURITY, Asylum	160.00	300.00	500.00
☐17c. 1795 Halfpenny, Dated, LIBERTY AND SECURITY, Plain Edge	75.00	175.00	280.00
☐18. Success Token, Large	65.00	140.00	225.00
☐19. Success Token, Small	65.00	140.00	225.00
☐20. 1795 Halfpenny, NORTH WALES	85.00	190.00	275.00

FRANKLIN PRESS TOKEN

This copper token was struck in England as a merchant piece and its use apparently restricted there. Because of its connection with Benjamin Franklin it has interest for collectors of American coinage. The obverse pictures an old-fashioned screw press (driven by jerking a lever), with the words "PAYABLE AT THE FRANKLIN PRESS LONDON" on the opposite side. It carries a date of 1794. As Franklin died in 1790 he could not have seen this token. Reproductions exist.

TYPE OF COIN	ABP	G-4 Good	F-12 Fine	EF-40 Ex. Fine
☐ 1794 Token	20.00	35.00	75.00	150.00

CASTORLAND

Royalists who fled France following the revolution's outbreak in 1791 scattered to many parts of the globe. A small colony settled in the New York State farmlands (near Carthage) and called the locality Castorland. The Castorland medal or token is said to be a pattern piece struck in France for a proposed currency. It never reached beyond the experimental stage and both varieties, in silver and copper, are extremely rare. They carry a date of 1796.

TYPE OF COIN	ABP	G-4 Good	VG-8 Very Good	F-12 Fine
☐ 1796 Silver Original, Reeded Edge				
☐ 1796 Copper Original, Reeded Edge		BOTH TYPES EXTREMELY RARE		

FUGIO CENTS

The Fugio Cents, so called because that word is a component in the obverse inscription, were the first officially sanctioned U.S. federal coinage. It was resolved by Congress in 1787 that a contract be put out with a private miller, James Jarvis, for 300 tons of copper coins. The arrangement was for Jarvis to secure the metal himself and pay all expenses, then sell the coins to the government at face value — his profit arising from the difference between his cost and the total face value. It was a venture of enormous proportions, considering that the U.S. had not previously authorized any coins. The matter of designing was not left to the contractor. Congress specifically spelled out what these coins should look like: "thirteen circles linked together, a small circle in the middle with the words United States around it, and in the center the words 'We are one'; on the other side of the same piece the following device, viz: a dial with the hours expressed on the face of it; a meridian sun above on one side of which is the word Fugio." Fugio is Latin for "time flies." As the obverse carries the saying "Mind your Business," often attributed to Benjamin Franklin, this is sometimes called the Franklin Cent; such terminology is, however, misleading and confusing. The dies were produced by Abel Buel of New Haven, Connecticut, and most of the striking was apparently carried out in that city.

1. 1787 CENT

2. 1787 CENT

3. 1787 CENT

4. 1787 CENT

TYPE OF COIN	ABP	G-4 Good	F-12 Fine
☐1. 1787 Cent, Club Rays, Rounded Ends	35.00	75.00	225.00
☐1a. 1787 Cent, Club Rays, Concave Ends, FUCIO (NOT ILLUS.)			
☐1b. 1787 Cent, Club Rays, Concave Ends, FUGIO	ALL VERY RARE		
☐1c. 1787 Cent, Club Rays, States United			
☐2. 1787 Cent, Pointed Rays, UNITED above, STATES below			
☐2a. 1787 Cent, Pointed Rays, UNITED STATES at side of circle (NOT ILLUS.)	25.00	40.00	125.00
☐3. 1787 Cent, Pointed Rays, STATES UNITED at side of circle; Cinquefoils	35.00	60.00	100.00
☐3a. 1787 Cent, Pointed Rays, STATES UNITED at sides, 8 pointed star on reverse band (NOT ILLUS.)	35.00	60.00	150.00
☐3b. 1787 Cent, Pointed Rays, STATES UNITED, raised edge on reverse band	30.00	75.00	175.00
☐3c. 1787 Cents, Pointed Ray, UNITED STATES, No Cinquefoils	50.00	100.00	375.00
☐3d. 1787 Cent, Pointed Rays, STATES UNITED, No Cinquefoils	65.00	125.00	400.00
☐4. 1787 Cent, AMERICAN CONGRESS, with Rays (NOT ILLUS.)	VERY RARE		

NEW HAVEN RESTRIKES

In 1858, C. Wyllys Betts found in New Haven 3 sets of dies. Restrikes in various metals were made. The restrikes were not made directly from these dies but copies fashioned from them.

TYPE OF COIN	ABP	MS-60 UNC
☐Copper	100.00	225.00
☐Silver	275.00	500.00
☐Brass	85.00	200.00
☐Gold	EXTREMELY RARE	

FIRST UNITED STATES OF AMERICA MINT ISSUES

1792 BIRCH CENT

The 1792 Birch Cent was the first coin to be struck at the newly established U.S. Mint in Philadelphia and the first governmental issue struck by the government as opposed to private contractors. This coin was not circulated but produced as a trial piece only. Along with it there were also trial or pattern pieces of half disme, disme, and quarter dollar denominations, all of which are extremely rare. A motion is said to have been made for placing George Washington's likeness of these pieces but that Washington, when informed of this plan, declined to be honored in such a manner. It was then decided to use a portrait of the Goddess of Liberty. The better-known version of the Birch Cent is large in size and composed entirely of copper. A smaller cent was also produced, containing a droplet of silver at the center. This was done entirely experimentally, in an effort to determine whether a penny coin in small size might be publicly more acceptable than one made exclusively of base metal. The pattern quarter dollar has more the appearance of a medal than a coin. The Birch Cent derives its name from Robert Birch, its designer. Birch is thought also to have been among the die-cutters for the half disme and disme.

1792 DISME

1792 BIRCH CENT

1792 DISME

TYPE OF COIN
☐ 1792 (Silver), DISME ....
☐ 1792 (Copper), DISME ....
☐ 1792 (Silver), HALF DISME ....
☐ 1792 BIRCH CENT (Copper) ....
☐ 1792 BIRCH CENT (White Metal) ....
☐ 1792 QUARTER DOLLAR (Pattern, Copper) ....
☐ 1792 QUARTER DOLLAR (Pattern, White Metal) ....

ALL COINS ARE RARE,
VERY RARE, OR UNIQUE
EXTREMELY RARE

1792 SILVER CENTER CENT

TYPE OF COIN
☐ 1792 Silver Center Cent ....
☐ 1792 Cent, No Silver Center ....

ALL COINS ARE VERY RARE, OR UNIQUE

HALF CENTS, 1793 - 1857

That the lowly half cent survived into the second half of the 19th century is looked upon as remarkable today by persons not well acquainted with the economic conditions of that time. Despite its minute face value, and the grumblings of many citizens that it did little but clutter their pockets, it served an important function in trade. Many articles in shops were priced fractionally and without the half cent difficulty would have been encountered in making change for such purchases. Their availability was, however frequently abused. Merchants, anxious to rid themselves of half cents, would often given them instead of pennies. As first introduced in 1793 the coin bore a portrait of Liberty facing left on its obverse and a wreathed reverse with the words "HALF CENT" and "UNITED STATES OF AMERICA." The designer was Adam Eckfeldt. The original weight was 6.74 grams and the composition pure copper. The coin has a diameter of 22 mm. and is stamped along the edge, "TWO HUNDRED FOR A DOLLAR." After being struck for a single year it was decided to redesign the coin (coin redesigning occured frequently in the Mint's early days of operation), the new design being the work of Robert Scot. Liberty was switched round to face right, her features streamlined, and her cap (the "cap of liberty," a reference to caps worn by freed slaves in Roman times) enlarged. The reverse was restyled but not materially altered. Planchets were of the same weight but slightly larger physically, measuring 23½ mm. Another fresh version was placed into use in 1795, this one the work of John S. Gardner; its specifications were the same as its predecessor's. It was later concluded that the weight had been set too high. This ushered in the so-called "thin planchet" half cent, weighing 5.44 grams and still measuring 23½ mm. "TWO HUNDRED FOR A DOLLAR" was removed from the edge. The varieties of this "Liberty Cap" half cent are numerous, despite the brief period of its manufacture.

The Liberty Cap half cent was followed in 1800 by introduction of the Draped Bust design, after a period of two years in which coins of this denomination were not minted (they could hardly have been in short supply as well over 200,000 had been circulated. Liberty's cap was removed and her hairstyle made somewhat more fashionable. The portrait was lengthened somewhat to include a suggestion of shoulders, over which a classical-style garment is placed. The designer was Robert Scot, who had done the 1794 version. Specifications remained the same as before. It was resolved to get these coins into very extensive circulation, resulting in a mintage quantity of more than one million in the year 1804 alone. By the end of 1808, the last year for this design, more than three million had been struck. The new half cent was the so-called "Classic Head" variety, designed by John Reich. Apparently this title was bestowed in the belief that Reich's Liberty more closely approximated Grecian sculpture than had the other types. The face, if stronger, became less physically attractive and more masculine. Stars were set at either side of the portrait and Liberty was given a band round her head with her name imprinted on it. The next design, and the last, was introduced in 1840 but used for proofs only, as the half cent did not return to general circulation until 1849. Christian Gobrecht was the designer and his rendition of Liberty has come to be known as the "Braided Hair Type." A sharp departure from the Reich approach, it pictured Liberty with Roman nose and considerable loss of bulk. This could well be considered the most attractive design, portrait-wise, of the half cent series.

HALF CENTS—LIBERTY CAP, 1793-1797

1793

1794-1797

1796 Pole to Cap

No Pole to Cap

DATE	MINTAGE	ABP	G-4 Good	F-12 Fine	VF-20 V. Fine
☐ 1793	31,534	575.00	750.00	1500.00	2250.00
☐ 1794	81,600	150.00	200.00	400.00	700.00
☐ 1795 Plain Edge		100.00	150.00	300.00	600.00
☐ 1795 Lettered Edge	25,600	120.00	175.00	325.00	650.00
☐ 1796 With Pole	5,090	900.00	1300.00	3000.00	6500.00
☐ 1796 No Pole		EXTREMELY RARE			
☐ 1797 Plain Edge		120.00	175.00	325.00	650.00
☐ 1797 Lettered Edge	119,214	150.00	200.00	600.00	1400.00
☐ 1797 1 Above 1		100.00	150.00	300.00	600.00

HALF CENTS—DRAPED BUST, 1800-1808

1804

Plain 4 Crosslet 4 Spiked Chin Variety

DATE	MINTAGE	ABP	G-4 Good	F-12 Fine	VF-20 V. Fine	EF-40 Ex. Fine
☐ 1800	211,530	15.00	25.00	35.00	65.00	110.00
☐ 1802 with 1800 reverse	11 Known	1200.00	1400.00	5000.00	10000.00	—
☐ 1802	14,366	100.00	200.00	350.00	750.00	1800.00
☐ 1803	87,900	15.00	18.00	30.00	45.00	85.00
☐ 1804 Plain 4		15.00	20.00	30.00	50.00	85.00
☐ 1804 Crosslet	1,055,312	15.00	20.00	30.00	50.00	85.00

☐ 1804 Spiked Chin		15.0	25.00	40.00	80.00	125.00
☐ 1805	814,464	12.00	17.00	32.00	48.00	90.00
☐ 1806	356,000	15.00	20.00	35.00	50.00	110.00
☐ 1806 Small 6, Stems		111-111-115.00	45.00	140.00	240.00	500.00
☐ 1807	476,000	15.00	20.00	35.00	70.00	135.00
☐ 1808 Normal Date	400,000	12.00	17.00	35.00	65.00	125.00
☐ 1807 Over 7		30.00	45.00	115.00	225.00	700.00

HALF CENTS — TURBAN HEAD, 1809 - 1837

DATE	MINTAGE	ABP	G-4 Good	F-12 Fine	VF-20 V. Fine	EF-40 Ex. Fine
☐ 1809	1,154,572	12.00	16.50	20.00	35.00	60.00
☐ 1809 over 6		111-111-112.00	16.50	22.00	35.00	60.00
☐ 1809 Circle Inside 0		12.00	16.50	22.00	35.00	60.00
☐ 1810	215,000	12.00	18.00	28.00	50.00	125.00
☐ 1811	63,140	45.00	65.00	150.00	350.00	800.00
☐ 1811 Restrike with 1802 Reverse		EXTREMELY RARE				
☐ 1825	63,000	18.00	25.00	35.00	45.00	75.00
☐ 1826	234,000	12.00	16.00	25.00	30.00	50.00
☐ 1828 12 Stars	606,000	14.00	20.00	26.00	35.00	62.50
☐ 1828 13 Stars		14.00	16.50	25.00	30.00	40.00
☐ 1829	487,000	14.00	16.50	25.00	30.00	40.00
☐ 1831-8 known	2200	750.00	Business	Strikes-	Original	1200.00
☐ 1831 SMALL BERRIES		3000.00	Proof Only	Restrike		
☐ 1831 LARGE BERRIES		1750.00	Proof Only	Restrike		
☐ 1832	154,000	14.00	18.00	22.00	35.00	50.00
☐ 1833	120,000	14.00	18.00	22.00	35.00	50.00
☐ 1834	141,000	14.00	18.00	22.00	35.00	50.00
☐ 1835	398,000	14.00	18.00	22.00	35.00	50.00
☐ 1836		Proof Only	Original	1400.00	—Restrike	2500.00
☐ 1837 (Token) pure copper		25.00	30.00	45.00	60.00	150.00

HALF CENTS — BRAIDED HAIR, 1840 - 1857

DATE	MINTAGE	ABP		PRF-65 Proof
☐ 1840		2250.00	Proof Only	3650.00
☐ 1841		2250.00	Proof Only	3650.00
☐ 1842	ORIGINAL	2250.00	Proof Only	3650.00
☐ 1843	AND RESTRIKE	2250.00	Proof Only	3650.00
☐ 1844	PROOFS ONLY	2250.00	Proof Only	3650.00
☐ 1845	1840-1849	2800.00	Proof Only	5000.00
☐ 1846	NO MINTAGE	2250.00	Proof Only	3650.00
☐ 1847	RECORDS	2250.00	Proof Only	3650.00
☐ 1848	AVAILABLE	2250.00	Proof Only	3650.00
☐ 1849		2250.00	Proof Only	

DATE	MINTAGE	ABP	G-4 Good	F-12 Fine	VF-20 V. Fine	EF-40 Ex. Fine
☐ 1849	39,864	18.00	25.00	30.00	38.00	75.00
☐ 1850	39,812	18.00	30.00	35.00	45.00	75.00
☐ 1851	147,672	12.00	25.00	35.00	40.00	65.00
☐ 1852		600.00	Proofs Only—Original and Restrike			1100.00
☐ 1853	129,964	12.00	22.00	40.00	50.00	75.00
☐ 1854	55,358	18.00	25.00	40.00	50.00	75.00
☐ 1855	56,500	18.00	25.00	40.00	50.00	75.00
☐ 1856	40,430	18.00	25.00	40.00	50.00	75.00
☐ 1857	35,180	25.00	35.00	45.00	75.00	100.00

LARGE CENTS — 1793 - 1857

The shrinkage of the cent from its introduction in 1793 to its present size is ample evidence of inflation; the present Lincoln cent weighs only about one third as much as its distant ancestor. But what the penny has lost in bulk and buying power has been compensated for, at least in part, by its greater convenience. The series began with the Flowering Hair/Chain Reverse type designed by Henry Voight. Its weight was set at 13.48 grams of pure copper, precisely twice that of the half cent. (The government set rigid standards of weight, fearing that without such regulations its coinage would not inspire confidence). There were no long suspensions of production, as with the half cent. A quantity — varying of course in number — was minted each year from the coin's exception until conclusion of the Large Cent in 1857, with the single exception of 1815 because of a metal shortage. The first design is aptly named as Liberty is shown with billowing hair that appears breeze-blown. Her features are delicate and the overall composition is pleasing. It will be noted that the reverse design bears very close resemblance to the Fugio cent or Franklin cent, struck in 1787. The diameter of this coin varies from 26 to 27 mm. It is consequently not very much smaller than the present 50¢ piece. After three months of striking coins from these dies, during which time more than 36,000 were produced, a new design was introduced. The work of Adam Eckfeldt, designer of the first half cent, it retained the Flowing Hair portrait on the obverse but employed a wreath rather than the chained reverse, enclosing the words "ONE CENT." Its weight was unchanged but the diameter varies from 26 to 28 mm. or slightly larger than its predecessor. Along the edge is stamped the inscription "ONE HUNDRED FOR A DOLLAR."

This design got somewhat further, resulting in a mintage of more than 60,000 pieces, but before the year was out another had taken its place. The Flowing Hair portrait, subjected to criticism in the press (to which the government seems to have been more sensitive than subsequently), was removed in favor of a "Liberty Cap" type, designed by Joseph Wright. Here the bust of Liberty is positioned somewhat to the right of center; over her left shoulder she balances a staff, on the tip of which rests of a conical-shaped cap — the "cap of liberty" symbolic of freedom from slavery in Roman times. This version, too, was assailed, but minters were so weary of making alterations that they continued using it until 1796. The staff and cap looked like an Indian arrow in the opinion of some; others fancied that Liberty was wearing an oversized bow in her hair. The weight was retained but the planchet grew slightly larger, to 29 mm. In 1795, still using the same design, the weight was dropped to 10.89 grams, diameter remained 29 mm., and new dies were engraved. The artist was John S. Gardner. His work is often said to be superior to other efforts. The "Draped Bust Type," first struck in mid 1796, was an effort to render more classicism to the portrait. Designed by Robert Scot, it deleted the much-maligned liberty cap and, while not materially altering Miss Liberty's facial features, gave her the appearance of chubbiness. Specifications remained as previously. In 1808 the so-called "Classic Head" made its bow, designed by John Reich. Here Liberty wears a coronet with the word "LIBERTY" spelled out upon it and the bust is shortened with drapery removed. She grows chubbier still. The reverse is very close to that of a modern "wheat" cent: the words "ONE CENT" encircled in laurel, surrounded by the legend "UNITED STATES OF AMERICA." There are numerous varieties, as enumerated below. The classic head survived until the copper shortage which followed close upon the heels of the War of 1812, when production of large cents was temporarily halted. When resumed in 1816 the design was new. The work of Robert Scot, it was referred to as "Matron Head," as Liberty appears to have taken on added years. She in fact was growing old with her coinage. A youth in 1792 when the series began, she had now advanced into middle age. The bust is shortened even further; stars now totally encircle it (except for the space containing the date); but the reverse remains the same.

In 1837 the last large cent design was put into production. The next two decades yielded many varieties of it, from die re-engravings. This is the

Gobrecht version, basically a handsome portrait which returns the youthful goddess image to Liberty and slims her down. The weight was 10.89 grams (the penny was never to return to its old weight-standard), the diameter 27½ mm. Chief variations are the Silly Head and Booby Head, neither of which really merited such ridicule. There was also a Petite Head and Mature Head and ample differences in letter and numeral sizes.

LARGE CENTS — FLOWING HAIR, 1793

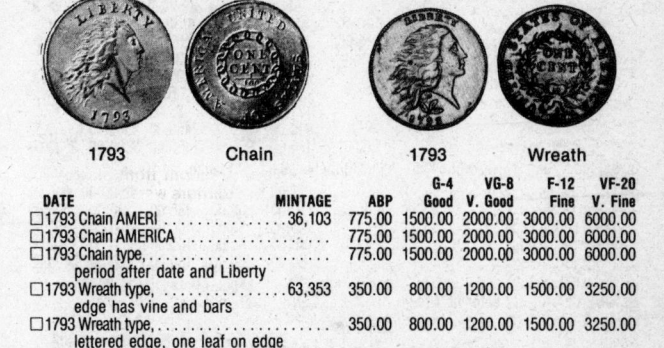

1793 Chain

1793 Wreath

DATE	MINTAGE	ABP	G-4 Good	VG-8 V. Good	F-12 Fine	VF-20 V. Fine
☐ 1793 Chain AMERI	36,103	775.00	1500.00	2000.00	3000.00	6000.00
☐ 1793 Chain AMERICA		775.00	1500.00	2000.00	3000.00	6000.00
☐ 1793 Chain type, period after date and Liberty		775.00	1500.00	2000.00	3000.00	6000.00
☐ 1793 Wreath type, edge has vine and bars	63,353	350.00	800.00	1200.00	1500.00	3250.00
☐ 1793 Wreath type, lettered edge, one leaf on edge		350.00	800.00	1200.00	1500.00	3250.00
☐ 1793 Wreath type lettered edge, double leaf on edge		350.00	800.00	1200.00	1500.00	3250.00

LARGE CENTS—LIBERTY CAP, 1793 - 1796

1793 LIBERTY CAP TYPE

JEFFERSON HEAD

One Cent
in Center of Wreath

High
in Wreath

DATE	MINTAGE	ABP	G-4 Good	VG-8 V. Good	F-12 Fine	VF-20 V. Fine
☐ 1793	11,056	375.00	750.00	1400.00	2250.00	6500.00
☐ 1794		16.00	75.00	100.00	200.00	400.00
☐ 1794* } ALL KINDS		40.00	150.00	300.00	400.00	950.00
☐ 1794**		19.00	45.00	65.00	175.00	425.00
☐ 1794*** } 918,521		27.00	55.00	75.00	165.00	425.00
☐ 1794****		600.00	1500.00	2450.00	4500.00	10000.00
☐ 1795 Jefferson Head		475.00	950.00	1450.00	3500.00	8500.00

*Head of 1793 **Head of 1795 ***No Fraction Bar ****Stars on Back

☐ 1795† Lettered Edge*		50.00	80.00	140.00	250.00	600.00
☐ 1795† Lettered Edge**		50.00	80.00	135.00	240.00	625.00
☐ 1795† Plain Edge*		40.00	80.00	100.00	150.00	350.00
☐ 1795†† Plain Edge**		40.00	80.00	100.00	200.00	350.00
☐ 1796††† Liberty Cap		50.00	80.00	100.00	200.00	400.00

†Total Mintage: 82,000   ††Total Mintage: 456,500   †††Total Mintage: 109,825
*"ONE CENT" in Center of Wreath   **"ONE CENT" High in Wreath

LARGE CENTS—DRAPED BUST, 1796 - 1800

Gripped or Milled Edge

LIBERTY 1796 (error)

DATE	MINTAGE	ABP	G-4 Good	VG-8 V. Good	F-12 Fine	VF-20 V. Fine
☐ 1796†		30.00	60.00	80.00	150.00	300.00
☐ 1796† "LIBERTY" (error)		34.00	65.00	115.00	180.00	350.00
☐ 1796†† Stems on Wreath		15.00	20.00	30.00	65.00	200.00
☐ 1797†† Stemless Wreath		27.00	50.00	90.00	190.00	300.00
☐ 1797†† Stems on Wreath			17.50	25.00	60.00	150.00
☐ 1797†† Gripped		18.00	20.00	30.00	65.00	135.00
☐ 1797†† Plain Edge		15.00	20.00	30.00	65.00	135.00
☐ 1798††† over 97		20.00	30.00	50.00	135.00	275.00

☐ 1798††† Small Date	8.50	17.00	20.00	55.00	95.00
☐ 1798††† Large Date	8.00	17.00	24.00	55.00	95.00
☐ 1798†††*	15.00	28.00	45.00	100.00	225.00
☐ 1799** over 98	200.00	550.00	950.00	2000.00	3500.00
☐ 1799** Normal Date	170.00	450.00	800.00	1750.00	2900.00
☐ 1800*** over 1798	15.00	25.00	40.00	90.00	200.00

†Total Mintage: 363,372   ††Total Mintage: 897,509   †††Total Mintage: 979,700
*Reverse of 96. Single leaf Reverse.   Total Mintage: 904,584   ***Part of 2,822,170

LARGE CENTS — DRAPED BUST, 1800 · 1801

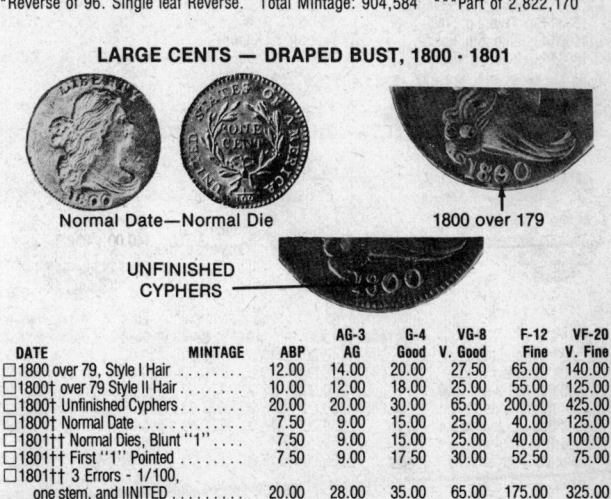

Normal Date—Normal Die   1800 over 179

UNFINISHED CYPHERS

DATE	MINTAGE	ABP	AG-3 AG	G-4 Good	VG-8 V. Good	F-12 Fine	VF-20 V. Fine
☐ 1800 over 79, Style I Hair		12.00	14.00	20.00	27.50	65.00	140.00
☐ 1800† over 79 Style II Hair		10.00	12.00	18.00	25.00	55.00	125.00
☐ 1800† Unfinished Cyphers		20.00	20.00	30.00	65.00	200.00	425.00
☐ 1800† Normal Date		7.50	9.00	15.00	25.00	40.00	125.00
☐ 1801†† Normal Dies, Blunt "1"		7.50	9.00	15.00	25.00	40.00	100.00
☐ 1801†† First "1" Pointed		7.50	9.00	17.50	30.00	52.50	75.00
☐ 1801†† 3 Errors - 1/100, one stem, and IINITED		20.00	28.00	35.00	65.00	175.00	325.00

Total Mintage: 2,822,170

LARGE CENTS — DRAPED BUST, 1801 · 1804

1801- $\frac{1}{100}$

ERROR $\frac{1}{100}$ over $\frac{1}{000}$

DATE	MINTAGE	ABP	AG-3 AG	G-4 Good	VG-8 V. Good	F-12 Fine	VF-20 V. Fine
☐ 1801†† 1/000		9.00	7.00	16.00	30.00	55.00	125.00
☐ 1801†† 1/100 Over 1/000		10.00	10.00	19.00	35.00	75.00	125.00
☐ 1802††† Normal Dies		8.50	10.00	14.00	25.00	35.00	100.00
☐ 1802††† Stemless Wreath		8.50	10.00	14.00	25.00	35.00	100.00
☐ 1802††† Fraction 1/000		8.50	10.00	14.00	25.00	35.00	200.00
☐ 1803* Sm. Date, Sm. Fract.		8.50	10.00	14.00	25.00	35.00	125.00
☐ 1803* Sm. Date, Lg. Fract.		8.50	10.00	14.00	25.00	35.00	125.00
☐ 1803* Lg. Date, Sm. Fract.	Rare (about 20 Known)						
☐ 1803* Lg. Date, Lg. Fract.		10.00	10.00	20.00	65.00	175.00	225.00

Total Mintage: ††1,362,837   †††3,435,100   *2,471,350

LARGE CENTS — DRAPED BUST, 1803 - 1804

"Mumps Obverse"   "Normal Obverse"

DATE	MINTAGE	ABP	AG-3 AG	G-4 Good	VG-8 V. Good	F-12 Fine	VF-20 V. Fine
☐ 1803† Mumps Obverse		8.00	10.00	16.00	20.00	40.00	100.00
☐ 1803† Stemless Wreath		8.00	10.00	16.00	29.00	60.00	125.00
☐ 1803† 1/100 over 1/000		9.00	12.00	20.00	35.00	125.00	200.00
☐ 1804 Normal Dies	756,837	250.00	275.00	325.00	410.00	675.00	1000.00
☐ 1804 Broken Obverse Die		250.00	275.00	325.00	410.00	675.00	1250.00
☐ 1804 Broken Obveerse & Reverse Die		250.00	275.00	325.00	410.00	675.00	1200.00

†Part of 2,471,350

LARGE CENTS — DRAPED BUST, 1804 - 1807

1804 Normal Die

1804 Restruck in 1860

Small Fraction    Large Fraction    COMET VARIETY, 1807

DATE	MINTAGE	ABP	AG-3 AG	G-4 Good	VG-8 V. Good	F-12 Fine	VF-20 V. Fine
☐ 1804 Restrike of 1860						UNC.	300.00
☐ 1805 Blunt "1" in Date	941,115	9.00	10.00	19.00	34.00	85.00	
☐ 1805 Pointed "1" in Date	941,115	9.00	10.00	17.00	22.00	35.00	85.00
☐ 1806	348,000	11.00	14.00	22.00	35.00	75.00	155.00
☐ 1807 over 6 lg. 7		9.00	10.00	15.00	25.00	40.00	100.00
☐ 1807 over 6 sm. 7	RARE-ABOUT 21 KNOWN						
☐ 1807 Small Fraction	727,000	8.00	10.00	14.00	25.00	40.00	100.00
☐ 1807 Large Fraction		8.00	10.00	14.00	25.00	40.00	100.00
☐ 1807 Comet Variety		12.00	15.00	20.00	30.00	60.00	125.00

LARGE CENTS — TURBAN HEAD, 1808 - 1814

DATE	MINTAGE	ABP	AG-3 AG	G-4 Good	VG-8 V. Good	F-12 Fine	VF-20 V. Fine
☐ 1808 13 Stars	1,109,000	8.00	8.00	16.00	30.00	75.00	200.00
☐ 1808 12 Stars		8.00	9.00	18.00	32.00	75.00	200.00
☐ 1809	222,867	40.00	45.00	60.00	100.00	220.00	350.00
☐ 1810 over 9	1,458,400	9.00	8.00	13.00	32.00	75.00	200.00
☐ 1810 Normal Date		5.00	6.00	13.00	22.00	65.00	175.00
☐ 1811 over 10	218,025	20.00	40.00	50.00	60.00	150.00	250.00
☐ 1811 Normal Date		25.00	35.00	45.00	65.00	125.00	350.00
☐ 1812 Small Date	1,075,500	20.00	22.00	45.00	65.00	125.00	350.00
☐ 1812 Large Date		6.00	8.50	13.00	22.00	35.00	110.00

☐ 1813 Close Stars	418,000	10.00	12.00	25.00	40.00	100.00	175.00
☐ 1813 Distant Stars		8.00	10.00	23.00	35.00	90.00	175.00
☐ 1814 Plain 4		8.00	10.00	23.00	35.00	90.00	175.00
☐ 1814 Crosslet 4	357,830	8.00	10.00	16.00	22.00	55.00	125.00

LARGE CENTS — CORONET, 1816 - 1838

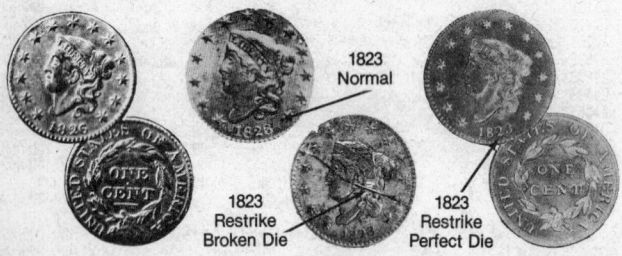

1823 Normal

1823 Restrike Broken Die

1823 Restrike Perfect Die

DATE	MINTAGE	ABP	G-4 Good	VG-8 V. Good	F-12 Fine	VF-20 V. Fine	MS-60 Unc.
☐ 1816	2,820,982	5.50	8.00	10.00	25.00	75.00	300.00
☐ 1817 Wide Date		5.50	8.00	10.00	25.00	75.00	300.00
☐ 1817	3,984,400	5.50	8.00	10.00	25.00	75.00	300.00
☐ 1817 (15 Stars)		4.00	7.00	20.00	40.00	40.00	375.00
☐ 1818	3,167,000	3.00	5.00	9.00	18.00	40.00	220.00
☐ 1819 over 18		3.00	5.50	9.00	20.00	80.00	400.00
☐ 1819 Large Date	2,671,000	3.00	5.00	9.00	20.00	80.00	300.00
☐ 1819 Small Date		3.00	5.00	9.00	20.00	40.00	300.00
☐ 1820 over 19		3.00	5.00	9.00	18.00	45.00	250.00
☐ 1820 Small Date	4,407,550	3.00	5.00	8.00	14.00	29.50	275.00
☐ 1820 Large Date		3.00	5.00	8.00	14.00	29.50	275.00
☐ 1821 Wide Date	389,000	10.00	11.00	18.00	50.00	175.00	1550.00
☐ 1821 Close Date		10.00	12.00	25.00	50.00	175.00	1550.00
☐ 1822 Wide Date	2,072,339	3.00	6.00	8.50	17.50	50.00	360.00
☐ 1822 Close Date		3.00	6.00	8.50	17.50	50.00	360.00
☐ 1823 over 22, Part of	855,730	15.00	25.00	45.00	100.00	215.00	4200.00
☐ 1823 Normal Date		20.00	35.00	55.00	100.00	200.00	6000.00
☐ 1823 Restrike from Broken Obv. Die .		85.00					250.00
☐ 1823 Restrike from Perfect Die	49 Known						
☐ 1824 over 22		16.00	20.00	25.00	60.00	125.00	3000.00
☐ 1824 Wide Date	1,262,090	3.00	5.50	9.50	25.00	45.00	900.00
☐ 1824 Close Date		3.00	5.50	9.50	25.00	45.00	900.00
☐ 1825 Small A's	1,461,000	3.00	5.50	9.50	20.00	32.50	450.00
☐ 1825 Large A's		3.00	5.50	9.50	20.00	32.50	450.00

DATE	MINTAGE	ABP	G-4 Good	VG-8 V. Good	F-12 Fine	VF-20 V. Fine	MS-60 Unc.
☐ 1826 over 25		7.00	10.00	20.00	45.00	80.00	650.00
☐ 1826 Wide Date	1,517,422	3.00	5.50	8.50	14.00	20.00	300.00
☐ 1826 Close Date		3.00	5.50	8.50	14.00	20.00	300.00
☐ 1827	2,357,733	3.00	5.50	9.50	14.00	20.00	300.00
☐ 1828 Small Date	2,260,625	3.50	7.00	10.00	22.50	45.00	300.00
☐ 1828 Large Date		3.00	5.50	7.50	12.00	25.00	300.00
☐ 1829 Small Letters	1,414,500	3.00	5.50	7.50	17.50	40.00	300.00
☐ 1829 Large Letters		3.00	5.50	7.50	16.50	35.00	300.00
☐ 1830 Small Letters	1,711,500	4.00	8.00	14.00	35.00	60.00	325.00
☐ 1830 Large Letters		3.00	5.00	7.00	10.00	15.00	300.00
☐ 1831 Small Letters	3,359,260	3.00	5.00	7.00	10.00	15.00	300.00
☐ 1831 Large Letters		3.00	5.00	7.00	10.00	15.00	300.00
☐ 1832 Small Letters	2,362,000	3.00	5.00	7.00	10.00	15.00	300.00
☐ 1832 Large Letters		3.00	5.00	7.00	10.00	15.00	300.00
☐ 1833 Small Letters	2,739,000	3.00	5.00	7.00	10.00	15.00	300.00
☐ 1833 Large Letters		3.00	5.00	7.00	10.00	15.00	300.00
☐ 1834*		3.00	6.75	11.00	20.00	32.00	300.00
☐ 1834**	1,855,110	3.00	5.00	7.00	13.00	15.00	300.00
☐ 1834***		3.00	5.00	7.00	13.00	22.00	300.00
☐ 1835 Sm. Date — Sm. Stars		3.00	5.00	7.00	12.00	17.00	325.00
☐ 1835 Lg. Date Lg. Stars	3,878,397	3.00	5.00	7.00	12.00	17.00	325.00
☐ 1835 Type of 1836		3.00	5.00	7.00	10.00	15.00	325.00
☐ 1836	2,111,000	3.00	5.00	7.00	10.00	15.00	325.00
☐ 1837 Plain Hair Cord Small Letters		5.00	6.00	9.00	15.00	25.00	315.00
☐ 1837 Plain Hair Cord Large Letters	5,558,301	5.00	5.00	7.00	10.00	20.00	315.00
☐ 1837 Beaded Hair Cord — Small Letters		5.00	5.00	7.00	10.00	20.00	315.00
☐ 1838	6,370,200	5.00	5.00	7.00	10.00	20.00	315.00

*Lg. Date — Lg. Stars — Lg. Letters Rev. **Sm. Date — Sm. Stars — Sm. Letters Rev.
***Lg. Date — Sm. Stars — Sm. Letters Rev.

LARGE CENTS — BRAIDED HAIR, 1839 - 1857

← Booby Head

1855 Knob on Ear    **1856 Slants**    **1857 Lg. Date**

DATE	MINTAGE	ABP	G-4 Good	VG-8 V. Good	F-12 Fine	VF-20 V. Fine	MS-60 Unc.
☐ 1839		60.00	175.00	250.00	300.00	500.00	1800.00
☐ 1839 Type 1838 Line under Cent	⎫	3.00	7.00	12.00	22.00	42.00	325.00
☐ 1839 Silly Head No Center Dot	⎬ ALL KINDS	5.00	9.00	14.00	25.00	40.00	565.00
☐ 1839 Booby Head	3,128,662	5.00	9.00	11.50	22.00	35.00	565.00
☐ 1839 Type of 1840	⎭	5.00	9.00	16.00	27.50	50.00	325.00
☐ 1839 Petite Head		5.00	9.00	11.50	22.00	30.00	425.00
☐ 1840 Small Date	⎫ 2,462,700	5.00	9.00	16.00	27.50	50.00	325.00
☐ 1840 Large Date	⎭	3.00	5.00	7.50	11.00	15.00	210.00
☐ 1841	1,597,366	3.00	5.00	7.50	11.00	15.00	240.00
☐ 1842 Small Date	⎫ 2,383,390	2.75	4.50	7.00	11.00	15.00	260.00
☐ 1842 Large Date	⎭	3.75	4.50	7.00	11.00	15.00	260.00
☐ 1843 Obv. and Rev. 1842		3.00	6.00	8.50	14.00	30.00	210.00
☐ 1843 Obv. 1842 Rev. 1844	2,428,319	15.00	22.00	40.00	80.00	275.00	950.00
☐ 1843 Obv. and Rev. 1844		2.75	5.50	11.50	15.00	32.00	225.00
☐ 1844	⎫ 2,398,752	2.75	4.00	5.00	7.00	9.00	220.00
☐ 1844 over 81	⎭	3.50	7.00	11.00	17.00	45.00	260.00
☐ 1845	3,894,805	2.75	6.00	8.00	9.50	11.00	225.00
☐ 1846 Small Date	⎫	2.75	6.00	8.00	9.50	10.00	225.00
☐ 1846 Med. Date	4,120,800	2.75	6.00	8.00	9.50	10.00	225.00
☐ 1846 Tall Date	⎭	2.75	6.00	8.00	9.50	10.00	235.00
☐ 1847	6,183,669	2.75	6.00	8.00	9.50	10.00	225.00
☐ 1847 7 over Small 7		4.00	10.00	15.00	20.00	30.00	300.00
☐ 1848	6,415,799	2.75	6.00	8.00	9.50	10.00	225.00
☐ 1849	4,178,500	2.75	6.00	8.00	9.50	10.00	225.00
☐ 1850	4,426,844	2.75	6.00	8.00	9.50	15.00	225.00
☐ 1851	⎫ 9,899,700	2.75	6.00	8.00	9.50	15.00	225.00
☐ 1851 over 81	⎭	3.75	7.50	10.00	15.00	30.00	250.00
☐ 1852	5,063,094	2.75	6.00	8.00	9.50	15.00	225.00
☐ 1853	6,641,131	2.75	6.00	8.00	9.50	15.00	225.00

☐ 1854	4,236,156	2.75	6.00	8.00	9.50	15.00	225.00
☐ 1855 Upright 5's		2.75	6.00	8.00	9.50	15.00	225.00
☐ 1855 Slanting 5's	1,574,829	2.75	6.00	8.00	9.50	15.00	225.00
☐ 1855 Slanting 5's Knob on Ear		3.50	7.50	10.50	15.00	25.00	225.00
☐ 1856 Upright 5	2,690,465	4.25	6.00	8.50	10.00	15.00	215.00
☐ 1856 Slanting 5		4.25	6.00	8.50	10.00	15.00	215.00
☐ 1857 Small Date	333,456	15.00	24.00	35.00	47.50	70.00	325.00
☐ 1857 Large Date		10.00	22.00	27.00	40.00	55.00	325.00

SMALL CENTS — FLYING EAGLE, 1856 - 1858

It would be hard to find a coin in the standard U.S. series that proved so unpopular as the Flying Eagle cent — unpopular, that is, originally. It has since become a favorite of collectors. During 1856, while the large cent continued in production, plans were underway to replace it with a smaller coin of the same value. A number of patterns of the Flying Eagle were struck that year at the Philadelphia Mint but were not circulated because the large cent was still current. In the early part of the following year the large cent was discontinued and minting switched over to this new piece, with a huge output in that one year of nearly 17,500,000 coins. The public balked. It charged that the government was forcing the small cent on it. Not only didn't the public care much for that idea, it was also not too fond of the coin. Instead of being struck in pure copper and have the substantial appearance that a cent was supposed to have, its composition was 88% copper and 12% nickel, yielding a coin that was sufficiently pale in color to be called white. (If one wonders about the bickerings over coin sizes, designs and compositions in the 18th and 19th centuries, it should be realized that far greater attention was focused upon money in those days, when few persons used checks and credit cards were unknown.) The Flying Eagle Cent was designed by James Longacre. Its weight was 4.67 grams and its diameter 19 mm. As a designer Longacre was not unskilled. He proved his abilities with the Indian Head Cent, which replaced the Flying Eagle in 1859.

Face Design   Back Design    Large Letters    Small Letters

DATE	MINTAGE	ABP	G-4 Good	F-12 Fine	EF-40 Ex. Fine	MS-60 Unc.	PRF-65 Proof
☐ 1856 Approx.	1,000	650.00	900.00	1100.00	1500.00	2000.00	7000.00
☐ 1857	17,450,000	7.50	12.00	18.00	75.00	350.00	7000.00
☐ 1858 Small Letters	24,600,000	7.50	12.00	18.00	75.00	350.00	7000.00
☐ 1858 Large Letters		7.50	12.00	18.00	75.00	350.00	7000.00

SMALL CENTS — INDIAN HEAD, 1859 - 1909

Probably the most famous of all U.S. coins (its only challenger for that honor being the Morgan Dollar), the Indian Head cent remained in production without change in design for half a century. After the disaster of the Flying Eagle Cent, rejected by the public because of its almost white color, the government knew that it must manufacture a cent whose appearance was that of good metal, even if it was not to return to the large cent. The question remained: would a small copper piece be accepted, when large cents, containing a much greater quantity of metal, were still widely circulating? The new cent had the same composition as its predecessor, 88% copper and 12% nickel. The first batch of Indian Heads, released in 1859, amounted to 36,400,000 pieces, more than had ever been coined of a single denomination in one year: $364,000 worth of pennies. Beginning in 1864 the copper content was increased to 95%, the nickel removed entirely and replaced with a 5% alloy of tin and zinc. This was so successfully absorbed into the copper that the resulting coin was hardly different in color than if copper alone were used. Finally the problem was solved, and the Indian Head Cent was on the road to a long successful existence. Its designer was James Longacre. The weight was 4.67 grams and the diameter 19 mm., these specifications being the same as the Flying Eagle Cent. The portrait is that of an Indian maiden. As first designed the reverse carried no shield but this was added in 1860, the second year of issue. The Indian Head became the first U.S. coin struck in a quantity of more than 100 million in a year, when 108 million specimens were turned out in 1907. This exceeded the country's population. It is interesting to note that the 1908 and 1909 editions, representing the last two years of this design, are the only dates to be found with mintmarks. The origin of the portrait has been for many years a matter of discussion. It was at one time thought that Longacre had taken it from life, using an Indian girl as his model. This was dismissed when the suggestion was advanced that the profile resembled Longacre's daughter. It is now generally believed that no live model sat for the likeness but that it was based upon classical statuary, of which Longacre was known to be a collector. The Indian Head Cent portrait is neither as realistic or impressive as that featured on the Buffalo Nickel, but this is nevertheless an important coin whose design represented a bold innovation.

1859
No Mint Mark

1860-1909.

Mint Mark "S" on 1908 and 1909, under Wreath on Reverse

DATE	MINTAGE	ABP	G-4 Good	F-12 Fine	EF-20 Ex. Fine	MS-60 Unc.	PRF-65 Proof
☐ 1859 Copper-Nickel	36,400,000	3.50	5.00	9.00	50.00	300.00	2750.00
☐ 1860 Copper-Nickel	20,566,000	2.00	4.00	7.00	20.00	130.00	2500.00
☐ 1861 Copper-Nickel	10,100,000	4.00	7.00	15.00	40.00	185.00	2500.00
☐ 1862 Copper-Nickel	28,075,000	1.50	2.75	5.00	18.00	110.00	2500.00
☐ 1863 Copper-Nickel	49,840,000	1.50	2.75	5.00	15.00	110.00	2500.00
☐ 1864 Copper-Nickel	13,740,000	3.00	5.00	11.00	32.00	150.00	2500.00
☐ 1864 Bronze	39,233,714	1.50	3.00	6.50	20.00	55.00	1800.00
☐ 1864 L on Ribbon		10.00	25.00	60.00	100.00	295.00	8000.00
☐ 1865	35,429,286	1.10	2.25	5.25	18.00	45.00	500.00
☐ 1866	9,826,500	8.00	15.00	27.50	70.00	150.00	500.00
☐ 1867	9,821,000	8.00	15.00	27.50	70.00	150.00	500.00
☐ 1868	10,266,500	8.00	15.00	27.50	70.00	150.00	500.00
☐ 1869	6,420,000	12.00	25.00	52.00	110.00	270.00	750.00
☐ 1869 over 8		40.00	60.00	185.00	400.00	1000.00	
☐ 1870	5,275,000	7.00	18.00	42.00	100.00	175.00	400.00
☐ 1871	3,929,500	15.00	25.00	50.00	100.00	200.00	425.00
☐ 1872	4,042,000	18.00	30.00	70.00	125.00	250.00	495.00
☐ 1873	11,676,500	3.00	6.50	15.00	40.00	100.00	300.00
☐ 1873 Doubled Liberty				EXTREMELY RARE			
☐ 1874	14,187,500	3.00	6.00	15.00	40.00	100.00	325.00
☐ 1875	13,528,000	3.00	6.00	15.00	40.00	100.00	300.00
☐ 1876	7,944,000	4.00	10.00	20.00	40.00	100.00	2500.00
☐ 1877	852,500	125.00	185.00	250.00	450.00	1000.00	280.00
☐ 1878	5,799,850	4.00	10.00	20.00	40.00	110.00	275.00
☐ 1879	16,231,200	1.50	3.00	8.00	20.00	40.00	225.00
☐ 1880	38,964,955	.45	1.00	4.00	15.00	50.00	225.00
☐ 1881	39,211,575	.45	1.00	3.50	15.00	50.00	225.00
☐ 1882	38,581,100	.45	1.00	3.50	15.00	50.00	225.00
☐ 1883	45,598,109	.45	1.00	3.50	18.00	50.00	225.00
☐ 1884	23,261,742	.45	1.75	6.50	30.00	50.00	300.00
☐ 1885	11,765,384	1.25	3.00	9.00	20.00	55.00	225.00
☐ 1886	17,654,290	1.00	2.25	6.00	10.00	50.00	225.00
☐ 1887	45,226,483	.50	1.00	2.25	10.00	35.00	225.00
☐ 1888	37,494,414	.50	1.00	2.25	10.00	35.00	225.00
☐ 1889	48,868,361	.50	1.00	2.25	10.00	35.00	225.00
☐ 1890	57,182,854	.50	.90	2.00	10.00	35.00	225.00
☐ 1891	47,072,350	.50	.90	2.00	10.00	35.00	225.00
☐ 1892	37,649,832	.50	.90	2.00	10.00	35.00	225.00
☐ 1893	46,642,195	.50	.90	2.00	10.00	35.00	225.00

DATE	MINTAGE	ABP	G-4 Good	F-12 Fine	EF-40 Ex. Fine	MS-60 Unc.	PRF-65 Proof
☐ 1894	16,752,132	.50	.80	6.75	20.00	60.00	225.00
☐ 1895	38,343,636	.50	.80	1.50	7.00	30.00	225.00
☐ 1896	39,057,293	.50	.80	1.50	7.00	30.00	225.00
☐ 1897	50,466,330	.50	.80	1.50	7.00	30.00	225.00
☐ 1898	49,923,079	.50	.80	1.50	7.00	30.00	225.00
☐ 1899	53,600,031	.50	.80	1.50	7.00	30.00	225.00
☐ 1900	66,833,764	.50	.80	1.50	6.75	20.00	225.00
☐ 1901	79,611,143	.40	.70	1.50	6.75	20.00	225.00
☐ 1902	87,376,722	.40	.70	1.50	6.75	20.00	225.00
☐ 1903	85,094,493	.40	.70	1.50	6.75	20.00	225.00
☐ 1904	61,328,015	.40	.70	1.50	6.75	20.00	225.00
☐ 1905	80,719,163	.40	.70	1.50	6.50	20.00	225.00
☐ 1906	96,022,255	.40	.70	1.50	6.50	20.00	225.00
☐ 1907	108,138,618	.40	.70	1.50	6.50	20.00	275.00
☐ 1908	32,327,987	.40	.70	1.50	6.50	35.00	300.00
☐ 1908S	1,115,000	9.00	20.00	20.00	150.00	150.00	
☐ 1909	14,370,645	.40	2.00	1.75	8.00	40.00	275.00
☐ 1909S	309,000	70.00	85.00	90.00	140.00	275.00	

SMALL CENTS — LINCOLN HEAD, 1909 to Date

It is quite likely that, despite having remained in use for 50 years, the Indian Head design would have been retained for the cent beyond 1909, had not President Roosevelt pressed for its removal. The year 1909 marked the 100th anniversary of Abraham Lincoln's birth and Roosevelt (who, not coincidentally, was a member of the same political party) wished to memorialize the anniversary by placing a likeness of Lincoln on the penny. His suggestion was adopted, the result being a design that has survived in continuous use longer than any other in the Mint's history: 72 years, with no indication that it will soon be replaced. The Indian Head Cents were so popular that criticism was risked by their removal. Had they been abandoned in favor of any other design a public outcry might have ensued. But for Lincoln, allowances could be made. This was incidentally the first time an American citizen appeared on coinage of the Mint, as George Washington, though depicted on numerous coins and tokens, was never portrayed on an issue of the federal Mint. Designer of the Lincoln Cent was Victor D. Brenner. Rather than using a close-up profile Brenner showed Lincoln in quarter-length, with beard, as he appeared in the last few years of his life. It is not known whether the likeness was adapted from a specific photograph, from statuary, or merely from a study of various photos and other artworks. As first struck the coin carried Brenner's initials and this variety is known as the VDB Cent. They were removed midway through production of the 1909 issue and not reinstated until 1918, when they were switched from the reverse to the obverse. Specimens of the 1909 coin with initials, especially those struck at San Francisco, where less than half a million were produced, eventually became favorite collectors' items. At the time little notice was taken of them.

Originally the reverse was composed of the wording "ONE CENT -UNITED STATES OF AMERICA" enshrouded by wheat sheaves. In 1959 a new reverse was introduced, on the occasion of the 150th anniversary of Lincoln's birth and the 50th of the coin's use. Designed by Frank Gasparro, it pictures the Lincoln Memorial building in Washington, D.C. As first issued the Lincoln Cent had a composition of 95% copper and 5% tin and zinc with a weight of 3.11 grams and a diameter of 19 mm. In 1962 its content was changed to 95% copper and 5% zinc, the tin being removed. Modification of the dies were made in 1969 and 1973.

Lincoln Head, 1909-1958

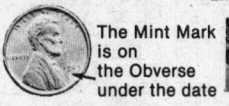

The Mint Mark is on the Obverse under the date

1909 Initials on Reverse

No V.D.B.

V.D.B. Restored

DATE	MINTAGE	ABP	G-4 Good	F-12 Fine	VF-20 V. Fine	EF-40 Ex. Fine	MS-60 Unc.	PRF-65 Proof
1909	72,702,618	.15	.30	.40	.60	1.50	10.00	245.00
1909 V.D.B.	27,995,000	1.00	1.50	2.00	2.25	3.00	13.00	1800.00
1909S	1,825,000	18.00	28.00	30.00	35.00	45.00	100.00	
1909S V.D.B.	484,000	120.00	150.00	200.00	225.00	250.00	400.00	
1910	146,801,218	.12	.25	.35	.50	1.50	15.00	275.00
1910S	6,045,000	3.75	6.00	7.50	8.00	12.00	60.00	
1911	101,177,787	.08	.15	.60	1.20	2.00	20.00	275.00
1911D	12,672,000	1.25	2.50	4.50	8.00	16.00	75.00	
1911S	4,026,000	6.50	9.00	11.00	13.00	20.00	75.00	
1912	68,153,060	.18	.25	1.50	3.50	6.00	30.00	250.00
1912D	10,411,000	1.50	2.50	5.00	10.00	20.00	65.00	
1912S	4,431,000	5.00	7.50	10.00	14.00	18.00	65.00	
1913	76,532,352	.12	.25	1.00	2.00	5.75	30.00	275.00
1913D	15,804,000	.80	1.25	3.00	7.00	16.00	70.00	
1913S	6,101,000	3.00	5.00	6.00	7.00	15.00	70.00	
1914	75,238,432	.15	.35	1.20	3.00	5.00	45.00	300.00
1914D	1,193,000	35.00	55.00	75.00	100.00	180.00	825.00	
1914S	4,137,000	4.00	6.00	8.00	9.50	19.00	125.00	
1915	29,092,120	.20	.40	4.00	8.50	22.00	100.00	350.00
1915D	22,050,000	.20	.40	1.00	4.50	10.00	40.00	
1915S	4,833,677	3.00	5.00	6.00	7.50	15.00	85.00	
1916	131,838,677	.07	.15	.35	.75	2.75	12.00	400.00
1916D	35,956,000	.12	.20	.85	1.50	5.25	30.00	
1916S	22,510,000	.28	.50	1.15	1.50	5.50	40.00	
1917	196,429,785	.07	.15	.30	.60	1.75	12.00	
1917D	55,120,000	.10	.20	.65	2.50	4.50	35.00	
1917S	32,620,000	.10	.20	.65	2.25	4.00	45.00	
1918	288,104,634	.07	.15	.30	.60	1.75	15.00	
1918D	47,830,000	.10	.20	.60	2.00	4.75	40.00	

DATE	MINTAGE	ABP	G-4 Good	F-12 Fine	VF-20 V. Fine	EF-40 Ex. Fine	MS-60 Unc.	PRF-65 Proof
☐ 1918S	34,680,000	.12	.25	.50	2.00	4.50	50.00	
☐ 1919	392,021,000	.07	.15	.25	.50	1.50	10.00	
☐ 1919D	57,154,000	.10	.20	.65	2.50	5.00	35.00	
☐ 1919S	139,760,000	.10	.20	.35	.75	2.00	30.00	
☐ 1920	310,165,000	.07	.15	.30	.50	1.50	11.50	
☐ 1920D	49,280,000	.07	.15	.50	1.25	4.00	45.00	
☐ 1920S	46,220,000	.07	.15	.50	1.25	3.75	50.00	
☐ 1921	39,157,000	.10	.20	.50	1.00	4.00	40.00	
☐ 1921S	15,274,000	.20	.50	1.00	2.25	8.50	155.00	
☐ 1922 Plain (No Mint Mark)		50.00	100.00	150.00	180.00	325.00	2500.00	
☐ 1922D	7,160,000	2.10	4.00	5.75	8.00	12.00	60.00	
☐ 1923	74,723,000	.07	.15	.30	.60	1.75	10.00	
☐ 1923S	8,700,000	.65	1.30	2.00	4.00	9.50	180.00	
☐ 1924	75,178,000	.07	.15	.30	.60	3.25	35.00	
☐ 1924D	2,520,000	4.50	8.00	10.00	14.00	30.00	225.00	
☐ 1924S	11,696,000	.25	.50	1.00	2.25	6.50	125.00	
☐ 1925	139,949,000	.07	.15	.30	.55	1.75	11.50	
☐ 1925D	22,580,000	.12	.25	.55	1.10	3.75	40.00	
☐ 1925S	26,380,000	.07	.15	.40	1.00	2.75	50.00	
☐ 1926	157,088,000	.07	.15	.30	.50	2.00	12.00	
☐ 1926D	28,022,022	.10	.20	.45	.80	3.00	45.00	
☐ 1926S	4,550,000	1.75	2.75	4.25	6.00	9.00	150.00	
☐ 1927	144,440,000	.07	.15	.30	.40	2.00	10.00	
☐ 1927D	27,170,000	.07	.15	.30	.40	2.50	32.50	
☐ 1927S	14,276,000	.12	.25	.50	1.50	3.75	60.00	
☐ 1928	134,116,000	.07	.15	.30	.40	1.50	8.50	
☐ 1928D	31,170,000	.10	.20	.30	.60	1.50	20.00	
☐ 1928S	17,266,000	.12	.25	.30	.65	2.00	55.00	
☐ 1929	185,262,000	.07	.15	.30	.40	1.20	8.50	
☐ 1929D	41,730,000	.07	.15	.30	.40	1.00	15.00	
☐ 1929S	50,148,000	.07	.15	.25	.40	1.00	10.00	
☐ 1930	157,415,000	.04	.10	.20	.30	1.00	10.00	
☐ 1930D	40,100,000	.04	.10	.20	.40	1.00	10.00	
☐ 1930S	24,286,000	.04	.10	.20	.40	1.00	5.00	
☐ 1931	19,396,000	.10	.20	.30	.40	1.65	18.00	
☐ 1931D	4,480,000	1.60	2.35	2.75	3.50	4.50	50.00	
☐ 1931S	866,000	15.00	24.00	26.00	30.00	35.00	60.00	
☐ 1932	9,062,000	.50	1.00	1.50	2.00	2.75	18.00	
☐ 1932D	10,500,000	.25	.50	1.20	2.00	2.50	16.00	
☐ 1933	14,360,000	.25	.50	.75	1.00	2.00	16.00	
☐ 1933D	6,200,000	.80	1.75	2.00	2.75	3.75	20.00	
☐ 1934	219,080,000	.04	.10	.20	.30	.45	1.75	
☐ 1934D	28,446,000	.07	.15	.25	.35	1.00	16.50	
☐ 1935	245,388,000	.05	.10	.15	.20	.25	1.25	
☐ 1935D	47,000,000	.04	.15	.25	.30	.40	2.50	
☐ 1935S	38,702,000	.04	.15	.25	.30	.45	3.75	
☐ 1936	309,637,569	.04	.10	.15	.20	.20	1.25	250.00
☐ 1936D	40,620,000	.03	.15	.25	.30	.35	1.25	
☐ 1936S	29,130,000	.04	.15	.25	.30	.35	1.50	

DATE	MINTAGE	ABP	G-4 Good	F-12 Fine	VF-20 V. Fine	EF-40 Ex. Fine	MS-60 Unc.	PRF-65 Proof
1937	309,179,320	.03	.07	.10	.15	.20	1.00	
1937D	50,430,000	.04	.08	.15	.20	.25	1.25	
1937S	35,500,000	.04	.10	.15	.20	.25	1.50	
1938	156,696,734	.03	.06	.08	.10	.15	1.50	55.00
1938D	20,010,000	.07	.15	.25	.30	.50	1.50	
1938S	15,180,000	.12	.25	.45	.55	.65	2.50	
1939	316,479,520	.03	.06	.08	.10	.15	1.00	25.00
1939D	15,160,000	.15	.30	.50	.60	.75	3.00	
1939S	52,070,000	.04	.10	.15	.20	.30	1.75	
1940	586,825,872	.03	.06	.08	.10	.30	1.00	25.00
1940D	81,390,000	.03	.06	.08	.10	.20	1.00	
1940S	112,940,000	.03	.06	.08	.10	.20	1.00	
1941	887,039,100	.03	.06	.08	.10	.20	1.00	25.00
1941D	128,700,000	.03	.06	.08	.10	.25	2.50	
1941S	92,360,000	.04	.08	.10	.15	.25	3.25	
1942	657,828,600	.04	.06	.08	.10	.20	.45	17.50
1942D	206,692,000	.03	.06	.08	.15	.20	.60	
1942S	85,590,000	.03	.06	.10	.20	.30	4.50	

WARTIME STEEL COMPOSITION

1943	684,628,670	.03	.06	.10	.15	.25	.65	
1943D	217,660,000	.04	.10	.15	.20	.35	.95	
1943S	191,550,000	.04	.10	.20	.30	.40	1.75	

"SHELL CASE" COPPER COMPOSITION

1944	1,435,400,000	.03			.10	.15	.25	
1944D	430,578,000	.03			.10	.15	.25	
1944S	282,760,000	.04			.12	.20	.30	

BRONZE — Regular Pre-War Composition Resumed

1945	1,040,515,000	.03			.08	.10	.30	
1945D	226,268,000	.03			.08	.10	.60	
1945S	181,770,000	.03			.08	.10	.50	
1946	991,655,000	.03			.08	.10	.25	
1946S	315,690,000	.03			.08	.10	.25	
1946S	198,100,000	.03			.08	.10	.60	
1947	190,555,000	.03			.08	.10	.50	
1947D	194,750,000	.03			.08	.10	.30	
1947S	99,000,000	.03			.10	.15	.75	
1948	317,570	.03			.08	.10	.50	
1948D	172,637,500	.03			.12	.15	.30	
1948S	81,735,000	.03			.15	.20	.30	
1949	217,490,000	.03			.08	.10	.75	
1949D	154,370,500	.03			.08	.10	.55	
1949S	64,290,000	.03			.10	.20	1.75	
1950	272,686,386	.03				.10	.40	38.00
1950D	334,950,000	.03				.10	.30	
1950S	118,505,000	.03			.08	.15	.50	
1951	294,633,500	.03				.10	1.75	15.00
1951D	625,355,000	.03				.10	.20	
1951S	100,890,000	.03			.08	.15	1.00	
1952	186,856,980	.03				.10	.50	12.00

DATE	MINTAGE	ABP	G-4 Good	F-12 Fine	VF-20 V. Fine	EF-40 Ex. Fine	MS-60 Unc.	PRF-65 Proof
☐ 1952D	746,130,000	.03				.10	.20	
☐ 1952S	137,800,004	.03			.08	.15	.65	
☐ 1953	256,883,800	.03				.10	.20	10.00
☐ 1953D	700,515,000	.03				.10	.20	
☐ 1953S	181,835,000	.03				.15	.45	
☐ 1954	71,873,350	.03			.12	.20	.30	6.00
☐ 1954D	251,552,500	.03				.10	.25	
☐ 1954S	96,190,000	.03			.08	.15	.35	
☐ 1955	330,958,200	.03				.10	.20	3.00
☐ 1955 Double Die		150.00		180.00	225.00	275.00	675.00	
☐ 1955D	563,257,500	.03					.05	.20
☐ 1955S	44,610,000	.10		.20	.25	.35	.60	
☐ 1956	421,414,384	.03					.05	.06	2.00
☐ 1956D	1,098,201,100	.03					.05	.06	
☐ 1957	283,787,952	.03					.05	.06	2.00
☐ 1957D	1,051,342,000	.03					.05	.06	
☐ 1958	253,400,652	.03					.05	.06	3.00
☐ 1958D	800,953,000	.03					.05	.06	

LINCOLN MEMORIAL DESIGN

1955/55 Double Die Obverse

1960 Small Date

1960 Large Date

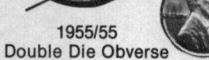

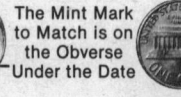

The Mint Mark to Match is on the Obverse Under the Date

Reverse: View of Lincoln Memorial in Washington

DATE	MINTAGE	ABP	EF-40 Ex. Fine	MS-60 Unc.	PRF-65 Proof
☐ 1959	610,864,291			.02	1.00
☐ 1959D	1,279,760,000			.02	
☐ 1960 Small Date	588,096,602	1.15	1.50	2.25	20.00
☐ 1960 Large Date				.10	
☐ 1960D Small Date	1,580,884,000			.35	
☐ 1960D Large Date				.15	
☐ 1961	756,373,244			.02	.80
☐ 1961D	1,753,266,700			.02	
☐ 1962	609,263,019			.02	.70
☐ 1962D	1,793,148,400			.02	
☐ 1963	757,185,645			.02	.70
☐ 1963D	1,744,020,400			.02	
☐ 1964	2,652,525,762			.02	.80

DATE	MINTAGE	ABP	EF-40 Ex. Fine	MS-60 Unc.	PRF-65 Proof
☐ 1964D	3,799,071,500			.02	
☐ 1965	1,497,224,900			.03	
☐ 1966	2,188,147,783			.03	
☐ 1967	3,048,667,077			.03	
☐ 1968	1,707,880,965			.04	
☐ 1968D	2,886,269,590			.02	
☐ 1968S	261,311,500			.02	.20
☐ 1969	1,136,910,000			.18	
☐ 1969D	4,002,832,200			.02	
☐ 1969S	547,309,631			.02	.20
☐ 1970	1,898,315,000			.03	
☐ 1970D	2,891,438,900			.02	
☐ 1970S	693,192,814			.02	.25
☐ 1971	1,919,490,000			.03	
☐ 1971D	2,911,045,600			.02	
☐ 1971S	528,354,192			.05	.20
☐ 1972	2,933,255,000			.02	
☐ 1972 Double Die		75.00	150.00	225.00	
☐ 1972D	2,665,071,400			.02	
☐ 1972S	380,200,104			.02	.20
☐ 1973	3,728,245,000			.02	
☐ 1973D	3,549,576,588			.02	
☐ 1973S	319,937,634			.02	.25
☐ 1974	4,232,140,523			.02	
☐ 1974D	4,235,098,000			.02	
☐ 1974S	412,039,228			.02	.25
☐ 1975	4,505,275,300			.02	
☐ 1975D	5,505,275,300			.02	
☐ 1975S Proof Only	2,909,369				8.00
☐ 1976	4,674,292,426			.02	
☐ 1976D	4,221,595,455			.02	
☐ 1976S Proof Only	4,149,945				2.00
☐ 1977	4,469,972,000			.02	
☐ 1977D	4,149,055,800			.02	
☐ 1977S Proof Only	3,250,895				2.00
☐ 1978	5,266,905,000			.02	
☐ 1978D	4,280,233,400			.02	
☐ 1978S Proof Only	3,127,781				2.75
☐ 1979P				.02	
☐ 1979D				.02	
☐ 1979S Proof Only					2.75

TWO-CENT PIECES — TWO-CENT (BRONZE), 1864-1873

The two cent piece was a short-lived coin whose impact upon the world fell far short of its impact on modern numismatists. Small change was growing increasingly scarce during the Civil War, to the point where postage stamps, encased in holders, were being used for money. The government sought to alleviate this by increased production of the penny and introduced the two cent piece to take the penny's place in areas where it might not be in sufficient supply. Enormous quantities were struck at the outset, approaching 20 million per year, the composition being the same as that of the penny, 95% copper to 5% of tin and zinc. The diameter was 23 mm. Designer of the two cent piece was James Longacre, who did most of the Mint's designing at that time. There is no portrait on the coin; it carries a U.S. shield on one side and a value statement on the other. The lack of portraiture was undoubtedly an effort to prevent this coin from being confused with the penny. Though larger by 4 mm. in diameter than the penny, it must be remembered that large cents were still found in circulation in 1864 — they had been discontinued less than ten years earlier — and one almost needed a scoreboard to keep track of the denominations of coins passing through his hands. Production totals of the two cent piece decreased each year of its minting, until only 65,000 were turned out in 1872 and nothing but proofs and restrikes the following year. It died a very silent death.

1864 Small Motto

1864 Large Motto

First Coin to Bear the Motto "In God We Trust"

DATE	MINTAGE	ABP	G-4 Good	F-12 Fine	EF-40 Ex. Fine	MS-60 Unc.	PRF-65 Proof
☐ 1864 Small Motto	19,847,500	20.00	40.00	60.00	150.00	400.00	
☐ 1864 Large Motto		3.00	5.00	8.00	25.00	165.00	1000.00
☐ 1865	13,640,000	3.00	4.00	6.00	35.00	165.00	1000.00
☐ 1866	3,177,000	3.00	5.00	7.50	35.00	175.00	1000.00
☐ 1867	3,915,000	3.00	5.00	7.00	35.00	175.00	950.00
☐ 1867 Double Die			EXTREMELY RARE				
☐ 1868	3,252,000	3.00	5.00	7.00	35.00	175.00	950.00
☐ 1869	1,546,500	3.00	6.00	7.00	32.00	250.00	1000.00
☐ 1870	861,250	3.00	6.00	15.00	40.00	300.00	1000.00
☐ 1871	721,250	3.50	7.00	15.00	45.00	325.00	1100.00
☐ 1872	65,000	30.00	60.00	115.00	225.00	500.00	1200.00
☐ 1873 Closed 3	600	1400.00	PROOFS ONLY				2500.00
☐ 1873 Open 3 (Restrike)	480	1400.00	PROOFS ONLY				2500.00

THREE-CENT PIECES — THREE CENT (SILVER), 1851 · 1873

America's burgeoning population, plus conditions brought about by the California gold strike, resulted in a shortage of small change during the middle 19th century. The decision was made to strike a coin in three cents denomination and to have its composition of silver, alloyed with 25% copper. Because of its low face value and precious metal content the coin was extremely small physically. Its designer was James Longacre. Rather than portraiture, a symbolic obverse was used, consisting of a six-pointed star and shield. This was done to avoid confusion with the half dime, whose size and color was similar. On the reverse was the Roman numeral III enclosed within an ornamental letter C (for "cents") and surrounded by small stars. The weight was only 4/5th of a gram — the lightest coin ever struck by the Mint — with a diameter of just 14 mm. It was tiny indeed. Undoubtedly the government expected that this coin, despite serving an important purpose, would not prove popular. It didn't. After striking about 35 million in the first three years of its production, quantities were sharply reduced thereafter. It was subsequently replaced by the "nickel" 3¢ piece following the Civil War, which contained no silver whatever. Though the basic design of the silver three cent piece was maintained throughout its lifetime — they continued being struck until 1873, though rarely circulated after 1862 — some minor changes were introduced. In 1854 the obverse star was redrawn with a triple border. The final version, put into use in 1859, has a double border. As there are no great rarities among the circulating dates of this series, a complete collection is well within the realm of possibility. In 1854 there was a change of composition to 90% silver/10% copper and the weight was brought down to 3/4ths of a gram. From then until conclusion of the series all minting was carried out in Philadelphia. Previously the manufacture of this coin had been divided between Philadelphia and New Orleans.

The Mint Mark "O" is on the Reverse to the right of the III

DATE	MINTAGE	ABP	G-4 Good	F-12 Fine	EF-40 Ex. Fine	MS-60 Unc.	PRF-65 Proof
☐ 1851	5,447,400	4.00	7.00	10.00	40.00	500.00	
☐ 1851 O	720,000	5.00	11.00	18.00	50.00	600.00	
☐ 1852	18,663,500	4.00	7.00	11.00	40.00	500.00	
☐ 1853	11,400,000	4.00	7.00	11.00	40.00	500.00	
☐ 1854	671,000	3.00	8.00	18.00	65.00	800.00	
☐ 1855	139,000	7.00	12.00	30.00	125.00	900.00	5000.00
☐ 1856	1,458,000	4.00	8.00	18.00	65.00	700.00	4500.00

DATE	MINTAGE	ABP	G-4 Good	F-12 Fine	EF-40 Ex. Fine	MS-60 Unc.	PRF-65 Proof
☐ 1857	1,042,000	4.00	8.00	18.00	65.00	650.00	4500.00
☐ 1858	1,604,000	4.00	8.00	18.00	65.00	650.00	4500.00
☐ 1859	365,000	5.00	10.00	18.00	50.00	400.00	4250.00
☐ 1860	287,000	5.00	10.00	18.00	50.00	400.00	4250.00
☐ 1861	498,000	5.00	10.00	18.00	50.00	400.00	4250.00
☐ 1862	363,550	5.00	10.00	18.00	50.00	400.00	4250.00
☐ 1862, 2 over 1		8.00	15.00	25.00	130.00	300.00	1000.00
☐ 1863	21,460	2500.00		PROOFS			4250.00
☐ 1863, 3 over 2		2500.00		PROOFS			4250.00
☐ 1864	470	2500.00		PROOFS			4250.00
☐ 1865	8,500	2500.00		PROOFS			4250.00
☐ 1866	22,725	2500.00		PROOFS			4250.00
☐ 1867	4,625	2500.00		PROOFS			4250.00
☐ 1868	4,100	2500.00		PROOFS			4250.00
☐ 1869	5,100	2500.00		PROOFS			4250.00
☐ 1870	4,000	2500.00		PROOFS			4250.00
☐ 1871	4,260	2500.00		PROOFS			4250.00
☐ 1872	1,950	2500.00		PROOFS			4250.00
☐ 1873	600	2500.00		PROOFS			4250.00

THREE-CENT PIECES — THREE CENT (NICKEL), 1865 - 1889

For all practical purposes the three cent piece had been out of circulation during most of the Civil War. Upon the war's conclusion its manufacture was resumed, but no longer was the composition chiefly of silver. In fact the new version contained no precious metal at all. It was composed of 75% copper and 25% nickel. What the three cent piece lost metallically it gained physically: its weight more than doubled, rising to 1.94 grams, and its diameter increased to 17.0 mm. It may be wondered why a coin containing 75% copper would be referred to as a "nickel" rather than a "copper." The explanation is that the term "copper" was already in use for the cent. Americans picked up this nickname from the British, who had long been calling their pennies "coppers." As the new three cent coin represented the greatest use made of nickel by the Mint up to that time, the name "nickel" seemed appropriate. The coin was somewhat better received than its predecessor, as there was not so much danger of confusing it with another denomination. The fact that its life was not particularly long (it was discontinued in 1889) can be attributed more to inflation than any fault of its own. By 1889 there was simply no longer a pressing need for three cent pieces. At least 20 million were in circulation at that time and this was deemed more than enough to meet whatever demand might exist. The five cent piece, which began in 1866 to be composed of the same copper-nickel ratio as the three cent, was adequately filling whatever need the three cent had earlier satisfied.

The three cent Nickel carried a Liberty head on its obverse and a large Roman numeral III on the reverse. Like the silver version it was designed by

James Longacre. All were struck at Philadelphia. Throughout the quarter-century of production no changes occured in its design.

DATE	MINTAGE	ABP	G-4 Good	F-12 Fine	EF-40 Ex. Fine	MS-60 Unc.	PRF-65 Proof
☐ 1865	11,382,000	3.00	4.00	6.00	12.00	180.00	5000.00
☐ 1866	4,801,000	3.00	4.00	6.00	12.00	180.00	2500.00
☐ 1867	3,915,000	3.00	4.00	6.00	12.00	180.00	2500.00
☐ 1868	3,252,000	3.00	4.00	6.00	12.00	180.00	2500.00
☐ 1869	1,604,000	3.00	5.00	7.00	15.00	180.00	2500.00
☐ 1870	1,335,000	3.00	5.00	8.00	15.00	180.00	2500.00
☐ 1871	604,000	3.00	5.00	8.00	15.00	180.00	2500.00
☐ 1872	862,000	3.00	5.00	8.00	15.00	180.00	2500.00
☐ 1873 Closed 3	1,173,000	3.00	5.00	8.00	15.00	180.00	2500.00
☐ 1873 Open 3		3.00	5.00	8.00	15.00	180.00	2500.00
☐ 1874	790,000	3.00	5.00	8.00	15.00	180.00	2500.00
☐ 1875	228,000	3.00	6.00	10.00	22.00	200.00	2500.00
☐ 1876	162,000	3.00	9.00	12.00	25.00	200.00	2500.00
☐ 1877	510	2750.00		PROOF			5000.00
☐ 1878	2,350	1500.00		PROOF			3500.00
☐ 1879	41,200	15.00	35.00	45.00	60.00	375.00	2500.00
☐ 1880	24,955	20.00	40.00	50.00	75.00	450.00	2500.00
☐ 1881	1,080,575	3.00	4.00	6.00	12.00	125.00	2500.00
☐ 1882	25,300	15.00	35.00	45.00	65.00	450.00	2500.00
☐ 1883	10,609	30.00	70.00	100.00	125.00	450.00	2500.00
☐ 1884	5,642	70.00	125.00	135.00	175.00	500.00	2500.00
☐ 1885	4,790	75.00	150.00	225.00	275.00	600.00	2500.00
☐ 1886	4,290	1200.00		PROOF			2500.00
☐ 1887	7,961	70.00	150.00	175.00	200.00	500.00	2500.00
☐ 1887 over 86		500.00					2500.00
☐ 1888	41,083	15.00	30.00	35.00	40.00	400.00	2500.00
☐ 1889	21,561	18.00	35.00	45.00	60.00	400.00	2500.00

A.B.P. is for coins in fine condition or better. Superbly struck uncirculated coins bring proportionately more than price listed.

NICKELS — SHIELD, 1866 - 1883

Though the silver half dime was still being struck in 1866 its production was too limited to serve as a general circulating coin. This noble old soldier, its origins dating back to the Mint's beginnings, was suffering the effects of general inflation and the bullion shortage of the Civil War, caused in part by a scarcity of laborers for the silver mines. Not knowing what the future might hold, the government had no wish to terminate the silver half dime but it wanted, at the same time, to introduce a coin of proportionate value made of base metal and attempt to popularize it. Thus was born the five cent piece Nickel or "true nickel," as opposed to the three cent coin that was also called a nickel. The five cent Nickel was authorized by Congress on May 16, 1866. It was to have a weight of 5 grams and be composed of three parts copper and one part nickel. The diameter was 20½ mm. James Longacre, chief engraver of the Mint, was called upon to design it and produced a portraitless coin consisting of a shielded obverse with arabic numeral "5" on the reverse surrounded by stars and rays (or bars). "IN GOD WE TRUST" appears on the obverse above the shield. Nearly 15,000,000 pieces were struck in the first year of issue. In the following year, 1867, after production had continued briefly, the rays were removed from the reverse, resulting in a rarity of moderate proportions for the "with rays" type. This is not, however, an expensive coin except in uncirculated condition. It may be asked why the 1867 variety with rays and the standard 1866 date are valued almost equally, when only 2,019,000 of the former and 14,742,500 of the latter were struck, yielding a scarcity ratio of 7-to-1. The answer is simply that the 1866 would *not* be worth so much, if it wasn't the first date of its series. There are many collectors buing "first dates" who buy no other coins or the series. For this reason the first year of minting of *any* U.S. coin carries a premium over and above the quantity struck or available in the market. (Compare the 1866 value with that of the 1872, of which fewer than half as many were struck; the former is more common but worth more.)

1866-83	1866-67 with rays	1867-83 without rays

DATE	MINTAGE	ABP	G-4 Good	F-12 Fine	EF-40 Ex. Fine	MS-60 Unc.	PRF-65 Proof
☐ 1866 w/rays	14,742,500	5.00	10.00	15.00	80.00	600.00	6000.00
☐ 1867 w/rays	30,909,500	5.00	10.00	20.00	100.00	600.00	12000.00
☐ 1867 no rays		4.00	7.00	10.00	25.00	175.00	2500.00
☐ 1868	28,817,000	4.00	7.00	10.00	25.00	175.00	2500.00
☐ 1869	16,395,000	4.00	7.00	10.00	25.00	175.00	2500.00
☐ 1870	4,806,000	4.50	9.00	12.00	30.00	175.00	2500.00
☐ 1871	561,000	16.00	30.00	40.00	75.00	300.00	2500.00
☐ 1872	6,036,000	4.00	9.00	11.00	30.00	175.00	2500.00
☐ 1873 closed 3	4,550,000	2.00	5.00	12.00	30.00	175.00	2500.00
☐ 1873 open 3		2.00	5.00	12.00	30.00	180.00	2500.00
☐ 1874	3,538,000	4.00	9.00	14.00	35.00	180.00	2500.00
☐ 1875	2,097,000	5.00	10.00	18.00	40.00	225.00	2500.00
☐ 1876	2,530,000	5.00	10.00	15.00	40.00	225.00	2500.00

DATE	MINTAGE	ABP	G-4 Good	F-12 Fine	EF-40 Ex. Fine	MS-60 Unc.	PRF-65 Proof
☐ 1877	.500	3000.00		PROOF			7000.00
☐ 1878	2,350	2200.00		PROOF			4000.00
☐ 1879	29,100	40.00	80.00	110.00	140.00	350.00	3500.00
☐ 1879 9 over 8				EXTREMELY RARE			
☐ 1880	19,955	40.00	80.00	110.00	150.00	325.00	3500.00
☐ 1881	72,375	30.00	60.00	80.00	110.00	300.00	2500.00
☐ 1882	11,476,600	3.00	7.00	10.00	28.00	175.00	2500.00
☐ 1883	1,456,919	4.00	8.00	10.00	28.00	175.00	2500.00
☐ 1883 over 2		25.00	30.00	50.00	125.00	250.00	2500.00

NICKEL — LIBERTY HEAD, 1883 - 1912

When production of the silver half dime picturing Liberty ceased in the 1870's, designers were free to transfer the likeness of this goddess to our nickel five cent piece. This, however, was not immediately done and when finally undertaken in 1883 the portrait was not the full figure used for half dimes but a profile bust. The new design was created by Charles E. Barber and gained for this piece the name "Barber Nickel," which was once used commonly but seems to have lost popularity. Like its predecessor it was made of 75% copper and 25% nickel and had a weight of 5 grams. The diameter was slightly larger, measuring 21.2 mm., and striking was done at Philadelphia, Denver and San Francisco. An embarrassing difficulty occured with this coin at the outset of production. As first designed the reverse carried the Roman numeral V (for 5) without the word "cents" or any sign indicating that cents was intended. Very shortly, unscrupulous persons began gilding the coin with gold wash and passing it to foreigners and other uninformed individuals as a $5 gold piece. The government put a halt to this acitivity by having the die re-engraved and the word "Cents" added. From then until 1913, when a new design was introduced (the famous Buffalo/Indian), no changes were made in designing. The Liberty Head was struck in great quantities throughout almost its entire run of production, with the total output reaching well into the hundreds of millions. It could still be found in general circulation, though not with much frequency, as late as the 1940's. The 1913 Liberty Head, America's most valuable basemetal coin, has long proved an enigma. The Mint claims not to have struck any Liberty Heads that year, asserting that its production consisted entirely of the Buffalo/Indian. It is certainly believable that no regular production occured, otherwise the total in existence would not be small as just five specimens. Even assuming that minting for the year was started with the Liberty Head design and was switched off to the new type after a few days, thousands of coins would by that time have been struck. There seems no logical way in which just five pieces could have been manufactured. The likelihood — though it may slightly tarnish this rarity's appeal — is that 1913 dies were produced, then put aside when the change of design was authorized and used (possibly clandestinely) to strike just a few specimens by a person or persons unknown. This theory is supported by the fact that originally, when first brought to public light, *all five* were owned by the same individual: Colonel Edward H. R. Green of New York, a noted collector of coins, stamps and art in the World War I era. If struck by the Mint and disbursed, it is almost beyond the realm of possibility that they could have been acquired by one collector within so short a period of time. (Colonel Green, incidentally, is equally noted for being the purchaser of the sheet of 24¢ inverted-center airmail stamps issued in 1918, which he *broke up and sold;* his approach to collecting was rather like that of a dealer or speculator, and one can only wonder at the reason for his association with the 1913 Liberty Head five cent piece.)

Without "CENTS"

Mint Mark under Dot

DATE	MINTAGE	ABP	G-4 Good	F-12 Fine	EF-40 Ex. Fine	MS-60 Unc.	PRF-65 Proof
☐ 1883 no cents	5,479,519	1.00	2.00	4.00	8.00	60.00	2000.00
☐ 1883 w/cents	16,032,983	2.50	5.00	15.00	35.00	150.00	1500.00
☐ 1884	11,273,942	3.00	6.00	15.00	35.00	150.00	1500.00
☐ 1885	1,476,490	40.00	100.00	175.00	250.00	600.00	3000.00
☐ 1886	3,330,290	135.00	30.00	70.00	135.00	425.00	1500.00
☐ 1887	15,263,652	2.00	4.00	12.00	32.00	150.00	1500.00
☐ 1888	10,720,483	2.50	5.00	14.00	40.00	150.00	1500.00
☐ 1889	15,881,361	2.00	4.00	12.00	30.00	150.00	1500.00
☐ 1890	16,259,272	2.00	4.00	12.00	32.00	150.00	1500.00
☐ 1891	16,834,350	2.00	4.00	12.00	32.00	150.00	1500.00
☐ 1892	11,699,642	2.25	4.50	15.00	40.00	150.00	1500.00
☐ 1893	13,370,195	2.25	4.00	12.00	35.00	150.00	1500.00
☐ 1894	5,413,132	3.00	6.00	16.00	50.00	150.00	1500.00
☐ 1895	9,979,884	2.00	5.00	14.00	38.00	125.00	1500.00
☐ 1896	8,842,920	2.00	5.00	15.00	55.00	125.00	1500.00
☐ 1897	20,428,735	.50	1.00	5.00	25.00	135.00	1500.00
☐ 1898	12,532,087	.50	1.00	5.00	25.00	125.00	1500.00
☐ 1899	26,029,031	.40	.75	3.00	22.00	150.00	1500.00
☐ 1900	27,255,995	.30	.70	3.00	20.00	200.00	1500.00
☐ 1901	26,480,213	.30	.70	3.00	20.00	200.00	1500.00
☐ 1902	31,480,579	.30	.70	3.00	20.00	200.00	1500.00
☐ 1903	28,006,725	.30	.70	3.00	20.00	200.00	1500.00
☐ 1904	21,404,984	.30	.70	3.00	20.00	200.00	1500.00
☐ 1905	29,827,276	.30	.70	3.00	20.00	200.00	1500.00
☐ 1906	38,613,725	.30	.70	3.00	20.00	200.00	1500.00
☐ 1907	39,214,800	.30	.70	3.00	20.00	200.00	1500.00
☐ 1908	22,686,177	.30	.70	3.00	20.00	200.00	1500.00
☐ 1909	11,590,526	.30	.70	3.00	20.00	200.00	1500.00

DATE	MINTAGE	ABP	G-4 Good	F-12 Fine	EF-40 Ex. Fine	MS-60 Unc.	PRF-65 Proof
☐ 1910	30,169,353	.30	.70	3.00	20.00	200.00	1500.00
☐ 1911	39,559,372	.30	.70	3.00	20.00	200.00	1500.00
☐ 1912	26,236,714	.30	.70	3.00	20.00	200.00	1500.00
☐ 1912D	8,474,000	.50	.90	5.00	35.00	200.00	
☐ 1912S	238,000	13.00	25.00	45.00	150.00	1000.00	

☐ 1913* Not a Regular Mint Issue—5 Known—SUPERIOR SALE 1978   200,000.00

NICKELS — BUFFALO OR INDIAN HEAD, 1913 - 1938

Undoubtedly the most dramatic, artistic and original set of designs employed for a U.S. coin, the Buffalo/Indian Head Nickel went into production in 1913. The composition was 75% copper and 25% nickel, with a weight of five grams. Its diameter was 21.2 mm. James E. Fraser, the designer, was not one to go half way. He hired an Indian to sit for the obverse portrait and took his sketching gear to the Bronx Zoo to get a likeness of a buffalo in the flesh. The artwork of this coin is little short of superb: each motif fully fills the planchet ground and is unencumbered by large inscriptions or miscellaneous symbols. Unfortunately the rate of wear in handling was such that few individuals aside from collectors had the opportunity to see the coin at its best. Just like the noble animal it pictured, the American bison, this coin proved to be a rapidly disappearing species. Within only 20 years after its discontinuation in 1938 it had all but vanished from circulation, despite enormous production output. Critics of the Buffalo/Indian Head Nickel were few. Those who spoke against it raised the objection that the buffalo was endangered by extinction because of its hunting by the Indians, and that to place both on the same coin was similar to picturing a woolly mastodon and a caveman. However, the intent, very well accomplished, was to use the medium of coinage to portray a subject genuinely Amercan rather than endlessly repeating such symbols of foreign origin as Liberty. So popular did the bison likeness become that the coin, unlike most others, came to be popularly known by its reverse rather than its obverse. In 1916 a Double Die error resulted on some specimens, producing a twin or ghost impression of the date. Of regularly struck pieces, those from the San Francisco mint in the early and middle 1920's are scarcest.

Mint Mark is on the Reverse, under "Five Cents"

1913-1938

1913-Type 1
Buffalo on High Mound

1913-Type 2
Buffalo on Level Ground

DATE	MINTAGE	ABP	G-4 Good	F-12 Fine	EF-40 Ex. Fine	MS-60 Unc.	PRF-65 Proof
☐ 1913 Type-1	30,993,520	1.25	2.00	4.00	10.00	35.00	3750.00
☐ 1913D Type-1	5,337,000	2.00	4.00	6.00	12.00	50.00	
☐ 1913S Type-1	2,105,000	2.50	5.00	10.00	20.00	75.00	
☐ 1913 Type-2	29,858,700	1.00	2.00	3.00	5.00	30.00	3000.00
☐ 1913D Type-2	4,156,000	10.00	20.00	35.00	60.00	100.00	
☐ 1913S Type-2	1,209,000	20.00	35.00	50.00	85.00	175.00	
☐ 1914	20,665,738	2.00	3.00	5.00	10.00	45.00	3000.00
☐ 1914D	3,912,000	7.00	15.00	25.00	60.00	175.00	
☐ 1914S	3,470,000	2.00	4.00	10.00	20.00	75.00	
☐ 1915	20,987,270	.50	1.00	2.00	8.00	35.00	3000.00
☐ 1915D	7,569,500	2.00	4.00	10.00	30.00	100.00	
☐ 1915S	1,505,000	2.75	6.00	18.00	55.00	175.00	
☐ 1916 Double Die Obverse				200.00	380.00	700.00	
☐ 1916	63,498,066	.20	.50	1.00	5.00	30.00	3000.00
☐ 1916D	13,333,000	3.00	3.00	6.00	22.00	90.00	
☐ 1916S	11,860,000	.85	3.00	6.00	22.00	90.00	
☐ 1917	51,424,029	.30	.70	1.25	8.00	30.00	
☐ 1917D	9,910,800	2.00	3.00	8.00	45.00	175.00	
☐ 1917S	4,193,000	2.00	4.00	8.00	42.00	175.00	
☐ 1918	32,086,314	.20	.60	2.25	10.00	70.00	
☐ 1918D	8,362,000	1.25	3.00	8.00	50.00	225.00	
☐ 1918D over 7		100.00	275.00	525.00	1800.00	9000.00	
☐ 1918S	4,882,000	2.00	3.00	8.00	50.00	200.00	
☐ 1919	60,868,000	.20	.45	1.00	7.00	32.00	
☐ 1919D	8,006,000	1.25	2.00	12.00	60.00	300.00	
☐ 1919S	7,521,000	1.25	2.00	8.00	50.00	275.00	
☐ 1920	63,093,000	.18	.40	1.00	7.00	38.00	
☐ 1920D	9,418,000	1.00	2.00	8.00	60.00	275.00	
☐ 1920S	9,689,000	1.00	2.00	6.00	55.00	225.00	
☐ 1921	10,683,000	.25	.60	2.25	10.00	75.00	
☐ 1921S	1,557,000	3.00	7.00	28.00	125.00	425.00	
☐ 1923	35,715,000	.18	.40	.80	7.00	32.00	
☐ 1923S	6,142,000	.70	1.00	4.50	35.00	200.00	
☐ 1924	21,620,000	.18	.40	.80	8.00	50.00	
☐ 1924D	5,258,000	1.00	2.00	7.00	40.00	225.00	
☐ 1924S	1,437,000	2.00	3.00	15.00	400.00	1800.00	
☐ 1925	35,565,100	.18	.40	.80	6.00	32.00	
☐ 1925D	4,450,000	1.50	3.00	10.00	50.00	225.00	
☐ 1925S	6,256,000	1.00	2.00	6.00	40.00	225.00	
☐ 1926	44,693,000	.18	.40	.80	4.00	28.00	

DATE	MINTAGE	ABP	G-4 Good	F-12 Fine	EF-40 Ex. Fine	MS-60 Unc.	PRF-65 Proof
☐ 1926D	5,638,000	1.00	2.00	8.00	60.00	125.00	
☐ 1926S	970,000	2.00	5.00	12.00	125.00	425.00	
☐ 1927	37,981,000	.18	.40	.80	4.00	25.00	
☐ 1927D	5,730,000	.25	.70	2.50	25.00	75.00	
☐ 1927S	3,430,000	.25	.80	4.00	40.00	200.00	
☐ 1928	23,411,000	.18	.40	.80	3.00	26.00	
☐ 1928D	6,436,000	.18	.50	1.50	8.00	42.00	
☐ 1928S	6,936,000	.18	.50	1.25	7.00	100.00	
☐ 1929	36,446,000	.18	.40	.80	3.00	22.00	
☐ 1929D	8,370,000	.18	.45	.90	8.00	45.00	
☐ 1929S	7,754,000	.18	.40	.80	5.00	35.00	
☐ 1930	22,849,000	.18	.40	.80	3.00	22.00	
☐ 1930S	5,435,000	.18	.50	.90	4.00	50.00	
☐ 1931S	1,200,000	1.00	2.50	3.50	10.00	50.00	
☐ 1934	20,313,000	.18	.40	.80	3.25	35.00	
☐ 1934D	7,480,000	.18	.45	.90	3.00	70.00	
☐ 1935	58,264,000	.18	.40	.80	1.25	18.00	
☐ 1935D	12,092,000	.18	.40	.80	2.00	60.00	
☐ 1935S	10,300,000	.18	.40	.80	1.75	25.00	
☐ 1936	119,001,420	.18	.40	.80	1.25	18.00	3500.00
☐ 1936D	24,418,000	.18	.40	.80	1.75	18.80	
☐ 1936S	14,390,000	.18	.40	.80	1.75	18.00	
☐ 1937	79,485,769	.18	.40	.80	1.75	12.00	3500.00
☐ 1937D	17,826,000	.18	.40	.90	1.50	12.00	
☐ 1937D—3 Legged Buffalo		65.00	115.00	140.00	180.00	450.00	
☐ 1937S	5,635,000	.18	.40	.90	1.25	14.00	
☐ 1938D	7,020,000	.18	.45	1.00	1.25	12.00	
☐ 1938D over S		2.00	4.00	6.00	9.00	25.00	

NICKELS — JEFFERSON, 1938 to Date

In 1938 Thomas Jefferson became the third President to be pictured on an American coin (preceded by Lincoln and Washington), when his likeness was installed on the five cent piece replacing the Buffalo/Indian Head. When the decision was made to use Jefferson's portrait on this coin a public competition was instituted to select the best design, accompanied by an award of $1,000. A total of 390 entries was received, the winning one being that of Felix Schlag. Jefferson is shown in profile facing left on the obverse with his home at Monticello pictured on the reverse. No alteration has ever been made in the design of this coin but some changes occurred in composition and modeling of the dies. In 1966 Schlag's initials were added, the feeling being that he deserved this honor as much as the designer of the Lincoln Cent, whose initials were incorporated into the design. The coin has always weighed five grams and measured 21.1 mm. Originally its content was 75% copper and 25% nickel. Due to a shortage of nickel during World War II, because of its use in military production, this metal was entirely removed from the coin in 1942 and substituted by a composition of

56% copper, 35% silver and 9% manganese. Wartime nickels consequently carry a premium value because of their silver content, though the silver additive was so small that the premium is only minimal. In 1946 the pre-war composition was resumed, and has since remained constant. Prior to 1968 the mint mark was on the reverse, to the right of the design. On wartime specimens (1942-45) it is considerably enlarged and placed above Monticello's dome. From 1968 on it appears on the obverse between the date and portrait.

Mint Mark from 1968

Felix Schlag (after 1966)

1938 to date

1938-1942, 1946 to 1968

1942-1945 Silver Content Type with Large Mint Mark over Dome

DATE	MINTAGE	ABP	G-4 Good	F-12 Fine	EF-40 Ex. Fine	MS-60 Unc.	PRF-65 Proof
☐ 1938	19,515,365			.25	.50	1.00	75.00
☐ 1938D	5,376,000	.50	1.00	1.50	2.25	5.00	
☐ 1938S	4,105,000	.50	2.00	2.50	3.50	6.00	
☐ 1939	120,627,535			.20	.40	1.25	40.00
☐ 1939D	3,514,000	2.50	4.00	4.50	7.50	50.00	
☐ 1939S	6,630,000	.25	.50	.75	2.00	12.00	
☐ 1940	176,499,158				.25	.75	40.00
☐ 1940D	43,540,000				.25	1.50	
☐ 1940S	39,690,000				.40	1.75	
☐ 1941	203,283,730				.20	.75	40.00
☐ 1941D	53,432,000				.30	1.25	
☐ 1941S	43,445,000				.30	1.40	
☐ 1942	49,818,600				.30	1.50	40.00
☐ 1942D	13,938,000	.12	.20	.30	2.00	12.50	
WARTIME SILVER NICKELS							
☐ 1942P	57,900,600	.50	.90	1.00	1.50	10.00	500.00
☐ 1942S	32,900,000	.50	.90	1.00	1.50	8.00	
☐ 1943P	271,165,000	.50	.90	1.00	1.50	2.00	
☐ 1943D	15,294,000	.60	1.20	1.60	2.25	2.50	
☐ 1943S	104,060,000		.90	1.00	2.75	2.50	
☐ 1944P	119,150,000	.50	.90	1.00	1.50	2.75	
☐ 1944D	32,309,000	.50	.90	1.00	1.00	2.50	
☐ 1944S	21,640,000	.50	.90	1.00	1.50	4.00	
☐ 1945P	119,408,100	.50	.90	1.00	1.50	5.00	
☐ 1945D	37,158,000	.50	.90	1.00	1.50	2.50	
☐ 1945S	58,939,000	.50	.90	1.00	1.50	2.00	

DATE	MINTAGE	ABP	G-4 Good	F-12 Fine	EF-40 Ex. Fine	MS-60 Unc.	PRF-65 Proof
REGULAR PRE-WAR TYPE							
☐ 1946	161,116,000				.20	.50	
☐ 1946D	45,292,200				.30	.70	
☐ 1946S	13,560,000				.40	1.00	
☐ 1947	95,000,000				.15	.30	
☐ 1947D	37,882,000				.25	1.00	
☐ 1947S	24,720,000			.25	.40	1.00	
☐ 1948	89,348,000				.15	.45	
☐ 1948D	44,734,000			.20	.35	1.00	
☐ 1948S	11,300,000			.25	.45	1.25	
☐ 1949	60,652,000				.20	1.00	
☐ 1949D	36,498,000			.20	.35	1.00	
☐ 1949S	9,716,000	.10	.20	.30	.75	2.00	
☐ 1950	9,847,386	.15	.30	.45	.90	1.50	32.50
☐ 1950D	2,530,000	6.00	8.00	8.50	9.00	10.00	
☐ 1951	28,689,500				.30	.75	18.00
☐ 1951D	20,460,000				.60	1.25	
☐ 1951S	7,776,000	.10	.25	.50	.80	2.50	
☐ 1952	64,069,980				.15	.40	12.00
☐ 1952D	30,638,000			.30	.60	2.00	
☐ 1952S	20,572,000			.10	.25	.50	
☐ 1953	46,772,800				.15	.20	7.00
☐ 1953D	59,878,600				.20	.30	
☐ 1953S	19,210,900			.15	.30	.50	
☐ 1954	47,917,350					.20	5.00
☐ 1954D	117,183,060					.20	
☐ 1954S	29,834,000			.10	.20	.35	
☐ 1954, S over D				6.00	12.00	30.00	
☐ 1955	8,266,200	.15	.30	.50	.60	1.25	3.00
☐ 1955D	74,464,100					.25	
☐ 1955, D over S				5.00	14.00	24.00	
☐ 1956	35,885,384					.25	1.50
☐ 1956D	67,222,940					.20	
☐ 1957	39,655,952					.25	1.15
☐ 1957D	136,828,900					.20	
☐ 1958	17,963,653				.25	.40	1.35
☐ 1958D	168,249,120				.15	.20	
☐ 1959	28,397,291					.06	1.10
☐ 1959D	160,738,240						
☐ 1960	57,107,602					.06	.90
☐ 1960D	192,582,180					.06	
☐ 1961	76,668,344					.06	.70
☐ 1961D	229,342,760					.06	
☐ 1962	100,602,019					.06	.70
☐ 1962D	280,195,720					.06	
☐ 1963	178,851,645					.06	.70
☐ 1963D	276,829,460					.06	
☐ 1964	1,028,622,762					.06	.60
☐ 1964D	1,787,297,160					.06	

DATE	MINTAGE	ABP	G-4 Good	F-12 Fine	EF-40 Ex. Fine	MS-60 Unc.	PRF-65 Proof
☐ 1965	136,131,380					.06	
☐ 1966	156,208,283					.06	
☐ 1967	107,324,750					.06	
☐ 1968D	91,227,800					.06	
☐ 1968S	103,437,510					.06	.50
☐ 1969D	202,807,500					.06	
☐ 1969S	128,099,631					.06	.50
☐ 1970D	515,485,380					.06	
☐ 1970S	241,464,814					.06	.60
☐ 1971	108,884,000					.25	
☐ 1971D	316,144,800					.06	
☐ 1971S	3,224,138						1.25
☐ 1972	202,036,000					.06	
☐ 1972D	351,694,600					.06	
☐ 1972S	3,267,667						1.25
☐ 1973	384,396,000					.06	
☐ 1973D	261,405,400					.06	
☐ 1973S	2,769,624						2.00
☐ 1974	601,752,000					.06	
☐ 1974D	277,373,000					.06	
☐ 1974S	2,617,350						3.00
☐ 1975	181,772,000					.06	
☐ 1975D	401,875,300					.06	
☐ 1975S Proof Only	2,909,369					.06	2.25
☐ 1976	376,124,000					.06	
☐ 1976D	563,964,147					.06	1.50
☐ 1976S Proof Only	4,149,945					.06	
☐ 1977	585,175,250					.06	
☐ 1977D	297,325,618						1.50
☐ 1977S	3,250,095						
☐ 1978	391,308,000					.06	
☐ 1978D	313,092,780					.06	
☐ 1978S Proof Only	3,127,781						1.25
☐ 1979						.06	
☐ 1979D						.06	
☐ 1979S Proof Only							1.00

HALF DIMES, 1794 - 1873

The terms "half dime" and "nickel" may be easily confused by the beginner, both seeming to have the same meaning. They were two distinctly different coins, whose production for a while overlapped. The nickel was at first a three cent piece composed in part of that metal, then a five cent piece as it remains today. The half dime was likewise worth five cents but was made of silver. It was not an emergency or experimental piece but was introduced as early as 1794 to be part of the standard denomination series. The first half dimes did not technically reach manufacture until 1795 but

164

carried a 1794 date as the dies had been engraved that year and there was no desire to redo this work. The weight was 1.35 grams, the composition consisting of .8924 silver and .1076 copper; or, to speak in rounded figures, nine parts silver to one part copper. After more than 40 years of being unchanged compositionally the silver content was raised to a full nine parts in 1837, which necessitated a weight reduction to 1.34 grams. The original obverse type was the Flowing Hair Liberty, similar to that of other silver coinage of the time. Its designer was Robert Scot. On the reverse appeared the standing eagle and legend "UNITED STATES OF AMERICA." This was replaced by the Draped Bust type with similar reverse in 1796, and the shield eagle reverse in 1800. Beginning in 1829 the Capped Bust was introduced, along with a modified version of the shield eagle (wings downward instead of upturned). The sharpest departure occured in 1837, with the introduction of a design that was to remain — with modifications — until the series closed out in 1873. This was the Seated Liberty, an attractive bit of classical portraiture but one to which some objection was voiced, on grounds that it closely resembled the figure of Britannia on British coins. The reverse carried the wording "HALF DIME" within an open wreath, encircled by "UNITED STATES OF AMERICA." There was initially no decoration of the obverse beyond the figure of Liberty. In 1838 a series of stars was added as a half-frame to the portrait. Arrows were placed by the date in 1853. The chief revision came in 1860 when the words "UNITED STATES OF AMERICA" were removed from the reverse and placed on the obverse, supplanting the stars. The reverse wreath was redesigned and made larger and frillier to fill the vacancy. The Half Dime was suspended in 1873 when sufficient quantities of the base-metal five cent coin had reached circulation.

1794-1795 LIBERTY WITH FLOWING HAIR

DATE	MINTAGE	ABP	G-4 Good	F-12 Fine	VF-20 V. Fine
☐ 1794		350.00	700.00	1000.00	1800.00
☐ 1795	86,416	350.00	700.00	1000.00	1800.00

HALF DIMES — DRAPED BUST, SMALL EAGLE, 1796 - 1797

DATE	MINTAGE	ABP	G-4 Good	F-12 Fine	VF-20 V. Fine
☐ 1796 over 5		325.00	700.00	1200.00	2000.00
☐ 1796	10,230	325.00	700.00	1200.00	2000.00
☐ 1796 LIKERTY		325.00	700.00	1200.00	2000.00
☐ 1797					
☐ (13 stars)		325.00	700.00	1200.00	2000.00
☐ (15 stars)	44,527	325.00	700.00	1200.00	2000.00
☐ (16 stars)		325.00	700.00	1200.00	2000.00

HALF DIMES — DRAPED BUST, LARGE EAGLE, 1800 - 1805

DATE	MINTAGE	ABP	G-4 Good	F-12 Fine	VF-20 V. Fine
☐ 1800	24,000	115.00	500.00	900.00	1400.00
☐ 1800 (LIREKTY)		150.00	500.00	900.00	1400.00
☐ 1801	33,910	115.00	500.00	900.00	1400.00
☐ 1802 (Very Rare)	13,010	1500.00	2200.00	6000.00	12500.00
☐ 1803	37,850	115.00	500.00	900.00	1400.00
☐ 1805	15,600	175.00	500.00	900.00	1400.00

HALF DIMES — LIBERTY CAP, 1829 - 1837

DATE	MINTAGE	ABP	G-4 Good	F-12 Fine	EF-40 Ex. Fine	MS-60 Unc.
☐ 1829	1,230,000	9.50	15.00	20.00	75.00	600.00
☐ 1830	1,240,000	9.50	15.00	20.00	75.00	600.00
☐ 1831	1,242,700	9.50	15.00	20.00	75.00	600.00
☐ 1832	965,000	9.50	15.00	20.00	75.00	600.00
☐ 1833	1,370,000	9.50	15.00	20.00	75.00	600.00
☐ 1834	1,480,000	9.50	15.00	20.00	75.00	600.00
☐ 1835*	2,760,000	9.50	15.00	20.00	75.00	600.00
☐ 1836	1,900,000	9.50	15.00	20.00	75.00	600.00
☐ 1837 large $.05	2,276,000	9.50	15.00	20.00	75.00	600.00
☐ 1837 small $.05		12.00	25.00	45.00	125.00	800.00

*1835 Large Date — Large $.05, Large Date — Small $.05, Same prices.
Small Date — Small $.05, Small Date — Large $.05, Same prices.

HALF DIMES — LIBERTY SEATED, 1837 - 1859

1837-1839O no Stars

1837-1859

1838-1859 with Stars

Mint Mark is on the Reverse under the Value

DATE	MINTAGE	ABP	G-4 Good	F-12 Fine	EF-40 Ex. Fine	MS-60 Unc.	PRF-65 Proof
☐ 1837** Small Date, No Stars		25.00	50.00	75.00	250.00	1000.00	
☐ 1837 Large Date, No Stars	2,250,000	25.00	50.00	75.00	250.00	800.00	
☐ 1838O No Stars	70,000	28.50	60.00	200.00	500.00	3,400.00	
☐ 1838 w/Stars	2,255,000	5.00	10.00	20.00	60.00	750.00	
☐ 1839	1,069,150	5.00	10.00	20.00	60.00	750.00	
☐ 1839O	1,096,550	7.00	15.00	25.00	80.00	850.00	
☐ 1840 No Drapery	1,344,085	5.00	10.00	20.00	60.00	800.00	
☐ 1840 Drapery		10.00	20.00	60.00	300.00	900.00	
☐ 1840O Drapery		15.00	30.00	100.00	600.00	1000.00	
☐ 1840O No Drapery		6.00	12.00	25.00	75.00	500.00	
☐ 1841	1,500,000	5.00	10.00	20.00	60.00	400.00	
☐ 1841O	815,000	6.00	12.00	25.00	70.00	600.00	
☐ 1842	815,000	5.00	10.00	20.00	60.00	500.00	
☐ 1842O	350,000	7.00	15.00	30.00	200.00	—	
☐ 1843	1,165,000	5.00	10.00	20.00	60.00	500.00	
☐ 1844	430,000	5.00	10.00	20.00	60.00	600.00	
☐ 1844O	220,000	20.00	40.00	150.00	750.00	—	
☐ 1845	1,564,000	5.00	10.00	20.00	60.00	500.00	
☐ 1846	27,000	30.00	65.00	250.00	700.00	—	
☐ 1847	1,274,000	5.00	10.00	20.00	60.00	500.00	
☐ 1848*	668,000	5.00	10.00	25.00	50.00	450.00	
☐ 1848**	600,000	5.00	10.00	25.00	50.00	450.00	
☐ 1849	1,309,000	5.00	10.00	20.00	60.00	350.00	
☐ 1849 over 46	1,309,000	6.00	12.00	20.00	65.00	425.00	
☐ 1849 over 48	1,309,000	10.00	20.00	30.00	70.00	475.00	
☐ 1849O	140,000	20.00	32.50	85.00	600.00	—	
☐ 1850	955,000	5.00	10.00	20.00	60.00	500.00	
☐ 1850O	690,000	7.00	15.00	30.00	80.00	600.00	
☐ 1851	781,000	5.00	10.00	20.00	60.00	350.00	
☐ 1851O	860,000	6.00	12.00	30.00	80.00	550.00	
☐ 1852	1,000,000	5.00	10.00	20.00	60.00	500.00	
☐ 1852O	260,000	15.00	30.00	60.00	200.00	—	
☐ 1853 w/arrows	13,210,020	4.00	7.00	9.00	45.00	400.00	
☐ 1853 no arrows	135,000	7.00	15.00	50.00	100.00	600.00	
☐ 1853O w/arrows	2,360,000	4.00	7.00	10.00	45.00	600.00	
☐ 1853O no arrows	2,360,000	60.00	115.00	200.00	800.00	—	
☐ 1854 w/arrows	5,740,000	4.00	7.00	9.00	45.00	600.00	
☐ 1854O w/arrows	1,560,000	4.50	8.00	15.00	75.00	900.00	

DATE	MINTAGE	ABP	G-4 Good	F-12 Fine	EF-40 Ex. Fine	MS-60 Unc.	PRF-65 Proof
☐ 1855 w/arrows	1,750,000	5.00	10.00	20.00	40.00	600.00	3500.00
☐ 1855O w/arrows	600,000	7.00	15.00	30.00	85.00	950.00	
☐ 1856	4,880,000	4.00	8.00	15.00	50.00	500.00	5000.00
☐ 1856O	1,100,000	5.00	10.00	20.00	60.00	500.00	
☐ 1857	7,280,000	4.00	8.00	15.00	50.00	350.00	4500.00
☐ 1857O	1,380,000	5.00	10.00	20.00	60.00	500.00	
☐ 1858	3,500,000	4.00	8.00	15.00	50.00	300.00	4500.00
☐ 1858 over inverted date							
☐ 1858O	1,660,000	5.00	10.00	20.00	60.00	500.00	
☐ 1859+	340,000	7.00	15.00	50.00	80.00	450.00	4500.00
☐ 1859O	560,000	7.00	15.00	30.00	70.00	700.00	

*Small Date & Lg. Date — Same Price   **Med. Date. Lg. Date — Same Price
+There are two recognized patterns in this series, the transitional pieces of 1859 and 1860:
1859 — proof: 10,000   1860 — unc: 3,500,000

HALF DIMES — LIBERTY SEATED, 1860-1873
with "UNITED STATES OF AMERICA" on Obverse

Mint Marks are Under or Within Wreath on Reverse

DATE	MINTAGE	ABP	G-4 Good	F-12 Fine	EF-40 Ex. Fine	MS-60 Unc.	PRF-65
☐ 1860 Legend	799,000	4.00	8.00	15.00	50.00	400.00	2500.00
☐ 1860O	1,060,000	4.00	8.00	20.00	60.00	400.00	
☐ 1861	3,361,000	4.00	8.00	15.00	40.00	200.00	3000.00
☐ 1862	1,492,550	4.00	8.00	15.00	40.00	200.00	3000.00
☐ 1863	18,460	30.00	60.00	100.00	200.00	400.00	1850.00
☐ 1863S	100,000	7.00	15.00	30.00	100.00	800.00	
☐ 1864	48,470	100.00	200.00	300.00	500.00	800.00	3000.00
☐ 1864S	90,000	12.00	25.00	75.00	150.00		
☐ 1865	13,500	50.00	100.00	150.00	200.00	600.00	2750.00
☐ 1865S	120,000	7.00	15.00	30.00	100.00	850.00	
☐ 1866	10,725	50.00	100.00	175.00	300.00	600.00	2750.00
☐ 1866S	120,000	7.00	15.00	30.00	125.00	850.00	
☐ 1867	8,625	75.00	150.00	200.00	400.00	1000.00	2000.00
☐ 1867S	120,000	7.00	15.00	35.00	125.00	750.00	
☐ 1868	89,2000	10.00	20.00	40.00	150.00	450.00	3000.00
☐ 1868S	280,000	4.00	8.00	18.00	60.00	325.00	
☐ 1869	208,600	5.00	10.00	25.00	60.00	400.00	3000.00
☐ 1869S	230,000	5.00	9.00	20.00	60.00	400.00	
☐ 1870	536,000	5.00	10.00	20.00	60.00	400.00	3000.00

1870S is unique — only one known.

DATE	MINTAGE	ABP	G-4 Good	F-12 Fine	EF-40 Ex. Fine	MS-60 Unc.	PRF-65 Proof
☐1871	1,873,960	4.00	8.00	15.00	60.00	400.00	3000.00
☐1871S	161,000	7.00	15.00	50.00	125.00	650.00	
☐1872	2,947,950	4.00	8.00	15.00	55.00	400.00	3000.00
☐1872S in wreath	837,000	5.00	10.00	20.00	50.00	400.00	
☐1872S below wreath		5.00	10.00	20.00	60.00	400.00	
☐1873	712,600	4.00	8.00	15.00	65.00	450.00	3000.00
☐1873S	324,000	5.00	10.00	20.00	50.00	450.00	

DIMES — EARLY DIMES, 1796 - 1891

A coin valued at 1/10th of a dollar was among the first to be authorized by the U.S. Mint, though production did not begin until 1796. Had the dime made its debut even just a year sooner there is every likelihood it would have carried the Flowing Hair design, but by 1796 there was no longer much enthusiasm for this rendition of Liberty and so the coin got its start with the Draped Bust portrait. This version of Liberty, familiar on other silver pieces, lacks the "cap of liberty" and shows the goddess with a somewhat more fashionable hairdo. On the reverse was the standing eagle, encircled by branches and the inscription "UNITED STATES OF AMERICA." Stars were placed in circular pattern on the obverse, ranging in number from 13 to 16. The designer was Robert Scot. The weight of this coin was 2.70 grams and its original composition was .8924 silver and .1076 copper, the same as that of the Half Dime (or, approximately, nine parts of silver to one part of copper). Its diameter was generally 19 mm. but slight variations are observed. In 1798 the standing eagle was replaced by the heraldic or shield eagle on the reverse, over which is a series of stars. Just like the stars on the original obverse, these too can vary in quantity from 13 to 16. In 1809 the portrait was changed to the Capped Bust, whose chief characteristic (aside from Liberty's headgear) is that the profile is switched round to face left instead of right. The reverse type is now the eagle-on-branch, still bearing a shield but with its wings down instead of opened wide. The year 1837 witnessed the most significant alteration up to the time; a likeness of Liberty seated replaced the bust type and the eagle's place on the reverse was taken by the wording "ONE DIME" within a wreath, surrounded by "UNITED STATES OF AMERICA." At first there were no stars on the obverse but these were added in 1838 and arrows were placed at the date in 1853. These, however, were of little duration as they disappeared in 1856. In 1860 the wording "UNITED STATES OF AMERICA" was removed from the reverse and placed on the obverse. Some change was made in the wreath's design to compensate for loss of the inscription. The arrows-at-date type was introduced again in 1873 but abandoned once more after two years. It composition was now precisely nine parts silver to one of copper, the weight was 2½ grams and the diameter 17.9 mm. The appearance and disappearance of arrows at the date may seem unexplainable. This was done for a logical purpose that was not in any way concerned with improving the design. They were added as indication that the coin had been compositionally changed.

DIMES — DRAPED BUST, 1796 - 1807
Eagle on Reverse

1798-1807

1796-1797
Small Eagle

1798-1807
Large Eagle

DATE	MINTAGE	ABP	G-4 Good	F-12 Fine	VF-20 V. Fine
☐ 1796	22,135	500.00	1000.00	1500.00	3000.00
☐ 1797 (13 stars)	25,261	500.00	1000.00	1500.00	3000.00
☐ 1797 (16 stars)		500.00	1000.00	1500.00	3000.00
☐ 1798*		250.00	500.00	800.00	1200.00
☐ 1798 over 97* w/13 stars on reverse	27,500		RARE		
☐ 1798 small 8*			RARE		
☐ 1798 over 97* w/16 stars on reverse		120.00	275.00	800.00	1200.00
☐ 1800	21,760	150.00	300.00	1500.00	6000.00
☐ 1801	34,640	150.00	300.00	1500.00	6000.00
☐ 1802	10,975	150.00	300.00	1500.00	6000.00
☐ 1803	33,040	150.00	300.00	1500.00	6000.00
☐ 1804 w/13 stars on reverse	8,265	400.00	750.00	1500.00	9000.00
☐ 1804 w/14 stars on reverse	8,265	400.00	750.00	1500.00	9000.00
☐ 1805 w/4 berries	120,780	150.00	300.00	1500.00	6000.00
☐ 1805 w/5 berries	120,780	150.00	300.00	1500.00	6000.00
☐ 1807	165,000	150.00	300.00	1500.00	6000.00

DIMES — LIBERTY CAP, 1809 - 1837

DATE	MINTAGE	ABP	G-4 Good	F-12 Fine	EF-40 Ex. Fine	MS-60 Unc.
☐ 1809	44,710	20.00	45.00	90.00	250.00	4000.00
☐ 1811 over 9	65,180	20.00	40.00	60.00	185.00	4000.00
☐ 1814	421,500	7.00	15.00	35.00	150.00	2000.00
☐ 1814 STATESOFAMERICA (No Breaks Between Words)		9.00	18.00	50.00	265.00	2000.00
☐ 1820	942,587	11.00	19.00	28.00	150.00	2000.00
☐ 1821	1,186,512	11.00	19.00	28.00	150.00	2000.00
☐ 1822	100,000	25.00	50.00	115.00	335.00	4000.00
☐ 1823 over 22	440,000	11.00	19.00	30.00	95.00	2000.00
☐ 1824 over 22	440,000	11.00	20.00	37.00	115.00	2000.00

DATE	MINTAGE	ABP	G-4 Good	F-12 Fine	EF-40 Ex. Fine	MS-60 Unc.
☐ 1825	510,000	11.00	19.00	30.00	90.00	2000.00
☐ 1827	1,215,000	11.00	19.00	25.00	80.00	2000.00
☐ 1828 Large Date	125,000	22.00	45.00	150.00	350.00	3000.00
☐ 1828 Small Date	125,000	11.00	20.00	37.50	115.00	2000.00
☐ 1829 Small $.10	770,000	6.00	12.00	20.00	125.00	2000.00
☐ 1829 Large $.10	770,000	6.00	12.00	20.00	125.00	2000.00
☐ 1830*	510,000	6.00	12.00	20.00	125.00	2000.00
☐ 1830, 30 over 29		25.00	38.00	140.00	375.00	1600.00
☐ 1831	771,350	6.00	12.00	20.00	125.00	2000.00
☐ 1832	522,500	6.00	12.00	20.00	125.00	2000.00
☐ 1833	485,000	6.00	12.00	20.00	125.00	2000.00
☐ 1834**	635,000	6.00	12.00	20.00	125.00	2000.00
☐ 1835	1,410,000	6.00	12.00	20.00	125.00	2000.00
☐ 1836	1,190,000	6.00	12.00	20.00	125.00	2000.00
☐ 1837 ALL KINDS	1,042,000	6.00	12.00	20.00	125.00	2000.00

*1830 — Small $.10, 1830 — Large $.10: Same Price
**1834 Small 4, 1834 — Large 4: Same Price

DIMES — LIBERTY SEATED, 1837 - 1860

1837-38O
no stars

1837-91

1838-60
with stars

Mint Mark is on the Reverse Under the Value

DATE	MINTAGE	ABP	G-4 Good	F-12 Fine	EF-40 Ex. Fine	MS-60 Unc.
☐ 1837 No Stars		20.00	40.00	85.00	350.00	1800.00
☐ 1838O No Stars	402,404	20.00	40.00	120.00	500.00	3000.00
☐ 1838 Small Stars	1,992,500	10.00	20.00	40.00	200.00	1500.00
☐ 1838 Large Stars		5.00	10.00	20.00	75.00	600.00
☐ 1838 Partial Drapery		10.00	25.00	50.00	180.00	1000.00
☐ 1839	1,053,115	5.00	10.00	18.00	70.00	600.00
☐ 1839O	1,243,272	6.00	12.00	20.00	100.00	800.00
☐ 1840 No Drape	1,358,580	4.00	8.00	10.00	70.00	600.00
☐ 1840O No Drape	1,175,000	7.00	15.00	40.00	100.00	1500.00
☐ 1840O	1,175,000	7.00	15.00	30.00	80.00	1500.00
☐ 1841	1,622,500	4.00	8.00	15.00	60.00	525.00
☐ 1841O	2,007,500	7.00	15.00	30.00	80.00	1200.00
☐ 1842	1,887,500	4.00	8.00	15.00	60.00	500.00
☐ 1842O	2,020,000	7.00	15.00	30.00	80.00	—

DATE	MINTAGE	ABP	G-4 Good	F-12 Fine	EF-40 Ex. Fine	MS-60 Unc.	PRF-65 Proof
☐ 1843	1,370,000	4.00	7.00	12.00	50.00	500.00	
☐ 1843O	150,000	20.00	40.00	100.00	700.00	—	
☐ 1844	72,500	12.00	25.00	75.00	300.00	1800.00	
☐ 1845	1,755,000	4.00	7.00	12.00	50.00	500.00	
☐ 1845O	230,000	10.00	20.00	50.00	750.00	—	
☐ 1846	31,300	25.00	60.00	150.00	500.00	—	
☐ 1847	245,000	7.00	15.00	50.00	200.00	1000.00	
☐ 1848	451,000	5.00	10.00	20.00	75.00	500.00	
☐ 1849	839,000	4.00	7.00	20.00	60.00	500.00	
☐ 1849O	300,000	7.00	15.00	30.00	250.00	—	
☐ 1850	1,931,500	4.00	7.00	12.00	50.00	500.00	
☐ 1850O	510,000	5.00	10.00	25.00	100.00	950.00	
☐ 1851	1,026,500	4.00	7.00	12.00	60.00	500.00	
☐ 1851O	400,000	5.00	10.00	25.00	60.00	1000.00	
☐ 1852	1,535,500	4.00	7.00	12.00	60.00	525.00	
☐ 1852O	430,000	4.50	12.00	35.00	150.00	1200.00	
☐ 1853 No arrows	95,000	20.00	30.00	50.00	200.00	950.00	
☐ 1853 w/arrows	12,173,010	5.00	7.50	12.00	50.00	525.00	10000.00
☐ 1853O	1,100,000	5.00	7.50	20.00	100.00	800.00	
☐ 1854	4,470,000	5.00	7.50	12.00	40.00	600.00	12000.00
☐ 1854O	1,770,000	5.00	7.50	18.00	100.00	600.00	
☐ 1855	2,075,000	5.00	7.50	12.00	45.00	600.00	7000.00
☐ 1856*	5,780,000	5.00	7.50	20.00	75.00	575.00	4000.00
☐ 1856O	1,180,000	4.00	7.00	12.00	60.00	550.00	
☐ 1856S	70,000	15.00	30.00	60.00	300.00	—	
☐ 1857	5,580,000	3.00	5.00	10.00	40.00	500.00	4500.00
☐ 1857O	1,540,000	4.00	7.00	12.00	50.00	500.00	
☐ 1858	1,540,000	4.00	7.00	10.00	50.00	500.00	4500.00
☐ 1858O	290,000	10.00	20.00	50.00	140.00	800.00	
☐ 1858S	60,000	15.00	30.00	75.00	300.00	—	
☐ 1859†	430,000	3.00	6.00	10.00	50.00	500.00	5000.00
☐ 1859O	480,000	3.00	6.00	15.00	60.00	500.00	
☐ 1859S	60,000	10.00	30.00	70.00	300.00	—	
☐ 1860S	140,000	4.50	15.00	30.00	175.00	—	

*1856 — Small Date, 1856 — Large Date: Same Price
†There is a recognized pattern in this series - 1859 Transitional Pattern Proof: 10,000

DIMES — LIBERTY SEATED, 1860-1891
with "UNITED STATES OF AMERICA" on Obverse

Mint Marks under or within Wreath on Reverse

DATE	MINTAGE	ABP	G-4 Good	F-12 Fine	EF-40 Ex. Fine	MS-60 Unc.	PRF-65 Proof
☐ 1860	607,000	2.50	5.00	17.00	40.00	275.00	3000.00
☐ 1860O	40,000	225.00	300.00	700.00	1,900.00		
☐ 1861	1,924,000	2.50	5.00	12.00	40.00	250.00	3000.00
☐ 1861S	172,500	10.00	20.00	40.00	175.00	—	
☐ 1862	847,550	2.50	4.00	12.00	40.00	250.00	3000.00
☐ 1862S	180,750	10.00	20.00	40.00	125.00	—	
☐ 1863	14,460	50.00	100.00	175.00	300.00	800.00	3000.00
☐ 1863S	157,000	10.00	20.00	35.00	165.00	1000.00	
☐ 1864	39,070	45.00	105.00	175.00	425.00	700.00	
☐ 1864S	230,000	7.00	15.00	30.00	150.00	1000.00	
☐ 1865	10,500	50.00	100.00	200.00	300.00	700.00	3000.00
☐ 1865S	175,000	7.00	15.00	30.00	140.00	—	
☐ 1866	8,725	60.00	120.00	200.00	400.00	900.00	3000.00
☐ 1866S	135,000	7.00	15.00	20.00	100.00	800.00	
☐ 1867	6,625	75.00	150.00	300.00	400.00	800.00	3000.00
☐ 1867S	140,000	7.00	15.00	30.00	100.00	1000.00	
☐ 1868	466,250	2.50	5.00	7.00	100.00	500.00	3000.00
☐ 1868S	260,000	5.00	10.00	20.00	150.00	800.00	3000.00
☐ 1869	256,600	2.50	5.00	18.00	120.00	600.00	3000.00
☐ 1869S	450,000	4.00	7.00	15.00	90.00	700.00	
☐ 1870	471,500	2.50	5.00	15.00	100.00	400.00	3000.00
☐ 1870S	50,000	30.00	60.00	125.00	300.00	2500.00	
☐ 1871	753,610	2.50	5.00	11.00	40.00	250.00	3000.00
☐ 1871CC	20,100	200.00	350.00	700.00	1800.00		
☐ 1871S	320,000	4.75	15.00	40.00	120.00	800.00	
☐ 1872	2,396,450	2.50	5.00	10.00	40.00	200.00	3000.00
☐ 1872CC	24,000	50.00	175.00	400.00	1000.00		
☐ 1872S	190,000	5.00	20.00	75.00	100.00	1000.00	
☐ 1873*	2,378,500	5.00	10.00	20.00	95.00	500.00	6000.00
☐ 1873** Open "3"	1,508,600	5.00	20.00	50.00	60.00	100.00	
☐ 1873** Close "3"	60,000	12.50	10.00	15.00	70.00	300.00	
☐ 1873CC**	12,400	UNIQUE—ONLY ONE KNOWN					
☐ 1873CC*	18,791	175.00	325.00	625.00	1400.00		
☐ 1873S*	455,000	10.00	18.00	35.00	100.00	800.00	
☐ 1874 w/arrows	2,940,000	7.50	12.00	22.00	100.00	800.00	6000.00
☐ 1874CC w/arrows	10,817	275.00	500.00	1200.00	2800.00		
☐ 1874S w/arrows	240,000	10.00	20.00	70.00	160.00	800.00	
☐ 1875	10,350,000	4.00	7.00	10.00	35.00	400.00	3000.00
☐ 1875CC in Wreath ☐ below Wreath	4,645,000	5.00 5.00	10.00 10.00	20.00 25.00	60.00 60.00	400.00 400.00	
☐ 18875S in Wreath ☐ below Wreath	9,070,000	5.00 3.00	10.00 5.00	20.00 10.00	50.00 40.00	400.00 400.00	
☐ 1876	11,461,150	2.50	5.00	10.00	40.00	400.00	3000.00
☐ 1876CC	8,270,000	2.50	5.00	10.00	40.00	400.00	
☐ 1876S	10,420,000	2.50	5.00	10.00	40.00	400.00	
☐ 1877	7,310,510	2.50	5.00	10.00	40.00	400.00	3000.00
☐ 1877CC	7,700,000	2.50	5.00	10.00	40.00	400.00	
☐ 1877S	2,340,000	2.50	5.00	10.00	40.00	400.00	
☐ 1878	1,678,300	2.50	5.00	10.00	40.00	400.00	3000.00

DATE	MINTAGE	ABP	G-4 Good	F-12 Fine	EF-40 Ex. Fine	MS-60 Unc.	PRF-65 Proof
☐1878CC	200,00	10.00	20.00	45.00	125.00	800.00	
☐1879	15,100	20.00	40.00	70.00	175.00	400.00	3000.00
☐1880	37,355	15.00	30.00	50.00	100.00	400.00	3000.00
☐1881	24,975	25.00	35.00	50.00	150.00	150.00	3000.00
☐18882	3,911,100	2.50	5.00	10.00	40.00	400.00	3000.00
☐1883	7,675,712	2.50	5.00	10.00	40.00	400.00	3000.00
☐1884	3,366,380	2.50	5.00	10.00	40.00	400.00	3000.00
☐1884S	564,969	5.00	10.00	20.00	75.00	400.00	
☐1885	2,533,427	3.00	6.00	12.00	40.00	400.00	3000.00
☐1885S	43,690	50.00	100.00	200.00	400.00	3000.00	
☐1886	6,377,570	2.50	5.00	10.00	35.00	400.00	3000.00
☐1886S	206,524	7.00	15.00	25.00	75.00	400.00	
☐1887	11,283,939	2.50	5.00	10.00	35.00	400.00	3000.00
☐1887S	4,454,450	2.50	5.00	10.00	35.00	400.00	
☐1888	5,496,487	2.50	5.00	10.00	35.00	400.00	3000.00
☐1888S	1,720.000	2.50	5.00	10.00	35.00	400.00	
☐1889	7,380,711	2.50	5.00	10.00	35.00	400.00	3000.00
☐1889S	972,678	4.25	9.00	18.00	50.00	400.00	
☐1890	9,911;541	2.50	5.00	10.00	35.00	400.00	3000.00
☐1890S	1,423,076	4.00	8.00	18.00	50.00	400.00	
☐1891	15,310,600	2.50	5.00	10.00	35.00	400.00	3000.00
☐18910	4,540,000	2.50	5.00	10.00	35.00	400.00	
☐1891S	3,196,116	2.50	5.00	10.00	35.00	400.00	

*With Arrows   **No Arrows

DIMES — LIBERTY HEAD OR BARBER, 1892 - 1916

After many years of using a seated figure of Liberty on the dime, it was decided in 1892 to return to a facial portrait. The designer was Charles E. Barber, resulting in the coin coming to be popularly known among collectors as the "Barber Dime." Liberty wears a wreath and is encircled by the inscription "UNITED STATES OF AMERICA," with the date appearing below the portrait. The reverse is unchanged from that used earlier, the words "ONE DIME" enclosed in a wreath. This coin's weight was set at 2½ grams. Its composition was nine parts silver to one part copper and its diameter 17.9 mm. It was struck at Philadelphia, Denver, San Francisco and New Orleans. The very rare 1894 San Francisco minting, of which only 24 were produced, is the stellar item of this series. In 1916 the Liberty Head design was replaced by the so-called Mercury Head.

Mint Mark is under Wreath on the Reverse

DATE	MINTAGE	ABP	G-4 Good	F-12 Fine	EF-40 Ex. Fine	MS-60 Unc.	PRF-65 Proof
☐1892	12,121,245	1.10	2.00	6.00	25.00	200.00	3000.00
☐1892O	3,841,700	2.00	4.00	12.00	30.00	175.00	
☐1892S	990,710	15.00	30.00	50.00	100.00	200.00	
☐1893	3,340,792	2.50	5.00	15.00	35.00	200.00	3000.00
☐1893, 3 over 2				EXTREMELY RARE			
☐1893O	1,760,000	6.00	12.00	60.00	100.00	200.00	
☐1893S	2,491,401	2.00	5.00	15.00	35.00	175.00	
☐1894	1,330,972	2.50	5.00	20.00	40.00	200.00	3000.00
☐1894O	720,000	12.00	25.00	75.00	100.00	700.00	
☐1894S		EXTREMELY RARE		PRIVATE SALE 1974			97,000.00
☐1895	690,880	20.00	40.00	90.00	175.00	400.00	4000.00
☐1895O	440,000	40.00	90.00	200.00	300.00	700.00	
☐1895S	1,120,000	6.00	12.00	25.00	75.00	225.00	
☐1896	2,000,672	4.00	7.00	18.00	50.00	175.00	3000.00
☐1896O	610,000	12.00	25.00	80.00	175.00	400.00	
☐1896S	575,056	15.00	30.00	75.00	150.00	400.00	
☐1897	10,869,264	1.10	2.00	5.00	30.00	175.00	3000.00
☐1897O	666,000	15.00	30.00	75.00	150.00	500.00	
☐1897S	1,342,844	2.50	5.00	15.00	60.00	200.00	
☐1898	16,320,735	1.10	1.50	5.00	25.00	175.00	3000.00
☐1898O	2,130,000	2.00	4.00	15.00	60.00	250.00	
☐1898S	1,702,507	1.50	3.00	10.00	35.00	175.00	
☐1899	19,580,846	1.00	1.50	5.00	25.00	175.00	3000.00
☐1899O	2,650,000	2.00	4.00	15.00	50.00	275.00	
☐1899S	1,867,493	2.00	4.00	12.00	40.00	200.00	
☐1900	17,600,912	1.10	1.50	5.00	25.00	175.00	3000.00
☐1900O	2,010,000	2.00	5.00	15.00	60.00	300.00	
☐1900S	5,168,270	1.10	1.50	5.00	25.00	175.00	
☐1901	18,860,478	1.10	1.50	4.00	20.00	180.00	3000.00
☐1901O	5,620,000	1.10	1.50	5.00	35.00	350.00	
☐1901S	593,022	15.00	35.00	80.00	175.00	800.00	
☐1902	21,380,777	1.10	1.50	4.00	15.00	175.00	3000.00
☐1902O	4,500,000	1.10	2.00	5.00	30.00	225.00	
☐1902S	2,070,000	1.25	3.00	12.00	40.00	300.00	
☐1903	19,500,755	1.10	1.50	4.00	25.00	175.00	3000.00
☐1903O	8,180,000	1.10	1.50	5.00	30.00	200.00	
☐1903S	613,300	12.00	25.00	50.00	150.00	500.00	
☐1904	14,601,027	1.10	1.50	5.00	25.00	175.00	3000.00
☐1904S	800,000	10.00	22.50	40.00	125.00	550.00	
☐1905	14,552,350	1.10	1.50	4.00	25.00	150.00	3000.00
☐1905O	3,400,000	1.10	1.50	10.00	40.00	200.00	
☐1905S	6,855,199	1.10	1.50	6.00	30.00	175.00	
☐1906	19,958,406	1.10	1.50	2.50	25.00	175.00	3000.00
☐1906D	4,060,000	1.10	1.50	6.00	30.00	175.00	
☐1906O	2,610,000	1.10	2.50	12.00	35.00	175.00	
☐1906S	3,136,640	1.10	2.00	7.00	32.00	175.00	
☐1907	22,220,575	1.10	1.50	3.00	25.00	175.00	3000.00
☐1907D	4,080,000	1.10	1.50	7.00	30.00	175.00	
☐1907O	5,058,000	1.10	1.50	6.00	28.00	175.00	

DATE	MINTAGE	ABP	G-4 Good	F-12 Fine	EF-40 Ex. Fine	MS-60 Unc.	PRF-65 Proof
☐1907S	3,178,470	1.10	1.50	7.00	32.00	300.00	
☐1908	10,600,545	1.10	1.50	4.00	25.00	300.00	3000.00
☐1908D	7,490,000	1.10	1.50	4.00	25.00	300.00	
☐1908O	1,789,000	1.00	3.25	12.00	35.00	200.00	
☐1908S	3,220,000	1.10	2.00	6.00	30.00	200.00	
☐1909	10,240,650	1.10	1.50	4.00	28.00	300.00	3000.00
☐1909D	954,000	1.10	3.25	14.00	52.00	225.00	
☐1909O	2,287,000	1.10	1.50	7.00	32.00	200.00	
☐1909S	2,000,000	1.25	4.00	18.00	55.00	225.00	
☐1910	11,520,551	1.10	1.50	3.00	25.00	300.00	3000.00
☐1910D	3,490,000	1.10	1.50	5.00	30.00	260.00	
☐1910S	1,240,000	1.10	2.50	7.00	35.00	200.00	
☐1911	18,870,543	1.10	1.25	2.50	25.00	300.00	3000.00
☐1911D	11,209,000	1.10	1.50	2.75	25.00	300.00	
☐1911S	3,530,000	1.10	1.50	4.00	32.00	300.00	
☐1912	19,350,700	1.10	1.25	2.50	25.00	300.00	3000.00
☐1912D	11,760,000	1.10	1.25	2.50	25.00	300.00	
☐1912S	3,420,000	1.10	1.50	3.50	30.00	250.00	
☐1913	19,760,000	1.10	1.25	2.50	25.00	180.00	3000.00
☐1913S	510,000	2.75	7.00	28.00	125.00	375.00	
☐1914	17,360,655	1.10	1.25	2.50	25.00	300.00	3500.00
☐1914D	11,908,000	1.10	1.25	2.50	25.00	300.00	
☐1914S	2,100,000	1.10	1.75	3.50	30.00	300.00	
☐1915	5,620,450	1.10	1.50	3.75	28.00	300.00	3000.00
☐1915S	960,000	1.10	2.50	8.00	35.00	225.00	
☐1916	18,490,000	1.10	1.25	2.50	25.00	300.00	
☐1916S	5,820,000	1.10	1.25	2.50	25.00	300.00	

DIMES — MERCURY DIMES, 1916 - 1945

The Mercury Dime is misnamed. The likeness on its obverse is not that of Mercury (a male god) but Liberty, the same mythological figure who had graced dimes since their introduction in 1796. Confusion resulted from the attachment of small wings to Liberty's headdress, which to students of Greek and Roman folklore could only represent Mercury, the "quick messenger," whom the gods equipped with wings to better execute his duties. To give Liberty wings was a bit of poetic license; the intended meaning was "liberty of thought," but so vague was this concept that its purpose remained unserved. On the reverse was an object that caused only slightly less confusion, a vertical column of some kind that only the most astute observers could identify. This was designed as a bundle of fasces or sticks with axe protruding. In Roman times, an imperial or senatorial procession was often accompnied by "fasces bearers" who carried these bundles of wood sticks throughout the streets. Their meaning was supposedly symbolic but they likewise served a practical function: when dusk fell they could be lighted to illuminate the path. Designer of the Mercury

Dime was Adolph Weinman. Its specifications are the same as those of the Barber Dime. The mintmark appears on the reverse, between the words "ONE" and "DIME," to the left of the fasces. The Mercury Dime was composed of 90% silver and 10% copper. It has a weight of 2½ grams and diameter of 17.9 mm.

Mint Mark is on Reverse at Bottom to Left of Branches

Enlargement Showing 1942 over 41 Dime

DATE	MINTAGE	ABP	G-4 Good	F-12 Fine	VF-20 V. Fine	EF-40 Ex. Fine	MS-60 Unc.
☐1916	22,180,000	1.10	1.25	2.00	3.00	7.00	22.00
☐1916D	264,000	250.00	375.00	600.00	800.00	1000.00	2500.00
☐1916S	10,450,000	1.10	2.25	4.50	6.00	10.00	32.00
☐1917	55,230,000	1.10	1.25	1.80	2.50	6.00	25.00
☐1917D	9,402,000	1.10	2.25	7.00	10.00	28.00	125.00
☐1917S	27,330,000	1.10	1.25	2.00	3.25	6.50	68.00
☐1918	26,680,000	1.10	1.25	3.75	7.00	18.00	65.00
☐1918D	22,674,800	1.10	1.75	4.00	6.00	15.00	125.00
☐1918S	19,300,000	1.10	1.25	2.50	5.00	11.00	135.00
☐1919	35,740,000	1.10	1.25	2.25	3.50	7.00	38.00
☐1919D	9,939,000	1.10	2.00	7.00	16.00	30.00	200.00
☐1919S	8,850,000	1.10	2.00	6.00	15.00	25.00	225.00
☐1920	59,030,000	1.10	1.25	1.50	2.25	4.00	22.00
☐1920D	19,171,000	1.10	1.25	2.50	5.00	10.00	100.00
☐1920S	13,820,000	1.10	1.25	2.00	4.00	10.00	100.00
☐1921	1,230,000	8.00	16.00	45.00	85.00	300.00	1200.00
☐1921D	1,080,000	12.00	25.00	60.00	100.00	180.00	1200.00
☐1923*	50,130,000	1.10	1.25	1.75	2.00	3.25	22.00
☐1923S	6,440,000	1.10	1.25	3.50	6.00	22.00	150.00
☐1924	24,010,000	1.10	1.25	1.75	2.00	5.00	45.00
☐1924D	6,810,000	1.10	1.25	3.50	5.25	15.00	175.00
☐1924S	7,120,000	1.10	1.25	3.50	5.25	15.00	175.00
☐1925	25,610,000	1.10	1.25	1.75	2.00	6.00	40.00
☐1925D	5,117,000	1.10	2.00	7.00	24.00	65.00	425.00
☐1925S	5,850,000	1.10	1.25	2.25	6.00	15.00	225.00
☐1926	32,160,000	1.10	1.25	1.50	2.00	4.00	22.00
☐1926D	6,828,000	1.10	1.25	2.00	4.00	14.00	120.00
☐1926S	1,520,000	3.50	6.00	10.00	20.00	60.00	700.00
☐1927	28,080,000	1.10	1.25	1.50	2.00	3.00	22.00
☐1927D	4,812,000	1.10	1.60	4.00	15.00	28.00	280.00
☐1927S	4,770,000	1.10	1.25	2.00	5.00	14.00	200.00
☐1928	19,480,000	1.10	1.25	1.75	2.00	3.00	30.00
☐1928D	4,161,000	1.10	1.25	3.50	12.00	32.00	150.00
☐1928S	7,400,000	1.10	1.25	2.00	3.00	10.00	100.00
☐1929	25,970,000	1.10	1.25	1.50	2.00	3.00	18.00

DATE	MINTAGE	ABP	G-4 Good	F-12 Fine	VF-20 V. Fine	EF-40 Ex. Fine	MS-60 Unc.	PRF-65 Proof
☐ 1929D	5,034,000	1.10	1.25	2.25	4.00	7.00	25.00	
☐ 1929S	4,730,000	1.10	1.25	2.00	2.50	4.00	50.00	
☐ 1930	6,770,000	1.10	1.25	2.00	2.50	4.00	50.00	
☐ 1930S	1,843,000	1.35	2.25	4.00	5.00	9.00	125.00	
☐ 1931	3,150,000	1.10	1.25	2.00	3.00	7.00	50.00	
☐ 1931D	1,260,000	3.75	6.00	8.00	12.00	20.00	125.00	
☐ 1931S	1,800,000	1.35	2.25	4.00	4.50	9.00	125.00	
☐ 1934	24,080,000	1.10	1.25	1.25	1.50	1.75	30.00	
☐ 1934D	6,772,000	1.10	1.25	1.50	1.75	5.00	75.00	
☐ 1935	58,830,000	1.10	1.25	1.50	1.75	2.00	20.00	
☐ 1935D	10,477,000	1.10	1.25	1.50	2.00	7.00	145.00	
☐ 1935S	15,840,000	1.10	1.25	1.50	1.65	2.15	32.00	
☐ 1936	87,504,130	1.10	1.25	1.50	1.65	2.25	16.00	1400.00
☐ 1936D	16,132,000	1.10	1.25	1.40	1.55	4.00	75.00	
☐ 1936S	9,210,000	1.10	1.25	1.40	1.50	2.00	30.00	
☐ 1937	56,865,756	1.10	1.25	1.40	1.50	2.00	10.00	1000.00
☐ 1937D	14,146,000	1.10	1.25	1.40	1.50	2.00	55.00	
☐ 1937S	9,740,000	1.10	1.25	1.40	1.50	2.00	38.00	
☐ 1938	22,198,728	1.10	1.25	1.40	1.50	2.00	10.00	800.00
☐ 1938D	5,537,000	1.10	1.25	1.40	1.50	2.00	40.00	
☐ 1938S	8,090,000	1.10	1.25	1.40	1.50	2.00	45.00	
☐ 1939	67,749,321	1.10	1.25	1.40	1.50	2.00	10.00	700.00
☐ 1939D	24,394,000	1.10	1.25	1.40	1.50	2.00	10.00	
☐ 1939S	10,540,000	1.10	1.25	1.40	1.50	2.00	32.00	
☐ 1940	65,361,827	1.10	1.25	1.40	1.50	2.00	9.00	500.00
☐ 1940D	21,560,000	1.10	1.25	1.40	1.50	2.00	25.00	
☐ 1940S	21,560,000	1.10	1.25	1.40	1.50	2.00	12.00	
☐ 1941	175,106,557	1.10	1.25	1.40	1.50	2.00	6.00	500.00
☐ 1941D	45,634,000	1.10	1.25	1.40	1.50	2.00	25.00	
☐ 1941S	43,090,000	1.10	1.25	1.40	1.50	2.00	10.00	
☐ 1942	205,432,329	1.10	1.25	1.40	1.50	1.75	6.00	500.00
☐ 1942 Part of Above over 41		60.00	175.00	200.00	225.00	300.00	1500.00	
☐ 1942/41-D		120.00	175.00	200.00	225.00	300.00	2000.00	
☐ 1942D	60,740,000	1.10	1.25	1.40	1.50	1.75	15.00	
☐ 1942S	49,300,000	1.10	1.25	1.40	1.50	1.75	25.00	
☐ 1943	191,710,000	1.10	1.25	1.40	1.50	1.75	25.00	
☐ 1943D	71,949,000	1.10	1.25	1.40	1.50	1.75	7.00	
☐ 1943S	60,400,000	1.10	1.25	1.40	1.50	1.75	25.00	
☐ 1944	231,410,000	1.10	1.25	1.40	1.50	1.75	25.00	
☐ 1944D	62,224,000	1.10	1.25	1.40	1.50	1.75	7.00	
☐ 1944S	49,490,000	1.10	1.25	1.40	1.50	1.75	7.00	
☐ 1945	159,130,000	1.10	1.25	1.40	1.50	1.75	5.00	
☐ 1945D	40,245,000	1.10	1.25	1.40	1.50	1.75	10.00	
☐ 1945S	41,920,000	1.10	1.25	1.40	1.50	1.75	10.00	
☐ (Micro S)		1.10	1.25	1.40	1.50	1.75	15.00	

*All Dimes with a 1923D Date are counterfeit.

DIMES — ROOSEVELT, 1946 TO DATE

The Roosevelt Dime series is significant for the change made to clad composition in 1965. Upon the death of President Roosevelt in 1945 there was considerable public sentiment to install his likeness on a coin. The penny, nickel and quarter were not seriously considered as they already carried portraits of former Presidents. As no dollars were being struck this left only the dime and half dollar, which both carried representations of Liberty, as suitable choices. The dime was selected, probably because of the much wider distribution of this coin. The designer was John Sinnock. Roosevelt is shown in profile facing left, with the word "LIBERTY" and the inscription "IN GOD WE TRUST." The bundle of fasces was retained as the central element for the reverse type, which was redrawn. Originally the mint mark appeared on the reverse, as it had on the Mercury Dime, then was switched to the obverse on clad pieces. The weight was 2½ grams. The composition of this coin, originally 90% silver and 10% copper, was altered in 1965 to three parts copper/one part nickel outer covering with an interior of pure copper, yielding a weight of 2.27 grams. The diameter remained 17.9 mm. In the first year of striking the clad pieces, more pieces were manufactured than had ever been turned out of a ten cent piece in the Mint's history, more than 1.6 billion. A serious shortage of dimes had resulted from spectators hoarding the silver coins and this abundant new supply was intended to replace those lost from circulation. A mintage figure of more than two billion was achieved in 1967, or more than $1 worth of dimes for every U.S. citizen.

Mint Mark is on Reverse of Left, Bottom of Torch.

From 1968 Mint Mark at Base of Neck.

DATE	MINTAGE	ABP	MS-60 Unc.	PRF-65 Proof
☐ 1946	255,250,000	1.10	5.00	
☐ 1946D	61,043,500	1.10	6.00	
☐ 1946S	27,900,000	1.10	5.00	
☐ 1947	121,500,000	1.10	5.00	
☐ 1947D	46,835,000	1.10	9.00	
☐ 1947S	34,840,000	1.10	5.00	
☐ 1948	74,950,000	1.10	5.00	
☐ 1948D	52,841,000	1.10	20.00	
☐ 1948S	35,520,000	1.10	6.00	
☐ 1949	30,940,000	1.10	25.00	
☐ 1949D	26,034,000	1.10	7.00	
☐ 1949S	13,510,000	1.10	40.00	
☐ 1950	50,181,500	1.10	5.00	80.00
☐ 1950D	46,803,000	1.10	5.00	
☐ 1950S	20,440,000	1.10	25.00	

DATE	MINTAGE	ABP	MS-60 Unc.	PRF-65 Proof
☐ 1951	103,937,602	1.10	5.00	
☐ 1951D	52,191,800	1.10	5.00	80.00
☐ 1951S	31,630,000	1.10	20.00	
☐ 1952	99,122,073	1.10	5.00	50.00
☐ 1952D	122,100,000	1.10	5.00	
☐ 1952S	44,419,500	1.10	5.00	
☐ 1953	53,618,920	1.10	5.00	30.00
☐ 1953D	156,433,000	1.10	5.00	
☐ 1953S	39,180,000	1.10	5.00	
☐ 1954	114,243,503	1.10	3.00	15.00
☐ 1954D	106,397,000	1.10	3.00	
☐ 1954S	22,860,000	1.10	3.00	
☐ 1955	12,828,381	1.10	4.00	15.00
☐ 1955D	13,959,000	1.10	3.00	
☐ 1955S	18,510,000	1.10	3.00	
☐ 1956	109,309,384	1.10	3.00	5.00
☐ 1956D	108,015,100	1.10	3.00	
☐ 1957	161,407,952	1.10	3.00	4.00
☐ 1957D	113,354,330	1.10	3.00	
☐ 1958	32,785,652	1.10	3.00	5.00
☐ 1958D	136,564,600	1.10	3.00	
☐ 1959	86,929,291	1.10	2.00	4.00
☐ 1959D	164,919,790	1.10	2.00	
☐ 1960	72,081,602	1.10	2.00	4.00
☐ 1960D	200,160,400	1.10	2.00	
☐ 1961	96,756,244	1.10	2.00	3.00
☐ 1961D	209,146,550	1.10	2.00	
☐ 1962	75,668,019	1.10	2.00	3.00
☐ 1962D	334,948,380	1.10	2.00	
☐ 1963	126,725,645	1.10	2.00	3.00
☐ 1963D	421,476,530	1.10	2.00	
☐ 1964	933,310,762	1.10	2.00	3.00
☐ 1964D	1,357,517,180	1.10	2.00	
☐ 1965 Clad Coinage Begins	1,652,140,570		.15	
☐ 1966	1,382,734,540		.15	
☐ 1967	2,244,077,300		.15	
☐ 1968	424,470,400		.15	
☐ 1968D	480,748,280		.15	
☐ 1968S Proof Only	3,041,508			.36
☐ 1969	145,790,000		.25	
☐ 1969D	563,323,870		.15	
☐ 1969S Proof Only	2,934,631			.36
☐ 1970	345,570,000		.15	
☐ 1970D	754,942,000		.15	
☐ 1970S Proof Only	2,632,810			.60
☐ 1971	162,690,000		.15	
☐ 1971D	377,914,240		.15	
☐ 1971S Proof Only	3,244,138			.36
☐ 1972	431,540,000		.15	

DATE	MINTAGE	MS-60 Unc.	PRF-65 Proof
☐ 1972D	330,290,000	.15	
☐ 1972S Proof Only	3,267,667		.36
☐ 1973	315,670,000	.15	
☐ 1973D	455,032,426	.15	
☐ 1973 Proof Only	2,769,624		.56
☐ 1974	470,248,000	.15	
☐ 1974D	571,083,000	.15	
☐ 1974S Proof Only	2,617,350		.70
☐ 1975	585,673,900	.15	
☐ 1975S Proof Only	2,909,369		.82
☐ 1976	568,760,000	.20	
☐ 1976D	695,222,774	.15	
☐ 1976S Proof Only	4,149,945		.42
☐ 1977	796,900,480	.15	
☐ 1977D	376,610,420	.15	
☐ 1977S Proof Only	3,250,895		.38
☐ 1978	663,908,000	.15	
☐ 1978D	282,847,540	.15	
☐ 1978S Proof Only	3,127,781		.48
☐ 1979		.15	
☐ 1979D		.15	
☐ 1979S Proof Only			.70

TWENTY-CENT PIECES — LIBERTY SEATED, 1875 - 1878

The 20¢ piece has the unenviable distinction of being the shortest-lived of any U.S. coin. Authorized by a Congressional Act on March 3, 1875, it was placed into production immediately thereafter, with manufacture divided up between the Philadelphia, San Francisco and Carson City mints (mints on the east and west coasts being employed in hopes the coin would distribute more evenly in circulation than if released exclusively from a single source of production). Designed by William Barber, it pictured a figure of the goddess Liberty seated on the obverse, framed by stars, with an eagle on the reverse. It was composed of nine-tenths silver and one-tenth copper, with a weight of five grams and a diameter of 22 mm. Despite high hopes the 20¢ piece never achieved popularity, the chief reason for its rejection being the physical similarity to the quarter. Production was greatly cut back in 1876 and discontinued two years thereafter. All told, less than a million and half were struck.

DATE	MINTAGE	ABP	G-4 Good	F-12 Fine	EF-40 Ex. Fine	MS-60 Unc.	PRF-65 Proof
☐ 1875	39,700	25.00	42.00	70.00	200.00	1400.00	6000.00
☐ 1875CC	133,290	25.00	46.00	62.50	160.00	850.00	
☐ 1875S	1,155,000	23.00	38.00	50.00	200.00	100.00	
☐ 1876	15,900	40.00	60.00	100.00	250.00	1400.00	6000.00
☐ 1876CC	10,000	(EXTREMELY RARE) A.N.A. SALE 1978 39,500.00					
☐ 1877	510	3500.00					7000.00
☐ 1878	600	3500.00					7000.00

QUARTERS — EARLY QUARTERS, 1796 - 1866

It became evident from a very early period that the quarter or 25¢ piece would be the most significant division of the dollar in everyday commerce. However, the effect was not fully felt until the 19th century. Striking of the quarter dollar was authorized in 1792 along with other denominations, upon establishment of a national currency. No actual specimens came into circulation until 1796. The earliest design was the Draped Bust portrait of Liberty, common to other silver coinage, with eagle reverse and the legend "UNITED STATES OF AMERICA." Stars appeared alongside Liberty on the obverse and her name was affixed above the portrait, with the date below. The designer was Robert Scot. The original quarter dollar was composed of .8924 silver alloyed with .1076 copper, or roughtly a nine-to-one ratio. Its weight was 6.74 grams and the diameter generally 27½ mm. with slight variations to be observed according to the flatness of the planchet. Only 6,146 pieces were struck in 1796 as a trial issue (influenced in some measure by a shortage of silver) and this date has become scarce, even in less than the best condition. Production of quarters was not resumed until 1804, when discontinuation of dollar coins increased the need for them. The Draped Bust type was retained but the reverse changed to the Heraldic or Shield Eagle design. John Reich designed a new quarter dollar in 1815, identical in composition to its predecessors but have a slightly smaller diameter, 27 mm. This was the Capped Bust type, with naturalistic shielded eagle on the reverse. Production got off to a small start but was rapidly expanded. No further change occured until 1831 when the coin was brought down in size to 24.3 mm. but was made a bit thicker, retaining the old weight of 6.74 grams. The designer of this new 25¢ piece was William Kneass (pronounced Niece) and all striking was done at Philadelphia. There is a "small letters" and "large letters" variety of this design, with little influence on value. The portrait is a somewhat streamlined Capped Liberty who appears more noble than previously. This design was of short duration, replaced by the Seated Liberty type in 1838. On the reverse was the shield eagle, beneath which appeared the words "QUAR. DOL." (The use of abbreviations did not fully meet the approval of artistic-minded persons.) There was an accompanying change in specifications as well. The silver content was slightly raised, to an even 90%; the copper dropped to an even 10%; and the weight went down to 6.68 grams. The diameter was the same as previously. Designer of this coin was Christian Gobrecht. It was stuck at both Philadelphia and New Orleans. A further reduction in weight was made to 6.22 grams in 1853; arrows were placed at the dates to remind users of the coin that it contained less silver than previously. Compositionally it was unaltered, with nine parts silver to one of copper. On the reverse, sunrays sprang from behind the eagle, an area of the design which previously had been blank. This addition was made for the same reason as the arrows.

QUARTERS — DRAPED BUST, 1796 - 1807

1796-1807

1796 Small Eagle

1804-1807 Large Eagle

DATE	MINTAGE	ABP	G-4 Good	F-12 Fine	VF-20 V. Fine	MS-60 Unc.
☐ 1796	5,894	850.00	1500.00	3000.00	6000.00	25000.00
☐ 1804	6,738	150.00	300.00	1500.00	2800.00	22000.00
☐ 1805	121,394	60.00	150.00	400.00	800.00	4000.00
☐ 1806	206,124	60.00	150.00	400.00	800.00	4000.00
☐ 1806 over 5		60.00	150.00	400.00	800.00	4000.00
☐ 1807	220,643	60.00	150.00	400.00	800.00	4000.00

QUARTERS — LIBERTY CAP, 1815 - 1838

1815-1838

1815-1828 Motto over Eagle

1831-1838 Without Motto

DATE	MINTAGE	ABP	G-4 Good	F-12 Fine	VF-20 V. Fine	MS-60 Unc.	PRF-65 Proof
☐ 1815	89,235	25.00	40.00	100.00	300.00	3500.00	
☐ 1818	361,174	25.00	40.00	100.00	300.00	3500.00	
☐ 1818 over 15	361,174	25.00	40.00	100.00	300.00	3500.00	
☐ 1819*	144,000	25.00	40.00	100.00	300.00	3500.00	
☐ 1820**	127,440	25.00	40.00	100.00	175.00	3500.00	
☐ 1821	216,850	25.00	40.00	100.00	200.00	3500.00	
☐ 1822	64,084	25.00	40.00	100.00	200.00	3500.00	
☐ 1822 (25 over $.50)		90.00	175.00	425.00	750.00	3500.00	
☐ 1823 over 22†	17,801	600.00	1200.00	6000.00	10000.00		32000.00
☐ 1824		20.00	40.00	75.00	175.00	3500.00	
☐ 1825 over dates	168,000	25.00	40.00	100.00	225.00	3500.00	
☐ 1827 (original)††	4,000		few pieces known — RARE				27000.00
☐ 1828	102,000	25.00	40.00	100.00	375.00	3500.00	
☐ 1828 (25 over $.50)	102,000	40.00	70.00	125.00	425.00	3500.00	
REDUCED SIZE — NO MOTTO ON REVERSE							
☐ 1831***	398,000	25.00	35.00	40.00	150.00	2000.00	
☐ 1832	320,000	25.00	35.00	40.00	150.00	2000.00	
☐ 1833	156,000	25.00	35.00	40.00	150.00	2000.00	

DATE	MINTAGE	ABP	G-4 Good	F-12 Fine	VF-20 V. Fine	MS-60 Unc.
☐1834	286,000	25.00	35.00	40.00	150.00	2000.00
☐1835	1,952,000	25.00	35.00	40.00	150.00	2000.00
☐1836	472,000	25.00	35.00	40.00	150.00	2000.00
☐1837	252,000	25.00	35.00	40.00	150.00	2000.00
☐1838 — Small 9, 1819	832,000	25.00	35.00	40.00	150.00	2000.00

*1819 — Small 9, 1819 — Large 9. **1820 — Small o, 1820 — Large 0: Same Price.
***1831 — Small Letters, 1831 — Large Letters: Same Price. †Stack's Auction, March 1977. ††Stack's Auction, 1977: also 1827 restrike proof 12,500.00.

QUARTERS — LIBERTY SEATED, 1838 - 1865
No Motto Above Eagle

1838-1865

1853 With Rays

Mint Mark is Below Eagle on Reverse
1838-1852
1854-1865
Without Rays

DATE	MINTAGE	ABP	G-4 Good	F-12 Fine	EF-40 Ex. Fine	MS-60 Unc.
☐1838*	832,000	8.00	15.00	25.00	150.00	3000.00
☐1839*	491,146	8.00	15.00	25.00	150.00	3000.00
☐1840**	188,127	10.00	20.00	40.00	150.00	2200.00
☐1840O	425,200	8.00	15.00	25.00	150.00	3000.00
☐1840O**		8.00	20.00	45.00	150.00	1500.00
☐1841	120,000	12.00	25.00	65.00	175.00	950.00
☐1841O	452,000	7.00	15.00	30.00	150.00	700.00
☐1842	88,000	25.00	55.00	125.00	325.00	1800.00
☐1842O Small Date	769,000	150.00	300.00	500.00	1400.00	
☐1842O Large Date		12.00	25.00	50.00	115.00	
☐1843	645,000	5.00	10.00	20.00	65.00	900.00
☐1843O Small "O"	968,000	10.00	20.00	50.00	300.00	
☐1843O Large "O"		10.00	20.00	50.00	300.00	
☐1844	421,000	6.00	12.00	20.00	75.00	600.00
☐1844O	740,000	6.00	12.00	20.00	75.00	1000.00
☐1845	922,000	6.00	12.00	20.00	75.00	600.00
☐1846	510,000	6.00	12.00	20.00	75.00	600.00
☐1847	734,000	6.00	12.00	20.00	75.00	600.00
☐1847O	368,000	10.00	20.00	45.00	165.00	600.00
☐1848	146,000	6.00	15.00	25.00	125.00	750.00
☐1849	340,000	6.00	15.00	25.00	125.00	700.00
☐1849O	16,000	125.00	325.00	725.00	2500.00	
☐1850	190,800	7.00	15.00	40.00	100.00	625.00
☐1850O	412,000	12.00	25.00	65.00	150.00	625.00
☐1851	160,000	12.00	25.00	65.00	150.00	625.00
☐1851O	88,000	80.00	165.00	325.00	1000.00	
☐1852	177,060	12.00	25.00	50.00	125.00	750.00
☐1852O	96,000	100.00	200.00	400.00	1100.00	

DATE	MINTAGE	ABP	G-4 Good	F-12 Fine	EF-40 Ex. Fine	MS-60 Unc.	PRF-65 Proof
☐1853***	15,210,020	4.00	8.00	12.00	125.00	1250.00	
☐1853/4		35.00	75.00	325.00	1000.00	4000.00	
☐1853††	44,200	5.00	10.00	20.00	100.00	1200.00	
☐1853O***	1,332,000	5.00	10.00	20.00	100.00	1200.00	
☐1854†	12,380,000	4.00	8.00	16.00	80.00	900.00	
☐1854†O Large "O"	1,484,000	4.00	8.00	16.00	80.00	900.00	
☐1854O Huge "O"		75.00	150.00	350.00	1200.00		
☐1855†	2,857,000	5.00	10.00	20.00	75.00	900.00	5000.00
☐1855O†	176,000	20.00	40.00	75.00	325.00	1200.00	
☐1855S†	396,400	15.00	32.00	70.00	275.00	1200.00	
☐1856	7,264,000	5.00	10.00	15.00	70.00	650.00	4000.00
☐1856O	968,000	10.00	20.00	40.00	125.00	700.00	
☐1856S		15.00	30.00	70.00	175.00		
☐1856S over S	286,000	45.00	100.00	400.00	1200.00		
☐1857	9,644,000	5.00	10.00	20.00	65.00	600.00	4000.00
☐1857O	1,180,000	7.00	15.00	30.00	100.00	625.00	
☐1857S	82,000	25.00	50.00	80.00	400.00		
☐1858	7,368,000	5.00	10.00	20.00	75.00	600.00	4000.00
☐1858O	520,000	10.00	20.00	40.00	125.00	650.00	
☐1858S	121,000	12.00	25.00	65.00	200.00		
☐1859	1,344,000	7.00	15.00	20.00	60.00	600.00	4000.00
☐1859O	260,000	15.00	35.00	75.00	200.00	650.00	
☐1859S	80,000	25.00	50.00	125.00	400.00		
☐1860	805,400	7.00	15.00	25.00	65.00	600.00	4000.00
☐1860O	388,000	10.00	20.00	40.00	150.00	700.00	
☐1860S	56,000	30.00	60.00	200.00	550.00		
☐1861	4,854,000	5.00	10.00	20.00	65.00	600.00	4000.00
☐1861S	96,000	12.00	25.00	50.00	200.00	2500.00	
☐1862	932,550	7.00	15.00	20.00	50.00	600.00	4000.00
☐1862S	67,000	15.00	30.00	70.00	250.00		
☐1863	192,060	8.00	15.00	30.00	75.00	700.00	4000.00
☐1864	94,070	15.00	30.00	50.00	125.00	1100.00	4000.00
☐1864S	20,000	60.00	125.00	300.00	1000.00		
☐1865	59,300	20.00	40.00	70.00	150.00	800.00	4000.00
☐1865S	41,000	20.00	35.00	75.00	250.00	1800.00	

☐1866 Only One Known — Hydeman Sale 1961 Proof — $24,500.00

*No Drapery **Drapery ***W/Arrows and Rays †W/Arrows and no Rays
††Over 53, No Arrows

QUARTERS — LIBERTY SEATED, 1866 - 1891
Motto Above Eagle

In 1866 the words "IN GOD WE TRUST" were added to the reverse, on a banner between the eagle and the inscription "UNITED STATES OF AMERICA." When the weight was changed slightly to 6.25 grams in 1873 the arrows were returned but no further use was made of sunrays on the reverse. The arrows were removed in 1875.

Arrows at Date

Motto Above Eagle

Mint Mark is Below Eagle on Reverse

DATE	MINTAGE	ABP	G-4 Good	F-12 Fine	EF-40 Ex. Fine	MS-60 Unc.	PRF-65 Proof
☐ 1866	17,525	80.00	175.00	300.00	500.00	1000.00	4000.00
☐ 1866S	28,000	20.00	45.00	120.00	300.00		
☐ 1867	20,625	40.00	80.00	150.00	295.00	725.00	4000.00
☐ 1867S	48,000	15.00	35.00	80.00	250.00	2800.00	
☐ 1868	30,000	20.00	40.00	100.00	200.00	600.00	4000.00
☐ 1868S	96,000	12.00	25.00	70.00	125.00	1600.00	
☐ 1869	16,600	80.00	175.00	300.00	500.00	1000.00	4000.00
☐ 1869S	76,000	10.00	25.00	70.00	125.00		
☐ 1870	87,400	10.00	20.00	45.00	170.00	850.00	4000.00
☐ 1870CC	8,340	300.00	700.00	1400.00	2800.00		
☐ 1871	171,232	5.50	10.00	30.00	80.00	800.00	4000.00
☐ 1871CC	10,890	1750.00	400.00	800.00	1800.00		
☐ 1871S	30,900	75.00	150.00	350.00	700.00	1800.00	
☐ 1872	182,950	5.50	10.00	30.00	100.00	500.00	4000.00
☐ 1872CC	9,100	100.00	200.00	425.00	1250.00		
☐ 1872S	103,000	75.00	150.00	350.00	700.00	3250.00	
☐ 1873*	1,263,700	10.00	20.00	30.00	150.00	1000.00	4000.00
☐ 1873** Open "3"	220,600	15.00	30.00	60.00	200.00	700.00	
☐ 1873** Closed "3"		30.00	65.00	175.00	350.00		4000.00
☐ 1873CC*	12,462	200.00	400.00	800.00	1800.00		
☐ 1873CC**	4,000	RARE—Unc. 80,000.00 Stack Sale, 1975					
☐ 1873S	15,600	10.00	20.00	40.00	200.00	900.00	
☐ 1874*	471,900	10.00	20.00	30.00	175.00	950.00	4000.00
☐ 1874S*	392,000	8.00	15.00	35.00	200.00	950.00	

Arrows Removed Starting 1875

☐ 1875	4,293,500	3.00	7.00	15.00	50.00	800.00	4000.00
☐ 1875CC	140,000	18.50	35.00	75.00	250.00	1200.00	
☐ 1875S	680,000	6.00	15.00	40.00	100.00	800.00	
☐ 1876	17,817,150	3.00	6.00	15.00	50.00	800.00	4000.00
☐ 1876CC	4,944,000	5.50	10.00	20.00	80.00	800.00	
☐ 1876S	8,596,000	4.00	8.00	15.00	50.00	800.00	
☐ 1877	10,911,710	3.00	6.00	15.00	50.00	800.00	4000.00
☐ 1877CC	4,192,000	5.50	10.00	20.00	75.00	800.00	
☐ 1877S	8,996,000	5.50	10.00	20.00	75.00	800.00	
☐ 1878	2,260,000	5.50	10.00	20.00	75.00	800.00	4000.00
☐ 1878CC	996,000	7.00	14.00	28.00	85.00	800.00	

DATE	MINTAGE	ABP	G-4 Good	F-12 Fine	EF-40 Ex. Fine	MS-60 Unc.	PRF-65 Proof
☐1878S	140,000	15.00	30.00	80.00	210.00	1400.00	
☐1879	14,700	30.00	60.00	100.00	175.00	800.00	4000.00
☐1880	14,955	30.00	60.00	100.00	175.00	800.00	4000.00
☐1881	12,975	30.00	60.00	100.00	175.00	800.00	4000.00
☐1882	16,300	30.00	60.00	100.00	175.00	800.00	4000.00
☐1883	15,439	30.00	60.00	100.00	175.00	800.00	4000.00
☐1884	8,875	40.00	80.00	150.00	250.00	800.00	4000.00
☐1885	14,530	40.00	80.00	150.00	250.00	800.00	4000.00
☐1886	5,886	75.00	150.00	225.00	375.00	800.00	4000.00
☐1887	10,710	40.00	75.00	125.00	225.00	800.00	4000.00
☐1888	10,833	40.00	75.00	125.00	225.00	800.00	4000.00
☐1888S	1,216,000	4.00	7.00	15.00	50.00	800.00	
☐1889	12,711	35.00	75.00	125.00	225.00	800.00	4000.00
☐1890	80,590	15.00	30.00	50.00	100.00	800.00	4000.00
☐1891	3,920,600	4.00	8.00	15.00	50.00	800.00	4000.00
☐1891O	68,000	60.00	115.00	200.00	500.00		
☐1891S	2,216,000	5.00	10.00	25.00	50.00	800.00	

*W/Arrows **No Arrows

QUARTERS — BARBER OR LIBERTY HEAD, 1892 - 1916

The Barber or Liberty Head Quarter with its classical portrait bust was introduced in 1892 after a design by Charles E. Barber. Liberty faces right and wears a cap and laurel wreath. On the reverse is a shield eagle holding arrows and branch, with (at long last) the words "QUARTER DOLLAR" spelled out without abbreviation. This was without doubt the handsomest design in the quarter dollar series and has become extremely popular with collectors. It was struck at Philadelphia, Denver, New Orleans and San Francisco. The Barber quarter has a composition of 90% silver and 10% copper with a weight of 6¼ grams and a diameter of 24.3 mm.

Mint Mark is below the Eagle on Reverse

DATE	MINTAGE	ABP	G-4 Good	F-12 Fine	EF-40 Ex. Fine	MS-60 Unc.	PRF-65 Proof
1892	8,237,245	2.75	4.50	10.00	60.00	400.00	4000.00
☐1892O	2,640,000	2.75	5.00	15.00	60.00	400.00	
☐1892S	964,079	5.50	10.00	30.00	100.00	400.00	
☐1893	5,444,815	2.75	4.00	12.00	65.00	450.00	4000.00
☐1893O	3,396,000	2.75	5.00	12.00	65.00	450.00	

DATE	MINTAGE	ABP	G-4 Good	F-12 Fine	EF-40 Ex. Fine	MS-60 Unc.	PRF-65 Proof
☐1893S	1,454,535	2.75	6.00	20.00	75.00	450.00	
☐1894	3,432,972	2.75	5.00	12.00	65.00	450.00	4000.00
☐1894O	2,852,000	2.75	6.00	20.00	65.00	450.00	
☐1894S	2,648,821	2.75	5.00	16.00	70.00	450.00	
☐1895	4,440,880	2.75	5.00	10.00	60.00	450.00	2000.00
☐1895O	2,816,000	2.75	5.00	15.00	65.00	400.00	
☐1895S	1,764,681	2.75	6.00	20.00	75.00	450.00	
☐1896	3,874,762	2.75	4.00	10.00	60.00	450.00	4000.00
☐1896O	1,484,000	2.75	6.00	18.00	75.00	590.00	
☐1896S	188,039	65.00	180.00	400.00	800.00	2200.00	
☐1897	8,140,731	2.75	4.00	10.00	60.00	450.00	4000.00
☐1897O	1,414,800	5.00	7.00	22.00	80.00	600.00	
☐1897S	542,229	5.50	12.00	30.00	100.00	500.00	
☐1898	11,100,735	2.75	4.00	9.00	60.00	450.00	4000.00
☐1898O	1,868,000	2.75	5.00	18.00	70.00	400.00	
☐1898S	1,020,592	2.75	5.00	15.00	60.00	400.00	
☐1899	12,624,846	2.75	4.00	8.00	55.00	450.00	4000.00
☐1899O	2,644,000	2.75	5.00	16.00	65.00	400.00	
☐1899S	708,000	4.25	7.00	25.00	75.00	400.00	
☐1900	10,016,912	2.75	4.00	8.00	60.00	450.00	4000.00
☐1900O	3,416,000	2.75	6.00	20.00	78.00	400.00	
☐1900S	1,858,585	2.75	5.00	10.00	55.00	450.00	
☐1901	8,892,813	2.75	4.00	10.00	60.00	450.00	4000.00
☐1901O	1,612,000	4.85	10.00	38.00	125.00	400.00	
☐1901S	72,664	200.00	500.00	800.00	1500.00	5500.00	
☐1902	12,197,744	2.75	4.00	9.00	55.00	450.00	4000.00
☐1902O	4,748,000	2.75	5.00	10.00	60.00	450.00	
☐1902S	1,524,612	2.75	8.00	20.00	75.00	450.00	
☐1903	9,670,064	2.75	5.00	9.00	60.00	350.00	4000.00
☐1903O	3,500,000	2.75	6.00	10.00	70.00	400.00	
☐1903S	1,036,000	2.75	9.00	20.00	80.00	400.00	
☐1904	9,588,813	2.75	5.00	10.00	50.00	325.00	4000.00
☐1904O	2,456,000	2.80	5.00	15.00	90.00	400.00	
☐1905	4,968,250	2.75	5.00	10.00	60.00	325.00	4000.00
☐1905O	1,230,000	2.75	7.00	20.00	100.00	470.00	
☐1905S	1,884,000	2.75	5.00	13.00	60.00	350.00	
☐1906	3,656,435	2.75	6.00	13.00	60.00	350.00	4000.00
☐1906D	3,280,000	2.75	6.00	13.00	60.00	350.00	
☐1906O	2,056,000	2.75	6.00	13.00	60.00	350.00	
☐1907	7,192,575	2.75	4.00	8.00	50.00	325.00	4000.00
☐1907D	2,484,000	2.75	6.00	15.00	70.00	350.00	
☐1907O	4,560,000	2.75	5.00	12.00	60.00	350.00	
☐1907S	1,360,000	2.75	5.00	12.00	60.00	350.00	
☐1908	4,232,545	2.75	4.00	9.00	63.00	325.00	4000.00
☐1908D	5,788,000	2.75	4.00	8.00	50.00	325.00	
☐1908O	6,244,000	2.75	4.00	8.00	50.00	325.00	
☐1908S	784,000	3.85	7.00	15.00	75.00	425.00	
☐1909	9,268,650	2.75	4.00	8.00	50.00	300.00	4000.00
☐1909D	5,114,000	2.75	4.00	8.00	50.00	325.00	

DATE	MINTAGE	ABP	G-4 Good	F-12 Fine	EF-40 Ex. Fine	MS-60 Unc.	PRF-65 Proof
☐ 19090	712,000	4.00	8.00	35.00	125.00	500.00	
☐ 1909S	1,348,000	2.75	4.00	8.00	60.00	350.00	
☐ 1910	2,244,551	2.75	4.00	9.00	65.00	325.00	4000.00
☐ 1910D	1,500,000	2.75	6.00	15.00	65.00	350.00	
☐ 1911	3,270,543	2.75	4.00	10.00	60.00	325.00	4000.00
☐ 1911D	933,600	2.75	5.00	18.00	75.00	375.00	
☐ 1911S	988,000	2.75	5.00	15.00	75.00	350.00	
☐ 1912	4,400,700	2.75	4.00	9.00	55.00	325.00	4000.00
☐ 1912S	708,000	2.75	5.00	15.00	70.00	375.00	
☐ 1913	484,613	5.00	7.00	35.00	200.00	600.00	4000.00
☐ 1913D	1,450,800	2.75	6.00	15.00	60.00	325.00	
☐ 1913S	40,000	60.00	200.00	400.00	900.00	4000.00	
☐ 1914	6,244,610	2.75	4.00	8.00	50.00	325.00	4000.00
☐ 1914D	3,046,000	2.75	4.00	8.00	50.00	325.00	
☐ 1914S	264,000	5.25	10.00	30.00	125.00	400.00	
☐ 1915	3,480,450	2.75	4.00	8.00	50.00	325.00	4000.00
☐ 1915D	3,694,000	2.75	4.00	8.00	50.00	325.00	
☐ 1915S	704,000	2.75	5.00	12.00	75.00	350.00	
☐ 1916	1,788,000	2.75	4.00	8.00	55.00	325.00	
☐ 1916D	6,540,000	2.75	4.00	8.00	55.00	325.00	

QUARTERS — STANDING LIBERTY, 1916 - 1930

The Standing Liberty Quarter was introduced in 1916 during World War I and its theme was intended to reflect the nation's sentiments at that time. The goddess is portrayed in full length holding a shield with which she, presumably, fends off the defilers of liberty. An eagle in flight is pictured on the obverse, with the words "UNITED STATES OF AMERICA" and "E PLURIBUS UNUM." The designer was Herman A. MacNeil. Specifications are the same as for the Barber Quarter. This design carried so much fine detailing that very moderate handling resulted in obvious wear, making uncirculated specimens more valuable, proportionately, than in the case of most other coins. The chief point of vulnerability was the date, so small in size, and positioned in such a way as to receive heavy wear, that many specimens lost their date after only a few years of circulation. The government wished to correct this fault without totally redesigning the obverse and in 1925 hit upon the plan of showing the date in incuse — that is, pressed into the coin rather than raised from its surface. While this did not totally prevent wear it helped keep the dates readable for a longer time. A series of minor alterations was made in 1917, the second year of issue, including a dressing up of Liberty to satisfy public criticism that the figure was displaying a scandalous amount of flesh. Three stars were added beneath the eagle on the reverse.

1916-30 — Mint Mark is to left of Date of Obverse

1916-1917 — No stars Under Eagle

1917-1930 — 3 Stars Under Eagle

DATE	MINTAGE	ABP	G-4 Good	VG-8 V. Good	F-12 Fine	EF-40 Ex. Fine	MS-60 Unc.
☐ 1916	52,000	350.00	700.00	800.00	1000.00	2000.00	3500.00
☐ 1917	8,792,000	3.00	7.00	10.00	15.00	50.00	300.00
☐ 1917D	1,509,200	4.00	8.00	10.00	15.00	60.00	300.00
☐ 1917S	1,952,000	4.00	8.00	10.00	15.00	60.00	300.00

STARS UNDER EAGLE

DATE	MINTAGE	ABP	G-4 Good	VG-8 V. Good	F-12 Fine	EF-40 Ex. Fine	MS-60 Unc.
☐ 1917	13,880,000	2.25	7.00	10.00	15.00	40.00	100.00
☐ 1917D	6,224,400	6.00	12.00	15.00	25.00	50.00	100.00
☐ 1917S	5,552,000	6.00	12.00	15.00	25.00	50.00	100.00
☐ 1918	12,240,000	4.00	8.00	10.00	15.00	40.00	100.00
☐ 1918D	7,380,000	5.00	10.00	12.00	18.00	40.00	100.00
☐ 1918S	11,072,000	4.00	8.00	10.00	15.00	45.00	110.00
☐ 1918S over 7	11,072,000	150.00	300.00	400.00	600.00	1500.00	7000.00
☐ 1919	11,324,000	9.00	18.00	22.00	25.00	40.00	200.00
☐ 1919D	1,944,000	15.00	30.00	40.00	60.00	125.00	275.00
☐ 1919S	1,836,000	15.00	30.00	45.00	60.00	125.00	275.00
☐ 1920	27,860,000	3.00	6.00	9.00	12.00	30.00	100.00
☐ 1920D	3,586,400	7.00	14.00	20.00	30.00	65.00	125.00
☐ 1920S	6,380,000	4.00	8.00	12.00	15.00	35.00	100.00
☐ 1921	1,916,000	15.00	30.00	40.00	70.00	160.00	275.00
☐ 1923	9,716,000	3.00	6.00	9.00	12.00	30.00	125.00
☐ 1923S*	1,360,000	20.00	40.00	60.00	80.00	150.00	375.00
☐ 1924	10,920,000	3.00	6.00	8.00	10.00	30.00	100.00
☐ 1924D	3,112,000	7.00	15.00	20.00	30.00	75.00	125.00
☐ 1924S	2,860,000	4.00	8.00	12.00	18.00	45.00	125.00
☐ 1925	12,280,000	2.75	4.00	6.00	7.50	30.00	100.00
☐ 1926	11,316,000	2.75	4.00	6.00	7.50	30.00	100.00
☐ 1926D	1,716,000	2.75	4.00	5.00	10.00	45.00	100.00
☐ 1926S	2,700,000	2.75	4.00	5.00	8.00	40.00	180.00
☐ 1927	11,912,000	2.75	4.00	4.00	7.00	30.00	100.00
☐ 1927D	976,400	2.75	5.00	6.00	12.00	50.00	125.00
☐ 1927S	396,000	3.00	7.00	8.00	25.00	200.00	1000.00
☐ 1928	6,336,000	2.75	4.00	6.00	8.00	30.00	175.00
☐ 1928D	1,627,600	2.75	4.00	6.00	8.50	30.00	175.00
☐ 1928S	2,644,000	2.75	4.00	6.00	8.50	30.00	175.00
☐ 1929	11,140,000	2.75	4.00	6.00	7.00	30.00	175.00
☐ 1929D	1,358,000	2.75	4.00	5.00	7.00	30.00	175.00
☐ 1929S	1,764,000	2.75	4.00	6.00	8.00	50.00	175.00
☐ 1930	5,632,000	2.75	4.00	6.00	8.50	28.00	175.00
☐ 1930S	1,556,000	2.75	4.00	6.00	6.00	30.00	175.00

*Check for altered Date.

QUARTERS — WASHINGTON, 1932 TO DATE

1932-1967 Mint Mark is on Reverse Below Eagle

1968 on — Mint Mark to Right of Hair Ribbon

DATE	MINTAGE	ABP	G-4 Good	F-12 Fine	EF-40 Ex. Fine	MS-60 Unc.	PRF-65 Proof
☐1932	5,404,000	2.75	4.00	6.00	7.00	40.00	
☐1932D	436,800	18.00	35.00	40.00	75.00	750.00	
☐1932S	408,000	15.00	32.00	37.00	50.00	360.00	
☐1934	31,912,052	2.75	4.00	6.00	7.00	20.00	
☐1934 Double Die			35.00	45.00	100.00	250.00	
☐1934D	3,527,200	2.75	4.00	6.00	15.00	150.00	
☐1935	32,484,000	2.75	4.00	6.00	7.00	50.00	
☐1935D	5,780,000	2.75	4.00	6.00	15.00	150.00	
☐1935S	5,550,000	2.75	4.00	6.00	7.00	125.00	
☐1936	41,303,837	2.75	4.00	6.00	7.00	50.00	800.00
☐1936D	5,374,000	2.75	4.00	6.00	40.00	325.00	
☐1936S	3,828,000	2.75	4.00	6.00	7.00	80.00	
☐1937	19,701,542	2.75	4.00	6.00	7.00	20.00	250.00
☐1937D	7,189,600	2.75	4.00	6.00	7.00	60.00	
☐1937S	1,652,000	2.75	4.00	6.00	20.00	150.00	
☐1938	9,480,045	2.75	4.00	6.00	8.00	80.00	225.00
☐1938S	2,832,000	2.75	4.00	6.00	8.50	90.00	
☐1939	33,548,795	2.75	4.00	6.00	7.00	40.00	100.00
☐1939D	7,092,000	2.75	4.00	6.00	7.00	45.00	
☐1939S	2,628,000	2.75	4.00	6.00	9.00	65.00	
☐1940	35,715,246	2.75	4.00	6.00	7.00	35.00	90.00
☐1940D	2,797,600	2.75	4.00	6.00	12.50	80.00	
☐1940S	8,244,000	2.75	4.00	6.00	7.00	60.00	
☐1941	79,047,287	2.75	4.00	6.00	7.00	12.00	85.00
☐1941D	16,714,800	2.75	4.00	6.00	7.00	40.00	
☐1941S	16,080,000	2.75	4.00	6.00	7.00	35.00	
☐1942	102,117,123	2.75		3.25	4.25	12.00	90.00
☐1942D	17,487,200	2.75		3.25	4.25	25.00	
☐1942S	19,384,000	2.75		3.25	4.25	125.00	
☐1943	99,700,000	2.75		3.25	4.25	12.00	
☐1943D	16,095,600	2.75		3.25	4.25	25.00	
☐1943S	21,700,000	2.75		3.25	4.25	100.00	
☐1943S Double Die			EXTREMELY RARE				
☐1944	104,956,000	2.75		3.25	4.25	12.00	
☐1944D	14,600,000	2.75		3.25	4.25	25.00	
☐1944S	12,560,000	2.75		3.25	4.25	35.00	
☐1945	74,372,000	2.75		3.25	4.25	25.00	
☐1945D	12,341,600	2.75		3.25	4.25	20.00	

DATE	MINTAGE	ABP	F-12 Fine	EF-40 Ex. Fine	MS-60 Unc.	PRF-65 Proof
☐ 1945S	17,004,001	2.75	3.25	4.25	25.00	
☐ 1946	53,436,000	2.75	3.25	4.25	10.00	
☐ 1946D	9,072,800	2.75	3.25	4.25	12.00	
☐ 1946S	4,204,000	2.75	3.25	4.25	10.00	
☐ 1947	22,556,000	2.75	3.25	4.25	12.00	
☐ 1947D	15,338,400	2.75	3.25	4.25	20.00	
☐ 1947S	5,532,000	2.75	3.25	4.25	12.00	
☐ 1948	35,196,000	2.75	3.25	4.25	12.00	
☐ 1948D	16,768,800	2.75	3.25	4.25	12.00	
☐ 1948S	15,960,000	2.75	3.25	4.25	20.00	
☐ 1949	9,312,000	2.75	3.25	4.25	25.00	
☐ 1949D	10,068,400	2.75	3.25	4.25	20.00	
☐ 1950	24,971,512	2.75	3.25	4.25	12.00	80.00
☐ 1950D	21,075,600	2.75	3.25	4.25	12.00	
☐ 1950S	10,284,004	2.75	3.25	4.25	25.00	
☐ 1951	43,505,602	2.75	3.25	4.25	12.00	50.00
☐ 1951D	35,354,800	2.75	3.25	4.25	12.00	
☐ 1951S	8,948,000	2.75	3.25	4.25	20.00	
☐ 1952	38,862,073	2.75	3.25	4.25	10.00	30.00
☐ 1952D	49,795,200	2.75	3.25	4.25	10.00	
☐ 1952S	13,707,800	2.75	3.25	4.25	14.00	
☐ 1953	18,664,920	2.75	3.25	4.25	10.00	18.00
☐ 1953D	56,112,400	2.75	3.25	4.25	10.00	
☐ 1953S	14,016,000	2.75	3.25	4.25	12.00	
☐ 1954	54,654,503	2.75	3.25	4.25	7.00	18.00
☐ 1954D	46,305,500	2.75	3.25	4.25	7.00	
☐ 1954S	11,834,722	2.75	3.25	4.25	8.00	
☐ 1955	18,558,381	2.75	3.25	4.25	8.00	15.00
☐ 1955D	3,182,400	2.75	3.25	4.25	8.00	
☐ 1956	44,813,384	2.75	3.25	4.25	7.00	12.00
☐ 1956D	32,334,500	2.75	3.25	4.25	7.00	
☐ 1957	47,779,952	2.75	3.25	4.25	7.00	12.00
☐ 1957D	77,924,160	2.75	3.25	4.25	7.00	15.00
☐ 1958	7,235,652	2.75	3.25	4.25	7.00	15.00
☐ 1958D	78,124,900	2.75	3.25	4.25	7.00	
☐ 1959	25,533,291	2.75	3.25	4.25	4.00	9.00
☐ 1959D	62,054,232	2.75	3.25	4.25	4.00	
☐ 1960	30,855,602	2.75	3.25	4.25	4.00	9.00
☐ 1960D	63,000,324	2.75	3.25	4.25	4.00	
☐ 1961	40,064,244	2.75	3.25	4.25	4.00	6.00
☐ 1961D	83,656,928	2.75	3.25	4.25	4.50	
☐ 1962	39,374,019	2.75	3.25	4.25	4.00	6.00
☐ 1962D	127,554,756	2.75	3.25	4.25	4.00	
☐ 1963	77,391,645	2.75	3.25	4.25	4.00	6.00
☐ 1963D	135,288,184	2.75	3.25	4.25	4.00	
☐ 1964	564,341,347	2.75	3.25	4.25	4.00	6.00
☐ 1964D	704,135,528	2.75	3.25		4.00	

DATE	MINTAGE		MS-60 Unc.	PRF-65 Proof
☐ 1965	1,819,717,540		.35	
☐ 1966	821,101,500		.35	
☐ 1967	1,524,031,840		.35	
☐ 1968	220,731,500		.45	
☐ 1968D	101,534,000		.35	
☐ 1968S	3,041,500	PROOF		
☐ 1969	176,212,000		.35	
☐ 1969D	114,372,000		.35	
☐ 1969S	2,934,631	PROOF		.75
☐ 1970	136,420,000		.35	
☐ 1970D	417,341,364		.35	
☐ 1970S	2,632,810	PROOF		1.00
☐ 1971	109,284,000		.35	
☐ 1971D	258,634,428		.35	
☐ 1971S	3,224,138	PROOF		.75
☐ 1972	215,048,000		.35	
☐ 1972D	311,067,732		.35	
☐ 1972S	3,267,667			.75
☐ 1973	346,924,000		.35	
☐ 1973D	232,977,400		.35	
☐ 1973S	2,796,624	PROOF		1.50
☐ 1974	801,456,000		.30	
☐ 1974D	363,160,300		.30	
☐ 1974S	2,612,568	PROOF		1.50
☐ 1976 Copper-Nickel Clad	809,780,016		.35	
☐ 1976D Copper-Nickel Clad	860,108,836		.35	
☐ 1976S Copper-Nickel Clad Proof	7,055,099			.50
☐ 1976S Silver Clad			2.00	
☐ 1976 Silver Clad Proof				5.25
☐ 1977	468,556,900		.30	
☐ 1977D	256,524,078		.30	
☐ 1977S Proof	2,909,269			1.00
☐ 1978	521,452,000		.30	
☐ 1978D	287,373,152		.30	
☐ 1978S Proof	3,127,781			1.00
☐ 1979P			.30	
☐ 1979D			.30	
☐ 1979S Proof				1.00

HALF DOLLARS — EARLY HALF DOLLARS, 1794 - 1838

As originally conceived the Half Dollar was to contain precisely — to the grain — half as much metal as the Dollar and was to be struck from metal of the same composition, .8924 silver alloyed with .1076 copper. It weighed 13.48 grams and was slightly larger in diameter than it subsequently became, 32½ mm. Its designer was Robert Scot and its obverse featured a profile portrait of Liberty facing right, the so-called Flowing Hair likeness used on other coins as well, backed by an eagle. Along the edge was stamped its value, as no statement of value appeared within the design: "FIFTY CENTS OR HALF A DOLLAR," the words set apart with small ornamental flourishes. Apparently the initial issue in 1794 was struck from just a single set of dies, but in the following year several dies were employed, resulting in a number of minor varieties. This was the final appearance of the Flowing Hair 50¢ piece. The design was replaced in 1796 by the Draped Bust version, to which the shielded eagle reverse was added in 1801. Because of the trading significance of this coin an effort was made to place as many half dollars as possible into circulation during its early years. It was temporarily discontinued in 1804 as a result of speculation, along with the silver dollar; but unlike the latter, which did not return for more than 30 years, production of the half dollar was resumed in 1805. In that year more than 200,000 were struck, followed by a striking exceeding 800,000 in 1806. The Capped Bust design was installed on the dollar in 1807, as it was on other coins. Its designer was a German-American named John Reich. The Capped Bust is sometimes referred to as "Turban Head." The word "LIBERTY" appears on the cap or turban band. On either side of the portrait is a series of stars, with the date positioned beneath it. The reverse as a modified shielded eagle (or heraldic eagle) with the motto "E PLURIBUS UNUM" on a banner and "50 C." This coin weighs 13.48 grams and has the same metallic composition as its predecessors. Varieties of the Capped Bust half dollar are so numerous, despite being in use for only about 30 years, that a large collection can be built around this coin. And it is, indeed, an ideal target for specialization, as nearly all specimens fall within the low to moderate range of price. Christian Gobrecht redesigned the coin in 1836, retaining the same types but modifying them somewhat. The composition was changed to provide a slightly higher content of silver and a slightly lower content of copper, the ratio now being nine parts silver/one part copper. Its weight was 13.36 grams and the diameter reduced to 30 mm. This design was replaced by Liberty Seated in 1839, which remained in use more than 50 years.

HALF DOLLARS — FLOWING HAIR, 1794 - 1795

DATE	MINTAGE	ABP	G-4 Good	F-12 Fine	VF-20 V. Fine
☐ 1794	5,300	250.00	500.00	2000.00	3000.00
☐ 1795	217,844	200.00	400.00	1000.00	1500.00
☐ 1795 Recut Date	317,844	200.00	350.00	1000.00	1500.00
☐ 1795*	317,844	225.00	450.00	800.00	1800.00

*3 leaves under each wing

HALF DOLLARS — DRAPED BUST, SMALL EAGLE 1796 - 1797

DATE	MINTAGE	ABP	G-4 Good	F-12 Fine	VF-20 V. Fine
☐ 1796 (15 stars)		4000.00	7500.00	15000.00	20000.00
☐ 1796 (16 stars)		4000.00	7500.00	15000.00	20000.00
☐ 1797	3,918	4000.00	7500.00	15000.00	20000.00

HALF DOLLARS — DRAPED BUST, 1801 - 1807
Eagle on Reverse

DATE	MINTAGE	ABP	G-4 Good	F-12 Fine	VF-20 V. Fine	MS-60 Unc.
☐ 1801	30,289	45.00	100.00	700.00	1000.00	9000.00
☐ 1802	29,890	40.00	80.00	700.00	1000.00	9000.00
☐ 1803 Large 3	188,234	25.00	45.00	125.00	300.00	8000.00
☐ 1803 Small 3		40.00	75.00	180.00	400.00	8000.00
☐ 1805		20.00	40.00	150.00	325.00	8000.00
☐ 1805 over 4	211,722	35.00	50.00	200.00	400.00	8000.00
☐ 1806		20.00	40.00	100.00	200.00	8000.00
☐ 1806 over 5	839,576	25.00	40.00	100.00	250.00	8000.00
☐ 1806 inverted (over 6)		33.00	50.00	125.00	225.00	8000.00
☐ 1806 Knobbed 6, Lg. Stars		30.00	45.00	100.00	190.00	8000.00
☐ 1806 Knobbed 6, Stem not through Claw			EXTREMELY RARE			
☐ 1807	301,076	20.00	40.00	80.00	200.00	8000.00

HALF DOLLARS — TURBAN HEAD or "CAPPED BUST", 1807 - 1836

Motto Above Eagle, Lettered Edge, Large Size

DATE	MINTAGE	ABP	G-4 Good	F-12 Fine	VF-20 V. Fine	MS-60 Unc.
☐ 1807 Sm./Stars		15.00	25.00	35.00	70.00	1000.00
☐ 1807 Lg./Stars	750,500	10.00	20.00	30.00	60.00	800.00
☐ 1807 .50 over .20		10.00	20.00	30.00	60.00	1000.00
☐ 1808	1,368,600	10.00	20.00	25.00	30.00	700.00
☐ 1808 over 7		10.00	20.00	25.00	30.00	700.00
☐ 1809	1,405,810	10.00	20.00	25.00	30.00	700.00
☐ 1810	1,276,276	13.00	20.00	25.00	30.00	700.00
☐ 1811	1,203,644	13.00	20.00	25.00	30.00	700.00
☐ 1812	1,628,059	13.00	20.00	25.00	30.00	700.00
☐ 1812 over 11		13.00	20.00	30.00	50.00	700.00
☐ 1813	1,241,903	13.00	20.00	25.00	30.00	700.00
☐ 1814	1,039,075	13.00	20.00	25.00	30.00	700.00
☐ 1814 over 13		13.00	20.00	35.00	50.00	700.00
☐ 1815 over 12	47,150	100.00	225.00	400.00	550.00	3250.00
☐ 1817	1,215,567	13.00	20.00	25.00	30.00	700.00
☐ 1817 over 13		15.00	30.00	50.00	65.00	1000.00
☐ 1818	1,960,322	13.00	20.00	25.00	30.00	700.00
☐ 1818 over 17		13.00	20.00	30.00	40.00	500.00

TYPE OF COIN	MINTAGE	ABP	G-4 Good	F-12 Fine	VF-20 V. Fine	MS-60 Unc.
☐ 1819	2,208,000	13.00	20.00	25.00	30.00	700.00
☐ 1819 over 18 Large 9		13.00	20.00	25.00	30.00	800.00
☐ 1820	751,122	12.00	25.00	40.00	50.00	800.00
☐ 1820 over 19		13.00	20.00	30.00	35.00	800.00
☐ 1821	1,305,797	13.00	20.00	25.00	30.00	700.00
☐ 1822	1,559,573	13.00	20.00	25.00	30.00	700.00
☐ 1822 over 21		15.00	30.00	50.00	80.00	800.00
☐ 1823	1,694,200	13.00	20.00	25.00	30.00	700.00
☐ 1823 Ugly 3		15.00	25.00	35.00	50.00	500.00
☐ 1824	3,504,954	8.00	15.00	20.00	25.00	700.00
☐ 1824 over 21 & others		13.00	20.00	25.00	30.00	800.00
☐ 1825	2,943,166	8.00	15.00	20.00	25.00	700.00
☐ 1826	4,044,180	8.00	15.00	20.00	25.00	700.00
☐ 1827*	5,493,400	8.00	15.00	20.00	25.00	700.00
☐ 1827 over 6 curled 2		8.00	15.00	25.00	30.00	700.00
☐ 1828	3,075,200	13.00	20.00	30.00	60.00	700.00
☐ 1829	3,712,156	8.00	15.00	20.00	25.00	700.00
☐ 1829 over 27		8.00	15.00	22.00	28.00	700.00
☐ 1830**	4,764,800	8.00	15.00	20.00	25.00	700.00
☐ 1831	5,873,660	8.00	15.00	20.00	25.00	700.00
☐ 1832***	4,797,000	8.00	15.00	20.00	25.00	600.00
☐ 1833	5,206,000	8.00	15.00	20.00	25.00	600.00
☐ 1834	6,412,000	8.00	15.00	20.00	25.00	600.00
☐ 1835	5,352,006	8.00	15.00	20.00	25.00	600.00
☐ 1836 ALL KINDS	6,546,200	8.00	15.00	20.00	25.00	600.00

*Square—Based 2. **Sm. O, in Date, Lg. O, in Date: Same Price.
***Sm. Ltrs., Lg. Ltrs.: Same Price.

HALF DOLLARS — TURBAN HEAD or "CAPPED BUST", 1836 - 1839
No Motto Above Eagle, Reeded Edge, Reduced Size

1836-1837 "50 cents"

1838-1839 "half dol."

DATE	MINTAGE	ABP	G-4 Good	F-12 Fine	EX-40 Ex. Fine	MS-60 Unc.	PRF-65 Proof
☐ 1836*		15.00	30.00	50.00	60.00	700.00	
☐ 1836 Reeded Edge		150.00	250.00	450.00	1500.00	4000.00	
☐ 1837	3,629,820	10.00	20.00	40.00	125.00	2000.00	
☐ 1838	3,546,000	10.00	20.00	35.00	125.00	2000.00	
☐ 1838O	Approx. 20	EXTREMELY RARE-Stack's Sale 1975					50000.00
☐ 1839	3,334,500	10.00	20.00	35.00	175.00	2000.00	
☐ 1839O	179,000	30.00	70.00	150.00	400.00	3000.00	

*Ltd. edge 50 over 00

HALF DOLLAR — LIBERTY SEATED, 1839 - 1866
Without Motto Above Eagle

The Seated Liberty half dollar was based on the now-celebrated design of Christian Gobrecht. The goddess sits looking left, holding a shield on which the word "LIBERTY" appears and, in the other hand, a staff. The upper portion of the design is encircled by stars. On the reverse is a shield or heraldic eagle holding arrows and branch. Beneath the eagle are the words "HALF DOL." After some minor modification of both the obverse and reverse design, the numerals used for giving the date were enlarged in 1846 and a major change occured in 1853. Because the California gold strikes of 1849 had brought great quantities of this metal into circulation, public confidence in silver was gradually eroding. To inspire greater acceptance of silver coinage their composition was revised to include a higher proportion of bullion. The new ratio — not just for half dollars but silver pieces in general — was nine parts silver to one of copper, the one part of copper being necessary to give this undurable metal a fair stability. The weight was 12.44 grams and the diameter 30.6 mm. A pair of arrows was placed on the obverse beside the date, as warning that the metal content had changed, and — in the event this was overlooked — sunrays were installed on the reverse, radiating from behind the eagle. These were discontinued in 1856. Beginning in 1866, and probably not coincidentally because the Civil War had recently ended, the motto "IN GOD WE TRUST" was incorporated into the reverse design, on a banner that flies above the eagle's head. When the weight was increased 6/10th of a gram in 1873, resort was again made to arrows at the date, but no sunrays adorned the reverse. The arrows were removed in 1875. The Seated Liberty Half Dollar continued to be struck until 1891, though throughout the 1880's its output was very limited.

Mint Mark is Below Eagle on Reverse

DATE	MINTAGE	ABP	G-4 Good	F-12 Fine	Ex-40 Ex. Fine	MS-60 Unc.	PRF-65 Proof
☐ 1839 no drapery from elbow		15.00	30.00	60.00	400.00	10000.00	
☐ 1839	3,334,560	5.50	10.00	25.00	65.00	825.00	
☐ 1840	1,435,008	5.50	10.00	20.00	50.00	825.00	
☐ 18400	855,100	5.50	10.00	20.00	70.00	825.00	
☐ 1841	310,000	12.00	25.00	50.00	150.00	825.00	
☐ 18410	401,000	7.00	15.00	30.00	80.00	825.00	
☐ 1842	2,012,764	5.50	10.00	25.00	65.00	825.00	
☐ 18420 small date		100.00	200.00	400.00	1800.00		
☐ large date		5.50	10.00	20.00	75.00	825.00	
☐ 1843	3,844,000	5.50	10.00	20.00	60.00	825.00	
☐ 18430	2,268,000	5.50	10.00	20.00	75.00	825.00	
☐ 1844	1,766,000	5.50	10.00	20.00	50.00	825.00	
☐ 18440	2,005,000	5.50	10.00	20.00	75.00	900.00	
☐ 1845	589,000	15.00	30.50	00.00	175.00	900.00	
☐ 18450	2,094,000	5.50	10.00	20.00	80.00	1000.00	
☐ 1846	2,110,000	5.50	10.00	20.00	60.00	825.00	
☐ 1846 over horizontal 6		15.00	30.00	70.00	80.00	825.00	
☐ 18460	2,304,000	5.50	10.00	20.00	65.00	825.00	
☐ 1847	1,156,000	5.50	10.00	20.00	60.00	825.00	
☐ 1847 over 6		325.00	700.00	2000.00			
☐ 18470	2,584,000	5.50	10.00	20.00	60.00	825.00	
☐ 1848	580,000	15.00	30.00	50.00	180.00	825.00	
☐ 18480	3,180,000	5.50	10.00	20.00	60.00	825.00	
☐ 1849	1,252,000	5.50	10.00	20.00	60.00	825.00	
☐ 18490	2,310,000	5.50	10.00	20.00	60.00	825.00	
☐ 1850	227,000	15.00	30.00	90.00	280.00	900.00	
☐ 18500	2,456,000	5.50	10.00	20.00	80.00	900.00	
☐ 1851	200,750	20.00	40.00	100.00	325.00	850.00	
☐ 18510	402,000	10.00	20.00	30.00	80.00	850.00	
☐ 1852	77,130	30.00	60.00	120.00	480.00	1200.00	
☐ 18520	144,000	15.00	30.00	50.00	150.00	800.00	
☐ 1853**	3,532,708	5.50	10.00	20.00	200.00	4000.00	
☐ 1853**	1,328,000	5.50	10.00	20.00	200.00	4000.00	
☐ 18530 NO ARROW — EXTREMELY RARE		STACK'S SALE 1975			FINE $24,000.00		
☐ 1854***	2,982,000	7.50	10.00	15.00	70.00	1400.00	
☐ 18540***	5,240,000	5.50	10.00	15.00	70.00	1400.00	
☐ 1855***	759,500	5.50	10.00	15.00	70.00	1400.00	10000.00
☐ 18550	3,688,000	5.50	10.00	15.00	70.00	1400.00	
☐ 1855S***	129,950	60.00	120.00	300.00	1000.00	2500.00	
☐ 1856	938,000	5.50	10.00	15.00	50.00	800.00	6250.00
☐ 18560	2,658,000	5.50	10.00	15.00	50.00	800.00	
☐ 1856S	211,000	7.50	15.00	30.00	250.00	1200.00	
☐ 1857	1,988,000	5.50	10.00	15.00	50.00	800.00	6250.00
☐ 18570	818,000	5.50	10.00	15.00	50.00	800.00	
☐ 1857S	158,000	9.00	15.00	35.00	125.00	700.00	
☐ 1858	4,226,000	5.50	10.00	15.00	50.00	800.00	6250.00
☐ 18580	7,294,000	5.50	10.00	15.00	50.00	800.00	

DATE	MINTAGE	ABP	G-4 Good	F-12 Fine	Ex-40 Ex. Fine	MS-60 Unc.	PRF-65 Proof
☐ 1858S	476,000	7.50	12.00	25.00	100.00	700.00	
☐ 1859	748,000	5.50	10.00	15.00	50.00	800.00	6250.00
☐ 1859O	2,834,000	5.50	10.00	15.00	50.00	800.00	
☐ 1859S	566,000	6.00	12.00	25.00	100.00	700.00	
☐ 1860	303,700	10.00	20.00	40.00	150.00	800.00	6250.00
☐ 1860O	1,290,000	5.50	10.00	15.00	50.00	800.00	
☐ 1860S	472,000	5.50	10.00	20.00	75.00	800.00	
☐ 1861	2,888,400	5.50	10.00	15.00	50.00	800.00	6250.00
☐ 1861O	330,000	5.50	10.00	15.00	50.00	800.00	
☐ 1861S	939,500	5.50	10.00	15.00	50.00	800.00	
☐ 1862	252,350	15.00	30.00	75.00	175.00	800.00	6250.00
☐ 1862S	1,352,000	5.50	10.00	15.00	50.00	800.00	
☐ 1863	503,660	10.00	20.00	50.00	150.00	750.00	6250.00
☐ 1863S	916,000	5.50	10.00	15.00	50.00	800.00	
☐ 1864	379,570	10.00	20.00	50.00	150.00	750.00	6250.00
☐ 1864S	658,000	5.50	10.00	20.00	75.00	800.00	
☐ 1865	511,900	12.00	25.00	50.00	150.00	730.00	6250.00
☐ 1865S	675,000	5.50	10.00	20.00	75.00	800.00	
☐ 1866S†		20.00	40.00	60.00	250.00	700.00	

**With Arrows and Rays   ***With Arrows
†Part of Total Mintage: 1,054,000

HALF DOLLARS — LIBERTY SEATED, 1866 - 1891
With Motto on Reverse

Arrows at Date    No Arrows at Date    Mint Mark is Below Eagle on Reverse

DATE	MINTAGE	ABP	G-4 Good	F-12 Fine	EF-40 Ex. Fine	MS-60 Unc.	PRF-65 Proof
☐ 1866	745,625	10.00	20.00	50.00	150.00	800.00	5000.00
☐ 1866S***		5.50	10.00	15.00	60.00	800.00	
☐ 1867	424,325	15.00	30.00	60.00	150.00	800.00	5000.00
☐ 1867S	1,196,000	5.50	10.00	12.00	50.00	800.00	
☐ 1868	378,000	20.00	40.00	75.00	175.00	800.00	5000.00
☐ 1868S	1,160,000	5.50	10.00	15.00	50.00	800.00	
☐ 1869	795,900	5.50	10.00	15.00	50.00	800.00	5000.00
☐ 1869S	656,000	7.00	15.00	20.00	75.00	800.00	

DATE	MINTAGE	ABP	G-4 Good	F-12 Fine	EF-40 Ex. Fine	MS-60 Unc.	PRF-65 Proof
☐ 1870	600,900	7.00	15.00	20.00	75.00	800.00	5000.00
☐ 1870CC	54,617	100.00	200.00	750.00	1500.00	Unknown in BU	
☐ 1870S	1,004,000	10.00	20.00	30.00	80.00	800.00	
☐ 1871	1,165,360	5.50	10.00	15.00	50.00	800.00	5000.00
☐ 1871CC	139,950	20.00	40.00	120.00	500.00	3000.00	
☐ 1871S	2,178,000	5.50	10.00	15.00	50.00	800.00	
☐ 1872	881,550	5.50	10.00	15.00	50.00	800.00	5000.00
☐ 1872CC	272,000	12.00	25.00	70.00	300.00	1200.00	
☐ 1872S	580,000	7.00	15.00	20.00	90.00	800.00	
☐ 1873 w/arrows	1,815,700	7.00	15.00	30.00	150.00	800.00	10000.00
☐ 1873 no arrows	801,800	5.50	10.00	15.00	50.00	800.00	5000.00
☐ 1873CC w/arrows	214,560	15.00	30.00	100.00	300.00	2000.00	
☐ 1873CC no arrows	122,500	25.00	40.00	120.00	375.00	1800.00	
☐ 1873S w/arrows	288,000	10.00	20.00	40.00	150.00	2000.00	
☐ 1873S no arrows	5,000		UNKNOWN		EXTREMELY RARE		
☐ 1874	2,360,300	7.00	15.00	30.00	150.00	700.00	10000.00
☐ 1874CC	59,000	30.00	75.00	200.00	600.00	1500.00	
☐ 1874S	394,000	10.00	20.00	50.00	150.00	900.00	
☐ 1875	6,027,500	5.00	10.00	16.00	50.00	700.00	5000.00
☐ 1875CC	1,008,000	5.00	10.00	16.00	50.00	700.00	
☐ 1875S	3,200,000	5.00	10.00	16.00	50.00	700.00	
☐ 1876	8,419,150	5.00	10.00	16.00	50.00	700.00	5000.00
☐ 1876CC	1,956,000	5.00	10.00	16.00	50.00	700.00	
☐ 1876S	4,528,000	5.00	10.00	16.00	50.00	700.00	
☐ 1877	8,304,510	5.00	10.00	16.00	50.00	700.00	5000.00
☐ 1877CC	1,420,000	5.00	10.00	16.00	50.00	700.00	
☐ 1877S	5,356,000	5.00	10.00	16.00	50.00	700.00	
☐ 1878	1,378,400	5.00	10.00	16.00	50.00	700.00	5000.00
☐ 1878CC	62,000	80.00	175.00	400.00	800.00	2800.00	
☐ 1878S	12,000	1200.00	2500.00	4000.00	7000.00	15000.00	
☐ 1879	5,900	50.00	100.00	125.00	200.00	1000.00	5000.00
☐ 1880	1,355	40.00	80.00	100.00	175.00	900.00	5000.00
☐ 1881	10,975	40.00	80.00	100.00	175.00	900.00	5000.00
☐ 1882	5,500	50.00	100.00	120.00	200.00	900.00	5000.00
☐ 1883	9,039	50.00	100.00	120.00	220.00	900.00	5000.00
☐ 1884	5,275	50.00	100.00	120.00	220.00	900.00	5000.00
☐ 1885	6,130	50.00	100.00	120.00	220.00	900.00	5000.00
☐ 1886	5,886	50.00	100.00	120.00	220.00	900.00	5000.00
☐ 1887	5,710	50.00	100.00	120.00	220.00	900.00	5000.00
☐ 1888	12,833	50.00	100.00	120.00	220.00	900.00	5000.00
☐ 1889	12,711	50.00	100.00	120.00	220.00	900.00	5000.00
☐ 1890	12,590	50.00	100.00	120.00	220.00	900.00	5000.00
☐ 1891	200,600	8.00	15.00	25.00	80.00	600.00	5000.00

***Part of Total Mintage: 1,054,000

HALF DOLLARS — LIBERTY HEAD or BARBER, 1892 · 1915

These coins, which resemble the Morgan Dollar in portraiture, were prepared from designs by Charles E. Barber and really have no connection with the Morgan Dollar aside from the possibility that Barber may have been inspired by it. The face of Liberty, which faces right, is strong and classical, suggesting the portraiture of Greek coins of ancient time. The weight is somewhat greater than the final version of the Seated Liberty half, 12½ grams, but its composition is the same, 90% silver and an alloy of 10% copper. The reverse has an attractive eagle with shield and wings spread wide; it holds the traditional arrows and branch. The mintmark appears directly beneath the eagle's tail feathrs. Without question this was artistically the finest coin of the half dollar series. It was struck at Philadelphia, New Orleans, Denver and San Francisco. Not a single rarity is to be found among the Barber halves, with the result that if offers splendid opportunities for completion — even if one wishes to include all the mintmarks.

Mint Mark is Below Eagle on Reverse

DATE	MINTAGE	ABP	G-4 Good	F-12 Fine	EF-40 Ex. Fine	MS-60 Unc.	PRF-65 Proof
☐1892	935,245	5.50	12.00	35.00	150.00	2000.00	5500.00
☐1892O	390,000	40.00	90.00	150.00	275.00	900.00	
☐1892S	1,029,028	30.00	75.00	140.00	250.00	900.00	
☐1893	1,826,792	5.50	10.00	35.00	150.00	700.00	5500.00
☐1893O	1,389,000	6.00	12.00	45.00	180.00	800.00	
☐1893S	740,000	30.00	60.00	125.00	225.00	800.00	
☐1894	1,148,972	5.50	10.00	35.00	150.00	700.00	5500.00
☐1894O	2,138,000	5.50	10.00	35.00	150.00	700.00	
☐1894S	4,048,690	5.50	12.00	25.00	125.00	800.00	
☐1895	1,835,218	5.50	12.00	30.00	150.00	750.00	5500.00
☐1895O	1,766,000	5.50	12.00	35.00	150.00	850.00	
☐1895S	1,108,086	7.00	15.00	45.00	175.00	800.00	
☐1896	950,762	5.50	10.00	35.00	150.00	800.00	5500.00
☐1896O	924,000	6.00	12.00	40.00	180.00	1000.00	
☐1896S	1,140,948	20.00	45.00	90.00	200.00	1000.00	
☐1897	2,480,731	5.50	12.00	15.00	140.00	700.00	5500.00
☐1897O	632,000	25.00	50.00	80.00	200.00	1200.00	
☐1897S	933,900	25.00	50.00	100.00	200.00	1000.00	
☐1898	2,956,735	5.50	12.00	15.00	125.00	700.00	5500.00

DATE	MINTAGE	ABP	G-4 Good	F-12 Fine	EF-40 Ex. Fine	MS-60 Unc.	PRF-65 Proof
☐ 1898O	874,000	6.00	12.00	40.00	225.00	900.00	
☐ 1898S	2,358,550	5.50	10.00	25.00	125.00	800.00	
☐ 1899	5,538,846	5.50	12.00	15.00	125.00	700.00	5500.00
☐ 1899O	1,724,000	5.50	12.00	28.00	135.00	900.00	
☐ 1899S	1,686,411	5.50	12.00	20.00	125.00	850.00	
☐ 1900	4,762,912	5.50	8.00	15.00	125.00	700.00	5000.00
☐ 1900O	2,744,000	5.50	8.00	15.00	125.00	1000.00	
☐ 1900S	2,560,322	5.50	9.00	15.00	120.00	800.00	
☐ 1901	4,268,813	5.50	8.00	16.00	130.00	725.00	5000.00
☐ 1901O	1,124,000	5.50	8.00	25.00	185.00	1200.00	
☐ 1901S	847,044	5.50	10.00	50.00	275.00	1400.00	
☐ 1902	4,922,777	5.50	8.00	15.00	115.00	800.00	5000.00
☐ 1902O	2,526,000	5.50	8.00	15.00	130.00	800.00	
☐ 1902S	1,460,670	5.50	9.00	20.00	135.00	800.00	
☐ 1903	2,278,755	5.50	8.00	18.00	135.00	800.00	5000.00
☐ 1903O	2,100,000	5.50	8.00	20.00	140.00	800.00	
☐ 1903S	1,920,772	5.50	8.00	18.00	140.00	800.00	
☐ 1904	2,992,670	5.50	8.00	16.00	120.00	800.00	5000.00
☐ 1904O	1,117,600	5.50	9.00	28.00	180.00	900.00	
☐ 1904S	553,038	5.50	10.00	45.00	200.00	900.00	
☐ 1905	662,727	5.50	10.00	40.00	175.00	800.00	5000.00
☐ 1905O	505,000	5.50	10.00	40.00	200.00	850.00	
☐ 1905S	2,494,000	5.50	8.00	15.00	125.00	800.00	
☐ 1906	1,638,675	5.50	7.00	12.00	100.00	800.00	5000.00
☐ 1906D	4,028,000	5.50	7.00	12.00	100.00	800.00	
☐ 1906O	2,446,000	5.50	7.00	12.00	100.00	800.00	
☐ 1906S	1,740,154	5.50	8.00	20.00	125.00	800.00	
☐ 1907	2,598,575	5.50	7.00	12.00	120.00	800.00	5000.00
☐ 1907D	3,856,000	5.50	7.00	12.00	120.00	800.00	
☐ 1907O	3,946,600	5.50	7.00	12.00	120.00	800.00	
☐ 1907S	1,250,000	5.50	8.00	15.00	130.00	800.00	
☐ 1908	1,354,545	5.50	8.00	20.00	125.00	800.00	5000.00
☐ 1908D	3,280,000	5.50	7.00	12.00	100.00	800.00	
☐ 1908O	5,360,000	5.50	7.00	12.00	100.00	800.00	
☐ 1908S	1,644,828	5.50	7.00	12.00	100.00	800.00	
☐ 1909	2,368,650	5.50	7.00	12.00	120.00	800.00	5000.00
☐ 1909O	925,400	5.50	8.00	15.00	120.00	800.00	
☐ 1909S	1,764,000	5.50	7.00	12.00	100.00	800.00	
☐ 1910	418,551	5.50	9.00	30.00	200.00	800.00	5000.00
☐ 1910S	1,948,000	5.50	8.00	15.00	120.00	800.00	
☐ 1911	1,406,543	5.50	8.00	15.00	120.00	800.00	5000.00
☐ 1911D	696,080	5.50	8.00	15.00	125.00	800.00	
☐ 1911S	1,272,000	5.50	8.00	15.00	120.00	800.00	
☐ 1912	1,550,700	5.50	7.00	15.00	120.00	800.00	5000.00
☐ 1912D	2,300,800	5.50	7.00	12.00	120.00	800.00	
☐ 1912S	1,370,000	5.50	7.00	12.00	100.00	800.00	
☐ 1913	188,627	7.00	15.00	40.00	200.00	800.00	5000.00
☐ 1913D	534,000	5.50	9.00	24.00	150.00	800.00	

DATE	MINTAGE	ABP	G-4 Good	F-12 Fine	EF-40 Ex. Fine	MS-60 Unc.	PRF-65 Proof
☐ 1913S	604,000	5.50	8.00	20.00	135.00	700.00	
☐ 1914	124,610	8.00	20.00	60.00	250.00	800.00	5000.00
☐ 1914S	992,000	5.50	8.00	15.00	130.00	700.00	
☐ 1915	138,450	7.25	20.00	50.00	225.00	900.00	5000.00
☐ 1915D	1,170,400	5.50	7.00	12.00	100.00	800.00	
☐ 1915S	1,604,000	5.50	7.00	12.00	100.00	800.00	

HALF DOLLARS — LIBERTY WALKING, 1916 - 1947

This attractive design, introduced in 1916, pictured a full-length representation of Liberty on the obverse, dressed in a diaphonous gown and strolling along a field, her right arm upraised as if in acknowledgment of the splendors of nature. In the distance the sun rises (or sets). The designer was A. Weinman, whose initials may be observed — if one has a coin with virtually no wear — on the reverse. His rendition of the eagle on the coin's reverse, a naturalistic type bearing little resemblance to the previously employed shield or heraldic eagle, is a noteworthy piece of art. Sadly the Liberty Walking half dollar suffered a great deal from rubbing in circulation and much of its delicate linework wore down rapidly, resulting in a shortage of presentable specimens. The collector who wishes to build up a set would be well advised to seek the finest condition obtainable, and be prepared to give a slight premium for coins of the best quality, rather than collect "average" specimens which are, truly, mere shadows of their original selves. The Liberty Walking 50¢ piece was struck at Philadelphia, San Francisco and Denver. Its composition is 90% silver and 10% copper with a weight of 12½ grams and diameter of 30.6 mm.

NOTE: The sale of Liberty Walking halves as silver bullion should be approached with care. While the majority of common dates in average condition are of no special numismatic value, this series, though modern, does include scarce dates and mintmarks which deserve a better fate than the smelter's pot. The silver in these coins amounts to .36169 ounce, or slightly more than one-third of an ounce.

Mint Mark is Under "In God We Trust" on 1916 and Early 1917. Later Left of "H" on Reverse

DATE	MINTAGE	ABP	G-4 Good	F-12 Fine	EF-40 Ex. Fine	MS-60 Unc.	PRF-65
☐ 1916	608,000	6.50	12.00	40.00	125.00	500.00	
☐ 1916D on obv.	1,014,400	5.50	10.00	20.00	105.00	500.00	
☐ 1916S on obv.	508,000	15.00	25.00	70.00	225.00	900.00	
☐ 1917	12,292,000	5.50	7.00	8.00	30.00	200.00	
☐ 1917D on obv.	765,400	5.50	8.00	25.00	125.00	600.00	
☐ 1917D on rev.	1,940,000	5.50	7.00	10.00	100.00	600.00	
☐ 1917S on obv.	952,000	5.50	8.00	30.00	225.00	700.00	
☐ 1917S on rev.	6,554,000	5.50	7.00	8.00	35.00	300.00	
☐ 1918	6,634,000	5.50	6.50	10.00	125.00	500.00	
☐ 1918D	3,853,040	5.50	6.50	10.00	100.00	1000.00	
☐ 1918S	10,282,000	5.50	6.50	8.00	40.00	400.00	
☐ 1919	962,000	5.50	8.00	20.00	225.00	1200.00	
☐ 1919D	1,165,000	5.50	7.00	20.00	300.00	2000.00	
☐ 1919S	1,552,000	5.50	6.50	12.00	300.00	2750.00	
☐ 1920	6,372,000	5.50	6.50	8.00	40.00	300.00	
☐ 1920D	1,551,000	5.50	6.50	10.00	175.00	1800.00	
☐ 1920S	4,624,000	5.50	6.50	8.00	100.00	1500.00	
☐ 1921	246,000	18.00	40.00	100.00	600.00	2500.00	
☐ 1921D	208,000	35.00	60.00	120.00	700.00	3000.00	
☐ 1921S	548,000	5.50	8.00	25.00	1000.00	12000.00	
☐ 1923S	2,178,000	5.50	6.50	9.00	125.00	1500.00	
☐ 1927S	2,393,000	5.50	6.50	8.00	75.00	1000.00	
☐ 1928S	1,940,000	5.50	6.50	8.00	80.00	1000.00	
☐ 1929D	1,001,200	5.50	6.50	8.00	60.00	500.00	
☐ 1929S	1,902,000	5.50	6.50	8.00	60.00	500.00	
☐ 1933S	1,786,000	5.50	6.50	8.00	60.00	500.00	
☐ 1934	6,964,000	5.50	6.50	8.00	11.00	150.00	
☐ 1934D	2,361,400	5.50	6.50	8.00	30.00	300.00	
☐ 1934S	3,652,000	5.50	6.50	8.00	25.00	450.00	
☐ 1935	9,162,000	5.50	6.50	8.00	15.00	80.00	
☐ 1935D	3,003,800	5.50	6.50	8.00	30.00	300.00	
☐ 1935S	2,854,000	5.50	6.50	8.00	20.00	375.00	
☐ 1936	12,617,901	5.50	6.50	8.00	10.00	75.00	2500.00
☐ 1936D	4,252,400	5.50	6.50	8.00	20.00	200.00	
☐ 1936S	3,884,000	5.50	6.50	8.00	20.00	200.00	
☐ 1937	9,527,728	5.50	6.50	8.00	10.00	75.00	1600.00
☐ 1937D	1,760,001	5.50	6.50	8.00	30.00	300.00	
☐ 1937S	2,090,000	5.50	6.50	8.00	20.00	300.00	
☐ 1938	4,118,152	5.50	6.50	8.00	10.00	200.00	1400.00
☐ 1938D	491,600	15.00	20.00	25.00	75.00	675.00	
☐ 1939	6,820,808	5.50	6.50	8.00	10.00	80.00	1200.00
☐ 1939D	4,267,800	5.50	6.50	8.00	10.00	125.00	
☐ 1939S	2,552,000	5.50	6.50	8.00	12.00	225.00	
☐ 1940	9,167,279	5.50	6.50	8.00	10.00	80.00	800.00
☐ 1940S	4,550,000	5.50	6.50	8.00	10.00	200.00	
☐ 1941	24,207,412	5.50	6.50	8.00	10.00	60.00	800.00
☐ 1941D	11,248,400	5.50	6.50	8.00	10.00	100.00	
☐ 1941S	8,098,000	5.50	6.50	8.00	10.00	325.00	

DATE	MINTAGE	ABP	G-4 Good	F-12 Fine	EF-40 Ex. Fine	MS-60 Unc.	PRF-65 Proof
☐ 1942	47,839,120	5.50	6.50	8.00	10.00	50.00	800.00
☐ 1942D	10,973,800	5.50	6.50	8.00	10.00	100.00	
☐ 1942S	12,708,000	5.50	6.50	8.00	10.00	275.00	
☐ 1943	53,190,000	5.50	6.50	8.00	10.00	60.00	
☐ 1943D	11,346,000	5.50	6.50	8.00	10.00	100.00	
☐ 1943S	13,450,000	5.50	6.50	8.00	10.00	225.00	
☐ 1944	28,206,000	5.50	6.50	8.00	10.00	75.00	
☐ 1944D	9,769,000	5.50	6.50	8.00	10.00	100.00	
☐ 1944S	8,904,000	5.50	6.50	8.00	10.00	225.00	
☐ 1945	31,502,000	5.50	6.50	8.00	10.00	60.00	
☐ 1945D	9,966,500	5.50	6.50	8.00	10.00	100.00	
☐ 1945S	10,156,000	5.50	6.50	8.00	10.00	245.00	
☐ 1946	12,118,000	5.50	6.50	8.00	10.00	80.00	
☐ 1946D	2,151,000	5.50	6.50	8.00	10.00	175.00	
☐ 1946S	3,724,000	5.50	6.50	8.00	10.00	225.00	
☐ 1947	4,094,000	5.50	6.50	8.00	10.00	100.00	
☐ 1947D	3,900,000	5.50	6.50	8.00	10.00	100.00	

HALF DOLLARS — FRANKLIN or "LIBERTY BELL", 1948 · 1963

The likeness of Benjamin Franklin, which had not previously appeared on a U.S. coin, was installed on the half dollar in 1948. Franklin was — and to this date is — the only non-President to be depicted on our coins, not counting colonial issues and tokens. That he was not President can be accounted for by mere circumstance. Had the federal government been formed ten or twenty years sooner, before Franklin had advanced into old age, there is little doubt but that he would have attained the office. Like the Roosevelt dime, introduced two years earlier, this coin was designed by John R. Sinnock. On the reverse is a large representation of the Liberty Bell, adapted from the artwork on the 1926 Sesquicentennial medal celebrating the 150th anniversary of our Declaration of Independence. Franklin is shown in profile facing right. The mintmark is atop the Liberty Bell on the reverse, directly below the words "UNITED STATES OF AMERICA." Composition is 90% silver, 10% copper, with a weight of 12½ grams. The diameter is 30.6 mm. It contains .36169 ounce of pure silver, or slightly more than one-third of an ounce.

Mint Mark is Above Liberty Bell on Reverse

DATE	MINTAGE	ABP	F-12 Fine	EF-40 Ex. Fine	MS-60 Unc.	PFR-65 Proof
☐ 1948	3,006,814	5.50	6.25	8.00	50.00	
☐ 1948D	4,028,600	5.50	6.25	8.00	40.00	
☐ 1949	5,714,000	5.50	6.25	8.00	100.00	
☐ 1949D	4,120,600	5.50	6.25	8.00	100.00	
☐ 1949S	3,744,000	5.50	9.00	20.00	400.00	
☐ 1950	7,793,509	5.50	6.25	8.00	75.00	500.00
☐ 1950D	8,031,600	5.50	6.25	8.00	50.00	
☐ 1951	16,859,602	5.50	6.25	8.00	25.00	400.00
☐ 1951D	9,475,200	5.50	6.25	8.00	100.00	
☐ 1951S	13,696,000	5.50	6.25	8.00	75.00	
☐ 1952	21,274,074	5.50	6.25	8.00	25.00	275.00
☐ 1952D	25,394,600	5.50	6.25	8.00	40.00	
☐ 1952S	5,526,000	5.50	6.25	8.00	65.00	
☐ 1953	2,796,920	5.50	6.25	8.00	40.00	150.00
☐ 1953D	20,900,400	5.50	6.25	8.00	25.00	
☐ 1953S	4,148,000	5.50	6.25	8.00	35.00	
☐ 1954	13,421,503	5.50	6.25	8.00	15.00	80.00
☐ 1954D	25,445,580	5.50	6.25	8.00	15.00	
☐ 1954S	4,993,400	5.50	6.25	8.00	20.00	
☐ 1955	2,876,381	5.50	6.25	8.00	20.00	75.00
☐ 1956	4,701,384	5.50	6.25	8.00	15.00	25.00
☐ 1957	6,361,952	5.50	6.25	8.00	15.00	15.00
☐ 1957D	19,996,850	5.50	6.25	8.00	14.00	15.00
☐ 1958	4,917,652	5.50	6.25	8.00	14.00	15.00
☐ 1958D	23,962,412	5.50	6.25	8.00	14.00	18.00
☐ 1959	7,349,291	5.50	6.25	8.00	14.00	18.00
☐ 1959D	13,053,750	5.50	6.25	8.00	14.00	
☐ 1960	7,715,602	5.50	6.25	8.00	14.00	18.00
☐ 1960D	18,215,812	5.50	6.25	8.00	12.00	
☐ 1961	11,318,244	5.50	6.25	8.00	10.00	15.00
☐ 1961D	20,276,442	5.50	6.25	8.00	10.00	
☐ 1962	12,932,019	5.50	6.25	8.00	10.00	
☐ 1962D	35,473,281	5.50	6.25	8.00	10.00	
☐ 1963	25,239,645	5.50	6.25	8.00	10.00	
☐ 1963D	67,069,292	5.50	6.25	8.00	10.00	

HALF DOLLARS — JOHN F. KENNEDY, 1964 TO DATE

Following the death of President Kennedy in 1963 there was considerable public sentiment for honoring his memory on coinage. As all coins except the half dollar already carried portraits of Presidents it was decided to install his likeness on this coin, even though its design had been changed as recently as 1948. The portrait was designed by Gilroy Roberts and Frank Gasparro, the reverse featuring a shield eagle surrounded by stars. As introduced in 1964 the coin was of regular silver composition (90% silver, 10% copper, .36169 ounces of silver by weight) but was altered in 1965 to the clad standard, consisting of a 21% silver/79% copper interior covered with 80% silver/20% copper, total weight of silver being .14792 ounces. Its weight was 11½ grams, down from 12½. In 1971 the silver was removed from its core and a new composition used for the exterior, comprising three parts copper to one of nickel. The silver had been entirely replaced and the weight fell to 11.34 grams. The only alteration in design occured in 1976 when a figure of Independence Hall in Philadelphia was added to the reverse, supplanting the eagle, as part of the Bicentennial program. On the obverse the date appeared as "1776-1976." In the following year the normal reverse was readopted. A quantity of silver-clad pieces were struck in 1976, the first (and last) in this series since 1970. This has been termed a difficult coin on which to find the mintmark. As first issued it may be observed on the reverse, above the "L" and "F" in the word "HALF." In 1968 it was brought to the obverse, beneath the portrait and above the date. Scarcest Kennedy half dollar is the 1970D, not minted for general circulation. The Kennedy half dollar has a diameter of 30.6 mm.

Mint Mark 1964-1967

Mint Mark 1968 on.

DATE	MINTAGE	ABP	EF-40 Ex. Fine	MS-60 Unc.	PRF-65 Proof
☐ 1964	277,254,766	5.50	8.00	9.00	10.00
☐ 1964D	156,205,446	5.50	8.00	9.00	
CLAD COINAGE					
☐ 1965	65,879,366		3.50	4.00	
☐ 1966	108,984,933		3.50	4.00	
☐ 1967	295,045,968		3.50	4.00	
☐ 1968D	246,951,930		3.50	4.00	
☐ 1968S PROOFS	3,041,508				4.00
☐ 1969D	129,881,800		3.50	3.00	
☐ 1969S PROOFS	2,934,631				4.00
☐ 1970D	2,150,000			45.00	
☐ 1970S PROOFS	2,632,810				10.00
☐ 1971	155,164,000			.70	
☐ 1971D	302,097,424			.70	
☐ 1971S PROOFS	3,224,138				3.75
☐ 1972	153,180,000			.70	
☐ 1972D	141,890,000			.70	
☐ 1972S PROOF	3,224,138				3.75
☐ 1973	64,964,000			.70	
☐ 1973D	83,171,400			.70	

DATE	MINTAGE	ABP	EF-40 Ex. Fine	MS-60 Unc.	PRF-65 Proof
☐ 1973S PROOF	2,769,624				6.00
☐ 1974	201,588,250			.70	
☐ 1974D	79,088,210			.70	
☐ 1974S	2,617,350				5.50
☐ 1976 Copper-nickel clad	234,318,200			1.10	
☐ 1976D Copper-nickel clad	287,565,290			1.10	
☐ 1976S Copper-nickel clad	7,123,300				4.00
☐ 1976S Silver clad	4,250,000			4.25	
☐ 1976S Silver clad	3,215,730				6.00
☐ 1977	43,569,000			.60	
☐ 1977D	31,450,250			.60	
☐ 1977S PROOFS	3,450,895				3.55
☐ 1978	14,350,000			.60	
☐ 1978D	13,765,799			1.25	
☐ 1978S PROOFS	3,127,781				7.50
☐ 1979				.60	
☐ 1979D					
☐ 1979S PROOFS					6.50

SILVER DOLLARS — EARLY, 1794 - 1804; Patterns, 1836 - 1839; Regular Issue, 1840 - 1873

The silver dollar, probably the most significant U.S. coin of the 19th century, was authorized on April 2, 1792 and intended as the chief currency piece or standard for other silver coinage. Striking was not however begun until 1794. The word "dollar" is a corruption of Taler or Thaler, a large silver coin widely distributed in Europe and well known to Colonial America. Prior to use of this term in domestic coinage it had become common to refer to Spain's "pieces of eight" as dollars, so it was natural that this crown-like silver piece should likewise be called a dollar. The first design, the Flowing Hair variety, was executed by Robert Scot and may be observed on other coinage of that era. Its reverse was an eagle surrounded by the words "UNITED STATES OF AMERICA." The composition was .8924 silver and .1076 copper, the addition of this roughly one-tenth part of base-metal being needed to provide ruggedness. It weighed 26.96 grams and was the heaviest U.S. silver coin excepting the Trade Dollar of much later vintage. Its diameter varies between 39 and 40 mm. Along the edge is impressed the words "HUNDRED CENTS ONE DOLLAR OR UNIT," interspersed with typographical ornament. There was very limited striking of dollars in the initial year of their appearance, less than 2,000 being turned out. The following year, 1795, witnessed greatly increased production, but because of the surface softness of these coins and the extensive handling to which they were subjected it is not easy finding specimens in the best grades of condition. "Average" examples can be had rather easily. There are two reverse varieties of the 1795 Flowing Hair dollar, one in which three leaves appear beneath the eagle's wings on either side, another with two leaves. Toward the end of 1795 the Flowing Hair obverse was replaced by the Draped Bust, with the so-called "Small Eagle" reverse (the eagle's wings and body in general being scaled smaller than previously). The Draped Bust obverse is found with dates in small or large numerals, and with the legend "UNITED STATES OF AMERICA" in small or large letters on the reverse. There are also differences in the number of stars on the obverse. In 1798 the shield eagle reverse was introduced, still with the Draped Bust portrait. These types were continued until 1803 when the striking of silver dollars was suspended. It was at one time believed that the Mint coined a few dollars in 1804 but it has now been established beyond reasonable doubt that silver dollars dated 1804 were struck in the 1830's for inclusion in proof sets. Apparently the die for an 1804 coin was prepared before any decision was reached to discontinue production and it was stored away at the Mint for those 30 years. In any case the 1804 dollar is an extremely rare piece whose popularity (and price) has not suffered in the least by results of research into its origins. A handful of restrikes were made later, in 1859. There is scarcely any difference in rarity or value between the 1830's proofs and the 1859 restrikes. Of all 1804 silver dollars (both types), 15 exist.

In 1836 Christian Gobrecht prepared designs for a new silver dollar, which at first was struck in limited numbers to test public response. A seated figure of Liberty appeared on the obverse with a flying eagle reverse. The obverse carried no wording whatever. On the reverse were the words "UNITED STATES OF AMERICA" and "ONE DOLLAR," the eagle set within a ground of stars. There are some varieties of this reverse containing no stars. Full-scale output of silver dollars was not resumed until 1840. For this issue, and for many years following, the shield or heraldic eagle was used for the reverse and the face value was abbreviated into "ONE DOL." In 1866 the motto "IN GOD WE TRUST" was added to the reverse, on a banner flowing above the eagle. The mintmark is located below the eagle and above the statement of value. Striking of dollars in this design ceased in 1873.

SILVER DOLLARS — LIBERTY WITH FLOWING HAIR, 1794 · 1795

DATE	MINTAGE	ABP	G-4 Good	F-12 Fine	VF-20 V. Fine	MS-60 Unc.
☐ 1794	1,758	2500.00	3500.00	7500.00	12000.00	25000.00
☐ 1795* Part of	184,013	275.00	600.00	1000.00	1800.00	16500.00

SILVER DOLLARS — DRAPED BUST, 1795 - 1798
Small Eagle on Reverse

DATE	MINTAGE	ABP	G-4 Good	F-12 Fine	VF-20 V. Fine	MS-60 Unc.
☐ 1795* Part of	184,013	265.00	500.00	700.00	1000.00	15000.00
☐ 1796	72,920	265.00	500.00	700.00	1000.00	15000.00
☐ 1797 sm. letters		265.00	500.00	500.00	12000.00	18000.00
☐ 1797 lg. letters	7,776	265.00	500.00	725.00	800.00	16000.00
☐ 1797 9 stars left, 7 right		250.00	425.00	900.00	15000.00	25000.00
☐ 1798 (Small eagle)	327,536	265.00	500.00	725.00	800.00	16000.00

*Total mintage for Flowing Hair & Draped Bust — 184,013

SILVER DOLLARS — DRAPED BUST, 1798 - 1804
Large Eagle on Reverse

DATE	MINTAGE	ABP	G-4 Good	F-12 Fine	VF-20 V. Fine	MS-60 Unc.
☐ 1798		275.00	500.00	700.00	1000.00	15000.00
☐ 1799	423,515	275.00	500.00	700.00	1000.00	15000.00
☐ 1800	220,920	275.00	500.00	700.00	1000.00	15000.00
☐ 1801	54,454	275.00	500.00	700.00	1000.00	15000.00
☐ 1802	41,650	275.00	500.00	700.00	1000.00	15000.00
☐ 1802 over 1		275.00	500.00	700.00	1000.00	15000.00
☐ 1803	66,064	275.00	500.00	700.00	1000.00	15000.00

☐ 1804 One of the most valued coins in the world — Less than 15 known. Last one sold was GARRETT COLLECTION March 1980 $400,000.00.

SILVER DOLLARS — LIBERTY SEATED (GOBRECHT), 1836 - 1839
With Flying Eagle on Reverse

DATE	MINTAGE	ABP	VF-20 V. Fine	EF-40 Ex. Fine	PRF-65 Proof
☐ 1836 approx.	1,025	750.00	1500.00	2500.00	6000.00
☐ 1838 approx.	31	6000.00	PROOF ONLY		10000.00
☐ 1839 approx.	303	3500.00	PROOF ONLY		7000.00

SILVER DOLLARS — LIBERTY SEATED, 1840 - 1865
No Motto Over Eagle

Mint Mark is Below Eagle on Reverse

DATE	MINTAGE	ABP	VG-8 V. Good	F-12 Fine	VF-20 V. Fine	MS-60 Unc.
☐ 1840	61,005	55.00	100.00	125.00	150.00	1200.00
☐ 1841	173,000	45.00	75.00	85.00	95.00	1200.00
☐ 1842	184,618	45.00	75.00	85.00	95.00	1200.00
☐ 1843	165,100	45.00	75.00	85.00	95.00	1200.00
☐ 1844	20,000	60.00	125.00	150.00	175.00	1400.00
☐ 1845	24,500	60.00	125.00	150.00	175.00	1400.00
☐ 1846	110,600	40.00	75.00	85.00	95.00	1200.00
☐ 18460	59,000	60.00	125.00	150.00	200.00	1200.00
☐ 1847	140,750	45.00	75.00	85.00	95.00	1200.00
☐ 1848	15,000	50.00	100.00	125.00	175.00	900.00
☐ 1849	62,600	40.00	80.00	100.00	125.00	800.00
☐ 1850	7,500	60.00	150.00	200.00	250.00	1200.00
☐ 18500	40,000	125.00	150.00	200.00	325.00	3200.00

DATE	MINTAGE	ABP	VG-8 V. Good	F-12 Fine	VF-20 V. Fine	MS-60 Unc.	PRF-65 Proof
☐ 1851	1,300	150.00	300.00	950.00	1500.00	6000.00	
☐ 1852	1,100	600.00	850.00	1050.00	1700.00	6000.00	
☐ 1853	46,110	40.00	80.00	95.00	135.00	900.00	
☐ 1854	33,140	60.00	125.00	200.00	300.00	1200.00	
☐ 1855	26,000	125.00	250.00	300.00	400.00	1500.00	10000.00
☐ 1856	63,500	60.00	120.00	200.00	225.00	1000.00	9000.00
☐ 1857	94,000	50.00	100.00	150.00	200.00	1000.00	9000.00
☐ 1858 PROOFS ONLY	80						8500.00
☐ 1859	256,500	40.00	75.00	100.00	150.00	800.00	5000.00
☐ 1859O	360,000	40.00	75.00	85.00	95.00	800.00	
☐ 1859S	20,000	60.00	125.00	150.00	225.00	1000.00	
☐ 1860	218,930	50.00	100.00	125.00	150.00	800.00	8000.00
☐ 1860O	515,000	40.00	75.00	85.00	95.00	800.00	
☐ 1861	78,500	40.00	90.00	100.00	130.00	900.00	8000.00
☐ 1862	12,090	125.00	250.00	350.00	500.00	1500.00	8000.00
☐ 1863	27,660	50.00	100.00	150.00	225.00	1200.00	8000.00
☐ 1864	31,170	60.00	125.00	175.00	225.00	1000.00	8000.00
☐ 1865	47,000	60.00	125.00	150.00	200.00	1200.00	8000.00

☐ 1866 No Motto — 2 Known — PROOF — 50,000.00

SILVER DOLLARS — LIBERTY SEATED, 1866 - 1873
Motto "IN GOD WE TRUST" Added

DATE	MINTAGE	ABP	VG-8 V. Good	F-12 Fine	VF-20 V. Fine	MS-60 Unc.	PRF-65
☐ 1866	49,625	70.00	150.00	175.00	200.00	1500.00	8000.00
☐ 1867	47,525	60.00	125.00	165.00	200.00	1500.00	8000.00
☐ 1868	162,700	40.00	80.00	100.00	150.00	1500.00	8000.00
☐ 1869	424,300	50.00	90.00	100.00	100.00	1500.00	8000.00
☐ 1870	416,000	48.00	90.00	100.00	120.00	1500.00	8000.00
☐ 1870CC	12,462	75.00	150.00	200.00	300.00	2000.00	
☐ 1870S			RARE — $62,500.00: 1973 Sale				
☐ 1871	1,074,760	48.00	75.00	85.00	95.00	1000.00	8000.00
☐ 1871CC	1,376	250.00	500.00	750.00	1100.00	5800.00	
☐ 1872	1,106,450	48.00	75.00	85.00	100.00	1000.00	8000.00
☐ 1872CC	3,150	105.00	200.00	375.00	700.00	3250.00	

DATE	MINTAGE	ABP	VG-8 V. Good	F-12 Fine	VF-20 V. Fine	MS-60 Unc.	PRF-65 Proof
☐ 1872S	9,000	55.00	85.00	150.00	750.00	2500.00	
☐ 1873	193,600	48.00	75.00	85.00	95.00	1000.00	8000.00
☐ 1873CC	2,300	375.00	600.00	850.00	1000.00	8000.00	
☐ 1873S	700		UNKNOWN IN ANY COLLECTION				

SILVER DOLLARS — TRADE, 1873 - 1885

In the early 1870's there was mounting pressure to increase the silver dollar's weight, as American commerce with Japan was being hindered by the fact that our silver dollar was somewhat smaller than European crowns. It was decided to strike a special coin, known as the "Trade Dollar," to weigh 27.22 grains and be composed of nine parts silver to one part copper. Much agitation to retain the silver dollar as a domestic circulating coin resulted in the government authorizing this new enlarged version to pass as legal tender (for its $1 face value) in transactions of $5 or less. This caused confusion and dissatisfaction, and in 1878 striking of a separate domestic silver dollar, based upon the pre-Trade Dollar standard, was resumed. For a while they were issued simultaneously until the Trade Dollar died a gradual death, its final year of striking being 1885. 1878 was the last year in which they were struck in numbers that could be termed sufficient for free circulation. The Trade Dollar has sometimes been called one of the handsomest U.S. coins of that denomination. True enough, the design is well drawn, but striking of circulating specimens was in such low relief that the slightest handling all but obliterated the more attractive detailing. Only when seen in proof state can the Trade Dollar's beauty be recognized. The designer was William Barber. On the reverse is a seated figure of Liberty, with an eagle reverse. The wording "TRADE DOLLAR" appears at the foot of the reverse. This is the only U.S. coin to proclaim its composition; the reverse is inscribed "420 GRAINS, 900 FINE." Meaning, of course, .900 silver to .100 base metal. Beginning in 1876 the Trade Dollar was no longer legal for domestic use. The Treasury Department (assailed from all sides in those days) left itself open to sharp criticism by not offering to redeem Trade Dollars until 1887, 11 years later. In diameter the Trade Dollar was no larger than the normal issues, 38.1 mm., but somewhat thicker. It was the heaviest U.S. silver coin ever minted. Only recently has it come into what might be termed popularity among collectors. In terms of mintage totals vs. regular dollars it is still rather underpriced.

Mint Mark is Below Eagle in Reverse

DATE	MINTAGE	ABP	F-12 Fine	EF-40 Ex. Fine	MS-60 Unc.**	PRF-65
☐ 1873	397,500	35.00	50.00	85.00	600.00	10000.00
☐ 1873CC	124,500	40.00	65.00	150.00	700.00	
☐ 1873S	703,000	38.00	55.00	90.00	600.00	
☐ 1874	987,800	35.00	48.00	65.00	500.00	10000.00
☐ 1874CC	1,373,200	38.00	60.00	125.00	600.00	
☐ 1874S	2,549,000	35.00	48.00	80.00	500.00	
☐ 1875	218,000	37.00	100.00	200.00	800.00	10000.00
☐ 1875CC	1,573,700	38.00	60.00	110.00	600.00	
☐ 1875S	4,487,000	35.00	48.00	65.00	500.00	
☐ 1875S over CC		100.00	250.00	535.00	1550.00	
☐ 1876	456,150	35.00	48.00	65.00	500.00	10000.00
☐ 1876CC	509,000	38.00	60.00	105.00	600.00	
☐ 1876S	5,227,000	35.00	48.00	80.00	500.00	
☐ 1877	3,039,710	35.00	48.00	80.00	500.00	10000.00
☐ 1877CC	534,000	40.00	80.00	155.00	675.00	
☐ 1877S	9,519,000	35.00	48.00	65.00	600.00	
☐ 1878	900	2000.00	PROOFS ONLY			10000.00
☐ 1878CC	97,000	115.00	205.00	450.00	2500.00	
☐ 1878S	4,162,000	35.00	48.00	75.00	500.00	
☐ 1879	1,541	2000.00	PROOFS ONLY			10000.00
☐ 1880	1,987	2000.00	PROOFS ONLY			10000.00
☐ 1881	960	2000.00	PROOFS ONLY			10000.00
☐ 1882	1,097	2000.00	PROOFS ONLY			10000.00
☐ 1883	979	1100.00	PROOFS ONLY			10000.00
☐ 1884	10		PROOFS ONLY		*	52500.00
☐ 1885	5		PROOFS ONLY—EXTREMELY RARE			

*KEISBERG AUCTION 1976
**Superbly struck pieces bring proportionately more than prices shown.

SILVER DOLLARS — LIBERTY HEAD or "MORGAN", 1878 - 1904, and 1921

For the resumption of the standard silver dollar series a new design was chosen. The work of George T. Morgan, and thereby popularly called Morgan Dollar, it showed a profile head of Liberty backed with an eagle holding arrows and branch. The motto "IN GOD WE TRUST" was installed above the eagle in Old English Gothic lettering. On the obverse appeared the slogan "E PLURIBUS UNUM." For many years the Morgan dollar was the best known and probably most respected silver "crown" in the world. Artistically the work is superb, rendered all the more impressive by the fact that its detailing did not become easily effaced with use. Morgan's goal was to fashion for this country a coin which, if it did not carry the financial power of ancient Greek silver pieces, might be regarded as their equal in design. The Morgan dollar remained unchanged in weight and composition throughout its history. It was comprised of nine parts silver to one part copper and weighed 412.5 grains. The diameter is 38.1 mm. After having been struck in large quantities for two and a half decades, production sometimes exceeding 30 million pieces annually, it was suspended in 1904 because of a shortage of silver. Striking was resumed in 1921, but only briefly, as the new Peace Dollar was introduced that same year. However there were more Morgan dollars coined in 1921 — over 80 million — than in any previous year. The mintmark is placed below the eagle on the reverse.

Beginning collectors should not be unduly influenced by the rising prices of common-date Morgan dollars. Market prices on these coins are set mainly by the value of silver bullion and do not indicate any special or increased demand for the coins by numismatists. It is quite likely, however, that if wholesale smelting of common Morgan dollars continues at the present pace, these coins will grow scarcer. The Morgan dollar contains .77344 ounce of silver, or slightly more than three-quarters of an ounce.

Mint Mark is Below Eagle on Reverse

DATE	MINTAGE	ABP	F-12 Fine	EX-40 Ex. Fine	MS-60 Unc.	PRF-65 Proof
☐ 1878 7 Tail Feathers	416,000	14.00	17.00	20.00	60.00	8000.00
☐ 1878 8 Tail Feathers	750,000	14.00	19.00	28.00	60.00	7000.00
☐ 1878 7 over 8 Tail Feathers		14.00	20.00	36.00	75.00	
☐ 1878CC	2,212,000	14.00	28.00	38.00	90.00	
☐ 1878S	9,774,000	14.00	17.00	18.00	45.00	
☐ 1879	14,807,100	14.00	16.00	18.00	45.00	7000.00
☐ 1879CC	756,000	20.00	38.00	200.00	900.00	
☐ 18790	2,887,000	14.00	16.00	18.00	60.00	
☐ 1879S	9,110,000	14.00	16.00	18.00	45.00	
☐ 1880	12,601,355	14.00	16.00	18.00	45.00	7000.00

DATE	MINTAGE	ABP	F-12 Fine	EX-40 Ex. Fine	MS-60 Unc.	PRF-65 Proof
☐ 1880CC	591,000	25.00	45.00	75.00	165.00	
☐ 1880 over 79CC		28.00	60.00	100.00	225.00	
☐ 1880O	5,305,000	14.00	16.00	18.00	85.00	
☐ 1880S	8,900,000	14.00	16.00	18.00	45.00	
☐ 1881	9,163,975	14.00	16.00	18.00	45.00	7000.00
☐ 1881CC	206,000	30.00	70.00	90.00	175.00	
☐ 1881O	5,708,000	14.00	16.00	18.00	45.00	
☐ 1881S	12,760,000	14.00	16.00	18.00	45.00	
☐ 1882	11,101,000	14.00	16.00	18.00	48.00	7000.00
☐ 1882CC	1,133,000	14.00	30.00	36.00	90.00	
☐ 1882O	6,090,000	14.00	16.00	18.00	45.00	
☐ 1882S	9,250,000	14.00	16.00	18.00	45.00	
☐ 1883	12,191,039	14.00	16.00	18.00	45.00	7000.00
☐ 1883CC	1,204,000	14.00	30.00	36.00	60.00	
☐ 1883O	8,725,000	14.00	16.00	18.00	35.00	
☐ 1883S	6,250,000	14.00	16.00	29.00	500.00	
☐ 1884	14,070,875	14.00	16.00	18.00	60.00	7000.00
☐ 1884CC	1,136,000	14.00	35.00	45.00	60.00	
☐ 1884O	9,730,000	14.00	16.00	18.00	35.00	
☐ 1884S	3,200,000	14.00	16.00	30.00	1200.00	
☐ 1885	17,787,767	14.00	16.00	18.00	35.00	7000.00
☐ 1885CC	228,000	80.00	125.00	150.00	200.00	
☐ 1885O	9,185,000	14.00	16.00	18.00	35.00	
☐ 1885S	1,497,000	14.00	18.00	30.00	175.00	
☐ 1886	19,963,886	14.00	16.00	18.00	35.00	7000.00
☐ 1886O	10,710,000	14.00	16.00	20.00	500.00	
☐ 1886S	750,000	14.00	26.00	45.00	275.00	
☐ 1887	20,290,710	14.00	16.00	18.00	35.00	7000.00
☐ 1887O	11,550,000	14.00	16.00	18.00	50.00	
☐ 1887S	1,771,000	14.00	18.00	22.00	130.00	
☐ 1888	19,183,833	14.00	16.00	18.00	40.00	7000.00
☐ 1888O	12,150,000	14.00	16.00	20.00	45.00	
☐ 1888S	657,000	14.00	28.00	55.00	275.00	
☐ 1889	21,726,811	14.00	16.00	20.00	40.00	7000.00
☐ 1889CC	350,000	85.00	165.00	600.00	6250.00	
☐ 1889O	11,875,000	14.00	16.00	20.00	135.00	
☐ 1889S	700,000	14.00	30.00	50.00	162.00	
☐ 1890	16,802,590	14.00	16.00	18.00	55.00	7000.00
☐ 1890CC	2,309,041	14.00	28.00	40.00	200.00	
☐ 1890O	10,701,000	14.00	16.00	20.00	80.00	
☐ 1890S	8,230,373	14.00	18.00	22.00	78.00	
☐ 1891	8,694,206	14.00	18.00	20.00	190.00	7000.00
☐ 1891CC	1,618,000	16.00	28.00	40.00	150.00	
☐ 1891O	7,954,529	14.00	18.00	21.00	165.00	
☐ 1891S	5,296,000	14.00	18.00	23.00	90.00	
☐ 1892	1,037,245	14.00	18.00	25.00	170.00	7000.00
☐ 1892CC	1,352,000	28.00	38.00	76.00	330.00	
☐ 1892O	2,744,000	14.00	18.00	25.00	250.00	
☐ 1892S	1,200,000	16.00	26.00	170.00	5500.00	

DATE	MINTAGE	ABP	F-12 Fine	EX-40 Ex. Fine	MS-60 Unc.	PRF-65 Proof
☐ 1893	378,792	20.00	45.00	100.00	600.00	7000.00
☐ 1893CC	667,000	35.00	50.00	300.00	1200.00	
☐ 1893O	300,000	35.00	55.00	250.00	1100.00	
☐ 1893S	100,000	750.00	1000.00	3000.00	25000.00	
☐ 1894	110,972	150.00	250.00	450.00	1500.00	7000.00
☐ 1894O	1,723,000	14.00	20.00	35.00	600.00	
☐ 1894S	1,260,000	14.00	28.00	100.00	500.00	
☐ 1895*	12,880		PROOF ONLY		35000.00	
☐ 1895O	450,000	25.00	60.00	300.00	3000.00	
☐ 1895S	400,000	40.00	80.00	500.00	1800.00	
☐ 1896	9,976,762	14.00	25.00	20.00	40.00	8000.00
☐ 1896O	4,900,000	14.00	16.00	25.00	900.00	
☐ 1896S	5,000,000	14.00	25.00	100.00	900.00	
☐ 1897	2,822,731	14.00	16.00	20.00	50.00	7000.00
☐ 1897O	4,004,000	14.00	16.00	20.00	525.00	
☐ 1897S	5,825,000	14.00	18.00	24.00	90.00	
☐ 1898	5,884,725	14.00	16.00	20.00	40.00	7000.00
☐ 1898O	4,440,000	14.00	16.00	20.00	40.00	
☐ 1898S	4,102,000	14.00	18.00	24.00	325.00	
☐ 1899	330,846	14.00	50.00	72.00	115.00	8000.00
☐ 1899O	12,290,000	14.00	16.00	20.00	40.00	
☐ 1899S	2,562,000	14.00	20.00	35.00	450.00	
☐ 1900	8,830,912	14.00	16.00	20.00	40.00	8000.00
☐ 1900O	12,590,000	14.00	16.00	20.00	40.00	
☐ 1900S	3,540,000	14.00	18.00	24.00	250.00	
☐ 1901	6,962,813	14.00	28.00	45.00	1100.00	10000.00
☐ 1901O	13,320,000	14.00	16.00	20.00	45.00	
☐ 1901S	2,284,000	14.00	20.00	35.00	450.00	
☐ 1902	7,994,777	14.00	18.00	22.00	75.00	8000.00
☐ 1902O	8,636,000	14.00	16.00	20.00	50.00	
☐ 1902S	1,530,000	14.00	35.00	100.00	400.00	
☐ 1903	4,652,755	14.00	18.00	20.00	80.00	7000.00
☐ 1903O	4,450,000	50.00	165.00	225.00	350.00	
☐ 1903S	1,241,000	14.00	25.00	145.00	2250.00	
☐ 1904	2,788,650	14.00	18.00	20.00	350.00	7000.00
☐ 1904O	3,720,000	14.00	16.00	20.00	40.00	
☐ 1904S	2,304,000	14.00	40.00	125.00	1300.00	
☐ 1921	44,690,000	14.00	16.00	18.00	35.00	
☐ 1921D	20,345,000	14.00	16.00	18.00	45.00	
☐ 1921S	21,695,000	14.00	16.00	18.00	65.00	

*Check carefully for removed Mint Mark.

NOTE: Superbly struck specimens with few bag marks bring substantially more than the prices listed.

SILVER DOLLARS — PEACE, 1921 - 1935

It was decided, following the Armistice of 1918, to issue a coin commemorating world peace, and to make this a circulating coin rather than a limited issue. As production of silver dollars was being resumed in 1921 this was the logical denomination. This coin, known as the Peace Dollar, was designed by Anthony DeFrancisci, who had some reputation as a designer of medals. Its obverse pictured a profile head of Liberty, quite different in character from those on other coins, and a standing eagle (perched on a mound) on its reverse. The word "Peace" was incorporated into the reverse. As originally engraved the dies were similar in nature to those of a medal, intended to strike in high relief. The following year modified dies were introduced. Coining of silver dollars was halted in 1935 and never resumed, the subsequent Ike and Anthony dollars being of a different metallic composition. Mintmark appears beneath the word "ONE" in "ONE DOLLAR" on the reverse. The Peace dollar is composed of 90% silver and 10% copper and has a weight of 412½ grains. The diamter is 38.1 mm. and the silver content is .77344 of an ounce.

Mint Mark — Below "One" and to Left of Wingtip

DATE	MINTAGE	ABP	F-12 Fine	EX-40 Ex. Fine	MS-60 Unc.
☐1921	1,006,473	20.00	35.00	60.00	600.00
☐1922	51,737,000	14.00	16.00	18.00	35.00
☐1922D	15,063,000	14.00	16.00	18.00	65.00
☐1922S	17,475,000	14.00	16.00	18.00	65.00
☐1923	30,800,000	14.00	16.00	18.00	35.00
☐1923D	6,811,000	14.00	16.00	18.00	60.00
☐1923S	19,020,000	14.00	16.00	18.00	110.00
☐1924	11,811,000	14.00	16.00	18.00	40.00
☐1924S	1,728,000	14.00	18.00	28.00	250.00
☐1925	10,198,000	14.00	16.00	18.00	38.00
☐1925S	1,610,000	14.00	17.00	25.00	325.00
☐1926	1,939,000	14.00	17.00	22.00	65.00
☐1926D	2,348,700	14.00	17.00	25.00	150.00
☐1926S	6,980,000	14.00	17.00	21.00	75.00

DATE	MINTAGE	ABP	F-12 Fine	EX-40 Ex. Fine	MS-60 Unc.
☐ 1927	848,000	14.00	25.00	32.00	125.00
☐ 1927D	1,268,900	14.00	18.00	30.00	325.00
☐ 1927S	866,000	14.00	19.00	28.00	435.00
☐ 1928	360,649	85.00	150.00	200.00	375.00
☐ 1928S	1,632,000	14.00	18.00	26.00	325.00
☐ 1934	954,057	14.00	25.00	30.00	150.00
☐ 1934D	1,569,500	14.00	18.00	26.00	200.00
☐ 1934S	1,011,000	14.00	20.00	135.00	2800.00
☐ 1935	1,576,000	14.00	18.00	24.00	100.00
☐ 1935S	1,964,000	14.00	18.00	26.00	250.00

DOLLARS — EISENHOWER, 1971 - 1978

Throughout most of the 1960's plans were variously put forward to resume striking $1 coins. In 1964 production was actually started up, using the old Peace design. After more than 300,000 specimens were coined it was decided to withhold the dollar coin until a more appropriate time and all were scrapped. Then in 1971, following the death of President Eisenhower, a dollar piece with his likeness on the obverse, backed by an adaption of the Apollo 11 insignia, was placed into circulation. Our astronauts had landed on the moon just two years earlier and this was commemorated by the reverse. Frank Gasparro, chief engraver of the Mint, was its designer. Due to the greatly increased price of silver bullion it was not possible to mint this coin as a "silver dollar." Its size was equivalent to that of earlier silver dollars but the composition bore little resemblance to the old standard. Two versions were struck, a collector's edition with an 80% silver exterior and ordinary circulating coins with an outer layer of three parts copper and one part nickel enclosing an interior of pure copper. The former had a weight of 24.59 grams, of which .31625 of an ounce was pure silver. The latter weighed 22.68 grams. Both have a 38.1 mm. diameter. In 1976 a special reverse design was applied, featuring a representation of the Liberty Bell superimposed against the moon, in connection with the Bicentennial. The obverse carried a double date, 1776-1976. Some silver-clad specimens were struck, their specification the same as stated above. In the following year the original reverse was reinstated. The final year of production was 1978.

DATE	MINTAGE	MS-60 Unc.	PRF-65 Proof
☐ 1971 Copper-nickel clad	47,799,000	2.10	
☐ 1971D Copper-nickel clad	68,587,424	2.10	
☐ 1971S Silver clad	11,133,764	9.00	10.00
☐ 1972 Copper-nickel clad	75,390,000	2.25	
☐ 1972D Copper-nickel clad	92,548,511	2.10	
☐ 1972S Silver clad	4,004,657	16.00	28.00
☐ 1973 Copper-nickel clad	2,000,056	16.00	
☐ 1973D Copper-nickel clad	2,000,000	16.00	
☐ 1973S Copper-nickel clad	2,760,339	15.00	
☐ 1973S Silver clad	1,883,140		5.00
☐ 1974 Copper-nickel clad	27,366,000	1.50	
☐ 1974D Copper-nickel clad	45,520,175	1.50	
☐ 1974S Copper-nickel clad	2,617,350	16.00	
☐ 1974S Silver clad	3,216,420		5.00
☐ 1976 Copper-nickel clad Variety I	4,021,250	2.75	
☐ 1976 Copper-nickel clad Variety II	113,325,000	1.25	
☐ 1976D Copper-nickel clad Variety I	21,048,650	1.50	
☐ 1976D Copper-nickel clad Variety II	82,179,355	1.25	
☐ 1976S Copper-nickel clad Variety I	2,845,390		13.00
☐ 1976S Copper-nickel clad Variety II	4,149,675		4.00
☐ 1976S Silver clad (40%)	4,239,460	9.00	11.50
☐ 1977 Copper-nickel clad	12,598,220	2.00	
☐ 1977D Copper-nickel clad	32,985,000	1.80	
☐ 1977S Copper-nickel clad	3,250,895		3.75
☐ 1978 Copper-nickel clad	25,702,000	1.50	
☐ 1978D Copper-nickel clad	33,012,890	1.50	
☐ 1978S Copper-nickel clad	3,127,781		13.00

DOLLARS — SUSAN B. ANTHONY, 1979 TO DATE

In 1979 the Eisenhower dollar was replaced by one picturing Susan B. Anthony, agitator for female suffrage in the earlier part of this century. The new coin, the target of much controversy, had the distinction of a number of "firsts":

*First U.S. coin to picture a female (excluding mythological and symbolic types)
*First non-gold dollar coin of small size.
*First U.S. coin with non-circular edge.

The Anthony dollar measures 26½ mm., or about the size of a quarter. To avoid its confusion with coins of that denomination, the edge was not made circular but squared out into sections. Its composition is: exterior, three parts copper to one part nickel; interior, pure copper. The weight is eight and 1/10th grams. On the reverse appears the Apollo 11 insignia used for the Eisenhower dollar. Public dissatisfaction with the coin has placed its future in doubt. The designer was Frank Gasparro.

DATE	MINTAGE	MS-60 Unc.	PRF-65 Proof
☐ 1979 Copper-nickel clad		1.05	
☐ 1979D Copper-nickel clad		1.05	
☐ 1979S Copper-nickel clad			12.00

GOLD DOLLARS, 1849 - 1889

No gold dollars were struck in the Mint's early years. It was felt (logically enough, based upon conditions that existed then) that silver would serve adequately for this denomination, and that gold should be restricted to coins of a higher face value. However a series of events occured, following the California gold strikes of 1849, which rendered gold dollars a necessity. Chief among them was the growing practice of citizens, especially in the West, to trade with bullion rather than coinage. So in 1849 a gold dollar was introduced. Designed by James Longacre, it carried a Liberty head on the obverse and was backed by a simple reverse featuring a wreath and the numeral one in arabic. A series of stars encircled the obverse portrait. As this coin was by necessity of diminutive size, elaborate designing was not possible. The Liberty Gold Dollar weighed 1.672 grams and was composed of 90% gold and 10% copper. It had a diameter of 13 mm. The mintmark appears below the wreath. In 1854 the obverse was given over to an Indian Head and the coin made flatter, its diameter increased to 15 mm. The weight was unaltered. There was a further change in 1856 when a new die was cast for the obverse, showing the Indian Head a bit larger. This was the final variety for the gold dollar, whose last year of coining was 1889. The gold content by weight for all three types was .04837 of an ounce.

GOLD DOLLARS — LIBERTY HEAD WITH CORONET, SMALL SIZE
1849 - 1854

Mint Mark is Below Wreath on Reverse

DATE	MINTAGE	ABP in F-12	F-12 Fine	EF-40 Ex. Fine	MS-60 Unc.
☐ 1849	688,600	200.00	275.00	400.00	1000.00
☐ 1849C Closed Wreath	11,634	250.00	325.00	425.00	1800.00
☐ 1849C Open Wreath	4 Known		EXTREMELY RARE		
☐ 1849D	21,588	200.00	275.00	850.00	2000.00
☐ 1849O	215,000	200.00	275.00	400.00	900.00
☐ 1850	481,953	200.00	275.00	400.00	900.00
☐ 1850C	6,966	250.00	325.00	700.00	2250.00
☐ 1850D	8,382	250.00	325.00	900.00	2500.00
☐ 1850O	14,000	200.00	275.00	400.00	900.00
☐ 1851	3,317,671	200.00	275.00	400.00	900.00
☐ 1851C	41,267	200.00	275.00	525.00	1500.00
☐ 1851D	9,832	200.00	275.00	925.00	2500.00
☐ 1851O	290,000	200.00	275.00	400.00	900.00
☐ 1852	2,045,351	200.00	275.00	400.00	900.00
☐ 1852C	9,434	200.00	325.00	700.00	2250.00
☐ 1852D	6,360	200.00	325.00	925.00	2500.00
☐ 1852O	140,000	200.00	275.00	400.00	900.00
☐ 1853	4,076,051	200.00	275.00	400.00	900.00
☐ 1853C	11,515	250.00	325.00	625.00	1800.00
☐ 1853D	6,583	250.00	325.00	925.00	2500.00
☐ 1853O	290,000	200.00	275.00	400.00	900.00
☐ 1854*	1,639,445	200.00	275.00	400.00	900.00
☐ 1854D	2,935	250.00	325.00	1400.00	5000.00
☐ 1854S	14,635	250.00	325.00	400.00	2500.00

*Includes Indian Headress Dollars of 1854 Type II

GOLD DOLLARS — SMALL LIBERTY HEAD, FEATHER HEADDRESS, LARGE SIZE, 1854 - 1856

Mint Mark is Below Wreath on Reverse

DATE	MINTAGE	ABP in F-12	F-12 Fine	EF-40 Ex. Fine	MS-60 Unc.
☐ *1854**	1,639,445	250.00	325.00	825.00	5200.00
☐ 1854C	4		UNKNOWN		
☐ 1855	758,269	250.00	325.00	825.00	5000.00
☐ 1855C	8,903	250.00	400.00	1200.00	9000.00
☐ 1855D	1,811	1250.00	1800.00	5000.00	10000.00
☐ 1855O	55,000	275.00	350.00	1000.00	8000.00
☐ 1856S	24,600	275.00	350.00	850.00	7000.00

*Includes Indian Headdress Dollars of 1854 Type II
**Includes Mintage of Liberty Head of 1854 Type I

GOLD DOLLARS — LARGE LIBERTY HEAD, FEATHER HEADDRESS, LARGE SIZE, 1856 - 1889

Mint Mark is Below Wreath on Reverse

DATE	MINTAGE	ABP in F-12	F-12 Fine	EF-40 Ex. Fine	MS-60 Unc.	PRF-65 Proof
☐ 1856 Slant 5	1,762,936	175.00	225.00	300.00	900.00	
☐ 1856D	1,460	1750.00	2000.00	5000.00	15000.00	
☐ 1857	774,789	175.00	225.00	300.00	900.00	
☐ 1857C	13,280	175.00	225.00	600.00	2000.00	
☐ 1857D	3,533	250.00	325.00	1400.00	3500.00	
☐ 1857S	10,000	175.00	225.00	325.00	1500.00	
☐ 1858	117,995	175.00	225.00	300.00	900.00	15000.00
☐ 1858D	3,477	325.00	425.00	1400.00	4000.00	
☐ 1858S	10,000	175.00	225.00	300.00	1200.00	
☐ 1859	168,244	175.00	225.00	300.00	900.00	13500.00
☐ 1859C	5,235	175.00	225.00	700.00	2000.00	
☐ 1859D	4,952	200.00	265.00	1200.00	2500.00	
☐ 1859S	15,000	175.00	225.00	325.00	2000.00	
☐ 1860	36,688	175.00	225.00	300.00	900.00	12000.00
☐ 1860D	1,566	1800.00	2150.00	5500.00	11000.00	
☐ 1860S	13,000	175.00	225.00	325.00	1000.00	
☐ 1861	527,499	175.00	225.00	325.00	900.00	12000.00
☐ 1861D		2500.00	3200.00	12500.00	20000.00	
☐ 1862	1,326,865	175.00	225.00	300.00	900.00	12000.00
☐ 1863	6,250	175.00	225.00	700.00	4000.00	12000.00
☐ 1864	5,950	175.00	225.00	550.00	3000.00	12000.00
☐ 1865	3,725	175.00	225.00	650.00	3200.00	14000.00
☐ 1866	7,180	175.00	225.00	400.00	1500.00	13000.00
☐ 1867	5,250	175.00	225.00	375.00	1500.00	12000.00
☐ 1868	10,525	175.00	225.00	325.00	1500.00	12000.00
☐ 1869	5,925	175.00	225.00	350.00	1500.00	12000.00
☐ 1870	6,335	175.00	225.00	350.00	1300.00	12000.00
☐ 1870S	3,000	250.00	325.00	1000.00	3500.00	
☐ 1871	3,930	175.00	225.00	400.00	1500.00	12000.00
☐ 1872	3,530	175.00	225.00	400.00	1800.00	12000.00
☐ 1873 open 3	125,125	175.00	225.00	500.00	900.00	
☐ 1873 closed 3		175.00	225.00	500.00	1500.00	12000.00
☐ 1874	198,820	175.00	225.00	300.00	900.00	12000.00
☐ 1875	420	1750.00	2000.00	3250.00	9000.00	14000.00
☐ 1876	3,245	175.00	225.00	350.00	1600.00	12000.00
☐ 1877	3,920	175.00	225.00	500.00	1800.00	12000.00
☐ 1878	3,020	175.00	225.00	500.00	1600.00	10000.00

DATE	MINTAGE	ABP in F-12	F-12 Fine	EF-40 Ex. Fine	MS-60 Unc.	PRF-65 Proof
☐1879	3,030	175.00	225.00	525.00	1500.00	10000.00
☐1880	1,636	175.00	225.00	525.00	1400.00	10000.00
☐1881	7,660	175.00	225.00	325.00	900.00	7000.00
☐1882	5,040	175.00	225.00	325.00	900.00	7000.00
☐1883	10,840	175.00	225.00	300.00	900.00	7000.00
☐1884	6,206	175.00	225.00	325.00	900.00	6000.00
☐1885	12,205	175.00	225.00	300.00	900.00	6000.00
☐1886	6,016	175.00	225.00	325.00	900.00	6000.00
☐1887	8,543	175.00	225.00	325.00	800.00	6000.00
☐1888	16,080	175.00	225.00	300.00	800.00	6000.00
☐1889	30,729	175.00	225.00	300.00	800.00	6000.00

Many gold dollars in the 1880's were hoarded and appear in gem prooflike condition. Beware of these pieces being sold as proofs.

QUARTER EAGLES — $2.50 GOLD PIECES

The $2.50 gold piece, authorized on April 2, 1792, was known as a "Quarter Eagle" (i.e., the quarter part of an Eagle or $10 gold piece). Striking was not begun until 1796. As early production was extremely limited — in no year were as many as 10,000 struck until 1834 — these are scarce and valuable coins. Designed by Robert Scot, the original type featured a capped Liberty on the obverse and shield eagle reverse. The portrait is quite different than that used on silver coinage and in general the engraving may be said to be somewhat superior. No wording other than "LIBERTY" adorns the obverse, with "UNITED STATES OF AMERICA" on the obverse. The composition was .9167 gold to .0833 copper, or more than 9/10ths gold, with a weight of 4.37 grams and a diameter which varied slightly but normally was about 20 mm. There are two obverse types, one with and one without a circular border of stars. In 1808 the portrait, while retaining the cap, was entirely redesigned. It was shifted around to face left instead of right, the cap was de-emphasized, Liberty's features were redrawn in an effort at greater femininity, her hair was made curlier, and the eagle was likewise refurbished. John Reish was the designer. From 1809 to 1820 no quarter eagles were minted. When the series was resumed in 1821 it was with modified obverse and reverse types and the diameter had shrank to 18½ mm. However, the coin contained fully as much gold as previously and the decreased diameter was compensated for by a slight increase in thickness. The obverse was changed in 1834 to the so-called "Classic Head" type, a more stylish rendition of Liberty, designed by the Mint's chief designer, William Kneass (pronounced Niece). The weight was reduced to 4.18 grams and the composition altered to contain less than 9/10ths gold: .8992 to .1008 copper. The diameter was 18.2 mm. Christian Gobrecht made some alterations to this design in 1840 but it was not materially changed. However, the gold content was increased to an even .900 and the diameter brought down to 18 mm. Total gold content by weight was .12094. This design remained in use for 67 years, surpassed for longevity only by the Lincoln Penny (1909-present). An interesting variation occurred in 1848, the so-called "California Quarter Eagle." In that year Colonel Mason, the Military Governor of California, shipped about 230 ounces of gold to Secretary of War Marcy in Washington, D.C. March had the bullion melted down and struck into quarter eagles, distinguished by the abbreviation, "CAL.", above the eagle's head on the reverse. This was not an integral part of the design but was stamped separately. As little more than 1,000 specimens were struck it became a choice collector's item. Purchasers should be on guard against fakes. The Gobrecht Quarter Eagle was discontinued in 1907. Specimens dated after 1900, and some earlier ones, are valued primarily for their bullion content.

QUARTER EAGLES — LIBERTY HEAD, 1796 - 1807

1808
Draped
Bust
Round Cap

1821-1834
Undraped
Liberty
Round Cap

1808-1834
Motto
Over Eagle

DATE	MINTAGE	ABP in F-12	F-12 Fine	EF-40 Ex. Fine	MS-60 Unc.
☐ 1796 No Stars	963	6000.00	7250.00	18000.00	35000.00
☐ 1796 With Stars	432	4500.00	6000.00	14000.00	32000.00
☐ 1797	427	3000.00	4000.00	9000.00	18000.00
☐ 1798	1,094	2000.00	2500.00	6500.00	14000.00
☐ 1802 over 1	3,033	1200.00	1600.00	6000.00	12000.00
☐ 1804 14 Star Reverse	3,327	1500.00	2000.00	6000.00	12000.00
☐ 1804 13 Star Reverse		2500.00	3200.00	10000.00	16000.00
☐ 1805	1,781	1500.00	2000.00	6000.00	12000.00
☐ 1806 over 4	1,616	1200.00	2000.00	6000.00	12000.00
☐ 1806 over 5		3000.00	3750.00	10000.00	18000.00
☐ 1807	6,812	1000.00	1500.00	5500.00	10000.00

QUARTER EAGLES — BUST TYPE, ROUND CAP, 1808 - 1834

1796
No Stars

1797-1807
With Stars

1796-1807

DATE	MINTAGE	ABP in F-12	F-12 Fine	EF-40 Ex. Fine	MS-60 Unc.
☐ 1808	2,710	4500.00	6000.00	16000.00	30000.00
REDUCED SIZE					
☐ 1821	6,448	2000.00	2500.00	7000.00	15000.00

☐ 1824 over 21	2,600	2000.00	2500.00	7000.00	15000.00
☐ 1825	4,434	2000.00	2500.00	7000.00	15000.00
☐ 1826 over 25	760	2200.00	3000.00	9500.00	18000.00
☐ 1827	2,800	2000.00	2500.00	7000.00	12000.00
☐ 1829	3,403	1500.00	2000.00	7000.00	12000.00
☐ 1830	4,540	1500.00	2000.00	7000.00	12000.00
☐ 1831	4,520	1200.00	1500.00	5000.00	12000.00
☐ 1832	4,400	1200.00	1500.00	5000.00	12000.00
☐ 1833	4,160	1200.00	1500.00	5000.00	12000.00
☐ 1834 Motto	4,000	2500.00	3250.00	10000.00	24500.00

QUARTER EAGLES — LIBERTY HEAD WITH RIBBONS, 1834 - 1839
No Motto Over Eagle

Mint Mark is above Date on Obverse

DATE	MINTAGE	ABP in F-12	F-12 Fine	EF-40 Ex. Fine	MS-60 Unc.
☐ 1834 No Motto	112,234	175.00	225.00	475.00	4000.00
☐ 1835	131,402	175.00	225.00	475.00	4000.00
☐ 1836	547,986	175.00	225.00	475.00	4000.00
☐ 1837	45,080	175.00	225.00	475.00	4000.00
☐ 1838	47,030	175.00	225.00	475.00	4000.00
☐ 1838C	7,908	250.00	325.00	800.00	5000.00
☐ 1839	27,021	200.00	250.00	475.00	4000.00
☐ 1839C	18,173	175.00	225.00	700.00	5000.00
☐ 1839D	13,674	550.00	700.00	1400.00	7000.00
☐ 18390	17,781	225.00	300.00	700.00	4000.00

QUARTER EAGLES — LIBERTY HEAD WITH CORONET, 1840 - 1907

Mint Mark is below Eagle on Reverse

DATE	MINTAGE	ABP in F-12	F-12 Fine	EF-40 Ex. Fine	MS-60 Unc.
☐ 1840	18,859	160.00	200.00	275.00	700.00
☐ 1840C	12,838	175.00	225.00	600.00	1400.00
☐ 1840D	3,532	175.00	225.00	900.00	2000.00
☐ 1840O	26,200	160.00	200.00	275.00	625.00
☐ 1841		Stack's 1976 $40,000 in Proofs			
☐ 1841C	10,297	160.00	200.00	500.00	1400.00
☐ 1841D	4,164	175.00	225.00	1200.00	3500.00
☐ 1842	2,823	175.00	225.00	750.00	1800.00
☐ 1842C	6,737	160.00	200.00	500.00	1200.00
☐ 1842D	4,643	175.00	225.00	1000.00	3250.00
☐ 1842O	19,800	175.00	225.00	275.00	600.00
☐ 1843	100,546	175.00	200.00	300.00	500.00
☐ 1843C Small Date	26,096	575.00	700.00	2250.00	7000.00
☐ 1843C Large Date	26,096	175.00	200.00	500.00	1200.00
☐ 1843D	36,209	175.00	200.00	600.00	1500.00
☐ 1843O Small Date	368,002	175.00	200.00	300.00	500.00
☐ 1843O Large Date	368,002	175.00	200.00	300.00	675.00
☐ 1844	6,784	175.00	200.00	500.00	1400.00
☐ 1844C	11,622	175.00	200.00	500.00	1200.00
☐ 1844D	17,332	175.00	200.00	600.00	1500.00
☐ 1845	91,051	175.00	200.00	300.00	500.00
☐ 1845D	19,460	175.00	200.00	600.00	1500.00
☐ 1845O	4,000	275.00	350.00	1200.00	3000.00
☐ 1846	21,598	175.00	200.00	300.00	500.00
☐ 1846C	4,808	185.00	225.00	800.00	2000.00
☐ 1846D	19,303	275.00	250.00	750.00	1600.00
☐ 1846O	66,000	175.00	200.00	300.00	500.00
☐ 1847	29,814	175.00	200.00	300.00	500.00
☐ 1847C	23,226	185.00	225.00	500.00	1200.00
☐ 1847D	15,784	200.00	275.00	700.00	1600.00
☐ 1847O	124,000	175.00	200.00	300.00	500.00
☐ 1848	8,886	200.00	275.00	800.00	1600.00
☐ 1848 Cal. above Eagle	1,389	2250.00	3000.00	8000.00	18000.00
☐ 1848C	16,788	185.00	225.00	500.00	1200.00
☐ 1848D	13,771	200.00	275.00	700.00	1600.00
☐ 1849	23,294	175.00	200.00	300.00	500.00
☐ 1849C	10,220	185.00	225.00	500.00	1200.00
☐ 1849D	10,945	200.00	225.00	700.00	1800.00
☐ 1850	252,923	175.00	200.00	300.00	500.00
☐ 1850C	9,148	185.00	225.00	500.00	1200.00
☐ 1850D	12,148	185.00	225.00	700.00	1800.00
☐ 1850O	84,000	160.00	200.00	300.00	500.00
☐ 1851	1,372,748	175.00	200.00	300.00	500.00
☐ 1851C	14,923	185.00	225.00	475.00	1200.00
☐ 1851D	11,264	185.00	225.00	700.00	1800.00
☐ 1851O	148,000	175.00	200.00	300.00	550.00
☐ 1852	1,159,681	175.00	200.00	300.00	500.00
☐ 1852C	9,772	185.00	225.00	525.00	1200.00
☐ 1852D	4,078	185.00	225.00	700.00	2000.00

DATE	MINTAGE	ABP in F-12	F-12 Fine	EF-40 Ex. Fine	MS-60 Unc.
☐ 1852O	140,000	175.00	200.00	300.00	500.00
☐ 1853	1,404,668	175.00	200.00	300.00	500.00
☐ 1853D	3,178	185.00	225.00	800.00	2000.00
☐ 1854	596,258	160.00	200.00	300.00	500.00
☐ 1854C	7,295	175.00	200.00	500.00	1200.00
☐ 1854D	1,760	1000.00	1200.00	3200.00	7000.00
☐ 1854O	153,000	160.00	200.00	300.00	600.00
☐ 1854S	246	EXTREMELY RARE—EF-40 $30,000.00			
☐ 1855	235,480	160.00	200.00	300.00	500.00
☐ 1855C	3,677	400.00	500.00	1200.00	3000.00
☐ 1855D	1,123	900.00	1000.00	3500.00	7000.00

DATE	MINTAGE	ABP in F-12	F-12 Fine	EF-40 Ex. Fine	MS-60 Unc.	PRF-65 Proof
☐ 1856	384,240	140.00	175.00	275.00	525.00	
☐ 1856C	7,913	175.00	200.00	525.00	1200.00	
☐ 1856D	874	1500.00	1800.00	5500.00		
☐ 1856O	21,100	140.00	175.00	300.00	575.00	
☐ 1856S	71,120	140.00	175.00	300.00	600.00	
☐ 1857	214,130	140.00	175.00	275.00	500.00	20000.00
☐ 1857D	2,364	185.00	225.00	1000.00	4000.00	
☐ 1857O	34,000	140.00	175.00	275.00	500.00	
☐ 1857S	68,000	140.00	175.00	275.00	750.00	
☐ 1858	9,056	185.00	225.00	450.00	1625.00	
☐ 1858	47,377	140.00	175.00	275.00	600.00	25000.00
☐ 1859	39,444	140.00	175.00	275.00	600.00	20000.00
☐ 1859D	2,244	185.00	225.00	800.00	2000.00	
☐ 1859S	15,200	140.00	175.00	275.00	700.00	
☐ 1860	22,675	140.00	175.00	275.00	500.00	17000.00
☐ 1860C	7,469	185.00	225.00	550.00	1800.00	
☐ 1860S	35,600	140.00	175.00	275.00	600.00	
☐ 1861	1,272,518	140.00	175.00	275.00	500.00	17000.00
☐ 1861S	24,000	140.00	175.00	275.00	600.00	
☐ 1862	112,353	140.00	175.00	275.00	500.00	18000.00
☐ 1862S	8,000	140.00	175.00	350.00	1000.00	
☐ 1863	30	PROOFS ONLY		**		36000.00
☐ 1863S	10,800	140.00	175.00	275.00	600.00	
☐ 1864	2,874	400.00	500.00	1800.00	3000.00	20000.00
☐ 1865	1,545	375.00	425.00	1500.00	2800.00	20000.00
☐ 1865S	23,376	140.00	175.00	275.00	500.00	
☐ 1866	3,110	175.00	200.00	450.00	1000.00	15000.00
☐ 1867	3,250	175.00	200.00	425.00	900.00	15000.00
☐ 1867S	28,000	140.00	175.00	275.00	500.00	
☐ 1868	3,625	185.00	225.00	350.00	1000.00	15000.00
☐ 1868S	34,000	140.00	175.00	300.00	600.00	
☐ 1869	4,343	140.00	175.00	300.00	725.00	15000.00
☐ 1869S	29,500	140.00	175.00	275.00	700.00	
☐ 1870	4,555	140.00	175.00	325.00	725.00	12000.00
☐ 1870S	16,000	140.00	175.00	375.00	600.00	

**Auction 1976 Garrett Collection.

DATE	MINTAGE	ABP in F-12	F-12 Fine	EF-40 Ex. Fine	MS-60 Unc.	PRF-65 Proof
☐ 1871	5,350	140.00	175.00	300.00	700.00	12000.00
☐ 1871S	22,000	140.00	175.00	275.00	625.00	
☐ 1872	3,030	175.00	200.00	375.00	800.00	12000.00
☐ 1872S	18,000	140.00	175.00	275.00	500.00	
☐ 1873	178,025	140.00	175.00	275.00	525.00	12000.00
☐ 1873S	27,000	140.00	175.00	275.00	500.00	
☐ 1874	3,940	175.00	200.00	350.00	700.00	15000.00
☐ 1875	420	1000.00	1400.00	5000.00	9000.00	20000.00
☐ 1875S	11,600	140.00	175.00	275.00	500.00	
☐ 1876	4,221	140.00	175.00	275.00	800.00	12000.00
☐ 1876S	5,000	140.00	175.00	300.00	1000.00	
☐ 1877	1,652	225.00	300.00	600.00	1800.00	15000.00
☐ 1877S	35,000	140.00	175.00	275.00	500.00	
☐ 1878	286,260	140.00	175.00	275.00	525.00	14000.00
☐ 1878S	55,000	140.00	175.00	275.00	525.00	
☐ 1879	88,900	140.00	175.00	275.00	525.00	12000.00
☐ 1879S	43,500	140.00	175.00	275.00	525.00	
☐ 1880	2,996	140.00	175.00	300.00	700.00	12000.00
☐ 1881	680	400.00	500.00	1600.00	3200.00	15000.00
☐ 1882	4,040	140.00	175.00	300.00	600.00	12000.00
☐ 1883	1,960	140.00	175.00	375.00	700.00	12000.00
☐ 1884	1,993	140.00	175.00	375.00	700.00	12000.00
☐ 1885	887	400.00	500.00	1500.00	2750.00	12000.00
☐ 1886	4,088	140.00	175.00	275.00	600.00	12000.00
☐ 1887	6,282	140.00	175.00	275.00	500.00	12000.00
☐ 1888	16,098	140.00	175.00	275.00	525.00	12000.00
☐ 1889	17,648	140.00	175.00	275.00	525.00	12000.00
☐ 1890	8,813	140.00	175.00	275.00	525.00	10000.00
☐ 1891	11,040	140.00	175.00	275.00	525.00	10000.00
☐ 1892	2,545	140.00	175.00	300.00	700.00	10000.00
☐ 1893	30,106	140.00	175.00	275.00	525.00	10000.00
☐ 1894	4,122	140.00	175.00	275.00	700.00	10000.00
☐ 1895	6,119	140.00	175.00	275.00	600.00	10000.00
☐ 1896	19,202	140.00	175.00	275.00	525.00	9000.00
☐ 1898	24,165	140.00	175.00	275.00	525.00	9000.00
☐ 1899	27,350	140.00	175.00	275.00	525.00	9000.00
☐ 1900	67,205	140.00	175.00	275.00	525.00	9000.00
☐ 1901	91,323	140.00	175.00	275.00	525.00	9000.00
☐ 1902	133,733	140.00	175.00	275.00	525.00	9000.00
☐ 1903	201,257	140.00	175.00	275.00	525.00	9000.00
☐ 1904	160,960	140.00	175.00	275.00	525.00	9000.00
☐ 1905	217,944	140.00	175.00	275.00	525.00	9000.00
☐ 1906	179,490	140.00	175.00	275.00	525.00	9000.00
☐ 1907	336,448	140.00	175.00	275.00	525.00	9000.00

QUARTER EAGLES — INDIAN HEAD, 1908 - 1929

The quarter eagle was redesigned in 1908 by Bela Lyon Pratt. Liberty was removed from its obverse and replaced by a portrait of an Indian wearing a war bonnet. A standing eagle adorned the reverse. The coin has no raised edge and the designs plus inscriptions are stamped in incuse, or recessed beneath the surface, rather than being shown in high relief. The composition is .900 gold., .100 copper, with a weight of 4.18 grams. Its diameter is 18 mm. with total gold content by weight remaining at .12094 ounce. Quarter eagles were last struck in 1929, the year of this nation's financial difficulties.

Mint Mark is to Left of Value on Reverse

DATE	MINTAGE	ABP in F-12	F-12 Fine	EF-40 Ex. Fine	MS-60 Unc.	PRF-65 Proof
☐ 1908	565,057	125.00	150.00	250.00	325.00	2500.00
☐ 1908	441,899	125.00	150.00	250.00	325.00	2500.00
☐ 1910	492,682	125.00	150.00	250.00	325.00	2500.00
☐ 1911	404,191	125.00	150.00	250.00	325.00	2500.00
☐ 1911D	55,680	400.00	500.00	1200.00	1400.00	2500.00
☐ 1912	616,197	125.00	150.00	250.00	325.00	2500.00
☐ 1913	722,165	125.00	150.00	250.00	325.00	2500.00
☐ 1914	240,117	125.00	150.00	250.00	325.00	2500.00
☐ 1914D	448,000	125.00	150.00	250.00	325.00	
☐ 1915	606,100	125.00	150.00	250.00	325.00	2500.00
☐ 1925D	578,000	125.00	150.00	250.00	325.00	
☐ 1926	446,000	125.00	150.00	250.00	325.00	
☐ 1927	388,000	125.00	150.00	250.00	325.00	
☐ 1928	416,000	125.00	150.00	250.00	325.00	
☐ 1929	532,000	125.00	150.00	250.00	325.00	

$3.00 GOLD PIECES
LIBERTY HEAD WITH FEATHER HEADDRESS, 1854 - 1889

Introduction and apparent public acceptance of the gold dollar in 1849 led to speculation on the possible usefulness of gold coinage in other denominations. The $3 gold piece, composed of 9/10ths gold with an alloy of 1/10th copper, was introduced in 1854. It carried an Indian Head on the obverse and a wreathed reverse. Its diameter was 20½ mm. and the weight 5.015 grams. Though the $3 gold piece continued to be struck until 1889 it had become obvious as early as pre-Civil War years that no great demand or popularity was enjoyed by this coin. The designer was James Longacre. In 1854 the word "DOLLARS" was set in smaller characters than subsequently. Total gold content by weight was .14512 ounce.

Mint Mark is Below Wreath on Reverse

DATE	MINTAGE	ABP in F-12	F-12 Fine	EF-40 Ex. Fine	MS-60 Unc.	PRF-65 Proof
☐ 1854	136,618	350.00	450.00	1200.00	3500.00	
☐ 1854D	1,120	1500.00	1800.00	7000.00	12000.00	
☐ 1854O	24,000	350.00	450.00	1250.00	3500.00	
☐ 1855	50,555	350.00	450.00	1200.00	3500.00	**35000.00
☐ 1855S	6,000	400.00	500.00	1400.00	3800.00	
☐ 1856	26,010	350.00	450.00	1200.00	3500.00	**21000.00
☐ 1856*	34,500	350.00	450.00	1200.00	3500.00	
☐ 1857	20,891	350.00	450.00	1200.00	3500.00	**17000.00
☐ 1857S	14,000	350.00	450.00	1200.00	4000.00	
☐ 1858	2,133	400.00	500.00	1400.00	4000.00	**14000.00
☐ 1859	15,638	350.00	450.00	1200.00	4000.00	20000.00
☐ 1860	7,155	400.00	500.00	1200.00	4000.00	28000.00
☐ 1860	7,000	350.00	450.00	1200.00	4000.00	
☐ 1861	6,072	350.00	450.00	1200.00	4000.00	20000.00
☐ 1862	5,785	350.00	450.00	1200.00	4000.00	20000.00
☐ 1863	5,039	400.00	500.00	1200.00	4500.00	20000.00
☐ 1864	2,680	400.00	500.00	1400.00	6000.00	20000.00
☐ 1865	1,165	500.00	600.00	1400.00	8000.00	30000.00
☐ 1866	4,030	350.00	450.00	1200.00	3800.00	20000.00
☐ 1867	2,650	400.00	500.00	1400.00	4000.00	20000.00
☐ 1868	4,875	350.00	450.00	1200.00	4000.00	20000.00
☐ 1869	2,525	350.00	450.00	1200.00	3500.00	20000.00
☐ 1870	3,535	400.00	500.00	1200.00	4000.00	20000.00
☐ 1870S	2	One piece is in the Eliasburg Collection. The other piece is in the corner stone of the San Francisco Mint.				
☐ 1871	1,330	400.00	500.00	1600.00	4000.00	20000.00
☐ 1872	2,030	350.00	450.00	1500.00	4000.00	20000.00
☐ 1873 Open 3	25	PROOF ONLY				45000.00
☐ 1873*** Closed 3					8000.00	20000.00
☐ 1874	41,820	350.00	450.00	1200.00	4000.00	20000.00
☐ 1875 Proofs Only	20	**Auction Sale $40,000.00				
☐ 1876 Proofs Only	†45	Bowers and Ruddy				27000.00
☐ 1877	1,488	400.00	500.00	1500.00	5000.00	20000.00
☐ 1878	82,324	350.00	450.00	1200.00	3500.00	14000.00
☐ 1879	3,030	400.00	500.00	1200.00	4000.00	14000.00

DATE	MINTAGE	ABP in F-12	F-12 Fine	EF-40 Ex. Fine	MS-60 Unc.	PRF-65 Proof
☐1880	1,036	400.00	500.00	1400.00	4000.00	12000.00
☐1881	550	700.00	800.00	2000.00	6000.00	12000.00
☐1882	1,540	400.00	500.00	1200.00	4000.00	12000.00
☐1883	940	400.00	500.00	1400.00	4000.00	12000.00
☐1884	1,106	400.00	500.00	1200.00	4000.00	12000.00
☐1885	910	400.00	500.00	1200.00	4250.00	12000.00
☐1886	1,142	400.00	500.00	1200.00	4000.00	12000.00
☐1887	6,160	350.00	450.00	1200.00	4000.00	12000.00
☐1888	5,291	350.00	450.00	1200.00	4000.00	12000.00
☐1889	2,429	350.00	450.00	1200.00	4000.00	12000.00

*Found in Small, Medium and Large S Varieties. **Stack's Sale 1976.
***All Restrikes †45 Originals 150 Restrikes, Bowers and Ruddy Sale 1979.
Beware of deceiving counterfeits with the following dates 1855, 1857, 1878, 1882, and 1888.

"STELLA" — $4.00 GOLD PIECES
LIBERTY HEAD WITH FLOWING or COILED HAIR, 1879 - 1880

In 1879 and 1880 proofs were struck, in limited quantities, of a $4 gold coin that never reached circulation. It was called "Stella" and was coined not only in gold but various other metals. The gold specimens are extremely valuable. There are two obverse types, one designed by Barber and the other by Morgan.

Flowing Hair

Coiled Hair

DATE	MINTAGE	ABP in PRF-65	PRF-65 Proof
☐1879 Flowing Hair (PROOFS ONLY)	415	27500.00	45000.00
☐1879 Coiled Hair (PROOFS ONLY)	10	85000.00	120000.00
☐1880 Flowing Hair (PROOFS ONLY)	15	50000.00	75000.00
☐1880 Coiled Hair (PROOFS ONLY)	10	80000.00	100000.00

HALF EAGLES — $5.00 GOLD PIECES, 1795 - 1908

The Half Eagle or $5 gold piece was authorized on April 2, 1792, and first struck in 1795. It has the distinction of being the first gold coin struck by the U.S. Mint. Production was limited in the early years. Its designer was Robert Scot. The composition was .9167 gold to .0833 copper alloy, yielding a weight of 8.75 grams and a diameter of (generally) 25 mm. A capped portrait of Liberty facing right adorned the obverse, with stars and date appearing below the portrait; on the reverse is a spread-winged eagle holding in its beak a wreath, surrounded by the wording "UNITED STATES OF AMERICA." Some alterations in the number of stars and size of figures in the date will be observed. These should be taken close account of as they can have a considerable bearing on value. In 1807 John Reich redesigned the Half Eagle. The bust, now "capped and draped," was turned round to face left and the eagle modified. A shortened bust was introduced in 1913. A further modification was made in 1829 but with the same basic design retained. By this time the Quarter Eagle had become an important circulating as well as banking piece, whose significance was to later increase. The year 1834 brought a revised design known as the "Classic Head," the work of William Kneass. The weight of this new coin was 8.36 grams and its composition .8992 gold to .1008 copper, with a diameter of 22½ mm. The slogan "IN GOD WE TRUST," previously used on the reverse, was dropped, probably because of a shortage of space. This was followed by Gobrecht's "Coronet" head in 1839, used until 1908. Its gold content was raised slightly to 9/10ths and the copper reduced to 1/10th. Gold content by weight was .24187 ounce. There are small and large date varieties of this coin. In 1866, following the Civil War, "IN GOD WE TRUST" was added to the rather cramped sapce between the eagle's head and the legend "UNITED STATES OF AMERICA." Composition was as before but the weight was changed to 8.359 grams and the diameter reduced to 21.6 mm. One of the longest lived of coin designs, it remained in use a full 70 years, to be replaced by Pratt's Indian head in 1908.

HALF EAGLES — LIBERTY HEAD, 1795 - 1807
Eagle on Reverse

Head Right
1795-1807

1795-1798
Small Eagle

1795-1807
Large Eagle

DATE	MINTAGE	ABP in F-12	F-12 Fine	EF-40 Ex. Fine	MS-60 Unc.
☐ 1795 Small Eagle	8,707	2250.00	3000.00	8000.00	20000.00
☐ 1795 Large Eagle		3000.00	4000.00	1000.00	25000.00
☐ 1895 over 95*	3,399	2750.00	3500.00	10000.00	20000.00
☐ 1797 over 95**	6,406	3000.00	4000.00	8000.00	15000.00
☐ 1798 Small Eagle	6 Known				
☐ 1798 Large Eagle	24,867	700.00	900.00	4000.00	9000.00
☐ 1799	7,451	700.00	900.00	4000.00	12000.00
☐ 1800	37,620	675.00	875.00	3500.00	10000.00
☐ 1802 over 1	53,176	675.00	875.00	3500.00	10000.00
☐ 1803 over 2	33,506	675.00	875.00	3500.00	10000.00

DATE	MINTAGE	ABP in F-12	F-12 Fine	EF-40 Ex. Fine	MS-60 Unc.
☐ 1804†	30,475	675.00	875.00	3500.00	8500.00
☐ 1805	33,183	675.00	875.00	3500.00	9000.00
☐ 1806†† (Round Top 6)	64,093	675.00	875.00	3000.00	8000.00
☐ 1807 (Head Right)	33,496	675.00	875.00	3000.00	8000.00

*Small Eagle **Large Eagle. 1970 DiBello Auction. †Large 8—Unc. 800.00
††Pointed Top 6—Unc. 800.00

HALF EAGLES — DRAPED BUST, 1807 - 1812
Value 5D on Reverse

HEAD LEFT

"Round Cap"

DATE	MINTAGE	ABP in F-12	F-12 Fine	EF-40 Ex. Fine	MS-60 Unc.
☐ 1807	50,597	650.00	1000.00	3000.00	7000.00
☐ 1808	55,578	650.00	1000.00	3000.00	6000.00
☐ 1809/8	33,875	650.00	1000.00	3000.00	6000.00
☐ 1810	100,287	650.00	1000.00	3000.00	6000.00
☐ 1811	99,581	650.00	1000.00	3000.00	6000.00
☐ 1812	58,087	650.00	1000.00	3000.00	6000.00

HALF EAGLES — LIBERTY HEAD, ROUND CAP, 1813 - 1834
Motto Over Eagle

DATE	MINTAGE	ABP in F-12	F-12 Fine	EF-40 Ex. Fine	MS-60 Unc.
☐ 1813	95,428	1000.00	1200.00	3250.00	8000.00
☐ 1814 (over 13)	15,454	1500.00	2000.00	6000.00	12000.00
☐ 1815	635		EXTREMELY RARE		
☐ 1818	48,588	1500.00	2000.00	4000.00	8000.00
☐ 1819	51,723		RARE 50,000.00		
☐ 1820	263,806	800.00	1200.00	3000.00	8000.00
☐ 1821	34,641	2000.00	2800.00	7000.00	10000.00
☐ 1822		Only 3 Known EXTREMELY RARE			

DATE	MINTAGE	ABP in F-12	F-12 Fine	EF-40 Ex. Fine	MS-60 Unc.
☐ 1823	14,485	2200.00	3000.00	8000.00	14000.00
☐ 1824	17,340	5500.00	6000.00	15000.00	25000.00
☐ 1825 over 21	29,060	2250.00	3000.00	7000.00	16000.00
☐ 1825 over 24	29,060	EXTREMELY RARE			
☐ 1826	18,069	2000.00	3000.00	5000.00	12000.00
☐ 1827	24,913	4500.00	7000.00	35000.00	50000.00
☐ 1828	28,029	RARE			
☐ 1828 over 27	28,029	7000.00	9000.00	20000.00	35000.00
☐ 1829 Small Date	57,442	RARE			
☐ 1829 Large Date		1976 STACK'S AUCTION 65,000			
☐ 1830	126,351	1200.00	1500.00	5000.00	12000.00
☐ 1831	140,594	1200.00	1500.00	5000.00	12000.00
☐ 1832**	157,487	1400.00	2000.00	8000.00	16000.00
☐ 1833	193,630	1200.00	1500.00	5000.00	12000.00
☐ 1835***	50,141	1200.00	1500.00	5000.00	12000.00

**1832 Square Based 2, 13 Stars   ***1834 Crosslet 4: Same Price

HALF EAGLES — LIBERTY HEAD WITH RIBBON, 1834 - 1838
No Motto Over Eagle

4 Plain 4

4 Crosslet 4

Mint Mark is Above Date on Obverse

DATE	MINTAGE	ABP in F-12	F-12 Fine	EF-40 Ex. Fine	MS-60 Unc.
☐ 1834 Plain 4*	682,028	225.00	300.00	500.00	5000.00
☐ 1835	371,534	225.00	300.00	600.00	5000.00
☐ 1836	553,147	225.00	300.00	500.00	5000.00
☐ 1837	207,121	225.00	300.00	500.00	5000.00
☐ 1838	286,588	225.00	300.00	500.00	5000.00
☐ 1838C	12,913	550.00	700.00	1500.00	5500.00
☐ 1838D	20,583	550.00	700.00	1500.00	6000.00

*1834 Crosslet 4 Worth More. Unc. $6000.00

HALF EAGLES — LIBERTY HEAD WITH CORONET, 1839 - 1908

1839-1908

1839-66 No Motto

1866-1908 With Motto

Mint Mark is Below Eagle on Reverse

DATE	MINTAGE	ABP in F-12	F-12 Fine	EF-40 Ex. Fine	MS-60 Unc.	PRF-65 Proof
☐ 1839	118,143	125.00	150.00	300.00	1400.00	
☐ 1839C	23,467	150.00	175.00	700.00	2250.00	
☐ 1839D	18,939	150.00	175.00	1000.00	3000.00	
☐ 1840	137,382	125.00	150.00	250.00	1400.00	
☐ 1840C	19,028	125.00	150.00	500.00	1800.00	
☐ 1840D	22,896	125.00	150.00	750.00	3250.00	
☐ 1840O	30,400	125.00	150.00	275.00	1600.00	
☐ 1841	15,833	125.00	150.00	250.00	1400.00	
☐ 1841C	21,511	125.00	150.00	500.00	1800.00	
☐ 1841D	30,495	125.00	150.00	700.00	3000.00	
☐ 1841O	50		EXTREMELY RARE 2 Known			
☐ 1842	27,578	125.00	150.00	275.00	1500.00	
☐ 1842C (Large Date)*	27,480	125.00	150.00	500.00	3000.00	
☐ 1842D (Small Date)**	59,608	125.00	150.00	700.00	3800.00	
☐ 1842O	16,400	125.00	150.00	500.00	1400.00	
☐ 1843	611,205	125.00	150.00	250.00	1400.00	
☐ 1843	611,205	125.00	150.00	250.00	1400.00	
☐ 1843C	44,353	125.00	150.00	475.00	1800.00	
☐ 1843D	98,452	125.00	150.00	700.00	2500.00	
☐ 1843O	101,075	125.00	150.00	300.00	1400.00	
☐ 1844	340,330	125.00	150.00	250.00	1400.00	
☐ 1844C	23,631	125.00	150.00	500.00	3000.00	
☐ 1844D	88,982	125.00	150.00	700.00	2600.00	
☐ 1844O	364,600	125.00	150.00	275.00	1400.00	
☐ 1845	417,099	125.00	150.00	250.00	1400.00	
☐ 1845D	90,629	125.00	150.00	700.00	2500.00	
☐ 1845O	41,000	125.00	150.00	275.00	1400.00	
☐ 1846	395,942	125.00	150.00	250.00	1400.00	
☐ 1846C	12,995	125.00	150.00	600.00	2000.00	
☐ 1846D	80,294	200.00	250.00	700.00	2800.00	
☐ 1846O	58,000	125.00	150.00	250.00	1400.00	
☐ 1847	915,981	125.00	150.00	250.00	1400.00	
☐ 1847 Impression of extra 7				VERY RARE		
☐ 1847C	84,151	150.00	200.00	500.00	1800.00	
☐ 1847D	64,405	125.00	150.00	700.00	2500.00	
☐ 1847O	12,000	150.00	175.00	700.00	1800.00	

DATE	MINTAGE	ABP in F-12	F-12 Fine	EF-40 Ex. Fine	MS-60 Unc.	PRF-65 Proof
☐ 1848	260,775	125.00	150.00	250.00	1400.00	
☐ 1848C	64,472	125.00	150.00	500.00	1800.00	
☐ 1848D	47,465	150.00	175.00	700.00	3000.00	
☐ 1849	133,070	125.00	150.00	250.00	1400.00	
☐ 1849C	64,823	125.00	150.00	500.00	1800.00	
☐ 1849D	39,036	140.00	175.00	700.00	3000.00	
☐ 1850	64,941	125.00	150.00	250.00	1600.00	
☐ 1850C	63,591	125.00	150.00	500.00	1600.00	
☐ 1850D	53,950	125.00	150.00	700.00	2500.00	
☐ 1851	377,505	125.00	150.00	250.00	1400.00	
☐ 1851C	49,176	125.00	150.00	500.00	1600.00	
☐ 1851D	62,710	125.00	150.00	700.00	2500.00	
☐ 1851O	41,000	125.00	150.00	250.00	1500.00	
☐ 1852	573,901	125.00	150.00	250.00	1400.00	
☐ 1852C	72,574	125.00	150.00	500.00	1600.00	
☐ 1852D	91,452	125.00	150.00	700.00	2500.00	
☐ 1853	305,770	125.00	150.00	250.00	1400.00	
☐ 1853C	65,571	125.00	150.00	500.00	1600.00	
☐ 1853D	89,687	125.00	150.00	700.00	2500.00	
☐ 1854	160,675	125.00	150.00	250.00	1500.00	
☐ 1854C	39,291	125.00	150.00	500.00	1600.00	
☐ 1854D	56,413	125.00	150.00	700.00	2500.00	
☐ 1854O	46,000	125.00	150.00	300.00	1400.00	
☐ 1854S	268		EXTREMELY RARE			
☐ 1855	117,098	125.00	150.00	250.00	1400.00	
☐ 1855C	39,788	125.00	150.00	500.00	1600.00	
☐ 1855D	22,432	125.00	150.00	700.00	2500.00	
☐ 1855O	11,100	150.00	175.00	600.00	1600.00	
☐ 1855S	61,000	125.00	150.00	300.00	1400.00	
☐ 1856	197,990	125.00	150.00	250.00	1400.00	
☐ 1856C	28,457	125.00	150.00	500.00	2000.00	
☐ 1856D	19,786	125.00	150.00	700.00	2800.00	
☐ 1856O	10,000	150.00	175.00	700.00	1600.00	
☐ 1856S	105,100	125.00	150.00	250.00	1400.00	
☐ 1857	98,188	125.00	150.00	250.00	1400.00	
☐ 1857C	31,360	150.00	175.00	500.00	1800.00	
☐ 1857D	17,046	125.00	150.00	750.00	3200.00	
☐ 1857O	13,000	125.00	150.00	400.00	1600.00	
☐ 1857S	87,000	125.00	150.00	250.00	1400.00	
☐ 1858	15,136	125.00	150.00	300.00	1400.00	45000.00
☐ 1858C	38,856	125.00	150.00	500.00	1800.00	
☐ 1858D	15,362	150.00	175.00	800.00	3200.00	
☐ 1858S	18,600	125.00	150.00	250.00	1400.00	
☐ 1859	16,814	125.00	150.00	250.00	1400.00	20000.00
☐ 1859C	31,487	125.00	150.00	500.00	1800.00	
☐ 1859D	10,366	150.00	175.00	800.00	3200.00	
☐ 1859S	13,220	150.00	175.00	500.00	1400.00	
☐ 1860	19,825	125.00	150.00	250.00	1400.00	20000.00

DATE	MINTAGE	ABP in F-12	F-12 Fine	EF-40 Ex. Fine	MS-60 Unc.	PRF-65 Proof
☐ 1860C	14,813	125.00	150.00	600.00	2000.00	
☐ 1860D	14,635	125.00	150.00	700.00	3200.00	
☐ 1860S	21,200	125.00	150.00	300.00	1400.00	
☐ 1861	639,950	125.00	150.00	250.00	1400.00	20000.00
☐ 1861C	6,879	300.00	400.00	1400.00	2800.00	
☐ 1861D	1,597	2000.00	2400.00	5000.00	10000.00	
☐ 1861S	9,500	125.00	150.00	500.00	1800.00	
☐ 1862	4,465	150.00	175.00	600.00	1800.00	20000.00
☐ 1862S	9,500	125.00	150.00	400.00	1800.00	
☐ 1863	2,472	400.00	500.00	1400.00	2800.00	20000.00
☐ 1863S	17,000	125.00	150.00	500.00	1800.00	
☐ 1864	4,220	275.00	300.00	900.00	3200.00	28000.00
☐ 1864S	3,888	800.00	1000.00	1800.00	5000.00	
☐ 1865	1,295	400.00	500.00	1400.00	2800.00	22500.00
☐ 1865S	27,612	125.00	150.00	500.00	1000.00	
☐ 1866S No Motto	43,020	125.00	150.00	500.00	1000.00	
☐ 1866S With Motto	43,020	225.00	275.00	400.00	1200.00	
☐ 1866***	6,720	250.00	300.00	600.00	1200.00	20000.00
☐ 1867	6,920	250.00	300.00	600.00	1200.00	18000.00
☐ 1867S	29,000	125.00	150.00	350.00	1200.00	
☐ 1868	5,725	225.00	275.00	500.00	1000.00	20000.00
☐ 1868S	52,000	125.00	150.00	250.00	1000.00	
☐ 1869	1,785	400.00	600.00	1000.00	2000.00	20000.00
☐ 1869S	31,000	125.00	150.00	300.00	1000.00	
☐ 1870	4,035	250.00	300.00	625.00	1200.00	18000.00
☐ 1870CC	7,675	1400.00	2000.00	3500.00	Unknown in UNC	
☐ 1870S	17,000	125.00	175.00	275.00	1000.00	
☐ 1871	3,230	225.00	300.00	500.00	1200.00	18000.00
☐ 1871CC	20,770	400.00	500.00	725.00	2500.00	
☐ 1871S	25,000	125.00	175.00	275.00	1000.00	
☐ 1872	1,690	500.00	625.00	1000.00	2400.00	17500.00
☐ 1872CC	16,980	500.00	625.00	1000.00	2400.00	
☐ 1872S	36,400	125.00	150.00	250.00	900.00	
☐ 1873	112,505	125.00	150.00	250.00	450.00	18000.00
☐ 1873CC	7,416	725.00	900.00	1200.00	2400.00	
☐ 1873S	31,000	125.00	150.00	250.00	600.00	
☐ 1874	3,508	250.00	325.00	500.00	1000.00	22500.00
☐ 1874CC	21,198	300.00	400.00	800.00	3200.00	
☐ 1874S	16,000	125.00	175.00	275.00	725.00	
☐ 1875	220	VERY RARE				†81000.00
☐ 1875CC	11,828	425.00	675.00	1000.00	2000.00	
☐ 1875S	9,000	225.00	325.00	625.00	2000.00	
☐ 1876	1,477	425.00	600.00	1000.00	2000.00	18000.00
☐ 1876CC	6,887	475.00	750.00	1000.00	2000.00	
☐ 1876S	4,000	1250.00	1600.00	2250.00	4000.00	
☐ 1877	1,152	550.00	700.00	1000.00	2400.00	18000.00
☐ 1877CC	8,680	485.00	675.00	1200.00	2500.00	
☐ 1878	131,740	125.00	150.00	240.00	400.00	18000.00

DATE	MINTAGE	ABP in F-12	F-12 Fine	EF-40 Ex. Fine	MS-60 Unc.	PRF-65 Proof
☐ 1878CC	9,054	1000.00	1500.00	2500.00	6000.00	
☐ 1878S	144,700	125.00	150.00	225.00	400.00	
☐ 1879	301,950	125.00	150.00	225.00	400.00	18000.00
☐ 1879CC	17,281	225.00	250.00	500.00	1000.00	
☐ 1879S	426,200	125.00	150.00	225.00	400.00	
☐ 1880	3,166,436	125.00	150.00	225.00	400.00	15000.00
☐ 1880CC	51,017	125.00	150.00	500.00	900.00	
☐ 1880S	1,348,900	125.00	150.00	225.00	400.00	
☐ 1881	5,708,800	125.00	150.00	225.00	400.00	15000.00
☐ 1881CC	13,886	225.00	300.00	500.00	900.00	
☐ 1881S	969,000	125.00	150.00	225.00	400.00	
☐ 1882	2,514,560	125.00	150.00	225.00	400.00	15000.00
☐ 1882CC	82,817	125.00	150.00	400.00	9500.00	
☐ 1882S	969,000	125.00	150.00	225.00	400.00	
☐ 1883	233,440	125.00	150.00	225.00	400.00	12000.00
☐ 1883CC	12,958	125.00	150.00	375.00	900.00	
☐ 1883S	83,200	125.00	150.00	225.00	400.00	
☐ 1884	191,048	125.00	150.00	225.00	400.00	12000.00
☐ 1884CC	16,402	125.00	150.00	400.00	800.00	
☐ 1884S	177,000	125.00	150.00	225.00	400.00	
☐ 1885	601,506	125.00	150.00	225.00	400.00	12000.00
☐ 1885S	1,211,500	125.00	150.00	225.00	400.00	
☐ 1886	388,432	125.00	150.00	225.00	400.00	12000.00
☐ 1886S	3,268,000	125.00	150.00	225.00	400.00	
☐ 1887	87		RARE			20000.00
☐ 1887S	1,912,000	125.00	150.00	225.00	400.00	
☐ 1888	18,296	125.00	150.00	225.00	400.00	12000.00
☐ 1888S	293,900	125.00	150.00	225.00	400.00	
☐ 1889	7,565	200.00	300.00	375.00	700.00	14000.00
☐ 1890	4,328	125.00	150.00	375.00	700.00	12000.00
☐ 1890CC	53,800	125.00	150.00	525.00	800.00	
☐ 1891	61,413	125.00	150.00	225.00	400.00	12000.00
☐ 1891CC	208,000	125.00	150.00	400.00	800.00	
☐ 1892	753,572	125.00	150.00	225.00	400.00	12000.00
☐ 1892CC	82,968	125.00	150.00	500.00	800.00	
☐ 1892O	10,000	425.00	575.00	900.00	2150.00	
☐ 1892S	298,400	125.00	150.00	225.00	400.00	
☐ 1893	1,528,197	125.00	150.00	225.00	400.00	12000.00
☐ 1893CC	60,000	125.00	150.00	500.00	800.00	
☐ 1893O	110,000	125.00	150.00	275.00	600.00	
☐ 1893S	224,000	125.00	150.00	225.00	400.00	
☐ 1894	957,955	125.00	150.00	225.00	400.00	12000.00
☐ 1894O	16,660	125.00	150.00	275.00	625.00	
☐ 1894S	55,900	125.00	150.00	225.00	400.00	
☐ 1895	1,345,936	125.00	150.00	225.00	400.00	10000.00
☐ 1895S	112,000	125.00	150.00	225.00	400.00	
☐ 1896	59,063	125.00	150.00	225.00	400.00	10000.00
☐ 1896S	115,400	125.00	150.00	225.00	400.00	
☐ 1897	867,883	125.00	150.00	225.00	400.00	10000.00

DATE	MINTAGE	ABP in F-12	F-12 Fine	EF-40 Ex. Fine	MS-60 Unc.	PRF-65 Proof
☐ 1897S	345,000	125.00	150.00	225.00	400.00	
☐ 1898	633,495	125.00	150.00	225.00	400.00	10000.00
☐ 1898S	1,397,400	125.00	150.00	225.00	400.00	
☐ 1899	1,710,729	125.00	150.00	225.00	400.00	10000.00
☐ 1899S	1,545,000	125.00	150.00	225.00	400.00	
☐ 1900	1,405,730	125.00	150.00	225.00	400.00	10000.00
☐ 1900	329,000	125.00	150.00	225.00	400.00	
☐ 1901	616,040	125.00	150.00	225.00	400.00	10000.00
☐ 1901S	3,648,000	125.00	150.00	225.00	400.00	
☐ 1901S 1 over 0					1600.00	
☐ 1902	172,562	125.00	150.00	225.00	400.00	10000.00
☐ 1902S	939,000	125.00	150.00	225.00	400.00	
☐ 1903	227,024	125.00	150.00	225.00	400.00	10000.00
☐ 1903S	1,885,000	125.00	150.00	225.00	400.00	
☐ 1904	392,136	125.00	150.00	225.00	400.00	10000.00
☐ 1904S	97,000	125.00	150.00	225.00	400.00	
☐ 1905	302,308	125.00	150.00	225.00	400.00	10000.00
☐ 1905S	880,700	125.00	150.00	225.00	400.00	
☐ 1906	348,820	125.00	150.00	225.00	400.00	10000.00
☐ 1906D	320,000	125.00	150.00	225.00	400.00	
☐ 1906S	598,000	125.00	150.00	225.00	400.00	
☐ 1907	626,192	125.00	150.00	225.00	400.00	10000.00
☐ 1907D	888,000	125.00	150.00	225.00	400.00	
☐ 1908	421,874	125.00	150.00	225.00	400.00	

*1842C—Small Date, UNC. MS-60 $3000.00
**1842D—Large Date, Uncirculated: 2200.00
***1866 to 1908 — ALL WITH MOTTO OVER EAGLE
†Garrett Collection Auction 1976

INDIAN HEAD, 1908 - 1929

Bela Lyon Pratt's Indian Head design replaced the Libery Head half eagle in 1908. Like the Quarter Eagle these coins are uniquely without raised edges and have designs stamped in incuse or recess rather than raised from the surface. A standing eagle adorns the reverse, with mintmark beneath the wording "E PLURIBUS UNUM." These half eagles contained 90% gold and 10% copper with a weight of 8.359 grains. The diameter is 21.6 mm. and the gold content by weight is .24187 ounce each. Striking of half eagles was suspended during World War I and not resumed until 1929, their final year of production.

Mint Mark is to Left of Value on Reverse

DATE	MINTAGE	ABP in F-12	F-12 Fine	EF-40 Ex. Fine	MS-60 Unc.	PRF-65 Proof
☐ 1908	578,012	135.00	160.00	250.00	900.00	16000.00
☐ 1908D	148,000	135.00	160.00	250.00	900.00	
☐ 1908S	82,000	135.00	160.00	550.00	4000.00	
☐ 1909	627,138	135.00	160.00	250.00	900.00	16000.00
☐ 1909D	3,423,560	135.00	160.00	250.00	800.00	
☐ 1909O*	34,200	300.00	400.00	925.00	10000.00	
☐ 1909S	297,200	135.00	160.00	275.00	2800.00	
☐ 1910	604,250	135.00	160.00	250.00	825.00	16000.00
☐ 1910D	193,600	135.00	160.00	250.00	2000.00	
☐ 1910S	770,200	135.00	160.00	275.00	2500.00	
☐ 1911	915,139	135.00	160.00	250.00	800.00	
☐ 1911D	72,500	135.00	160.00	500.00	5500.00	16000.00
☐ 1911S	1,416,000	135.00	160.00	300.00	1800.00	
☐ 1912	790,144	135.00	160.00	275.00	900.00	
☐ 1912S	392,000	135.00	160.00	325.00	2250.00	
☐ 1913	916,099	135.00	160.00	275.00	800.00	18000.00
☐ 1913S	408,000	135.00	160.00	250.00	6000.00	
☐ 1914	247,125	135.00	160.00	250.00	900.00	18000.00
☐ 1914D	247,000	135.00	160.00	250.00	900.00	
☐ 1914S	263,000	135.00	160.00	250.00	2000.00	
☐ 1915**	588,075	135.00	160.00	250.00	800.00	18000.00
☐ 1915S	164,000	135.00	160.00	250.00	4000.00	
☐ 1916S	240,000	135.00	160.00	250.00	1800.00	
☐ 1929	662,000	1200.00	1600.00	2500.00	9500.00	

*Some "O" Mint Marks are false. **Coins dated 1915D are counterfeit.

EAGLES, $10 GOLD PIECES, 1795 - 1907

Gold pieces valued at $10 were released for general circulation in 1795. Despite the large face value and the super-large buying power ($10 in the 1790's was equivalent to about $200 in present-day money), this coin was struck in substantial numbers, chiefly as a banking piece. Though bullion shortages, speculation, and world economic conditions made the Eagle's career far from sedate, it retained great influence throughout most of its history. The first design, conceived by Robert Scot, comprised a capped bust of Liberty facing right with the so-called Small Eagle reverse, depicting an eagle holding a wreath in its beak. The shield or heraldic eagle replaced this type in 1797 and production was stepped up, output reaching more than 37,000 in 1799. The content was .9167 gold to .0833 copper, with a weight of 17½ grams and diameter generally of 33 mm. From 1805 to 1837 no eagles were struck. When production resumed in 1838 the portrait of Liberty had undergone a thorough alteration, at the hands of Christian Gobrecht. This was the Coronet type, with modified shielded eagle on the reverse. It weighed 16.718 grams with a 9-to-1 gold content (alloyed with copper) and diameter of 27 mm. The gold content by weight was .48375 ounces. The slogan "E PLURIBUS UNUM," previously used on the reverse, was dropped. For many years no motto appeared on the reverse until the installation, in 1866, of "IN GOD WE TRUST." The composition and other specifications remained unaltered. No change was made until 1907 when the Indian Head obverse, designed by Augustus Saint-Gaudens, was introduced.

EAGLES — LIBERTY HEAD WITH CORONET, 1838 - 1907

1838

1838-1866
No Motto

1866-1907
With Motto

Mint Mark is below Eagle on Reverse

DATE	MINTAGE	ABP in F-12	F-12 Fine	EF-40 Ex. Fine	MS-60 Unc.	PRF-65 Proof
☐1838	7,200	400.00	500.00	2500.00	10000.00	
☐1839	38,248	300.00	375.00	1800.00	7500.00	
☐1840	47,338	200.00	250.00	425.00	4500.00	
☐1841	63,131	200.00	250.00	425.00	4000.00	
☐1841O	2,500	300.00	375.00	1000.00	6000.00	
☐1842	81,507	200.00	250.00	425.00	4250.00	
☐1842O	27,400	200.00	250.00	425.00	4250.00	
☐1843	75,462	200.00	250.00	425.00	4250.00	
☐1843O	175,162	200.00	250.00	425.00	4250.00	
☐1844	6,361	200.00	250.00	425.00	5000.00	
☐1844O	118,700	200.00	250.00	425.00	5000.00	
☐1845	26,153	200.00	250.00	425.00	5000.00	
☐1845O	47,500	200.00	250.00	425.00	5000.00	
☐1846	20,095	200.00	250.00	425.00	5000.00	
☐1846O	81,780	200.00	250.00	425.00	5000.00	
☐1847	862,258	200.00	250.00	425.00	5000.00	
☐1847O	417,099	200.00	250.00	425.00	5000.00	
☐1848	145,484	200.00	250.00	425.00	5000.00	
☐1848O	35,850	125.00	250.00	425.00	4250.00	
☐1849	653,618	200.00	250.00	425.00	4250.00	
☐1849O	23,900	200.00	250.00	425.00	4250.00	
☐1850	291,451	200.00	250.00	425.00	4250.00	
☐1850O	57,500	200.00	250.00	425.00	4250.00	
☐1851	176,328	200.00	250.00	425.00	4250.00	
☐1851O	263,000	200.00	250.00	425.00	4250.00	
☐1852	263,106	200.00	250.00	425.00	4250.00	
☐1852O	18,000	200.00	250.00	425.00	4250.00	

DATE	MINTAGE	ABP in F-12	F-12 Fine	EF-40 Ex. Fine	MS-60 Unc.	PRF-65 Proof
☐ 1853	201,253	200.00	250.00	425.00	4250.00	
☐ 1853O	51,000	200.00	250.00	425.00	4250.00	
☐ 1854	54,250	200.00	250.00	425.00	4250.00	
☐ 1854O	52,500	200.00	250.00	425.00	4250.00	
☐ 1854S	123,826	200.00	250.00	425.00	4250.00	
☐ 1855	121,701	200.00	250.00	425.00	4250.00	30000.00
☐ 1855O	18,000	200.00	250.00	425.00	4250.00	
☐ 1855S	9,000	225.00	300.00	1000.00	5000.00	
☐ 1856	60,490	200.00	250.00	425.00	4250.00	25000.00
☐ 1856O	14,500	200.00	250.00	425.00	4250.00	
☐ 1856S	26,000	200.00	250.00	425.00	4250.00	
☐ 1857	16,606	200.00	250.00	425.00	4250.00	
☐ 1857O	5,500	450.00	525.00	1600.00	4250.00	
☐ 1857S	26,000	200.00	250.00	425.00	4250.00	
☐ 1858*	2,521	2000.00	2800.00	5000.00		30000.00
☐ 1858O	20,000	200.00	250.00	425.00	4250.00	
☐ 1858S	11,800	200.00	250.00	425.00	4250.00	
☐ 1859	16,093	200.00	250.00	425.00	4250.00	25000.00
☐ 1859O	2,300	850.00	1100.00	3250.00	4250.00	
☐ 1859S	7,007	350.00	400.00	1000.00	4250.00	
☐ 1860	11,783	200.00	250.00	425.00	4250.00	25000.00
☐ 1860O	11,100	200.00	250.00	600.00	4250.00	
☐ 1860S	5,500	400.00	500.00	1000.00	5500.00	
☐ 1861	113,233	200.00	250.00	425.00	4250.00	25000.00
☐ 1861S	15,500	200.00	250.00	450.00	4250.00	
☐ 1862	10,995	200.00	250.00	425.00	4250.00	30000.00
☐ 1862S	12,500	200.00	250.00	750.00	4250.00	
☐ 1863	1,248	1275.00	1800.00	4500.00	80000.00	30000.00
☐ 1863S	10,000	200.00	250.00	850.00	4250.00	
☐ 1864	3,580	400.00	500.00	1200.00	5000.00	40000.00
☐ 1864S	2,500	850.00	1100.00	1800.00	6000.00	
☐ 1865	4,005	325.00	475.00	1000.00	5500.00	25000.00
☐ 1865S	16,700	225.00	300.00	1000.00	4500.00	
☐ 1866 With Motto	3,780	225.00	275.00	400.00	1000.00	25000.00
☐ 1866S No Motto	20,000	575.00	800.00	1800.00	6000.00	
☐ 1866S With Motto	20,000	275.00	325.00	500.00	1200.00	
☐ 1867	3,140	250.00	300.00	400.00	900.00	25000.00
☐ 1867S	9,000	275.00	325.00	500.00	1000.00	
☐ 1868	10,655	275.00	325.00	375.00	700.00	30000.00
☐ 1868S	13,500	275.00	325.00	500.00	900.00	
☐ 1869	1,855	950.00	1200.00	2200.00	3500.00	30000.00
☐ 1869S	6,430	300.00	375.00	525.00	1200.00	
☐ 1870	2,535	300.00	375.00	700.00	1000.00	25000.00
☐ 1870CC	5,908	1000.00	1400.00	3000.00	10000.00	
☐ 1870S	8,000	300.00	400.00	500.00	1000.00	
☐ 1871S	1,780	850.00	1150.00	2000.00	3200.00	30000.00
☐ 1871CC	7,185	425.00	575.00	1200.00	2250.00	
☐ 1871S	16,500	275.00	325.00	500.00	850.00	
☐ 1872	1,650	725.00	1000.00	1750.00	3200.00	25000.00

DATE	MINTAGE	ABP in F-12	F-12 Fine	EF-40 Ex. Fine	MS-60 Unc.	PRF-65 Proof
☐ 1872CC	5,500	450.00	600.00	900.00	2250.00	25000.00
☐ 1872S	17,300	250.00	300.00	450.00	900.00	
☐ 1873	825	1000.00	1500.00	2150.00	4500.00	30000.00
☐ 1873CC	4,543	725.00	1000.00	1500.00	4500.00	
☐ 1873S	12,000	250.00	300.00	475.00	900.00	
☐ 1874	53,160	250.00	300.00	375.00	600.00	25000.00
☐ 1874CC	16,767	275.00	325.00	500.00	1200.00	
☐ 1874S	10,000	275.00	325.00	600.00	1000.00	
☐ 1875	120	1976 GARRET COLLECTION				91000.00
☐ 1875CC	7,715	500.00	625.00	1150.00	2250.00	
☐ 1876	732	1350.00	1800.00	3500.00	8000.00	25000.00
☐ 1876CC	4,696	700.00	900.00	1500.00	3000.00	
☐ 1876S	5,000	450.00	600.00	900.00	1800.00	
☐ 1877	817	1100.00	1600.00	4200.00	6800.00	30000.00
☐ 1877C	3,332	950.00	1200.00	2000.00	3800.00	
☐ 1877S	17,000	225.00	300.00	375.00	600.00	
☐ 1878	73,800	200.00	250.00	325.00	425.00	30000.00
☐ 1878CC	3,244	950.00	1200.00	2000.00	3500.00	
☐ 1878S	26,100	200.00	250.00	325.00	500.00	
☐ 1879	384,770	200.00	250.00	325.00	425.00	25000.00
☐ 1879CC	1,762	3200.00	4200.00	7000.00	10000.00	
☐ 1879O	1,500	1200.00	2000.00	3200.00	5500.00	
☐ 1879S	224,000	200.00	250.00	325.00	425.00	
☐ 1880	1,644,876	200.00	250.00	325.00	425.00	20000.00
☐ 1880CC	11,192	200.00	250.00	700.00	1200.00	
☐ 1880O	9,500	225.00	300.00	675.00	900.00	
☐ 1880S	506,205	200.00	250.00	325.00	425.00	
☐ 1881	3,877,260	200.00	250.00	325.00	425.00	20000.00
☐ 1881CC	24,015	200.00	250.00	325.00	1000.00	
☐ 1881O	8,350	200.00	250.00	325.00	800.00	
☐ 1881S	970,000	200.00	250.00	325.00	425.00	
☐ 1882	2,324,480	200.00	250.00	325.00	425.00	20000.00
☐ 1882CC	6,764	200.00	250.00	325.00	1200.00	
☐ 1882C	10,280	200.00	250.00	325.00	550.00	
☐ 1882S	132,000	200.00	250.00	325.00	425.00	
☐ 1883	208,740	200.00	250.00	325.00	425.00	20000.00
☐ 1883CC	12,000	200.00	250.00	325.00	1200.00	
☐ 1883S	800	2000.00	3000.00	4250.00	8500.00	
☐ 1883S	38,000	200.00	250.00	325.00	425.00	
☐ 1884	76,017	200.00	250.00	325.00	425.00	35000.00
☐ 1884CC	9,925	200.00	250.00	325.00	1200.00	
☐ 1884S	124,250	200.00	250.00	325.00	425.00	
☐ 1885	253,527	200.00	250.00	325.00	425.00	18000.00
☐ 1885S	228,000	200.00	250.00	325.00	425.00	
☐ 1886	236,160	200.00	250.00	325.00	425.00	18000.00
☐ 1886S	826,000	200.00	250.00	325.00	425.00	
☐ 1887	53,680	200.00	250.00	325.00	425.00	18000.00
☐ 1887S	817,000	200.00	250.00	325.00	425.00	

DATE	MINTAGE	ABP in F-12	F-12 Fine	EF-40 Ex. Fine	MS-60 Unc.	PRF-65 Proof
☐ 1888	132,996	200.00	250.00	325.00	425.00	18000.00
☐ 1888O	21,335	200.00	250.00	325.00	425.00	
☐ 1888S	648,700	200.00	250.00	325.00	425.00	
☐ 1889	4,485	275.00	375.00	600.00	1400.00	20000.00
☐ 1889S	425,400	200.00	250.00	325.00	425.00	
☐ 1890	58,043	200.00	250.00	325.00	425.00	18000.00
☐ 1890CC	17,500	225.00	350.00	475.00	800.00	
☐ 1891	91,868	200.00	250.00	325.00	425.00	18000.00
☐ 1891CC	103,732	225.00	350.00	475.00	800.00	
☐ 1892	797,552	200.00	250.00	325.00	425.00	18000.00
☐ 1892CC	40,000	200.00	250.00	325.00	425.00	
☐ 1892O	28,688	200.00	250.00	325.00	425.00	
☐ 1892S	115,500	200.00	250.00	325.00	425.00	
☐ 1893	1,840,895	200.00	250.00	325.00	425.00	18000.00
☐ 1893CC	14,000	200.00	250.00	325.00	425.00	
☐ 1893O	17,000	200.00	250.00	325.00	425.00	
☐ 1893S	141,350	200.00	250.00	325.00	425.00	
☐ 1894	2,470,782	200.00	250.00	325.00	425.00	18000.00
☐ 1894O	197,500	200.00	250.00	325.00	425.00	
☐ 1894S	25,000	200.00	250.00	325.00	425.00	
☐ 1895	567,826	200.00	250.00	325.00	425.00	18000.00
☐ 1895O	98,000	200.00	250.00	325.00	425.00	
☐ 1895S	49,000	200.00	250.00	325.00	425.00	
☐ 1896	76,348	200.00	250.00	325.00	425.00	18000.00
☐ 1896S	123,750	200.00	250.00	325.00	425.00	
☐ 1897	1,000,159	200.00	250.00	325.00	425.00	20000.00
☐ 1897O	42,500	200.00	250.00	325.00	425.00	
☐ 1897S	234,750	200.00	250.00	325.00	425.00	
☐ 1898	812,197	200.00	250.00	325.00	425.00	16000.00
☐ 1898S	473,600	200.00	250.00	325.00	425.00	
☐ 1899	1,262,305	200.00	250.00	325.00	425.00	16000.00
☐ 1899O	37,047	200.00	250.00	325.00	425.00	
☐ 1899S	841,000	200.00	250.00	325.00	425.00	16000.00
☐ 1900	293,960	200.00	250.00	325.00	425.00	16000.00
☐ 1900S	81,000	200.00	250.00	325.00	425.00	
☐ 1901	1,718,825	200.00	250.00	325.00	425.00	16000.00
☐ 1901O	72,041	200.00	250.00	325.00	425.00	
☐ 1901S	2,812,750	200.00	250.00	325.00	425.00	
☐ 1902	82,513	200.00	250.00	325.00	425.00	16000.00
☐ 1902S	469,500	200.00	250.00	325.00	425.00	
☐ 1903	125,926	200.00	250.00	325.00	425.00	16000.00
☐ 1903O	112,771	200.00	250.00	325.00	425.00	
☐ 1903S		200.00	250.00	325.00	425.00	
☐ 1904	162,038	200.00	250.00	325.00	425.00	16000.00
☐ 1904O	108,950	200.00	250.00	325.00	425.00	
☐ 1905	201,078	200.00	250.00	325.00	425.00	16000.00
☐ 1905S	369,250	200.00	250.00	325.00	425.00	
☐ 1906	165,496	200.00	250.00	325.00	425.00	16000.00
☐ 1906D	981,000	200.00	250.00	325.00	425.00	

DATE	MINTAGE	ABP in F-12	F-12 Fine	EF-40 Ex. Fine	MS-60 Unc.	PRF-65 Proof
☐ 19060	86,895	200.00	250.00	325.00	425.00	
☐ 1906S	457,000	200.00	250.00	325.00	425.00	
☐ 1907	1,203,973	200.00	250.00	325.00	425.00	16000.00
☐ 1907	1,020,000	200.00	250.00	325.00	425.00	
☐ 1907D	1,020,000	200.00	250.00	325.00	425.00	
☐ 1907S	210,000	200.00	250.00	325.00	425.00	

*Check For Removed Mint Mark
**Auction 1976 Garrett Collection

EAGLES — INDIAN HEAD, 1907 - 1933

A. Saint-Gaudens, a noted scultor and really the first artist of international repute to design an American coin, strove to inject a touch of creative feeling in coin design. True to the artistic spirit of the times he sacrificed such supposedly old-fashioned qualities as balance to achieve imagination of line and composition. His eagle, on the reverse, is totally stylized, its strength and symmetry purposely over-emphasized. At first the motto "IN GOD WE TRUST" was omitted, owing to President Theodore Roosevelt's opinion that the name of God was not suitable for use on coinage in any context. He was overruled by Congress in 1908 and the motto appeared shortly thereafter. Striking of eagles, which had reached as high as nearly 4½ million pieces in a single year ($45,000,000 face value), was discontinued in 1933. The Saint-Gaudens Eagle contained 90 percent gold and 10 percent copper, with a diameter of 27 mm. and a weight of 16,718 grams. The bullion weight is .48375 of an ounce.

1907-1908 Without Motto

1908-1933 With Motto

Mint Mark is Left of Value on Reverse

1907-1933

DATE	MINTAGE	ABP in F-12	F-12 Fine	EF-40 Ex. Fine	MS-60 Unc.	PRF-65 Proof
☐ 1907	239,406	225.00	400.00	500.00	1500.00	
☐ 1907 Wire Rim with Periods Before and After U.S.A.	500				10000.00	
☐ 1907 Rolled Rim, Periods	42				45000.00	
☐ 1908 No Motto	33,500	250.00	425.00	500.00	3500.00	
☐ 1908 W/Motto	341,486	250.00	425.00	500.00	1000.00	20000.00
☐ 1908D No Motto	210,000	250.00	425.00	500.00	2000.00	
☐ 1908D	386,500	250.00	425.00	500.00	1200.00	

DATE	MINTAGE	ABP in F-12	F-12 Fine	EF-40 Ex. Fine	MS-60 Unc.	PRF-65 Proof
☐1908S	59,850	275.00	450.00	750.00	5000.00	
☐1909	184,863	250.00	425.00	500.00	1000.00	20000.00
☐1909D	121,540	250.00	425.00	500.00	1800.00	
☐1909S	292,350	250.00	425.00	500.00	2500.00	
☐1910	318,704	250.00	425.00	500.00	1000.00	20000.00
☐1910D	2,356,640	250.00	425.00	500.00	1000.00	
☐1910S	811,000	250.00	425.00	500.00	2800.00	
☐1911	505,595	250.00	425.00	500.00	900.00	20000.00
☐1911D	30,100	450.00	600.00	1000.00	9000.00	
☐1911S	51,000	375.00	500.00	700.00	5000.00	
☐1912	405,083	250.00	425.00	500.00	900.00	20000.00
☐1912S	300,000	250.00	425.00	500.00	3500.00	
☐1913	442,071	250.00	425.00	500.00	900.00	20000.00
☐1913S	66,000	375.00	500.00	500.00	12000.00	
☐1914	151,050	250.00	425.00	500.00	1200.00	20000.00
☐1914D	343,500	250.00	425.00	500.00	1000.00	
☐1914S	208,000	250.00	425.00	500.00	3000.00	
☐1915	351,075	250.00	425.00	500.00	800.00	20000.00
☐1915S	59,000	250.00	425.00	500.00	5000.00	
☐1916S	138,500	250.00	425.00	500.00	3000.00	
☐1920S	126,500	5500.00	8000.00	15000.00	50000.00	
☐1926	1,014,000	250.00	425.00	500.00	900.00	
☐1930S	96,000	2250.00	3200.00	5000.00	15000.00	
☐1932	1,463,000	250.00	425.00	500.00	900.00	
☐1933	312,500		16000.00	55000.00		

The rare dates of this series are heavily counterfeited. Be sure that you buy from a reputable dealer.

DOUBLE EAGLES, $20.00 GOLD PIECES

LIBERTY HEAD, 1849 - 1866
No Motto on Reverse

EXTRA FINE:
Slight wear on beads of crown, slight wear on hair curls, minor

Scratches or digs - Lower Grade.

Mint Mark is below Eagle on Reverse

DATE	MINTAGE	ABP in F-12	F-12 Fine	EF-40 Ex. Fine	MS-60 Unc.	PRF-65 Proof
☐1849	....	Unique —	only 1 known in U.S. Mint Collection			
☐1850	1,170,261	400.00	500.00	750.00	3000.00	
☐1850O	141,000	400.00	500.00	825.00	3500.00	
☐1851	2,087,155	400.00	500.00	750.00	2750.00	
☐1851O	315,000	400.00	500.00	750.00	3000.00	
☐1852	2,053,026	400.00	500.00	750.00	2750.00	
☐1852O	190,000	400.00	500.00	775.00	3000.00	
☐1853	1,261,326	400.00	500.00	750.00	2800.00	
☐1853O	71,000	400.00	500.00	850.00	3500.00	
☐1854	757,899	400.00	500.00	750.00	2750.00	
☐1854O	3,250			40000.00	*52500.00	
☐1854S	141,469	400.00	500.00	750.00	3000.00	
☐1855	364,666	400.00	500.00	750.00	2750.00	
☐1855O	8,000	1000.00	1500.00	3000.00	9500.00	
☐1855S	879,675	400.00	500.00	750.00	2500.00	
☐1856	329,878	400.00	500.00	750.00	2500.00	
☐1856O	2,250			*70000.00		
☐1856S	1,189,750	400.00	500.00	750.00	2750.00	
☐1857	439,375	400.00	500.00	750.00	2500.00	
☐1857O	30,000	400.00	500.00	800.00	3000.00	
☐1857S	970,500	400.00	500.00	750.00	2500.00	
☐1858	211,714	400.00	500.00	750.00	2500.00	45000.00
☐1858O	35,250	400.00	500.00	1200.00	3500.00	
☐1858S	846,710	400.00	500.00	750.00	2500.00	
☐1859	43,597	400.00	500.00	825.00	3250.00	40000.00
☐1859S	636,445	400.00	500.00	2750.00	2500.00	
☐1859O	9,100	1000.00	1500.00	2800.00	7000.00	
☐1860	577,670	400.00	500.00	750.00	2500.00	40000.00
☐1860O	6,600	2000.00	2800.00	4000.00	7500.00	
☐1860O	544,950	400.00	500.00	750.00	2500.00	
☐1861	2,976,453	400.00	500.00	750.00	2500.00	45000.00
☐1861O	5,000	1000.00	1500.00	2000.00	7000.00	
☐1861S	768,000	400.00	500.00	750.00	2750.00	
☐1862	92,133	400.00	500.00	750.00	2750.00	35000.00
☐162S	854,173	400.00	500.00	750.00	2750.00	
☐1863	142,790	400.00	500.00	750.00	2750.00	40000.00
☐1863S	966,570	400.00	500.00	750.00	2750.00	
☐1864	204,285	400.00	500.00	750.00	2750.00	35000.00
☐1864S	793,660	400.00	500.00	750.00	2750.00	
☐1865	351,200	400.00	500.00	750.00	2750.00	40000.00
☐1865S	1,042,500	400.00	500.00	750.00	2750.00	
☐1866S Part of	842,250	400.00	550.00	1000.00	3750.00	

*Stack's Auction 1979

DOUBLE EAGLES — LIBERTY HEAD, 1866 - 1876
With Motto and "TWENTY D" on Reverse

Mint Mark is below Eagle on Reverse

DATE	MINTAGE	ABP in F-12	F-12 Fine	EF-40 Ex. Fine	MS-60 Unc.	PRF-65 Proof
☐ 1866	698,775	400.00	500.00	700.00	1400.00	35000.00
☐ 1866S Part of	698,775	400.00	500.00	700.00	1400.00	
☐ 1867	251,065	400.00	500.00	700.00	1000.00	30000.00
☐ 1867S	920,750	400.00	500.00	700.00	1400.00	
☐ 1868	98,600	400.00	500.00	700.00	1400.00	35000.00
☐ 1868S	837,500	400.00	500.00	700.00	1200.00	
☐ 1869	175,155	400.00	500.00	700.00	1000.00	35000.00
☐ 1869S	686,750	400.00	500.00	700.00	1000.00	
☐ 1870	155,185	400.00	500.00	700.00	1000.00	35000.00
☐ 1870CC	3,789	Auction — 1973 — $28,000.00*				
☐ 1870S	982,000	400.00	500.00	700.00	900.00	
☐ 1871	80,150	400.00	500.00	700.00	900.00	35000.00
☐ 1871CC	14,687	900.00	1200.00	2500.00	4000.00	
☐ 1871S	928,000	400.00	500.00	700.00	900.00	
☐ 1872	251,880	400.00	500.00	700.00	900.00	35000.00
☐ 1872CC	29,650	400.00	500.00	800.00	2250.00	
☐ 1872S	780,000	400.00	500.00	700.00	900.00	
☐ 1873	1,709,825	400.00	500.00	700.00		30000.00
☐ 1873CC	22,410	400.00	500.00	1200.00	2500.00	
☐ 1873S	1,040,600	400.00	500.00	700.00	900.00	
☐ 1874	366,800	400.00	500.00	700.00	900.00	30000.00
☐ 1874CC	115,085	400.00	500.00	700.00	1500.00	
☐ 1874S	1,241,000	400.00	500.00	700.00	900.00	
☐ 1875	295,740	400.00	500.00	700.00	900.00	30000.00
☐ 1875CC	111,151	400.00	500.00	800.00	1500.00	
☐ 1875S	1,230,000	400.00	500.00	700.00	900.00	
☐ 1876	583,905	400.00	500.00	700.00	900.00	50000.00
☐ 1876CC	138,441	400.00	500.00	700.00	1000.00	
☐ 1876	1,597,000	400.00	500.00	700.00	900.00	

1861 and 1861-S both with A. C. Paquet Rev.
61-S rare 61 ex. rare
Stack's Auction in AU-50 condition

DOUBLE EAGLES — LIBERTY, 1877 - 1907
With Motto and "TWENTY DOLLARS" on Reverse

Mint Mark is below Eagle on Reverse

DATE	MINTAGE	ABP in F-12	F-12 Fine	EF-40 Ex. Fine	MS-60 Unc.	PRF-65 Proof
☐ 1877	397,670	400.00	500.00	625.00	750.00	40000.00
☐ 1877CC	42,565	400.00	500.00	625.00	750.00	
☐ 1877S	1,735,000	400.00	500.00	625.00	750.00	
☐ 1878	534,645	400.00	500.00	625.00	750.00	35000.00
☐ 1878CC	13,180	400.00	500.00	625.00	2500.00	
☐ 1878S	1,739,000	400.00	500.00	625.00	750.00	
☐ 1879	207,5630	400.00	500.00	625.00	750.00	35000.00
☐ 1879CC	10,708	500.00	800.00	1200.00	3500.00	
☐ 18790	2,325	800.00	1500.00	2000.00	7000.00	
☐ 1879S	1,223,800	400.00	500.00	625.00	750.00	
☐ 1880	51,456	400.00	500.00	625.00	750.00	30000.00
☐ 1880S	836,000	400.00	500.00	625.00	750.00	
☐ 1881	2,260	800.00	1500.00	6000.00	10000.00	35000.00
☐ 1881S	727,000	400.00	500.00	625.00	750.00	
☐ 1882	630	5500.00	7000.00	12000.00	30000.00	50000.00
☐ 1882CC	39,140	400.00	500.00	625.00	1400.00	
☐ 1882S	1,125,000	400.00	500.00	625.00	750.00	
☐ 1883	40	PROOFS ONLY				95000.00
☐ 1883CC	59,962	400.00	500.00	625.00	1200.00	
☐ 1883S	1,189,000	400.00	500.00	625.00	750.00	
☐ 1884	71	PROOFS ONLY				45500.00
☐ 1884CC	81,139	400.00	500.00	625.00	1200.00	
☐ 1884S	916,000	400.00	500.00	625.00	750.00	
☐ 1885	828	3000.00	4000.00	7000.00	20000.00	50000.00
☐ 1885CC	9,450	625.00	800.00	1000.00	2500.00	
☐ 1885S	683,500	400.00	500.00	625.00	750.00	
☐ 1886	1,106	3000.00	4000.00	9000.00	20000.00	35000.00
☐ 1887	121	PROOFS ONLY				35000.00
☐ 1887S	283	400.00	500.00	625.00		
☐ 1888	226,266	400.00	500.00	625.00	750.00	25000.00
☐ 1888S	859,600	400.00	500.00	625.00	750.00	
☐ 1889	44,111	400.00	500.00	625.00	750.00	30000.00
☐ 1889CC	30,945	400.00	500.00	900.00	1200.00	
☐ 1889S	774,700	400.00	500.00	625.00	750.00	

DATE	MINTAGE	ABP in F-12	F-12 Fine	EF-40 Ex. Fine	MS-60 Unc.	PRF-65 Proof
☐ 1890	75,995	400.00	500.00	625.00	750.00	30000.00
☐ 1890CC	91,209	400.00	500.00	625.00	1200.00	
☐ 1890S	802,750	400.00	500.00	625.00	750.00	
☐ 1891	1,442	1200.00	1800.00	2500.00	7000.00	35000.00
☐ 1891CC	5,000	750.00	1000.00	1600.00	5000.00	
☐ 1891S	1,288,125	400.00	500.00	625.00	750.00	
☐ 1892	4,523	750.00	1000.00	1800.00	5000.00	30000.00
☐ 1892CC	27,265	400.00	500.00	625.00	2000.00	
☐ 1892S	930,150	400.00	500.00	625.00	750.00	
☐ 1893	344,399	400.00	500.00	625.00	750.00	30000.00
☐ 1893O	18,402	400.00	500.00	625.00	750.00	25000.00
☐ 1893S	996,175	400.00	500.00	625.00	750.00	
☐ 1894	1,368,990	400.00	500.00	625.00	750.00	30000.00
☐ 1894S	1,048,550	400.00	500.00	625.00	750.00	
☐ 1895	1,114,656	400.00	500.00	625.00	750.00	25000.00
☐ 1895S	1,143,500	400.00	500.00	625.00	750.00	
☐ 1896	792,663	400.00	500.00	625.00	750.00	25000.00
☐ 1896S	1,403,925	400.00	500.00	625.00	750.00	
☐ 1897	1,383,261	400.00	500.00	625.00	750.00	25000.00
☐ 1897S	1,470,250	400.00	500.00	625.00	750.00	
☐ 1898	170,470	400.00	500.00	625.00	750.00	25000.00
☐ 1898S	2,575,175	400.00	500.00	625.00	750.00	
☐ 1899	1,669,384	400.00	500.00	625.00	750.00	25000.00
☐ 1899S	2,010,300	400.00	500.00	625.00	750.00	
☐ 1900	1,874,584	400.00	500.00	625.00	750.00	25000.00
☐ 1900S	2,459,500	400.00	500.00	625.00	750.00	
☐ 1901	111,526	400.00	500.00	625.00	750.00	25000.00
☐ 1901S	1,596,000	400.00	500.00	625.00	750.00	
☐ 1902	31,254	400.00	500.00	625.00	750.00	25000.00
☐ 1902S	1,753,625	400.00	500.00	625.00	750.00	25000.00
☐ 1903	287,428	400.00	500.00	625.00	750.00	25000.00
☐ 1903S	954,000	400.00	500.00	625.00	750.00	
☐ 1904	6,256,797	400.00	500.00	625.00	750.00	25000.00
☐ 1904S	5,134,175	400.00	500.00	625.00	25000.00	
☐ 1905	59,011	400.00	500.00	625.00	750.00	25000.00
☐ 1905S	1,813,000	400.00	500.00	625.00	25000.00	
☐ 1906	69,690	400.00	500.00	625.00	750.00	25000.00
☐ 1906D	620,250	400.00	500.00	625.00	750.00	
☐ 1906S	2,065,750	400.00	500.00	625.00	750.00	
☐ 1907	1,451,864	400.00	500.00	625.00	750.00	25000.00
☐ 1907D	842,250	400.00	500.00	625.00	750.00	
☐ 1907S	2,165,800	400.00	500.00	625.00	750.00	

DOUBLE EAGLES, ST. GAUDENS, 1907-1933

The Longacre Liberty design was replaced by the Saint-Gaudens in 1907, featuring a striding figure of Liberty holding a torch on the obverse and an eagle in flight on the reverse. A fact seldom mentioned is that this, of all representations of Liberty on our coins, was the only full-face likeness, the others being profiles or semi-profiles. Composition and weight remained as previously. The motto "IN GOD WE TRUST," at first omitted on request of Theodore Roosevelt, was added by Act of Congress in 1908. Striking of Double Eagles ceased in 1933. This final version of the mighty coin had a 90% gold/10% copper composition, with a weight of 33.436 grams (of which .96750 of an ounce was pure gold — almost a full ounce. Its diameter was 34 mm.

As a speculative item for gold investors, the double eagle has enjoyed greater popularity and media publicity in recent months than ever in its history. This should not be surprising as it contains very nearly an exact ounce of gold and its worth as bullion can be figured easily based upon daily gold quotations.

LIBERTY STANDING — ST. GAUDENS
Roman Numerals MCMVII

EXTRA FINE: All details clear. Slight wear on Right Breast, Knee and Lower Feathers of Eagles Breast.

Roman Numeral High Relief, Wire Rim Plain Edge, 14 Rays Over Capitol. Three folds on Liberty's skirt.

DATE	MINTAGE	ABP in F-12	F-12 Fine	EF-40 Ex. Fine	MS-60 Unc.	PRF-65 Proof
☐ 1907-MCMVII Ex. High Relief—Lettered Edge			VERY RARE			435000.00
☐ 1907-MCMVII Ex. High Relief—Plain Engr.			UNIQUE-STACK'S 1974 $200000.00			
☐ 1907 Flat Rim	11,250	3500.00	4250.00	6000.00	12000.00	
☐ 1907 Wire Rim	11,250	3500.00	4250.00	6000.00	12000.00	

DOUBLE EAGLES — LIBERTY STANDING — ST. GAUDENS, 1907 - 1908
Date in Arabic Numerals, No Motto on Reverse

Mint Mark is Above Date on Obverse

DATE	MINTAGE	ABP in F-12	F-12 Fine	EF-40 Ex. Fine	MS-60 Unc.
☐ 1907*	361,667	400.00	525.00	650.00	1000.00
☐ 1908	4,271,551	400.00	525.00	650.00	1000.00
☐ 1908D	66,750	400.00	525.00	600.00	1000.00

*Small Letters on Edge. Large Letter on Edge-Unique.

DOUBLE EAGLES — LIBERTY STANDING — ST. GAUDENS, 1908 - 1933
With Motto on Reverse

Motto "In God We Trust"

Mint Mark is Above Date on Obverse

DATE	MINTAGE	ABP in F-12	F-12 Fine	EF-40 Ex. Fine	MS-60 Unc.	PRF-65 Proof
☐ 1908*	156,359	400.00	525.00	650.00	900.00	35000.00
☐ 1908D*	349,500	400.00	525.00	650.00	700.00	
☐ 1908S	22,000	400.00	525.00	1000.00	4000.00	
☐ 1909	161,282	400.00	525.00	650.00	1000.00	35000.00
☐ 1909 over 8	161,282	400.00	525.00	650.00	2000.00	
☐ 1909D	52,500	400.00	525.00	650.00	650.00	
☐ 1909S	2,774,925	400.00	525.00	650.00	850.00	
☐ 1910	482,167	400.00	525.00	650.00	700.00	35000.00
☐ 1910D	429,000	400.00	525.00	650.00	700.00	
☐ 1910S	2,128,250	400.00	525.00	650.00	700.00	

DATE	MINTAGE	ABP in F-12	F-12 Fine	EF-40 Ex. Fine	MS-60 Unc.	PRF-65 Proof
☐1911	197,350	400.00	525.00	650.00	700.00	
☐1911D	846,500	400.00	525.00	650.00	700.00	
☐1911S	775,750	400.00	525.00	650.00	700.00	
☐1912	149,824	400.00	525.00	650.00	1000.00	30000.00
☐1913	168,838	400.00	525.00	650.00	900.00	30000.00
☐1913D	393,500	400.00	525.00	650.00	700.00	
☐1913S	34,000	400.00	525.00	650.00	1600.00	
☐1914	95,320	400.00	525.00	650.00	900.00	30000.00
☐1914D	453,000	400.00	525.00	650.00	700.00	
☐1914S	1,498,000	400.00	525.00	650.00	700.00	
☐1915	152,050	400.00	525.00	650.00	1000.00	35000.00
☐1915S	567,500	400.00	525.00	650.00	700.00	
☐1916S	796,000	400.00	525.00	650.00	900.00	
☐1920	228,250	400.00	525.00	650.00	900.00	
☐1920S	558,000	3200.00	4000.00	8000.00	20000.00	
☐1921	528,500	8000.00	10000.00	18000.00	30000.00	
☐1922	1,375,500	400.00	525.00	650.00	700.00	
☐1922S	2,658,000	400.00	525.00	650.00	1200.00	
☐1923	566,000	400.00	525.00	650.00	700.00	
☐1923D	1,702,000	400.00	525.00	650.00	1200.00	
☐1924	4,323,500	400.00	525.00	650.00	700.00	
☐1924D	3,049,500	400.00	525.00	650.00	2000.00	
☐1924S	2,927,500	400.00	525.00	650.00	1750.00	
☐1925	2,831,750	400.00	525.00	650.00	700.00	
☐1925D	2,938,500	400.00	525.00	650.00	2750.00	
☐1925S	2,776,500	400.00	525.00	650.00	2750.00	
☐1926	816,750	400.00	525.00	650.00	700.00	
☐1926D	481,000	400.00	525.00	1000.00	2800.00	
☐1926S	2,041,500	400.00	525.00	900.00	2000.00	
☐1927	2,946,750	400.00	525.00	650.00	700.00	
☐1927D	180,000		Private Sale 1974 $17,500.00			
☐1927S	3,107,000	400.00	2500.00	4000.00	12000.00	
☐1928	8,816,000	400.00	525.00	650.00	700.00	
☐1929	1,779,750	400.00	1500.00	3000.00	10000.00	
☐1930S	74,000	400.00	5000.00	9000.00	20000.00	
☐1931	2,938,250	400.00	3750.00	7000.00	16000.00	
☐1931D	106,500	400.00	3500.00	6800.00	20000.00	
☐1932	1,101,750	400.00	4000.00	8000.00	21500.00	
☐1933	445,525		NEVER PLACED IN CIRCULATION			

THE SILVER COMMEMORATIVE COINAGE OF THE UNITED STATES

Commemorative coinage — that is, coins whose designs present a departure from the normal types for their denomination — was first struck in the ancient world. Roman emperors delighted in issuing coins portraying members of the family or tropical events; they served an important propaganda purpose. Commemorative coins must be distinguished from medals, as the former have a stated face value and can be spent as money while the latter serve a decorative function only. During the Mint's first century it coined no commemoratives whatever. Its first was the Columbian half dollar of 1892, issued in connecton with the Columbia Exposition. To date the total has reached 158 pieces, of which one is a silver dollar; one a silver quarter; 143 are half dollars (comprising 48 major types); two are $2.50 gold pieces, two are $50 gold pieces; and nine are $1 gold pieces. There is some objection to including the $50 "Quintuple Eagles" as commemorative *coins*, as regular coins of this denomination were never issued. They dow however bear a statement of face value and were spendable.

Commemorative coins are issued by a special act of Congress and overseen by a committee established for the purpose. Sale of commemoratives is made to the public (and coin dealers) at an advance in price over the face value, this advance being excused on grounds that specimens supplied as choice and uncirculated and have, presumably, sufficient collect appeal to be worth more than their stated denomination. While commemoratives, have certainly not all advanced in price at a comparable pace, all have shown very healthy increases and proved excellent investments for their original or early purchasers.

A pair of medals are traditionally collected in conjunction with commemorative silver coins and careful note should be taken of them. These are the "Octagonal Norse American Centennial, 1828-1925," designed by Opus Fraser, stuck on thick and thin planchets in a total issue of 40,000 (the latter are scarcer); and the "Wilson Dollar," designed by George T. Morgan of Morgan Dollar fame in connection with opening of the Phillipines Mint. The 2 Kroner commemorative of 1936 issued by Sweden is also frequently collected with our commemoratives, though small in size and quite plentiful, as it relates to the Delaware Tercentenary or 300th anniversary.

The extent to which commemorative coins have been used as money is not precisely determined but is thought to be very limited. As the original owners paid a premium for these coins it is not likely that many — except in time of dire need — would have cared to exchange them merely at face value. It should not automatically be presumed that specimens in less than uncirculated condition were indeed used as money and passed through many hands. Their substandard preservation could well be the result of injury, ill-advised cleaning or mounting procedures, or wear received from handling in traveling from collection to collection. Nevertheless, discriminatint buyers expect commemoratives to be in uncirculated state and anything inferior is worth much less (the discount being sharper than for a circulating coin)

The existence of proofs among the commemorative series has aroused much debate. Commemoratives are occasionally seen as proofs, notably the Columbian and Isabella quarters, but this is no evidence that all or even a majority of commemoratives were available in proof state. It is easy to be confused on this point as well-stuck uncirculated specimens frequently have a proof-like appearance.

SILVER COMEMORATIVE, 1892 - 1954
ISABELLA QUARTER DOLLAR

Comparitively little notice was at first taken of this handsome commemorative, because the Columbian Exposition (at which it was issued) had already produced a commemorative and a larger one, in 50¢ denomination. The Isabella Quarter Dollar, originally sold at the exposition for $1, soon became a popular favorite of collectors. Agitation for it was made by the fair's Board of Lady Managers, which may explain why it portrays a female on the obverse — Isabella of Spain, who helped finance Columbus' voyage round the world — and a symbol of "female industry" on its reverse. The coin was designed by C. E. Barber and struck in 1893.

DATE	MINTAGE	ABP in MS-60	MS-60 Unc.	MS-65 Unc.
☐ 1893	24,214	500.00	750.00	1800.00

LAFAYETTE DOLLAR

The celebrated Lafayette Dollar holds a special rank among commemoratives, being the first $1 denomination coin of its sort and the first to portray an American President. On its obverse is a profile bust of General Lafayette, the French officer so instrumental to our efforts in ending colonial domination, over which a profile of Washington is superimposed. The reverse carries a fine equestrian likeness of Lafayette, adapted from a statue put up at Paris as a gift from the American people. This coin was designed by C. E. Barber and struck in 1900. They were sold originally at twice the face value, with proceeds going to the Lafayette Memorial Commission.

DATE	MINTAGE	ABP in MS-60	MS-60 Unc.	MS-65 Unc.
☐ 1900	36,026	2400.00	4500.00	12000.00

SILVER COMMEMORATIVE HALF DOLLARS

COLUMBIAN EXPOSITION HALF DOLLAR

1892-1893

DATE	MINTAGE	ABP in MS-60	MS-60 Unc.	MS-65 Unc.
☐ 1892	950,000	18.00	30.00	175.00
☐ 1893	1,550,405	18.00	30.00	175.00

DATE	MINTAGE		ABP in MS-60	MS-60 Unc.	MS-65 Unc.
☐ 1921 Alabama Centennial	59,038		350.00	550.00	1200.00
☐ 1921 Same w/2 x 2 on Obverse	6,006		375.00	600.00	1500.00
☐ 1936 Albany, N.Y.	17,671		175.00	375.00	650.00
☐ Arkansas Centennial	Type		60.00	100.00	140.00
☐ 1935 Arkansas Centennial	13,012				
☐ 1935D Arkansas Centennial	5,505	SET	190.00	275.00	425.00
☐ 1935S Arkansas Centennial	5,506				
☐ 1936 Arkansas Centennial	9,660				
☐ 1936D Arkansas Centennial	9,660	SET	190.00	275.00	425.00
☐ 1936S Arkansas Centennial	9,662				
☐ 1937 Arkansas Centennial	5,505				
☐ 1937D Arkansas Centennial	5,505	SET	185.00	290.00	450.00
☐ 1937S Arkansas Centennial	5,506				
☐ 1938 Arkansas Centennial	3,156				
☐ 1938D Arkansas Centennial	3,155	SET	450.00	750.00	1250.00
☐ 1938S Arkansas Centennial	3,156				
☐ 1939 Arkansas Centennial	2,104				
☐ 1939D Arkansas Centennial	2,104	SET	950.00	1500.00	2400.00
☐ 1939S Arkansas Centennial	2,105				
☐ 1936 Arkansas (Robinson)	25,265		110.00	150.00	400.00
☐ 1937 Battle of Antietam	18,028		290.00	475.00	900.00
☐ 1936 Battle of Gettysburg	26,030		240.00	400.00	775.00
☐ Boone Bi-Centennial	Type		70.00	125.00	250.00
☐ 1934 Boone Bi-Centennial	10,007		85.00	150.00	250.00
☐ 1935 Boone Bi-Centennial	10,010				
☐ 1935D Boone Bi-Centennial	5,005	SET	225.00	400.00	600.00
☐ 1935S Boone Bi-Centennial	5,005				

DATE	MINTAGE		ABP in MS-60	MS-60 Unc.	MS-65 Unc.
☐ 1935 Boone Bi-Cent. Sm. 1934 Rev.	10,008				
☐ 1935D Type of 1934	2,003	SET	950.00	1600.00	2600.00
☐ 1935S Type of 1934	2,004				
☐ 1936 Type of 1934	12,012				
☐ 1936D Type of 1934	5,006	SET	190.00	385.00	600.00
☐ 1936S Type of 1934	5,005				
☐ 1937 Type of 1934	9,810				
☐ 1937D Type of 1934	2,506	SET	475.00	850.00	1450.00
☐ 1937S Type of 1934	2,506				
☐ 1938 Type of 1934	2,100				
☐ 1938D Same	2,100	SET	900.00	1500.00	2500.00
☐ 1938S Same	2,100				
☐ 1936 Bridgeport, Conn.	25,015		145.00	240.00	350.00
☐ 1925S California Diamond Jubilee	86,594		165.00	350.00	900.00
☐ 1938 Cinc. Music Center	Type		400.00	550.00	850.00
☐ 1936 Cinc. Music Center	5,005				
☐ 1936D Cinc. Music Center	5,005	SET	1175.00	1650.00	2500.00
☐ 1936 Cinc. Music Center	5,006				
☐ 1936 Cleveland Exposition	50,030		70.00	100.00	175.00
☐ 1936 Columbia, S.C.	Type		300.00	450.00	650.00
☐ 1936 Columbia, S.C.	9,007				
☐ 1936D Columbia, S.C.	8,009	SET	875.00	1350.00	1950.00
☐ 1936S Colubmia, S.C.	8,007				
☐ 1892 Columbian	1,550,405		16.00	32.50	190.00
☐ 1893 Columbian	950,000		15.00		175.00
☐ 1935 Conn. Tercentennial	25,018		225.00	375.00	650.00
☐ 1936 Delaware Tercentennial	20,993		210.00	350.00	600.00
☐ 1936 Elgin, Illinois	20,015		190.00	300.00	600.00
☐ 1925S Fort Vancouver	14,944		550.00	800.00	1900.00
☐ 1922 Grant Memorial	67,405		80.00	190.00	400.00
☐ 1922 Same w/Star on Obverse	4,256		900.00	1600.00	2900.00
☐ 1928 Hawaii Sesquicentennial	9,958		1400.00	2000.00	4250.00
☐ 1935 Hudson Sesquicentennial	10,008		750.00	1000.00	1950.00
☐ 1918 Illinois Centennial	100,058		70.00	140.00	275.00
☐ 1946 Iowa Centennial	100,057		60.00	110.00	190.00
☐ 1925 Lexington-Concord	162,013		65.00	115.00	190.00
☐ 1936 Long Island	81,826		50.00	90.00	150.00
☐ 1936 Lynchburg, Va.	20,013		160.00	300.00	600.00
☐ 1920 Maine Centennial	50,028		140.00	275.00	500.00
☐ 1934 Maryland Tercentennial	25,015		150.00	275.00	500.00
☐ 1921 Missouri Centennial	15,428		900.00	1600.00	2600.00
☐ 1923 Monroe Doctrine	274,077		65.00	140.00	300.00
☐ 1938 New Rochelle	15,226		350.00	600.00	950.00
☐ 1936 Norfolk, Va.	16,936		450.00	775.00	1100.00
☐ 1936 Oakland Bay Bridge	71,424		75.00	150.00	300.00
☐ 1935 Old Spanish Trail	10,008		675.00	1250.00	2600.00
☐ Oregon Trail	Type		70.00	150.00	300.00
☐ 1926 Oregon Trail	47,955		70.00	150.00	300.00

DATE	MINTAGE		ABP in MS-60	MS-60 Unc.	MS-65 Unc.
☐ 1926D Oregon Trail	83,055		70.00	150.00	300.00
☐ 1928 Oregon Trail	6,028		250.00	350.00	650.00
☐ 1933S Oregon Trail	5,008		275.00	375.00	750.00
☐ 1934D Oregon Trail	7,006		250.00	290.00	550.00
☐ 1936 Oregon Trail	10,006		100.00	200.00	650.00
☐ 1936S Oregon Trail	5,006		200.00	300.00	650.00
☐ 1937D Oregon Trail	12,008		90.00	165.00	325.00
☐ 1938 Oregon Trail	6,006				
☐ 1938D Oregon Trail	6,005	SET	375.00	595.00	1200.00
☐ 1938S Oregon Trail	6,006				
☐ 1939 Oregon Trail	3,004				
☐ 1939D Oregon Trail	3,004	SET	550.00	950.00	1950.00
☐ 1939S Oregon Trail	3,005				
☐ 1915S Pan Pacific Exposition	27,134			2500.00	7500.00
☐ 1920 Pilgrim Tercentennial	152,112		55.00	125.00	250.00
☐ 1921 Pilgrim Tercentennial	20,053		140.00	325.00	675.00
☐ Rhode Island	Type		100.00	250.00	375.00
☐ 1936 Rhode Island	20,013				
☐ 1936S Rhode Island	15,010	SET	300.00	675.00	1100.00
☐ 1936S Rhode Island	15,011				
☐ 1937 Roanoke Island, N.C.	29,030		80.00	175.00	650.00
☐ 1935S San Diego Exposition	70,132		50.00	80.00	225.00
☐ 1936D San Diego Exposition	30,082		75.00	125.00	375.00
☐ 1926 Sesquicentennial	141,120		45.00	75.00	250.00
☐ 1925 Stone Mountain	1,314,709		30.00	55.00	110.00
☐ Texas Centennial	Type		90.00	140.00	225.00
☐ 1934 Texas Centennial	61,413		75.00	145.00	250.00
☐ 1935 Texas Centennial	9,996				
☐ 1935D Texas Centennial	10,007	SET	180.00	325.00	700.00
☐ 1935S Texas Centennial	10,008				
☐ 1936 Texas Centennial	8,911				
☐ 1936D Texas Centennial	9,039	SET	180.00	325.00	700.00
☐ 1936S Texas Centennial	9,055				
☐ 1937 Texas Centennial	6,571				
☐ 1937D Texas Centennial	6,605	SET	210.00	375.00	750.00
☐ 1937S Texas Centennial	6,637				
☐ 1938 Texas Centennial	3,780				
☐ 1938D Texas Centennial	3,775	SET	550.00	950.00	1300.00
☐ 1938S Texas Centennial	3,814				
☐ 1927 Vermont (Bennington)	28,162		175.00	400.00	1000.00
☐ 1924 Hugenot Wallon	142,080		80.00	140.00	475.00
☐ Washington Carver	Type		7.50	17.50	35.00
☐ 1951 Washington Carver	110,018				
☐ 1951D Washington Carver	10,004	SET	70.00	140.00	225.00
☐ 1951S Washington Carver	10,004				
☐ 1952 Washington Carver	2,006,292				
☐ 1952D Washington Carver	8,006	SET	85.00	165.00	295.00
☐ 1952S Washington Carver	8,006				

DATE	MINTAGE		ABP in MS-60	MS-60 Unc.	MS-65 Unc.
☐ 1953 Washington Carver	8,003				
☐ 1953D Washington Carver	8,003	SET	130.00	225.00	375.00
☐ 1953S Washington Carver	108,020				
☐ 1954 Washington Carver	12,006				
☐ 1954D Washington Carver	12,006	SET	75.00	145.00	245.00
☐ 1954S Washington Carver	122,024				
☐ B. T. Washington	Type		7.50	17.50	35.00
☐ 1946 B. T. Washington	1,000,546				
☐ 1946D B. T. Washington	200,113	SET	35.00	55.00	110.00
☐ 1946S B. T. Washington	500,279				
☐ 1947 B. T. Washington	100,017				
☐ 1947D B. T. Washington	100,017	SET	70.00	115.00	190.00
☐ 1947S B. T. Washington	100,017				
☐ 1948 B. T. Washington	8,005				
☐ 1948D B. T. Washington	8,005	SET	125.00	275.00	450.00
☐ 1948S B. T. Washington	8,005				
☐ 1949 B. T. Washington	6,004				
☐ 1949D B. T. Washington	6,004	SET	275.00	450.00	700.00
☐ 1949S B. T. Washington	6,004				
☐ 1950 B. T. Washington	6,004				
☐ 1950D B. T. Washington	6,004	SET	225.00	375.00	575.00
☐ 1950S B. T. Washington	512,091				
☐ 1951 B. T. Washington	510,082				
☐ 1951D B. T. Washington	7,004	SET	110.00	275.00	450.00
☐ 1951S B. T. Washington	7,004				
☐ 1936 Wisconsin	25,015		125.00	275.00	650.00
☐ 1936 York County, Me.	25,015		120.00	275.00	625.00

SILVER COMMEMORATIVES

MEDALS COLLECTED WITH COMMEMORATIVES

NORTH AMERICAN CENTENNIAL

DATE	MINTAGE	ABP in MS-60	MS-60 Unc.	MS-65 Unc.
☐ 1925 (Thin)	40,000	40.00	70.00	120.00
☐ 1925 (Thick)	40,000	30.00	50.00	85.00

So-Called WILSON DOLLAR

DATE	MINTAGE	ABP in MS-60	MS-60 Unc.	MS-65 Unc.
☐ 1920 Silver	2,200	160.00	250.00	375.00

2 KRONER SWEDEN

DATE	MINTAGE	ABP in MS-60	MS-60 Unc.	MS-65 Unc.
☐ 1936 2 Kroner Delaware Swedish Tercentennial	500,000	15.00	25.00	40.00

GOLD COMMEMORATIVES
GOLD COMMEMORATIVES, 1903 - 1926

The gold commemorative series began not long after the silver, in 1903. Far fewer gold commemoratives were issued, as the large physical size necessary for impressive designing resulted in a coin of very high face value. Experiments were made with $1 gold commemoratives, which some critics called puny, and goliaths of $50 denomination, which were indeed eye-catching but well beyond the budgets of most citizens in those days. The final gold commemorative was coined for the 1926 Sesquicentennial or

150th anniversary of American freedom from Britain. Because of bullion market conditions it is extremely doubtful that any will ever again be attempted. The value of these pieces in extremely fine condition is about one-third the price for uncirculated — ample proof that most buying activity originates with numismatists rather than bullion speculators.

ONE DOLLAR GOLD

1903-Jefferson   1903-McKinley   1922-Grant

DATE	MINTAGE	ABP in MS-60	MS-60 Unc.	MS-65 Unc.
☐ 1903 Jefferson Dollar	17,500	550.00	950.00	2100.00
☐ 1903 McKinley Dollar	17,500	550.00	950.00	2100.00
☐ 1904 Lewis & Clark Dollar	10,025	1400.00	2500.00	5500.00
☐ 1905 Lewis & Clark Dollar	10,041	1400.00	2500.00	5500.00
☐ 1915* Panama-Pacific Dollar	15,000	650.00	1200.00	4250.00
☐ 1915* Panama-Pacific Dollar	6,766	2400.00	4000.00	12000.00
☐ 1916 McKinley Dollar	10,003	500.00	950.00	1950.00
☐ 1917 McKinley Dollar	10,004	450.00	1000.00	2000.00
☐ 1922 Grant Dollar	5,016	1200.00	2000.00	4500.00
☐ 1922 Grant Dollar w/star	5,000	1200.00	2000.00	4500.00

*Struck to Commemorate the Opening of the Panama Canal.

ONE DOLLAR GOLD

Panama-Pacific

$2.50 GOLD

Philadelphia

DATE	MINTAGE	ABP in MS-60	MS-60 Unc.	MS-65 Unc.
☐ 1926 Philadelphia Sesquicentennial $2.50	46,019	450.00	750.00	1250.00

PANAMA-PACIFIC FIFTY DOLLARS

This huge coin, containing nearly 2½ ounces of gold, was not the world's largest goldpiece but by far the most substantial coin of that metal struck by the U.S. government. (To give some indication of changes in the market from 1915, the date of issue, until today, $50 worth of gold today is about 1/10th of an ounce.) It was issued for the Panama-Pacific Exposition and was struck in two varieties, one with round and one with octagonal edge, the former being somewhat scarcer and more valuable. Minerva is pictured on the obverse and the Athenian state symbol, the owl, representative of wisdom, on the reverse. The place of issue was San Francisco and the designer Robert Aitken. This is definitely not a piece for bullion speculators as its value is many times that of the gold content and under no circumstances would a $50 Panama-Pacific — or any U.S. gold commemorative — be melted down.

ROUND

DATE	MINTAGE	ABP in MS-60	MS-60 Unc.	MS-65 Unc.
☐ 1915S Round	483	35000.00	45000.00	65000.00

OCTAGONAL

DATE	MINTAGE	ABP in MS-60	MS-60 Unc.	MS-65 Unc.
☐ 1915S Octagonal	645	32500.00	40000.00	60000.00

☐ COMPLETE SET, 50.00 Gold Round and Octagonal, 2.50 & 1.00 Gold and Half Dollar Silver UNC. - ABP 22,000.00

CONFEDERATE STATES OF AMERICA

Following its secession from the Union in 1861, the Confederate government of Louisiana took control of the federal mint at New Orleans (the only mint operating in southern territory), along with its materials and machinery. Jefferson Davis, President of the C.S.A., appointed C. G. Memminger his Secretary of the Treasury and authorized production of a "Confederate Half Dollar." This was presumably manufactured by taking ordinary half dollars and removing their reverse motif, to which was added a shield with seven stars (one for each state that had joined the C.S.A.), a Liberty cap, a wreath of sugar cane and cotton, and the wording "CONFEDERATE STATES OF AMERICAN HALF DOL." No serious effort was made to circulate this coin, only four specimens being struck. Restrikes were later made. J. W. Scott somehow got hold of the original reverse die and, having keen business aptitude, struck off 500 examples for sale to souvenir-hunters. He used his own obverse, consisting of wording without portraiture or other design.

1861
HALF DOL.

DATE	MINTAGE	ABP in MS-60	VF-20 V. Fine	MS-60 Unc.	MS-65 Unc.
☐ 1861 Half Dollar (Rare)	4		VERY RARE		
☐ 1861 Half Dollar Restrike	500	400.00	650.00	1400.00	2500.00
☐ 1861 Scott Token Obverse, Confederate Reverse	500	110.00	150.00	325.00	400.00

CONFEDERATE CENT

This was the only Confederate coin intended for general circulation — and it never got that far. Robert Lovett of Philadelphia was commissioned by agents of the C.S.A. to prepare coins in the denomination of 1¢ in 1861. He was to design the coin, engrave their dies, and do the acutal striking as well. After producing a certain quantity, of which only 12 have been discovered, Lovett ceased operations and hid both the coins and the dies from which they were struck, fearing, as a resident of the North, arrest by authorities on grounds of complicity with the enemy. Restrikes were subsequently made, in gold, silver and copper, by John Haseltine. The figures given here for mintages of the restrikes are based on best available information. Haseltine, in his memoirs of the affair, states that the die broke on the 59th coin. There are nevertheless believed to be 72 restrikes in existence. Haseltine made a point of striking no reproductions in nickel for fear they might be taken for originals.

ORIGINAL   RESTRIKE

DATE	MINTAGE		MS-60 Unc.	MS-65 Unc.
☐ 1861 Cent (original)	12		6000.00	9500.00
☐ 1861 Restrike, Gold (1964 Auction)	7		14000.00	20000.00
☐ 1861 Restrike, Silver	12	PROOF	3000.00	4000.00
☐ 1861 Restrike, Copper	55		1900.00	2500.00

U.S. PROOF SETS, 1936 TO DATE

The technical definition of a Proof is a coin made for presentation or collector purposes. Beginning in the second half of the 19th century the Mint struck proofs of many of its coins; some, but not a great number, appeared previously. A proof is not made from a specially manufactured die but rather an ordinary die set aside exclusively for use in proofs. The dies are cleaned and polished more frequently than those used for ordinary circulating coins. When any sign of wear or imperfection appears the die is scrapped. This is why proofs have a somewhat higher surface relief (bas-relief) than uncirculated specimens, leading to the conclusion — mistakenly — that more deeply engraved dies are employed. After coming from the press, proofs are not touched except with gloves or special tongs made for the purpose, and are inspected for uniformity. Any exhibiting flaws of any nature are rejected. Proofs that pass inspection are housed into holders, so that nothing may interfere with their finish.

Frosted proofs are no longer produced. These have a lustrous shining ground but the design and lettering is non-reflective or frosted. So-called "matte" proofs have a granular finish. These too are a thing of the past. Brilliant proofs, those struck from 1936 to date, are mirrorlike over the entire surface, not only the ground but design and lettering. It is well to keep in mind (for beginners) that a coin found in circulation is never a proof, regardless of its lustre or perfection of its condition. It is simply a "proof-like" coin.

Proof sets have been struck by the Mint since 1936, though none were issued in the years 1943-49. Beginning in 1968 they were issued in stiff plastic holders rather than pliable vinyl. Proof sets are not struck only at the San Francisco mint and all coins carry the "S" mintmark.

DATE	MINTAGE	ABP	MS-65 Proof
☐ 1936	3,837	8000.00	10000.00
☐ 1937	5,542	5000.00	6500.00
☐ 1938	8,045	2750.00	3500.00
☐ 1939	8,795	2250.00	3000.00
☐ 1940	11,246	1500.00	2000.00
☐ 1941	15,287	1500.00	2000.00
☐ 1942 One Nickel		1500.00	2000.00
☐ 1942 Two Nickels	21,120	1800.00	2400.00
☐ 1950	51,386	700.00	850.00
☐ 1951	57,500	625.00	700.00
☐ 1952	81,980	350.00	450.00
☐ 1953	128,800	200.00	250.00
☐ 1954	233,300	120.00	150.00
☐ 1955	378,200	100.00	125.00
☐ 1956	699,384	40.00	45.00
☐ 1957	1,247,952	20.00	25.00
☐ 1958	875,652	22.50	30.00
☐ 1959	1,149,291	16.00	20.00
☐ 1960 Small Date		30.00	35.00
☐ 1960 Large Date	1,691,602	12.00	15.00
☐ 1961	3,028,244	12.00	15.00
☐ 1962	3,218,019	12.00	15.00
☐ 1963	3,075,645	12.00	15.00
☐ 1964	3,949,634	12.00	15.00
☐ 1965MS*	3,360,000	3.75	5.00
☐ 1966MS*	2,261,573	3.75	5.00
☐ 1967MS*	1,863,344	7.50	10.00

DATE	MINTAGE	ABP	MS-65 Proof
☐ 1968S	3,041,508	4.00	6.00
☐ 1968S Without "S" 10S		8500.00	12000.00
☐ 1969S	2,360,000	4.00	6.00
☐ 1970S	2,600,000	4.00	6.00
☐ 1970S Small Date ¢	2,600,00	95.00	125.00
☐ 1970S Without "S" 10¢	2,200	1200.00	1600.00
☐ 1971S	3,244,138	3.00	4.50
☐ 1971S Without "S" 5¢	1,655	2000.00	2500.00
☐ 1972S	3,267,667	3.00	5.00
☐ 1973S	2,769,624	8.00	12.00
☐ 1974S	2,617,350	8.00	12.00
☐ 1975S	2,850,715	15.00	20.00
☐ 1976-S (40%-3 pieces)	3,215,730	15.00	20.00
☐ 1976-S	4,150,210	7.00	9.00
☐ 1977-S	3,251,125	7.50	10.00
☐ 1978-S	3,127,781	16.00	22.00
☐ 1979-S		15.00	20.00

*SPECIAL MINT SETS While no proof sets were issued for 1965, 1966, 1967, the Mint filled the void by issuing a five piece *UNCIRCULATED* coin set in a *RIGID PLASTIC HOLDER*, and labeled *"SPECIAL MINT SETS."*

DETECTING ALTERED COINS

For further details refer to HOW TO DETECT ALTERED AND COUNTERFEIT COINS AND PAPER MONEY by Bert Harsche. Distrubuted by House of Collectibles.

Available at your dealer

Removing Metal, some examples are:
1834 half cent altered to 1871, 1940s cent altered to 1910s, 1941 D or S cent altered to 1911 D or S, 1942 D or S cent altered to 1912 D or S, 1944 D or S altered to 1914 D or S, 1930 D or S, altered to 1936 D or S (some check for either), 1938 P or D cent altered to 1933 P or D, 1948 P D or S altered to 1943 P D or S Copper cent, 1924 P or D dime altered to 1921 P or D, 1934 D dime altered to 1931 D, 1928 S quarter altered to 1923 S etc.

Removing existing mint marks on coins where the "P" mint coin is worth considerably more than the branch mint coin. Some coins to watch are the 1922 P cent, 1960 small date cent, Barber halves of 1913, 1914, 1915, 1895 silver dollar, 1928 silver dollar, 1899 dollar, 1865 $5 gold, 1869 $5 gold, 1869 $5 gold, 1872 5 Denver gold, 1875 $5 gold, 1877 $5 gold, 1877 5 Denver gold, 1858 $10 gold, etc.

Examine the area of mint mark for evidence of tooling and buffing. On buffed coins the detail around the removed mint mark will be indistinct or blurred.

On an altered coin the field from which the mint mark was removed is often not level. You will see a slight depression by holding the coin at an angle.

Shaving Blob Mint Marks
Some examples of this are:
1912 D Liberty nickel altered to 1912 S. 1916 S dime altered to 1916 D. 1909 D $5.00 gold altered to 1909 O.

Splitting Coins
Examine coins with mint marks on the reverse for evidence of split rim, especially nickels as they do not have a reeded rim.

A plain obverse and a mint marked reverse are planed down and the halves are soldered together.

Coins with a reeded rim are usually split by hollowing out a coin then reducing the size and thickness of another so that the reduced half fits into the hollowed out portion and soldered into position.

Punched Mint Marks
A mint mark is punched on a plain coin and the metal around the mint mark is removed so the mint mark appears to be raised above the field.

Hold the coin at eye level and compare the height of the mint mark with detail around it.

Examine the area on the opposite side of the mint mark for a flat spot or a slight bulge.

Note: On the Indian head $2.50 gold and $5 gold the mint mark is the highest point on the coin as the design is incuse.

Another method is to raise metal on a plain coin by drilling a hole into the coin on the opposite side of the mint mark until the remaining metal is very thin.

The remaining metal is then pushed up to form the raised mint mark and the hole is filled in.

Examine the area on the opposite side of the mint mark for evidence of filling and buffing.

Soldered or Glued Mint Marks

Compare the size, shape and position of the mint mark with a genuine coin or photo of a genuine (the position will vary on the genuine).

Hold the coin at eye level and compare the mint mark's height with the other details around it. Also compare with other coins of the series to become familiar with the height, shape, and position of the mint marks.

Examine the base of the mint mark for a seam; you will need a good glass to see the thin line.

On silver coins look for evidence of removal of excess silver solder.

Use of Acid

Chemically pure (C.P.) nitric acid is used in the alteration of coins for several reasons. First is the use of the acid to remove a genuine mint mark from another coin. A genuine mint mark is taken from a coin that has been cut or ground down near the area of the mint mark. The acid is applied to totally remove the mint mark by eating away the material left in the mint mark area. The result is a clean mint mark that can now be used to alter another coin.

Acid etch is also responsible for dots, overdates, flagpoles or other added attractions on coins.

On copper and nickel coins C.P. nitric acid is used full strength. If the acid is used with water the etching process is slower with a rough appearance left of the coin's surface.

To produce a dot or whatever on any of these pieces a material that can not be eaten away by the acid must be used. This is normally something similar to asphalt paint. The dot is painted on the coin to be altered in the exact position and of the exact size as the genuine. The acid is applied to the complete surface of the coin and rubbed down so the coin's surface will receive an even etch. After several applications the asphalt paint is removed and the result will be a dot in the right place on the altered coin.

Silver coins that require this same treatment will be etched with a solution of one part C.P. nitric acid, two parts of water and some tri-sodium phosphite.

Acid etch will still leave the mint marks or digits with rounded base. A genuine coin will have features that have a square base and this squareness can not be easily produced by acid etch or photo engraving.

1874 INDIANHEAD CENT ALTERED TO 1871 INDIANHEAD CENT

GENUINE   ALTERED

Draw an imaginary line under the date, or use a piece of paper with a straight edge.

1. On the 1871, only the "8" and the "7" in the dat will touch the line.
2. The date on the altered 1874 is level so all the number will touch the line.

Note: Compare the top of the last "1" in the date of the genuine with the altered 1874.

ALTERED 1909S VDB

Altered 1909S VDBS are made in the following ways:
1. Combining a 1909-S obverse with a 1909 V.D.B. reverse by milling down the two coins and sweating together. Usually copper-flash plated and then rebrowned. Very difficult to detect. Becoming less predominant now that the price of 1909-S is high and with other methods explained below being used.
2. Combining a 1909-S obverse with 1909 V.D.B. reverse by inlaying the planed down V.D.B. reverse into a bored out 1908-S obverse. Hard to detect if copper-flash plated and then rebrowned.
3. Relief-etching a V.D.B. on the reverse of a regular 1909-S. Usually easy to detect with a magnifying glass by comparing with genuine piece.
4. Altering third numeral of 1939 S to a zero and then combining with V.D.B. reverse with one of the above methods.
   Altering third numeral of 1929 S and matching to V.D.B. reverse. Usually detected by uneven field in date area. All numerals in date may not appear equal in height.
5. Punched-up S mint mark on milled 1909 obverse and mated to V.D.B. reverse. Detectable by mint position and inspection of mint mark.
6. Die struck coins made on spark erosion dies. Detectable in "new" pieces by grain structure (similar to sandblast proof), color, and minute detail. Would be virtually impossible to detect in any grades below XF if wear and color were simulated and genuine blank planchets were used. At this writing no authenticated pieces produced by spark erosion have been reported.
7. Soldered on S mint mark on regular 1909 V.D.B. Detectable with strong magnifier on "older models". Would be difficult to detect if piece given copper-flash and then rebrowned.

8. **Glued on S mint mark.** The S glued on regular 1909 V.D.B. with resin glue. If proper 1909 V.D.B. reverse type was used and if position and tilt of mint mark is precise, these extremely skillful fakes are virtually impossible to detect by inspection alone (even under strong magnification). Test is to dissolve the resin glue with acetone and S will come off.
9. **Cast coins.** Generally poor quality. However, pieces produced by centrifugal casting can be of good quality. A valuable tool in their detection is a micrometer and fine balance scale to weigh coins in grains. Castings are underweight and slightly undersized.

1909 S CENTS

1    2    3

1909 S Cents
 Altered 1909 S are made in the following ways:
 1. Glued mint marks.
 2. Relief etching S minting mark.
 3. Cast and die struck phonies.

1944 D CENT ALTERED TO 1914 D

1. The genuine 1914 D cent has the numbers in the date evenly spaced.
2. The altered 1944 D cent has a wide space between the "9" and the second "1"
3. A genuine 1914 D does not have the initial VDB under the shoulder.

4. The altered date 1944 D may have the initial VDB on the shoulder, but this test is not conclusive as the VDB can be removed.

I have seen coins where the third number was entirely removed and a "1" glued between the "9" and "4" properly spaced. I have also seen a 1934 D altered to a 1914 D by the method described above.

This check will identify 1910 S, 1911 S, 1914 S, and 1915 S Lincoln cents.

1930 S OR D ALTERED TO 1931 S OR D

1. On a genuine 1931 S cent, the last "1" in the date is the same length as the first one.
2. On an altered 1936 S, the last "1" is shorter than the first "1".
3. On a genuine 1931 S, the top of the "3" is rounded and the end curves down.
4. On an altered 1936 S, the top of the "3" is straight; beware of tooling the top end to make it appear to curve.
5. The bottom curve of the "3" on the genuine 1931 S is long, pointed, and curves up close to the number "9".
6. On the altered 1936 S, the bottom of the "3" is short and does not curve as much as the genuine.

ALTERED 1931 S CENT

Glued Mint Marks

Beware! I have seen 1931 S cents with mint marks attached so skillfully and so perfectly positioned that it was impossible with a strong glass to detect any abnormality whatsoever.

Nevertheless, application of some acetone caused the S to fall off the coin.

Examine all 1931-S cents very carefully. If permission is obtained treat the mint mark with acetone; if not, beware.

1956 D OR 1959 D JEFFERSON NICKEL ALTERED TO 1950 D

1. On genuine 1950 D nickel, the numbers in the date are of the same size.
2. On the altered 1956 D or 1959 D, the "0" in the date is very small.
3. Beware of split coins. *Example:* a 1950 plain obverse and a "D" mint reverse.

This evidence could be on the rim as illustrated on the obverse or reverse next to the rim.

Specimens with evidence of tampering on the obverse or reverse are made by hollowing out a nickel and reducing the size and thickness of another nickel so that it fits inside the hollowed out portion, then soldered into position.

Beware of glued mint marks.

I have heard of a 1958 D being altered to a 50 D by punching out the center of the number "8". Inspection of the number should expose these fakes. If the zero in the date does not match the illustration of the genuine, it is fake.

ALTERED 1916 DIMES

Altered 1916 D dimes have been made in the following ways:
1. 1916 S dime altered to 1916 D by shaving a blob "S" mint mark to resemble a "D". Usually easy to detect by comparing size, shape, and position of mint mark with a genuine or photo of a genuine coin.

③　　　　　　　　　④

Examine the position of the D mint mark. Denver mint records indicate that there were four working used dies for the 1916D reverse; these are:
No. 1—high tilts right.
No. 2—high more vertical.
No. 3—medium high
No. 4—low.

2. A 1916 obverse hollowed out and "D" mint reverse inserted, or the other way around. This is very hard to detect if the size, shape, and position of the mint mark is like the genuine. Examine obverse and reverse next to the rim for the seam with a good glass. Compare mint mark position with a genuine.
3. A "D" mint mark is glued to a 1916 P coin. Examine the base of the mint mark for the seam. Beware of dark area around mint mark as this could hide the seam. Compare with genuine for mint mark position, size, etc. If it looks phony, treat mint mark with acetone.
4. A hole is drilled into the obverse opposite the mint mark until the metal is very thin. The thin metal is then punched up to form the mint mark and the hole filled in. Compare mint mark with genuine. Also examine obverse opposite mint mark for evidence of filled hole.
5. A 1916 P obverse and a "D" mint reverse are planed down and soldered or glued together. Usually easy to detect as the reeded edge is fouled up or very unlike the reeding on a genuine if touched up specimen.
6. The last number of a 1917D, 1918D, 1919D, or the third number of a 1926D is removed and replaced by a number making it a 1916D. Easy to detect by comparing position of numbers in date with a 1916 obverse and genuine reverse for mint mark, size, and position.

Examine the position of the D mint mark. Denver mint records indicate that there were four working dies used for the 1916D reverse.

To be genuine the mint mark must match one of these positions exactly. If you have a suspect coin, treat the mint mark area with acetone. If it is glued it can be removed by pushing the mint mark a few minutes after treating with acetone. Examine for evidence of soldered mint marks.

1932 P QUARTER ALTERED TO 1932 D OR S MINT MARK
SOLDERED OR GLUED TO PLAIN

ALTERED

1. Examine base of mint mark for a seam or very thin line.
2. Compare size, position, and height of mint mark with a genuine. The mint mark should never be higher than the detail around it.

If you have a suspected coin, treat the mint mark with acetone. If it is glued, it will fall off when you push it. Examine for evidence of removal of excess solder.

GENERAL INFORMATION ON SILVER DOLLARS

On larger pieces such as the silver dollar it is somewhat easier to detect some of the alterations which are quite a bit harder to find on the smaller pieces. This is due to the size of the field of silver dollars.

Glue specks or solder joints or the imperfect fit of a transplanted mint mark can usually be spotted without aid of a high powered glass.

Mint marks may appear to be more worn or to be newer than the rest of the coin if transplanted from another coin.

Comparison of a questioned coin with genuine coins of the same date can sometimes show up variations which might otherwise go unnoticed.

Silver dollars have been altered by machining one part to fit inside another machined coin. This will make the ring of the coin very flat and dull.

Fakes consisting of a genuine obverse and reverse muled together are also becoming more plentiful. Silver dollars are good subjects for this activity due to the mint mark and date being on opposite sides of the coin. These coins will normally be a little smaller in diameter and will not have a true ring. The telltale seam between the two halves is difficult to camouflage as the match of the reeding is a problem. These coins reproduce a dull flat sound also.

Studying the major die varieties of the silver dollar series is a must for collectors of these coins. The collector of the key coins in the silver dollar series should have a running knowledge of varieties and how alterations are produced.

Added mint marks or deletion of mint marks can sometimes be determined by knowing the type of variety minted at each of the mints involved. All genuine coins will have a square base for all the lettering, dates and mint marks.

WEIGHTS AND MEASURES
WEIGHTS OF U.S. COINS

DENOMINATION	DATE OF ISSUE	WEIGHT GRAINS	WT. TOL. + OR – GRAINS
Half Cent	1793-1795	104.0	
	1796-1857	84.0	
Large Cent	1793-1795	208.0	
	1795-1857	168.0	
Small Cent	1856-1864	72.0	2.0
	1864-	48.0	2.0
	1943	42.5	2.0
Two Cent	1864-1873	96.0	2.0
Three Cent Nic.	1865-1889	30.0	
Three Cent Sil.	1851-1854	12.345	
	1854-1873	11.574	
Half Dime	1794-1837	20.8	
	1837-1853	20.625	
	1853-1873	19.2	
Five Cents	1866-	77.16	3.0
Dime	1796-1837	41.6	
	1837-1853	41.25	1.5
	1853-1873	38.4	1.5
	1873-1964	38.58	1.5
	1965-	35.0	1.5
Twenty Cent	1875-1878	77.162	
Quarter	1796-1838	104.0	
	1838-1853	103.09	3.0
	1853-1873	95.99	3.0
	1873-1964	96.45	3.0
	1965-	87.5	3.0
Half Dollar	1794-1836	208.0	
	1836-1853	206.17	4.0
	1853-1873	192.0	4.0
	1873-1964	192.9	4.0
	1965-1970	177.5	4.0
	1971-	175.0	4.0
	1976S (Sil.)	177.5	4.0
Silver Dollar	1794-1803	416.0	
	1840-1935	412.5	6.0
Clad Dollar	1971-	350.0	8.0
40% Silver	1971-1976	379.5	8.0
Trade Dollar	1873-1885	420.0	
Gold Dollar 1	1849-1854	25.8	0.25
Gold Dollar 2	1854-1856	25.8	0.25
Gold Dollar 3	1865-1889	25.8	0.25
$2½ Gold	1796-1834	67.5	0.25
	1834-1929	64.5	0.25
$3 Gold	1854-1889	77.4	0.25
$5 Gold	1795-1834	135.0	0.25
	1834-1929	129.0	0.25
$10 Gold	1795-1834	270.0	0.50
	1834-1933	258.0	0.50
$20 Gold	1849-1933	516.0	0.50

1 Gram = 15.432 grains

FAST-FIND COIN REFERENCE INDEX

Colonial Coins, Patterns and Tokens 80
   Auctori Plebis Token 119
   Baltimore, Maryland Coinage ... 111
   Bar Cent 120
   Brasher Doubloons 107
   Castorland 126
   Colonial Plantation Token 87
   Confederatio Cent 117
   Connecticut Coinage 102
   Continental Dollar 113
   Elephant Token 88
   Franklin Press Token 126
   French Colonies in America 97
   Fugio Cents 127
   George Washington Coinage 121
   Georgius Triumpho Token 119
   Gloucester Token 91
   Higley Coinage 94
   Immune Colombia 116
   Kentucky Token 110
   Machin Coppers 118
   Mark Newby or St. Patrick Halfpence 86
   Maryland-Chalmers Tokens 111
   Maryland Coinage 85
   Massachusetts Coinage 108
   Massachusetts Halfpenny 110
   Massachusetts-New England Coinage 81
   Mott Token 120
   NE Shilling 82
   New Hampshire Coinage 100
   New Haven Restrikes 128
   New Jersey Coinage 104
   New York Coinage 106
   New Yorke Token 90
   North American Token 118
   Nova Constellatio Coppers 115
   Nova Constellatio Silvers 114
   Oak Tree Coins 83
   Pine Tree Coins-Bay Colony 84
   Pine Tree Copper-Massachusetts 109
   Rhode Island Token 112
   Rosa Americana 92
   Sommer Island Shilling (Hog Money) 80
   Specimen Patterns 117
   Standish Barry Coins 111
   Talbot, Allum and Lee Cents 121
   Vermont Coinage 101
   Virginia Coinage 100
   Voce Populi Coinage 96
   Willow Tree Coins 82
   Woods Coinage or Hibernia Coinage 93

Commemorative Medals 261
   2 Kroner Sweden 262
   North American Centennial 261
   So-Called Wilson Dollar 262

Confederate Coinage 265
   Confederate Cent 266
   Confederate Half Dollar 265

Dimes 169
   Barber 174
   Draped Bust 170
   Liberty Cap 170
   Liberty Seated 171
   Mercury 176
   Roosevelt 179

First U.S. Mint Issues 128
   Birch Cent 128
   Silver Center Cent 129

Five Cent Pieces 155
   Buffalo 159
   Jefferson 161
   Liberty Head 157
   Shield 155

Gold Commemorative Coinage 262
   Grant $1.00 263
   Jefferson $1.00 263
   Lewis & Clark $1.00 263
   McKinley $1.00 263
   Panama-Pacific $1.00 263
   Panama Pacific $50.00 264
   Philadelphia Sesquicentennial $2.50 263

Gold Dollars **222**	Flowing Hair 195
Liberty Head 222	Franklin 206
Large Liberty Head 224	Kennedy 207
Small Liberty Head 223	Liberty Seated 198
Gold $2.50 Pieces **225**	Turban Head 196
Indian Head $2.50 231	Walking Liberty 204
Liberty Head $2.50 226	**Large Cents** **133**
Liberty Head Bust Type $2.50 226	Flowing Hair 135
	Braided Hair 141
Liberty Head With Coronet $2.50 227	Coronet Head 140
	Draped Bust 136
Liberty Head With Ribbons $2.50 227	Liberty Cap 135
	Turban Head 139
Gold $3.00 Pieces **231**	**Quarters** **182**
Gold $4.00 Pieces **233**	Barber 187
Gold $5.00 Pieces **233**	Draped Bust 183
Indian Head $5.00 241	Liberty Cap 183
Liberty Head $5.00 234	Liberty Seated 184
Liberty Head With Coronet $5.00 237	Standing Liberty 189
	Washington 191
Liberty Head—Draped Bust 235	**Small Cents** **143**
Liberty Head With Ribbon $5.00 236	Flying Eagle 143
	Indian Head 144
Liberty Head—Round Cap 235	Lincoln Head Memorial 150
Gold $10.00 Pieces **242**	Lincoln Head Wheatline ... 146
Indian Head $10.00 247	**Silver Commemorative Coinage** **257**
Liberty Head With Coronet $10.00 243	Half Dollars 258
	Isabella Quarter Dollar ... 257
Gold $20.00 Pieces **248**	Lafayette Dollar 257
Liberty Head $20.00 248	**Dollars** **209**
St. Gaudens $20.00 253	Draped Bust 211
Half Cents **130**	Eisenhower 220
Braided Hair 133	Flowing Hair 210
Draped Bust 131	Liberty Seated 212
Liberty Cap 131	Morgan 215
Turban Head 132	Peace 219
Half Dimes **164**	Susan B. Anthony 221
Draped Bust 165	Trade 214
Liberty Cap 166	**Two Cent Pieces—Bronze** ... **151**
Liberty Seated 167	**Three Cent Pieces—Nickel** .. **154**
Half Dollars **194**	**Three Cent Pieces—Silver** .. **153**
Barber 202	**Twenty Cent Pieces** **181**
Capped Bust 196	**United States Proof Sets** **266**
Draped Bust 195	

QTY.	DATE	TYPE	CONDITION	DATE PURCHASED	COST	DATE SOLD	PRICE	REMARKS

THE OFFICIAL 1981 BLACKBOOK PRICE GUIDE OF UNITED STATES POSTAGE STAMPS
THIRD EDITION

NEW • ALL STAMPS ARE PICTURED IN A FULL COLOR, FAST-FIND PHOTO INDEX

- over 15,000 current selling prices
- covers ALL U.S. STAMPS - 1861 TO DATE - GENERAL ISSUES-AIRMAILS-UNITED NATIONS-FIRST DAY COVERS-HAWAIIAN ISSUES
- **EXCLUSIVE DETAILED GRADING SECTION**
- stamps are listed using THE SCOTT NUMBERING SYSTEM
- information on investments / rarities / trends
- glossary of terminology
- inventory checklist system

BUY IT – USE IT – BECOME AN EXPERT

THE OFFICIAL $2.50
1981
BLACKBOOK
PRICE GUIDE OF
UNITED STATES
POSTAGE
STAMPS
THIRD EDITION

NEW • ALL STAMPS IN COLOR
- STAMPS 1847 - TO DATE
- 15,000 CURRENT SELLING PRICES
- EXCLUSIVE STAMP GRADING SECTION
- FULLY ILLUSTRATED • INVENTORY CHECKLIST

$2.50

4-1/8" x 5-1/2" 224 pages
(paperback)

Send for our latest catalog or contact your local bookseller.

THE OFFICIAL
1981 BLACKBOOK
PRICE GUIDE OF UNITED STATES
PAPER MONEY
THIRTEENTH EDITION

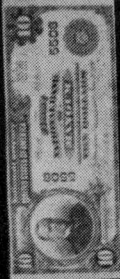

NEW • EXPANDED CONFEDERATE CURRENCY SECTION

- over **6,200 buying and selling prices**
- covers U.S. CURRENCY—1861 TO DATE—DEMAND-NATIONAL BANK-GOLD AND SILVER CERTIFICATES-TREASURY-FEDERAL RESERVE-FRACTIONAL MULES-FREAKS AND ERRORS
- comprehensive grading system
- fully illustrated for easy identification
- additional information on collecting paper money
- **FEDERAL RESERVE** district information
- inventory checklist system

$2.50 BUY IT — USE IT — BECOME AN EXPERT

4-1/8" x 5-1/2" 224 pages
(paperback)

Send for our latest catalog or contact your local bookseller.

EIGHTH EDITION

MAJOR **VARIETY**
AND **ODDITY**
GUIDE TO UNITED STATES COINS

OVER 3900 LISTINGS OF U.S. COINS
CURRENT PRICES
FULLY ILLUSTRATED • GAUGE WEIGHT AND MINTAGE
IMPORTANT SPECIFICATION CHARTS

EIGHTH EDITION

$3.95

BY FRANK G. SPADONE

5-3/8" x 8" 128 pages
(paperback)

MAJOR VARIETY AND ODDITY
GUIDE TO UNITED STATES COINS

IMPORTANT NEW GAUGE, WEIGHT AND MINTAGE SPECIFICATION CHARTS!

Authored by Frank Spadone, first published in 1962

- over **4,000 listings and current prices**
- This 8th edition contains the latest updated information. Various mint errors — filled dies, cracked dies, off-metals, over-dates, clipped planchets, rotated dies — are explained so that the beginning collector will better understand how these interesting pieces of numismatic oddities occur.

YOU CAN ENJOY A NEW PHASE OF THE COIN HOBBY with this helpful reference guide of major varieties and oddities of United States coins.

BUY IT – USE IT – BECOME AN EXPERT

Send for our latest catalog or contact your local bookseller.

FOURTEENTH EDITION

THE HEWITT-DONLON CATALOG OF U.S. SMALL SIZE PAPER MONEY

THE STANDARD REFERENCE GUIDE FOR OVER 14 YEARS.

- over **3,000 current selling prices** with detailed listings
- covers all U.S. small size currency - SPECIAL PRINTING ERRORS - FEDERAL RESERVE NOTES - NATIONAL BANK NOTES - GOLD AND SILVER CERTIFICATES - EMERGENCY NOTES - UNCUT SHEETS - U.S. NOTES
- a step-by-step description of the printing of small sized notes by the **BUREAU OF PRINTING AND ENGRAVING**
- detailed grading section
- fully illustrated

$3.50 BUY IT – USE IT – BECOME AN EXPERT

HEWITT-DONLON CATALOG

UNITED STATES SMALL SIZE
PAPER MONEY

VALUATIONS – DESCRIPTIONS – ILLUSTRATIONS

5-3/8" x 8" 192 pages
(paperback)

Send for our latest catalog or contact your local bookseller.

THE OFFICIAL PRICE GUIDE TO MINT ERRORS AND VARIETIES

ABSOLUTELY THE MOST AUTHORITATIVE BOOK ON THE SUBJECT OF MINT ERRORS AND VARIETIES PUBLISHED!

Authored by Alan Herbert, N.L.G., an officer of the Collectors of Numismatic Errors Club, a member of two other National Clubs devoted to coin error and variety collecting, and a national columnist on the subject.

- The official system of cataloging and identifying the 150 different classes of mint errors, developed by Mr. Herbert, is the standard accepted by the majority of collectors in the numismatic world
- Each listed mint error classification is fully illustrated and detailed to explain the **Planchet-Die-Striking System of Identification**
- Important information on how to **determine the authenticity and the value** of your mint errors and varieties

BUY IT – USE IT – BECOME AN EXPERT

SECOND EDITION

THE OFFICIAL PRICE GUIDE TO MINT ERRORS AND VARIETIES

- OVER 150 DIFFERENT VARIETIES OF MINT ERRORS
- P-D-S SYSTEM OF CLASSIFYING COINS
- HOW MINT ERRORS OCCUR THROUGH THE MINTING PROCESS
- HOW TO CATALOG AND AUTHENTICATE YOUR COLLECTION

BY ALAN HERBERT, N.L.G.

$3.95

5-3/8"x8" 182 pages (paperback)

Send for our latest catalog or contact your local bookseller.

HOW TO DETECT
ALTERED & COUNTERFEIT
COINS
AND
PAPER MONEY

CAN YOU TELL THE DIFFERENCE BETWEEN AUTHENTIC AND FAKE??? HERE'S HOW IT'S DONE...

Authored by Bert Harshe, this book is designed so beginner and professional can ascertain counterfeit from genuine, fully illustrated and easy to understand.

- Complete new section on counterfeit gold coins, detailed facts and techniques used in distinguishing authentic gold from "fakes"
- Every day the American public is victimized by counterfeit bills. Learn how you can protect yourself from accepting fraudulent **paper money**
- With the high prices commanded by misstruck coins, counterfeits have become increasingly more common. Learn to quickly identify imitations

BUY IT – USE IT – BECOME AN EXPERT

SIXTH EDITION

HOW TO DETECT ALTERED & COUNTERFEIT COINS AND PAPER MONEY

- FREQUENTLY ALTERED U.S. CENTS THRU GOLD COINS
- NEW SECTION ON COUNTERFEIT GOLD COINS AND PAPER MONEY
- HOW TO RECOGNIZE COUNTERFEIT MINT ERRORS

BY BERT HARSHE

$2.95

SIXTH EDITION   60 pages
5-3/8" x 8"
(paperback)

Send for our latest catalog or contact your local bookseller.

the original...
THE OFFICIAL GUIDE TO COIN COLLECTING
AN ABSOLUTE MUST FOR EVERY
BEGINNING COIN COLLECTOR **FIRST EDITION**

A comprehensive and thoughtful analysis of all aspects of collecting. Commencing with "Basic Approach" and concluding with "Numismatics Today"

25 chapters cover such topics as Rare versus Common Coins, Buying and Selling, Grading, Cleaning, Investment, Dealing, Developing a Balanced Coin Collection, Mint Errors, Medals and Tokens, Foreign Coins, Paper Money, Hoarding, Speculative Buying, Gold and Silver, and much more.

$2.95 - 5-3/8" x 7-1/8"
192 pages (hardback)

OFFICIAL GUIDE TO WORLD PROOF COINS
by Charles R. Hosch **ENLARGED SECOND EDITION**

Covering more than 540 proof sets and commemorative **issues.** Also included are mintage figures, mintmarks and mints, types of packaging, designers, all specifications including denomination, yeoman number, metallic content, diameter, weight, thickness, shape and edge design. This book also lists the **CURRENT VALUE** of each set, proof or specimen coin and explains noncirculating, legal tender "issues." Fully illustrated.

$10.50 - 7" x 9"
448 pages, (paperback)

CATALOG OF THE WORLD'S MOST POPULAR COINS
by Fred Reinfeld & Burton Hobson **NINTH EDITION**

This work has been widely acclaimed as the most comprehensive standard catalog for the coins of the world. **Listing the important coinage of every nation from Afars and Issas to Zanzibar,** it illustrates the major types with more than 5000 photographs. The appendix covers coins of ancient Egypt, Greece and Rome. No other single book provides this information on such a wide range.

$9.95 - 6½" x 10"
480 pages, (paperback)

GOLD COINS OF THE AMERICAS
by Robert P. Harris **FIRST EDITION**

Most comprehensive **listing** of gold coins issued in the **Western Hemisphere - 1750 to date** - by country, denomination and date. Over 1500 illustrations. Valuable information on grading, mints and mintmarks, counterfeits and terminology. Gold-stamped cover.

$7.95 - 6" x 9"
280 pages, (hardback)

CROWNS OF THE BRITISH EMPIRE
by Richard J. Troubridge **SECOND EDITION**

The scope of this work covers the period fom the *minting of the first British crown - the hand struck Edward VI issue of 1551 - down to the present.* Crowns issued in the name of member states of the British empire are also included. Complete with valuations, illustrated.

$5.00 - 6" x 9"
170 pages, (paperback)

VERMONT OBSOLETE NOTES & SCRIP
by Mayre Burnes Coulter **FIRST EDITION**

This book contains a complete history of the early political system in Vermont and covers **ALL notes, imprints, rarities and values.** Also included is a complete geographical index of Vermont banks.

$10.00 - 9" x 12"
164 pages, (hardbound)

Send for our latest catalog or contact your local bookseller.

BECOME AN EXPERT

The **HOUSE OF COLLECTIBLES** *is the exclusive publisher of* **THE OFFICIAL PRICE GUIDE** *series.*

KEEPING UP WITH THE EVER-EXPANDING MARKET IN COLLECTIBLES IS OUR BUSINESS. Our series of OFFICIAL PRICE GUIDES covers virtually every facet of collecting with subjects that range from ALMANACS to ZEPPELIN STAMPS. Each volume is devoted to a particular subject area and is written by an expert in that field. The information is presented in an organized, easily understood format with the utmost care given to accuracy. This comprehensive approach offers valuable information to both the novice and the seasoned collector.

Send for our latest catalog or contact your local bookseller.

BUY IT • USE IT • BECOME AN EXPERT

House of Collectibles
773 Kirkman Road, No. 120, Orlando, FL 32811
Phone: (305) 299-9343